The Sociology of Religion

The Sociology of Religion
A Canadian Focus

Edited by W.E. Hewitt

Butterworths
Toronto Vancouver

The Sociology of Religion

Printed and bound in Canada.

The Butterworth Group of Companies

CANADA	Butterworths Canada Ltd., 75 Clegg Road, MARKHAM, Ontario L6G 1A1 and 409 Granville St., Ste. 1455, VANCOUVER, British Columbia V6C 1T2
AUSTRALIA	Butterworths, SYDNEY, MELBOURNE, BRISBANE, ADELAIDE, PERTH, CANBERRA and HOBART
IRELAND	Butterworths (Ireland) Ltd., DUBLIN
NEW ZEALAND	Butterworths of New Zealand Ltd., WELLINGTON and AUCKLAND
PUERTO RICO	Butterworth of Puerto Rico, Inc., SAN JUAN
SINGAPORE	Butterworths Asia, SINGAPORE
UNITED KINGDOM	Butterworth & Co. (Publishers) Ltd., LONDON and EDINBURGH
UNITED STATES	Butterworth Legal Publishers, AUSTIN, Texas; CLEARWATER, Florida; ORFORD, New Hampshire; ST. PAUL, Minnesota; SALEM, New Hampshire

Canadian Cataloguing in Publication Data

Main entry under title:

The Sociology of religion: a Canadian focus

Includes bibliographical references and index.
ISBN 0-409-90724-3

1. Religion and sociology — Canada. I. Title.

BL60.S63 1993   306.6'0971   C93-093679-5

For our students

Preface

As a sociologist, I have long been fascinated by how religion shapes social behaviour, especially its connection with social movements and various other forms of overt political action. This interest has been instructed, for the most part, by the classical tradition in sociology, in particular, by Max Weber's prolific studies of the effect of religious belief on the acting individual in the everyday world.

As I have pursued my interest in this area, I have come to realize just how complex the religious enterprise really is. In our world, there is a vast array of religious beliefs and expressions, a variety of religious structures or institutions existing both within and across societal boundaries, and a myriad of ways in which religious prescriptions have been acted upon in given social circumstances.

Unlike many other social phenomena, religion also possesses an intensely personal dimension. Various beliefs and religious groups have given rise to fierce loyalties among their followers. This in turn has led not only to differences of opinion or harsh words between religious "competitors," but also to open conflict and war. Even analyses and interpretations of the phenomenon itself — what it is and what it should be — have given rise to heated debate, between believers and nonbelievers, and also between and within religious organizations.

Given the volatility and especially the complexity of the terrain, the religious enterprise presents itself as an obvious and important subject for careful sociological study. Yet, precisely because of its principal characteristics, undertaking sociological research on the global dimensions of religion has often represented an extremely daunting task. This certainly appears to be true of the study of religion in Canada, which to date has been only partially — and selectively — explored from a social-scientific point of view.

At the level of university instruction, the underdeveloped state of research on the domestic religious market is clearly evidenced by the lack, to this point, of an undergraduate sociology text in the area. For many years now, in fact, the sociology of religion has stood somewhat alone in this regard. Since the late 1960s, there has been a move to include a greater portion of Canadian-produced teaching and resource materials in all course areas of the discipline. This may be seen especially at the introductory level, where the number of textbooks written by Canadians has grown exponentially during the past two decades.

With its comprehensive academic treatment of the religious enterprise in Canada, this book fills a significant gap in the advanced-level sociological study of religion in this country. In producing this book, the goal has been to produce an instructional resource that, in its treatment of both theory and data, speaks clearly and directly to the everyday experiences of its audience: Canadian university students. It is our hope that by making the subject matter more familiar, the sociological study of religion will "come alive" and assume a greater importance and relevance to the student than would be the case otherwise.

The book's individual chapters are written by Canada's best-known sociologists of religion. They include academics with long-time teaching and research experience in the area, and some new faces with different angles on new and old topics. In bringing this group together, I have made no attempt to force a unified "front" in favour of one sociological perspective or another. In fact, a wide variety of orientations and perspectives are brought to the theoretical discussions of the role and importance of the religious enterprise in Canada. Structured this way, it is hoped that the authors' contributions will provide not only a solid source of information on the topics that they themselves know best, but also stimulate discussion among students about the past, present and future role of religion in this country.

In terms of presentation and format, the book has been structured as a "text with readings." As editor, I have attempted to strike a balance between the major theoretical issues within the field — such as the scope and nature of religious organizations, and secularization — and more empirical descriptions of the state of religion (in both institutional and non-institutional form) in Canada. Discussion of these dimensions and areas are undertaken in a language that assumes training in sociology. The book should be suitable for both junior-level full- and half-year courses in the sociology of religion, and also, owing to its more in-depth treatment of specific issues and processes, for senior-level seminar courses.

To further assist in the instructional task, the book also possesses a number of key features. In order to encourage further reading and research, each chapter concludes with a list of readings seminal to its subject area. As well, the Works Cited section provides an extensive listing of books and articles dealing with the sociology of religion and, undoubtedly, is the best up-to-date catalogue of titles in the socio-logical study of religion in Canada. The Conclusion, finally, contains specific suggestions for group discussion, research paper preparation and other types of projects, which I hope will be of benefit and use to students at all levels.

The actual task of assembling a text of such magnitude and scope was for me a formidable challenge. Fortunately, I was able to rely on a number of people without whose assistance this project might never have gotten off the ground.

First and foremost, I should like to express my heartfelt thanks to the contributors themselves. All were extremely supportive of the project from the very beginning. They have put considerable effort into their chapters, and were most gracious in their endurance of my occasional questions, criticisms and friendly reminders. I am par-ticularly indebted to Roger O'Toole, who went above and beyond the call of duty in producing not one, but three chapters in this book, and still part of another.

I would further like to thank all those involved in the physical production of the book. Lisa Charters at Butterworths first convinced me to undertake the project in late 1990. Since that time, Lisa and her colleague Linda Kee have consistently proved ready, willing and able to prod the work to fruition. The editorial skills of Cy Strom and Tracy Bordian of The Editorial Centre in Toronto were also in-valuable in rendering the book "user-friendly" to its intended audience.

Closer to home, I would like to express my gratitude to a host of long-time colleagues, friends and relatives who have accompanied me along what has been to date a rather long, and sometimes bumpy, academic road. The list includes my mentors, Bob Blumstock and Howard Brotz; stalwart friends and colleagues Reg Bibby, Ken Westhues, Tom Bruneau and Jim Teevan; my wife Sara and my mother Bess, and my son Christopher.

Finally, I must offer a word of thanks to those whose early works opened the doors to the sociological study of religion in Canada, among them S.D. Clark, W.E. Mann and Stewart Crysdale. Without question, it is the pioneering effort and commitment to the subdiscipline made by these individuals that made this book possible.

Certainly, this work is not the final word in the sociology of religion in Canada. In attempting to speak directly to the day-to-day experiences of Canadian students, the book does cover considerable territory. Yet, more could be offered. This is especially true of the sociology of non-Western religions, especially those faiths that are less well-known and frequently misunderstood, having been recently added to the religious mosaic by the growing ranks of new Canadians.

Nevertheless, with the publication of this first edition, the door is now open, and the evaluations and criticisms of its readers are openly invited. I see the project not as an end, but as a beginning, with the potential to adapt and transform itself as needs be to speak to the full spectrum of the Canadian religious experience.

Contributors

PETER BEYER teaches in the Department for the Study of Religion at the University of Toronto. He is author of the forthcoming book, *Religion and Globalization*, and has contributed to *Studies in Religion/Sciences Religieuses*, *Sociological Analysis* and *Theory, Culture and Society*.

REGINALD W. BIBBY is Professor of Sociology at the University of Lethbridge. He is a frequent contributor to sociology journals and has written a number of best-selling books, including *The Emerging Generation* (1985), *Fragmented Gods* (1987), *Mosaic Madness* (1990) and *Teen Trends* (1992). His most recent work is entitled *Fragmented Gods: The Updated Story of Religion in Canada* (1993).

ROBERT BLUMSTOCK is Associate Professor of Sociology at McMaster University. He has written two books, *Public Opinion in European Socialist Systems* (1977) and *Bekevar: A Hungarian-Canadian Prairie Community* (1979). His articles on religion and Eastern European topics have appeared in *Canadian Review of Sociology and Anthropology, Hungarian Studies Review, Jewish Social Studies* and *Revista di Studie Ungheress.*

MERLIN B. BRINKERHOFF is Professor of Sociology and Director of the Division on International Development at the University of Calgary. Along with several sociology books and articles, he has written extensively on the sociology of religion in such journals as *The Journal for the Scientific Study of Religion, Sociological Analysis, Canadian Journal of Sociology, Social Forces* and *Social Indicators Research.*

DOUGLAS F. CAMPBELL is Associate Professor of Sociology at Erindale College, University of Toronto. He is author of *Beginnings* (1983) and co-author of *Beyond the Atlantic Roar* (1974) and *Ties That Bind* (1979). In addition, he has contributed to *Canadian Review of Sociology and Anthropology, International*

Journal of Comparative Religion, International Journal of Canadian Studies, Journal of Church and State, Sociological Analysis and *Social Compass.*

JOHN A. HANNIGAN is Associate Professor of Sociology at the University of Toronto. Along with extensive work on social movements, he has recently contributed articles on the sociology of religion in *Review of Religious Research* and *Sociological Analysis.*

W.E. HEWITT is Associate Professor of Sociology at the University of Western Ontario. He is author of *Base Christian Communities and Social Change in Brazil* and has contributed articles to numerous periodicals including *Journal for the Scientific Study of Religion, Sociological Analysis, Journal of Church and State, Canadian Review of Sociology and Anthropology* and *Journal of Developing Areas.*

IRVING HEXHAM is Associate Professor in the department of Religious Studies at the University of Calgary. He has written numerous scholarly articles on religious subjects and several books, including *The Irony of Apartheid* (1981) and *Texts on Zulu Religion* (1987). In addition, he has co-authored *Understanding Cults and New Religions* (1986) and has edited four works dealing with African religion.

STEPHEN A. KENT is Associate Professor of Sociology at the University of Alberta. He has written extensively in the sociology of religion in such journals as *Sociological Inquiry, Religion, British Journal of Sociology, Sociological Analysis, Comparative Social Research* and *Canadian Journal of Sociology.*

DAVID L. LEWIS is a lecturer in sociology at McMaster University and is the principal of a research firm. He has co-authored articles in the sociology of religion appearing in such periodicals as *Journal of Church and State,* and has written extensively on religion and social issues in the popular press in Canada.

MARLENE MACKIE is Professor of Sociology at the University of Calgary. She is author of *Constructing Women and Men: Gender Socialization* (1987) and *Gender Relations in Canada* (1991). She has written articles in a large number of academic journals, among them *Canada Review of Sociology and Anthropology, Canada Journal of Sociology, Canadian Ethnic Studies, Review of Religious Research, Sociology and Social Research* and *Social Problems.* Prof. Mackie is also the current Sociology Editor of the *Canadian Review of Sociology and Anthropology.*

NANCY NASON-CLARK is Associate Professor of Sociology at the University of New Brunswick. She has contributed articles on the sociology of religion to such journals as *Review of Religious Research, Sociological Analysis, Canadian Ethnic Studies* and *Canadian Journal of Criminology.*

DAVID A. NOCK is Professor of Sociology at Lakehead University. He is author of *A Victorian Missionary and Canadian Indian Policy* (1988) and is co-author of *Reading, Writing, and Riches: Education and the Socio-Economic Order in North America* (1978). He has also contributed articles to *Sociological Analysis, Canadian Review of Sociology and Anthropology, Canadian Ethnic Studies* and *Sociological Review.*

ROGER O'TOOLE is Professor in the Department of Sociology and the Graduate Centre for the Study of Religion at the University of Toronto. He is author of *The Precipitous Path: Studies in Political Sects* (1977) and *Religion: Classic Sociological Approaches* (1984). He has edited *Sociological Studies in Roman Catholicism* (1989) and co-edited *Philosophy, History and Social Action* (1988). He has also contributed articles to a number of journals, among them *Journal for the Scientific Study of Religion, Sociological Analysis, Studies in Religion/Sciences Religieuses* and *Canadian Review of Sociology and Anthropology.*

JOHN H. SIMPSON is Professor and Chair in the Department of Sociology at the University of Toronto. His many articles on the sociology of religion have appeared in *Canadian Issues, Sociological Analysis, Review of Religious Research, Journal for the Scientific Study of Religion, Religious Studies Review, American Journal of Sociology, British Journal of Sociology, Social Forces* and *Sociology and Social Research*.

KENNETH WESTHUES is Professor of Sociology at the University of Waterloo. He has written *First Sociology* (1982) and *Basic Principles for Social Science in Our Time* (1987). He has co-written *Village in Crisis* (1974) and *In Search of Community* (1992). In addition, he has contributed articles on the sociology of religion to a number of journals, among them *Canadian Review of Sociology and Anthropology, Canadian Journal of Sociology, American Journal of Sociology, Sociological Analysis* and *Social Forces*.

Contents

PART I

THE SOCIOLOGICAL STUDY OF RELIGION

Introduction

W.E. Hewitt

WHY STUDY RELIGION?

You're taking a course in what? All too frequently this is the question that greets undergraduate students when announcing that they intend to pursue studies in the sociology of religion. Many people presume that students electing courses in this area have "found religion" or intend to pursue a career in the ministry. While this may be true for some, most students elect courses in the sociology of religion for the same reasons they take courses in other areas: the subject matter interests them; friends have recommended the instructor; or the course fits in nicely with their schedule.

Students in sociology of religion courses are not the only ones to whom non-academic motives are ascribed. Many of those who teach and do research in the sociology of religion are also often typecast as "religious." Within the local academic community, stories abound that one instructor or another was "kicked out of the seminary," is a former priest or is a devotee of Shirley MacLaine's mystical odysseys. So convinced are they by the rumours affirming the religious roots of people working in the area that students and colleagues are often shocked to hear the instructors use even mild profanity. This in turn has prompted many an instructor to swear openly now and again, if only to show that the link between their chosen area of research and their personal status religiosity is much weaker than many presume.

Along with this "you are what you study" syndrome — which in many respects represents a subtle (or perhaps not so subtle) attack on the academic credentials of those working in the field — the sociology of religion has been increasingly subject to marginalization within the wider sociological enterprise. While it is clearly an important concern within the works of the classical sociological theorists, religion has come to be seen by many sociologists today as less than worthy of full-time research. After all, it is often held, few people go to church anymore, and religion is assuming less and less importance in the daily lives of individuals. In short, the world is becoming increasingly secular. Consequently, many are asking, why study a phenomenon that few people care about anymore?

Such claims of increasing irrelevance are easily refuted. The fact is that religion is far from dead in contemporary society. Rather than disappearing, sociologists of religion would assert, religion is simply changing.

Without question, if we look at trends for this century, there is certainly evidence of a decline in the importance of things religious. Rates of church attendance, in particular, are unquestionably at an all-time low. In Canada, one survey demonstrated that in 1986, only one-third of church-affiliated Canadians attended religious services weekly. This compares with over two-thirds at the time of the Second World War (Bibby 1987, 17).

Nevertheless, if we look at factors other than simple attendance at church, religion continues to play an important part in the everyday lives of Canadians. For example, in surveys conducted during 1980-85, 93 percent of Canadians identified themselves as affiliated with a range of specific religious groups or churches. Nine out of ten Canadians expressed belief in God or a supreme being, three out of four prayed privately, and seven out of ten had some rite of passage (for example, baptism, wedding) performed for them by a church (Bibby 1987, 64, 68, 76). There is also strong public interest in religious issues. Internal church squabbles continue to make the news in Canada on a regular basis (such as the recent United Church difficulties over the ordination of homosexuals), as does international conflict based in whole or in part on religion. Take, for instance, media coverage of the perpetual strife between populations in Israel and the occupied territories, the religious dimensions of revolution in Iran or the religious roots of the "troubles" in Northern Ireland.

Among university undergraduates, religion also appears to have retained its currency. While, like other Canadians, students may not go to church very often, religion has remained an important subject of interest. Courses in the sociology of religion are far from empty. Student essays in sociological theory courses often focus on the religious emphases within the works of the great masters — Karl Marx, Max Weber and Emile Durkheim. Moreover, in student projects assigned in methods courses, religion is very frequently one of a number of important independent variables examined to explain some social phenomenon or other.

RELIGIOUS SOCIOLOGY VERSUS THE SOCIOLOGY OF RELIGION

Admittedly, general misconceptions about the study of religion have been generated at least in part by some of those doing research in the area. Certainly, not all those who investigate religion using sociological methods are doing so out of curiosity or to further knowledge.

Many students of religion, in fact, are directly affiliated with churches or religious groups and have an interest in studying the dimensions and consequences of matters of faith for the sole purpose of furthering institutional ends. These church-based researchers may want to know how many people are affiliated with their group or about who they are. They may also be interested in male and female rates of church attendance or in whether or not the children of members and younger people generally are joining the church. They may even want to learn something about people's attitudes towards their church or about the kinds of changes church members might seek in church services or organizational format.

Overall, the goal of this type of research is self-serving: to improve the church organization or the offering of church "services," generally speaking. Such improvements, in turn, are designed to enhance the church's popular appeal and, thus, its ability to attract and retain new members. For the church, these are critical objectives, insofar as they relate directly to its ability to survive, or, especially in the case of the Christian churches, its ability to offer the gift of eternal salvation to the largest number of people.

For some observers, this church-based research is what the sociological study of religion is really all about. Nothing, however, could be farther from the truth. While such research does involve the use of the sociological method, it is directed first and foremost to the furtherance of inherently religious, as opposed to intellectual, ends. For this reason, it has been known as, and is best denominated as, "religious sociology" — with the emphasis on "religious."

By comparison, the sociology of religion is another pursuit altogether. Sociologists of religion are typically trained academicians resident in secular institutions (such as universities), who, in seeking to uncover the essential role of matters of faith in society, put aside any and all identification or empathy with church structures and goals. Indeed, the sociology of religion is no more a product of, or tied to, the existing religious milieu than the sociology of deviance is to deviant subcultures. Sociologists of deviance study deviant behaviour because the subject matter has aroused their intellectual curiosity. The same can be said of sociologists who study stratification, culture, minorities, socialization or virtually any of the myriad topics listed in introductory sociology texts.

As is the case with all other "sociologies," the sociology of religion involves the scientific study of a particular set of structures and processes — in this instance, related to matters of faith. Overall, its aims are to discover the origins or empirical dimensions of religious phenomena, and/or to theorize about the past, present or future role of religion in society. As in the case of other sociological sub-fields, all of this is conducted objectively, with safeguards applied as necessary to ensure that values play as little a role as possible in the interpretation of research findings.

WHAT IS RELIGION?

Obviously, when attempting to assess the scope and worth of any sociological sub-field, it is important to consider just what the object of study is. For Canadians, most of whom profess Christianity, the answer to "what is religion?" is probably fairly elementary. Many would argue that religion is simply the worship of God or the quest for salvation. A few, perhaps recognizing the plurality of religious beliefs and practices in Canada and elsewhere, might allow that religion involves the worship of "gods" or "spirits" more generically conceived.

For social scientists, however, defining religion has been much more problematic. The essential difficulty is one of scope. Clearly, a good definition must be broad enough to include all or most of the world's faiths. Yet, it must be precise enough so that the "religious" becomes clearly distinguishable from secular or inherently non-religious belief systems or ideologies.

Generally speaking, those who have made the attempt to define religion have opted for one of two basic strategies. Some use *substantive* definitions, in which religion is defined in terms of what it is or what it represents. Others use *functional* definitions, in which religion is defined in terms of what it does, or what it stands for, both in societal and individual terms.

One often-cited definition is found in the work of anthropologist Melford Spiro. On the basis of his own extensive research, Spiro has dubbed religion "an institution consisting of culturally patterned interaction with culturally postulated superhuman beings" (1966, 96). For Spiro, religion involves some form of organized or patterned social behaviour, wherein religious adherents respond, both in daily activities and specific rituals, to the perceived will of some entity that is seen as having greater power than themselves.

Sociologist Roland Robertson provides another substantive definition. For Robertson, it is not religion per se but religious *content* that must be deciphered. Religious content consists of religious culture and religious action. Religious culture, claims Robertson, "is that set of beliefs and symbols (and values deriving directly thereof) pertaining to a distinction between an empirical [everyday] and non-empirical, transcendent [other-worldly or supernatural] reality" (1970, 47). In this scheme, Robertson relates, the empirical or everyday takes a back seat to the non-empirical or other-worldly. Religious action, for Robertson, simply involves "action shaped by the empirical/super-empirical distinction."

One final example of a substantive definition of religion is provided in the work of Peter Berger. For Berger, religion represents the highest order of legitimation in society. It is a powerful and pervasive sheltering canopy that by its very existence serves to render meaningful and legitimate all societal institutions and belief systems to present and future generations. In his words, "religion is the human enterprise by which a sacred cosmos is established" (1967, 25). This cosmos, or overarching societal meaning system, is sacred insofar as its constitutive elements are believed to possess "a quality of mysterious and awesome power, other than man and yet related to him, which is believed to reside in certain objects of experience."

Functional definitions of religion are of two varieties. The first concerns itself more with the function or role of religion within society, per se. The second emphasizes the function or role of religion in terms of how it affects the individual.

Perhaps the best example of the first variety is contained in the work of Emile Durkheim (1976). As a sociologist, Durkheim was concerned with "social facts"; in other words, phenomena operating at the societal level that are both exterior to, and constrain, the individual. Religion is just such a social fact, whose primary function or role in society has been to enforce and maintain social cohesion or solidarity. Durkheim defined religion as "a unified system of beliefs and practices relative to sacred things, that is to say things set apart and forbidden — beliefs and practices which unite into one single moral community called a church, all those who adhere to them." In his view, both the beliefs and the practices associated with reverence for the supernatural — in the form of religious rituals involving collective celebration or denial — help to bring people together and enforce the societal mould.

Karl Marx also maintained a definition of religion that emphasized its function or role in society generally. For Marx, society itself is a terrain of conflict, within which social groups or classes — determined by their position within the division of labour — are locked in a continuous struggle for control of societal resources. In this struggle, one set of classes is clearly dominant. This dominance is sealed not only by ownership of the means employed to produce the commodities required for survival, but also by a corresponding control over cultural products such as ideology (especially religious ideology). As part of the dominant classes' arsenal in the battle for social control, religion functions as a narcotic. It acts as an other-worldly escape for the subordinate classes, directing their minds and actions away from revolutionary pursuits that could upset the balance of class power. As he states, "religion is the sigh of the oppressed creature, the heart of a heartless world and the soul of soulless conditions. It is the *opium* of the people" (Marx 1975, 244).

Alongside these definitions emphasizing religion's broader societal functions, a range of definitions that focus on religion's role in the day-to-day lives of individuals is equally in evidence. One of the best-known functional definitions has been developed by Milton Yinger who sees religion as a tool that is used by the individual to cope with life's fundamental dilemmas. "Religion," claims Yinger, "can be defined as a system of beliefs and practices by means of which a group of people struggles with [the] ultimate problems of human life. It expresses their refusal to capitulate to death, to give up in the face of frustration, to allow hostility to tear apart their human associations" (1970, 7).

In a similar vein, anthropologist Clifford Geertz has emphasized the personal satisfactions or rewards of religion. For Geertz, the essence of religion lies in its ability to produce, by way of the view of the world it provides, certain feelings and, consequently, predispositions to engage in certain specific actions — actions that individuals would not otherwise undertake. Specifically, he defines religion as "a system of symbols which act to ... establish powerful, pervasive, and long-lasting moods and motivations in men by ... formulating conceptions of a general order of existence and ... clothing these conceptions with such an aura of factuality that ... the moods and motivations seem uniquely realistic" (1966, 4).

One of sociology's major figures, Max Weber, has also emphasized the personal side of religious function. While it is true that for Weber defining religion does not appear to be a central concern, it is clear in his work that his conception of religion is very much tied to the role it plays in everyday life. Specifically, as demonstrated in much of his work in the area (including his now famous thesis on the religious roots of modern economic enterprise, *The Protestant Ethic and the Spirit of Capitalism*), religion for Weber must be understood in terms of how it motivates individual action in the political, economic or other spheres. Thus, religion is best studied "from the viewpoint of the subjective experiences, ideas, and purposes of the individuals concerned — in short, from the viewpoint of the religious behaviour's 'meaning'" (1963, 1).

As types or categories, both substantive and functional definitions of religion possess certain strengths and weaknesses. By interpreting religion in terms of attributional categories, substantive definitions offer precision and clarity. They leave little doubt as to what does or does not constitute religion. The problem is that in doing so, they may exclude phenomena that in some respects may possess religious properties. For example, in many countries of the former Soviet bloc, communism, as the official or state ideology, possessed a number of features in common with religious systems in other settings. It had its gods (Marx), saints (Lenin and Mao), icons and statues, and its own belief system. Nevertheless, depending upon the substantive definition invoked, communism may be lacking in certain specific attributes that would effectively disqualify it from status as a religion.

Functional definitions go some distance towards solving this problem. Rather than attempting to provide all-inclusive and universal categorizations, these definitions focus more on the role of religious phenomena in society, or in other words, on what religion offers. Thus, a greater range of belief systems might qualify as religious, depending on whether or not they perform certain specific functions for either the individual or society as a whole. However, functional definitions may leave the door too wide open in this regard. While science, for example, may perform certain quasi-religious functions in society (for example, it provides meaning and a belief system) and thus satisfy the conditions of a functional definition, most people (including many sociologists of religion) would probably not equate science to religion.

Constitutive Elements of Religion

Given these advantages and disadvantages, it is not surprising that no one type of definition has really "won out" among sociologists of religion. For the most part, students of religion pick one definition or the other, and then conduct research guided by their choice.

This is not to suggest that once a definitional choice is made, sociologists of religion are no longer able to share any common ground about what precisely a religion is or isn't, or to discuss and examine their research findings on a comparative basis. Fortunately, they do share a common language in a set of universal characteristics or constitutive elements of religion. While not all students of religious phenomena may see all of these elements as necessary, certainly there is broad agreement that most should be present if a phenomenon is to be dubbed "religious."

To begin with, religions are generally seen as possessing some concept of the sacred or supernatural. In other words, there is very commonly a distinction made by faith groups between what they consider ordinary or everyday and what they believe calls for special treatment or reverence. Often as well, a mystical element is associated with these sacred objects or processes, insofar as thinking about them or being near them invokes a special feeling, whether it be fear, awe or joy.

Religions are also typically seen as maintaining belief systems that serve to explain the participants' world and their place in it. On the one hand, these belief systems provide a kind of ideological filter through which worldly events may be interpreted. On the other hand, they also provide a sense of what is right and what is wrong. This moral code often influences individual and collective action on a day-to-day basis.

According to most observers, ritual is another important element of most religious categories. Religious ceremonies or rituals typically involve a high degree of symbolism, as special words, objects and actions whose meaning is known only to the participants are invoked. Frequently, these rituals follow time-honoured guidelines and are held at specific times in special places.

Finally, religious behaviour is commonly assumed to be group based. In most cases, individuals collectively share religious symbols and beliefs, and participate jointly in ritual. Religious groups are thus "communities" of the faithful, consisting of individuals who come together to celebrate their faith jointly and who identify with each other as members of a particular social entity.

Religion and Magic

Even given this quasi-universal characterization, not all definitional problems — especially those associated with the distinction between religion and other phenomena — disappear. This is especially true in the case of magic, which very often tends to be seen as a special, or perhaps a more primitive, form of religion. Are these two phenomena distinct, sociologists of religion still ask, or are they different versions of the same thing?

Some researchers, such as Roland Robertson (1970, 47-50), see the distinction between religion and magic as less than problematic, and are reluctant to draw a firm line between the two. After all, magic does involve the supernatural, has certain beliefs and rituals attached to it, and is often undertaken in groups. Consequently, there may be a case for the suggestion that magic is just a subset or a variant of the broader category known as "religion."

Others have taken a more definitive stance on differences between the two. While arguing that religion and magic may share certain elements in common, Ronald Johnstone (1992, 17-18) argues that important contrasts are evident.

To begin with, religion tends to deal with the broader complexities of life, while magic often concerns itself with specific everyday issues and problems. For example, in religion, the quest for ultimate meaning (in terms of our place as human beings in the universe) is a central preoccupation, as is the concern for our life after death (salvation). For its part, magic sees such issues as non-problematic.

Secondly, magic is oriented towards problem solving in the here and now, while religion is future-oriented. Certainly this is the case with the preoccupation with life after death, which for religions is a central problem. Even more generally, however, most religions are concerned with the fate of humankind and the fate of the world.

Thirdly, as previously mentioned, religion tends to be a community affair, involving joint worship and ritual. While often undertaken in a group setting, magic tends to be more of an individual undertaking, as only one or two within the group possess special "powers."

Finally, and perhaps most importantly, religion is typically less of a manipulative or instrumental undertaking than magic. Within the religious group, members tend to subordinate themselves to the supernatural. They revere and fear it, and accept their fate in accordance with the perceived wishes of the other-worldly power. Magic's primary objective is to seek out and instrumentalize super-natural powers for some specific end. It is not a passive process, but one designed to make the powers of the other-world operate in a way that suits the magician.

STUDYING RELIGION AND RELIGIOUS PHENOMENA

Sociologists of religion are, of course, concerned with more than simple definitions and religious characterization. Yet, most observers, even within sociology, still want to know what issues sociologists of religion are concerned with and, more specifically, how these issues are studied.

Sociologists of religion are concerned with a range of issues, processes and organizational questions related to faith and the faithful. To a considerable extent, however, their research pursuits may be seen as falling within one of three broad categories.

For some, the object of study is the religious institution per se. Typically, sociologists of religion working in this area may look at the formation of formal religious groups, their internal structure and membership characteristics, or the factors that contribute to their maintenance or demise. Often, students of religion will also consider how religious institutions affect the broader society and vice versa.

Other sociologists of religion focus on religious belief systems and behaviour. Some look specifically at factors affecting the depth of adherents' religious faith or "religiosity," as measured by church attendance, frequency of prayer, adoption of specific religious beliefs or participation in religious practices. Still others concentrate on variables affecting conversion to, or defection from, established religious groups. Another common concern within this area has been with the way in which religious beliefs motivate particular types of behaviour day to day.

Finally, sociologists of religion are often involved in the study of inter-religious conflict or cooperation. As is well known, the contemporary world has been torn by strife promoted in whole or in part by religious considerations, and this has frequently become an object of concern. Competition between religious groups for membership or societal influence has also been a focus of study among students of religion. Conversely, religious cooperation in the form of ecumenical bodies and councils has been a source of continuing interest, especially where the pursuit of social-justice issues is concerned.

How do sociologists of religion study these and other phenomena? What methodological tools do they use? Certainly, they do more than simply "sit in church and take notes," as some would presume. Researchers in the area draw from a full range of methods currently in use within the sociological enterprise, carefully selected to capture the essence of the phenomenon at hand.

For some, qualitative research methods offer the best way of generating data for analysis. In the study of smaller religious groupings especially, participant observation is frequently the method of choice. Typically, this approach involves first-hand observation on the part of the researcher, who seeks to become a part of the structure he or she is studying. The researcher enters the field with as few preconceptions as possible about group organization or interaction, and then through intense observation over a prolonged period, attempts to draw out the essential characteristics of the phenomenon he or she is studying. The data collected in this manner are then organized and analyzed in order to develop more comprehensive explanations and theories of human behaviour within the specific context or case in question. One prominent example of this type of research is found in the work of John Lofland (1966), who in *Doomsday Cult*, conducted an in-depth study of membership recruitment and maintenance within one new religious movement in the United States.

Also within the qualitative mould, some researchers have used contemporary and historical or archival documents. In order to examine the relationship between religiosity and modern economic development, Weber (1958a), for example, undertook a detailed examination of the life and teachings of Protestant reformers Martin Luther and John Calvin. As part of this project, he was also very careful to research and trace out the essential features of both economic and religious life in post-Reformation Europe. Further, as part of an attempt to determine the social origins of religion, Durkheim (1976) used existing anthropological accounts of the life and practices of Australian Aborigines. This use of documents is often combined with cross-cultural analysis. Such is the case with Weber (1951, 1958b), who endeavoured to compare the effects of Christian teaching in Europe and North America with that of Hindu and Buddhist religion in India and China, respectively.

Intensive interviewing is still another popular qualitative research method. This involves often lengthy conversations with respondents who are encouraged to offer their thoughts on a variety of subjects related to the research question. While time-consuming, and often difficult to organize because of the sheer breadth and volume of material, such interviewing techniques can yield important information about how religious groups operate or how members themselves relate to their groups. Research by Stephen Kent (1991a) on contemporary religious groups is based in good measure on dozens of interviews with former group members throughout North America.

On the other side of the methodological coin, quantitative research methods are far from unknown in the sociological study of religion. For example, researchers have very often used census data to examine the demographic characteristics of group members or to study the relationship between variables such as age, social class or gender, and membership within specific religious groups. As part of their broader study of Canadian population attributes, W.E. Kalbach and W.W. McVey (1971) have analyzed the membership profile of the major religious denominations in Canada and the growth of these denominations since the Second World War.

Many sociologists of religion also undertake their own surveys. Drawing samples from church membership lists or the public at large, respondents may be contacted by mail, telephone or in person by trained interviewers. This approach allows for more flexibility in gathering and analyzing data than is the case with census material, which allows only for consideration of those classifications and variables employed by the census-taking agency. In effect, the researcher can develop questions to suit the particular research problem he or she has posed, and more importantly, directly target those in whom he or she is most interested.

One prominent Canadian sociologist of religion who has frequently employed the survey method is Reginald W. Bibby. Bibby has undertaken studies of religious attitudes and behaviours on a regular basis since 1975, and today their results provide an important source of data for Canadian and foreign researchers, as well as the public at large. At least two journals in the United States, *The Review of Religious Research* and *The Journal for the Scientific Study of Religion*, publish articles from time to time employing survey or other types of quantitative research methods in the study of religion in Canada.

THE SOCIOLOGY OF RELIGION: A CANADIAN FOCUS

As a text in the sociology of religion, this book reflects the broad range of research topics and methodologies within the field. Certainly, the treatment is not exhaustive. Over the course of its fifteen chapters, however, the book does attempt to deal with those topics that sociologists of religion in Canada most commonly grapple with.

The book is divided into three parts. Part I deals with more general theoretical concerns within the field, considered within the context of the Canadian reality. Chapter 1 opens the section with a comprehensive overview of the relationship between religion and society as it has been discussed within the classical sociological literature. Through an examination of the treatment of the religious question within the works of eminent sociologists such as Marx, Weber and Durkheim, the central importance of the subject area within the broader sociological enterprise is revealed. The chapter also considers classic sociological views of the nature and functions of religion, and sets the stage for discussion of specific concepts and issues to be dealt with in subsequent chapters. Expanding upon this theme, Chapter 2 describes the topics treated in some of the major works in the sociology of religion in Canada, and their connections with the classical tradition. Chapter 3 moves to the "nuts and bolts" of the theoretical enterprise, investigating existing forms of church organization from a historical and comparative perspective. Particular attention is paid to the types of religious organization that have arisen in Canada, the factors conducive to their development and their relationship to each other and society in general. Chapter 4 investigates the changing character of religion in contemporary society through a presentation and critical appraisal of the various conceptions of secularization (generally conceived as the rise of the secular or non-religious) that have appeared in the literature. Particular attention is paid here to the nature of the secularization process within Canadian society and the relative persistence of at least some types of religious beliefs and practices. Chapter 5 investigates the relatively recent emergence of new religious movements. The chapter examines the rise of various alternative faiths, such as the Unification Church, Hare Krishna and Scientology, and assesses the relationship that these groups have with each other and with the established churches. Particular attention is paid to the growth of new religious movements in Canada, as compared to other parts of the world.

Part II of the book deals substantively with social dimensions of religious belief and nonbelief in Canada. The section opens, in Chapter 6, with a discussion of the quality and distribution of religious "nones" or nonbelievers in this country. It also attempts to explain current patterns of nonbelief with reference to a host of key social variables. Chapter 7 extends the general tone of this discussion to the special case of Quebec. Long seen as the bastion of Canadian Catholicism, the rather tenuous character and uncertain future of religion in this part of Canada is examined in light of the new secular reality in Quebec and, in particular, the sovereigntist push. The remaining chapters of the section provide a striking contrast to discussion of religious decline in Canada by looking at religion's less apparent manifestations within Canadian society. Chapter 8 attempts to decode the implicit yet enduring presence of the "religious" within Canadian culture — in particular, within the literary field. Through an investigation of the works of major Canadian authors, such as Northrop Frye and Margaret Atwood, the chapter shows how religious conceptions are encoded within the national psyche, manifesting themselves subtly through authors' descriptions of the Canadian reality. Further developing the theme investigated in Chapter 8, Chapter 9 examines the religious content of popular and academic perceptions of the Canadian identity. Finally, Chapter 10 looks for connections between the environmental movement and religiosity.

Part III of the book looks at the current developments within a range of Canadian religious institutions, focusing especially on their attempts to deal with the range of human rights and social-justice issues facing Canadian society at large. Chapter 11 examines the changing attitudes and practices of women with respect to their churches, and, in particular, to the ways in which they have attempted to become more actively engaged in various aspects of institutional church life. It also considers the Canadian churches' response to women's demands. Chapter 12 presents an overview of the churches' thorny relationship with Canada's Native communities and describes the ways in which some religious groups are attempting to right the wrongs of the past. Chapter 13 looks at the one-time bastion of conservative values within Canadian society, the Roman Catholic church (Canada's largest denomination), and its emergence in recent years as supporter of many popular causes, including Native rights, income redistribution, world peace and women's rights. This chapter offers an assessment of this change in orientation within Catholicism, which is seen as partly rooted in more general religious concerns with social justice dating to the era of the Great Depression. In addition, the chapter deals with factors that may be pushing the Catholic church once again in a more conservative direction. Chapter 14 outlines recent developments within the United Church, Canada's largest Protestant denomination. The chapter discusses the rationale behind, and the institutional consequences of, church attempts to deal with the question of injustice, not only within Canadian society, but within the church itself. Particular attention is paid to the church's decision to allow the ordination of homosexuals, and the resultant conflict that ensued among church leaders and the laity. Chapter 15, finally, reviews the historical development of Canada's conservative Christian churches and attempts to account for their relative success within the current religious environment, as compared to some of Canada's larger, established denominations, which have been shrinking somewhat in recent years — both in size and influence.

The volume concludes with a summary and assessment of the state of the sociology of religion in Canada, as part of an attempt to generate further discussion among students of religion about the nature and future of religion in Canada. To this end as well, it provides a range of ideas for additional research by both students and academics.

Chapter 1

Classical Statements
on Religion and Society

Roger O'Toole

ORIGINS OF THE SOCIOLOGY OF RELIGION

The origins of the sociology of religion may readily be discerned in
the earliest formulations of sociology and proto-sociology. So central,
indeed, is religion in the doctrines of the widely acknowledged
founders of the discipline, Saint-Simon and Auguste Comte, that, in
the writings of each, the genesis of scientific sociology is inseparable
from the proclamation of a new, humanistic religion (Manuel 1965).
The foundation of the Saint-Simonian "New Christianity" and the
Comteian "Religion of Humanity" with their accompanying hierar-
chies, rituals and secular scriptures attests to an early sociological
appreciation of both the elusiveness of any definition of the substance
of religion and the universality of the functions performed by religion.
Having sensed from the very beginning the significance of religion in
both the maintenance and transformation of the social order,
sociologists still ponder the paradox that while religion is a social
phenomenon and thus a part of the study of society, society in its
entirety may be perceived as "religious" in nature.

An Enlightenment preoccupation with the idea of progress and a
nineteenth-century interest in the theory of evolution are indelibly
imprinted on the earliest works in the sociology of religion. Likewise
haunted by these notions, the founders of the new disciplines of
anthropology and comparative religion obsessively searched for the
origins of religion among the relics of "our rude forebears," in the
exotic rites of contemporary "savages" and within the arcane lexicons
of ancient languages. The works of such writers as Edward B. Tylor,

Max Müller, Herbert Spencer and James Frazer thus contain ingenious speculations on the genesis, development and prospects of religious phenomena, which they define in terms of their substance (Sharpe 1986; O'Toole 1984a, 52-62). With characteristic Victorian erudition, they engage in extensive imaginative reconstruction of an exotic primitive world of dreams, trances, ghosts, spells and animated natural forces as perceived through rudimentary philosophy and pseudo-science. Viewing them in essentially cognitive or intellectual terms, these authors identify magic and religion with the infancy of humanity; they smugly contrast the childish errors of these systems with the maturity of the modern scientific outlook. Though few of their assertions meet with the approbation of contemporary social scientists, the monumental encyclopedic labours of nineteenth-century evolutionary anthropologists, nature mythologists and folklorists deserve credit for an appreciation of the central historical role of religion in the structure and process of human societies. In this regard, they foreshadow modern neo-evolutionary social theories and merit highly critical, discriminating and selective attention in certain current research contexts even though scholarship has essentially evolved beyond them (Leach 1961; Horton 1968).

Among those whose works are considered to constitute the classics of sociological thought (see Chapter 2 for a critical discussion of this concept), Karl Marx, Emile Durkheim and Max Weber figure most prominently in the sociology of religion.

Karl Marx

No less in awe of Darwinism than his British contemporaries, Marx advanced the nineteenth-century understanding of religion in a manner that owed more to Hegelian philosophy than to recent discoveries in botany, biology, geology and zoology (Marx 1965; Marx and Engels 1958; Feuerbach 1957; O'Toole 1984a, 63-69, 188-194). While it was not Marx but Ludwig Feuerbach who originally "turned Hegel on his head" (or right way up) by reversing the relationship between God and humanity posited by Hegel, it was Marx who transposed this relationship into sociological terms. In Enlightenment fashion, Feuerbach viewed traditional religion as a colossal intellectual error in which the fantasies of human imagination dominated and demeaned the lives of their creators. For Marx, however, the false consciousness expressed in religious belief and activity constituted the inevitable consequence of a specific kind of economic, political and social order. The alienation of human beings through a process of fantastic reification reflected a more fundamental estrangement of humanity from itself. While he granted that Feuerbach had successfully resolved the spiritual world into its secular basis in intellectual terms, Marx denied that human liberation could emerge solely from a critical reorientation of human thinking. In Marx's view, liberation represented a historical rather than a mental process and involved nothing less than a revolutionizing of the existing world. It was impossible to extinguish the illusions of religion without first eradicating the social conditions that gave rise to them. The death of God required the prior demise of the very social order that demanded and sustained His existence.

The essentially sociological character of Marx's interpretation administers a necessary antidote to the intellectualist bias, not merely of Feuerbach, but of contemporaneous anthropological analyses of religion. Somewhat ironically, given his concern with class conflict and change, Marx's overriding concern with the social necessity of religion in existing societies, as well as its crucial role in the preservation of the status quo, gives his analysis a decidedly functionalist aspect. Regarding religion primarily as a brake against radical change frequently conscripted by ruling elites ("the opium of the people"), Marx stresses its character as a passive reflector of underlying social forces and a potent force of social stability. His uncharacteristic emphasis on statics rather than dynamics in this context does not, however, exclude awareness of the occasionally positive impact of religion on revolutionary movements. Thus, those contemporary thinkers (Marxist and non-Marxist alike) who reject a simplistic notion of religion as merely an epiphenomenal result of material causation can claim, with some justification, that Marx discerned and acknowledged the relative autonomy of religion in major social processes (Maduro 1977; O'Toole 1976; Beckford 1991). Neo-Marxian sociologists of religion overwhelmingly reject rigid economic determinism and affirm religion's creative role as an independent variable in social change. Such a stance renders these scholars, in many cases, indistinguishable from their Weberian rivals.

Emile Durkheim

If Marx deserves credit for situating religion firmly within social structure, it is Durkheim who pursues the link between religion and society in the most relentless sociologistic manner (Durkheim 1976; O'Toole 1984a, 76-100, 194-202). In this respect, and despite his conservative reputation, Durkheim's theory of religion is far more intellectually radical than that of Marx. The notion that God is nothing more nor less than society itself is a proposition breathtaking in its audacity no matter how many qualifications, questions or doubts surround it. Like Marx, Durkheim focuses on religion primarily as a source of social stability, integration and reproduction rather than as an agent of social transformation whether in the intimacy of primitive, communal, mechanical solidarity or in the organic, individualized anonymity of modern complex social forms.

Viewing the distinction between sacred and profane as a ubiquitous human dichotomy, Durkheim denotes sacred things as the universal substantive focus of religious belief and ritual. The distinctiveness and originality of his definitional strategy, however, is derived from his firm functionalist insistence that religion is recognizable not by what it *is* but what it *does*. The fact that religion unites its adherents into a moral community is no less essential than its preoccupation with the sacred; its inseparability from social collectivities is a defining rather than contingent characteristic. Through incisive investigation of the totemic practices of Australian Aborigines, Durkheim discerns the fundamental forms, as opposed to the evolutionary origins, of religious belief and practice. Explaining totemic dual symbolism of god and group by the notion that god and society are one and the same, he proclaims the eminently social nature of religion by asserting that religious mythologies are collective representations of underlying social realities. Perceiving the "universal and eternal objective cause" of religious experience in his conception of society, Durkheim promulgates his doctrine of the *sociological* truth of all religions. In this conception, there are no false religions; even the most fantastic myths and rituals "translate some human need, some aspect of life" while expressing "the given conditions of human existence." Convinced that no human institution can "rest upon an error and a lie," Durkheim transcends mere dismissal of religious symbolism as intellectual confusion. His concern is conspicuously more ambitious: to probe, expose and decipher the social truth hidden within such symbolic construction.

Durkheim's intellectual legacy is both confusing and challenging. His conservative preoccupation with the socially integrative consequences of collective ritual and the role of ceremony in securing individual commitment to existing social order demonstrates his interest in social statics and justifies his canonization as a founder of sociological functionalism. By contrast, his discernment of the genesis of religion in the "collective effervescence" of uninstitutionalized social gatherings clearly betrays a profound concern with social dynamics. Pondering the aptitude of society for creating new gods during the turbulent years of the French Revolution, Durkheim implies assent to a cyclical process of religious birth, death and renaissance rooted in fundamental social transformation. Peering prophetically into a future in which "creative effervescence" will once again generate novel ideas and formulas to serve as "guides to humanity," he exhibits appropriate sensitivity both to the eternal, universal aspect of religion and to the transitory symbols in which it clothes itself under changing social circumstances.

The elusive nature of Durkheim's concept of society has encouraged such divergent interpretations of his theory of religion that he has been depicted as both materialist and idealist, cultural determinist and structuralist, ultra-sociologist and covert psychologist (Evans-Pritchard 1965; Bottomore 1981; Swanson 1960; Winter 1973). If contemporary sociologists, influenced by Talcott Parsons and Robert Bellah (Parsons 1949, 1964, 1973; Bellah 1967, 1970, 1973), tend towards an idealistic and cultural reading of his work, its richness and subtlety ensures that such interpretation is by no means conclusive. Dissent and dispute rightly accompany current orthodoxy, and more than eighty years after its publication, Durkheim's *The Elementary Forms of the Religious Life* retains the power of a true classic. It provokes and stimulates a new generation of scholars to investigate "the capital role played by religion in social life."

Max Weber

Weber's contribution to the sociology of religion rivals and even surpasses that of Durkheim while presenting many sharp contrasts both in form and content (Weber 1951, 1952a, 1952b, 1958a, 1963;

O'Toole 1984a, 111-170, 202-205). Its encyclopedic erudition, its employment of the method of *Verstehen* (understanding human motivations) and its elusive, implicit definitional underpinnings all exemplify Weber's characteristically formidable brilliance and subvert his infamous claim to be tone-deaf to the music of religion.

For Weber, the central concern of religion is identical with the defining component of social action itself. Religious beliefs and rituals involve nothing less than the production of *meaning* (individual and collective, intellectual and moral) in an otherwise meaningless world (Steeman 1964). This notion of religion as a device that makes rational the irrationalities of the human condition is one that, though undeniably functional in conception, incites investigation of the dynamic as well as the static elements in social systems. Weber is undoubtedly more interested than Durkheim in religion's role in major social change than its part in maintaining the status quo. Indeed, even his lengthy penetrating analyses of the crucial contributions of Hinduism and Confucianism to the remarkably static character of India and China, respectively, are undertaken within the wider context of a pursuit of the religious sources of a social transformation with universal significance.

In many respects, Weber's renowned work *The Protestant Ethic and the Spirit of Capitalism* provides an ideal strategic framework for discerning the fundamental assumptions of his sociology of religion. Most broadly, it indicates his commitment to *Verstehen*, his focus on dynamics rather than statics, his obsession with "grounds of meaning" (or ultimate moral and cognitive reference points) and his appreciation of religion as a key to understanding society as a whole. More specifically, it reveals his undogmatic, indeterministic conception of the complex causal relationship between religious commitments and other social involvements. That this forthright rejection of an economically deterministic version of Marxist historical materialism now finds favour among neo-Marxian sociologists of religion is one of the ironies of intellectual history. Weber's erudite ruminations on the precise linkage between ascetic Protestantism and modern rational capitalism encapsulate and illuminate his vision of religion as a causal element of pivotal importance in the fate of past and present human societies of the most diverse character.

Weber's fascination with religion and his firm refusal to view it as an impotent epiphenomenon derive from a profound sense that something that, by definition, grapples with the meaning of life must inevitably play an important part in human affairs. It is as impossible, in these terms, to understand society without understanding religion as it is to understand religion without understanding society. In addition to his investigation of sixteenth- to eighteenth-century Calvinism, Weber's researches into the origins and influence of religious ideas range in subject matter from ancient cosmologies to modern mysticisms. They include meditations on the character of primitive agrarian beliefs, a monumental study of ancient Hebraic religiosity and reflections on the socio-economic composition of early Christianity. They also embrace widely admired book-length treatises on Chinese and Indian religion. Weber explores the role of theodicies (philosophies of divine justice) as resolutions of the existential problem of suffering and evil, especially in the context of under-developed Asiatic societies. In the Western context, in particular, he examines the process of rationalization of everyday life — its sys-tematization and ordering (the "disenchantment of the world"); he also studies the periodic occurrence of moral and intellectual breakthroughs throughout history.

Weber's methodology is ideal-typical analysis (1949). This involves the selection of phenomena that fit a particular schema and their synthesis into unified theoretical constructs, or ideal types. From this methodological perspective, he contrasts official and popular religion, priesthood and prophecy, mysticism and asceticism, church and sect. Then, using this methodology as a tool for moving from theoretical generalizations to particular instances, he further dichotomizes some of these elements as an aid to systematic, comparative analysis of empirical cases.

Weber's ideal-typical strategy imparts an underlying conceptual structure to the specificity and idiosyncrasy of the reality of religious life; it organizes and clarifies what might otherwise be a baffling, intellectually indigestible mass of information. Even so, his sociology of religion remains a daunting prospect, especially for those who reflect disconsolately on its supposedly stark contrast to Durkheim's carefully circumscribed experimental case study of a single, simple, small-scale society. While Weber's achievement may not readily serve as a practical example for contemporary imitation, it is nonetheless applauded by many distinguished scholars as the "most crucial contribution of our century to the comparative and evolutionary understanding of the relations between religion and society" (Parsons 1963a, xvii). Whether tone-deaf to the music of religion or not, Weber still inspires some of the most impressive inquiries in the scientific study of religion, nearly three-quarters of a century after his death. His intellectual influence is profound, widespread and growing.

CONCLUSION

Even the most cursory review of classic writings reveals a passionate concern with themes that still preoccupy sociological practitioners both in disciplinary and subdisciplinary contexts. The central problems of both the sociology of religion and sociological theory remain those originally identified and analyzed in these writings. In recent years, sociologists of religion have sought to regain a central role in the sociological enterprise as a whole and have adopted a strategy that reflects a "larger interest within sociology in building critically on classical theory." By combining "a thoughtful return to classical themes" with an ambition to go beyond the classics (McGuire 1992, 22; Glock and Hammond 1973), they reaffirm the fundamental conviction of their great precursors that society cannot be properly understood without the examination of religion. On this basis, they rightly proclaim that the sociological study of religion is indispensable to the systematic analysis of society a whole.

For Further Reading

Durkheim, Emile. 1976. *The Elementary Forms of the Religious Life.* London: George Allen and Unwin.

Marx, Karl, and Frederick Engels. 1958. *On Religion.* Moscow: Foreign Languages Publishing House.

O'Toole, Roger. 1984. *Religion: Classic Sociological Approaches.* Toronto: McGraw-Hill Ryerson.

Weber, Max. 1958. *The Protestant Ethic and the Spirit of Capitalism.* Translated by Talcott Parsons. London: Charles Scribner's Sons.

Weber, Max. 1963. *The Sociology of Religion.* Translated by Ernest Fischoff. Boston: Beacon Press.

Chapter 2

Beyond Classical Statements on Religion and Society: The Sociology of Religion in Canada

Roger O'Toole

Roger O'Toole

THE CLASSICS AND CONTEMPORARY SOCIOLOGY OF RELIGION

As the renowned German theorist Jürgen Habermas (1974) has indicated, the unity of theory and practice is easier in theory than in practice. Though the imprint of the sociological classics on current research in the subdiscipline sociology of religion is widely perceived, any attempt to trace their precise influence must settle for plausibility rather than proof. The mark of the classics — a body of work whose core is the writings of Karl Marx, Emile Durkheim and Max Weber — is discernible in the subdiscipline although, in many cases, it is faint or almost invisible. It may be detected more frequently in implicit affinities than in explicit lines of descent, a circumstance that reflects the condition of sociology as a whole.

While there appears to be general consensus concerning the continuing relevance of the sociological classics for current research practice (Rhea 1981; Coser 1981; Parsons 1981; Wallace and Wolf 1991; Kantrowitz 1992), there are powerful dissenting voices. Howard S. Becker, for example, interprets the "otherwise mysterious" contemporary concentration on the "Holy Trinity" of Marx, Durkheim and Weber as an ancestor cult that enables confused scholars to make sense *ex post facto* of a polycentric babel of contending, conflicting and often mutually incompatible theoretical assertions (Becker 1979, 24). In his view, such resort to the classics is therapeutic myth-making born of a yearning for theoretical integration and harmony. Yet the inference that the classics are nothing more than an artificially invented tradition is unconvincing (Hobsbawm and Ranger 1983). However difficult to document precisely, the conventional disciplinary wisdom promoting the continuing relevance of the classics appears, for good or ill, to be well founded (Schutz 1967; Garfinkel 1967; Glock and Hammond 1973).

In the broadest sense, the classics are relevant to contemporary research because they still supply the main "models" or "paradigms" that constitute the foundations of current discourse and debate.[1] Essentially in agreement with C. Wright Mills' assertion that the present generation of social scientists is "still living off their ideas," perceptive commentators such as Lawrence W. Sherman and Randall Collins attempt to sketch in detail the pervading influence of classic thinkers on the present concerns and conduct of sociology (Mills 1960; Sherman 1974; Collins 1985). Taking his lead from Habermas' (1971) delineation of three types of science, Sherman perceives contemporary sociology as encompassing three major paradigms, the nomological (or law-seeking), the interpretive and the critical, whose "fountainheads" are the ideas of Durkheim, Weber and Marx, respectively. Similarly, Collins discerns three core sociological traditions that "have a continuity in time and depth of thought matched by few others" (1985, 14). These are the "conflict" approach comprising the insights of Marx and Weber, the "Durkheimian" perspective, and the micro-level interactionist viewpoint to which both Durkheim and Weber have contributed significantly.

If sociologists in general are indebted to the classics and, to some extent, still governed by the preferences and priorities of the classical writers, sociologists of religion exhibit an especially pronounced classical bias for reasons not difficult to determine. Rightly or wrongly, contemporary sociological elites tend to neglect religion as a serious topic of inquiry and relegate its investigation to the margins of the subdiscipline (Ralston 1988; Martin 1966). By contrast, the subdiscipline's founders from Saint-Simon and Auguste Comte through to Marx, Durkheim and Weber accorded religion a paramount place in sociological concern, a commitment that is the first article of the creed binding sociologists of religion (O'Toole 1984a). Thus, if members of the subdiscipline are particularly preoccupied with the classics, it is only partly as a quest for status legitimation within their profession. Primarily, it is an act of faith in the shared classic proposition that the analysis of religion is indispensable to the systematic study of society. Sociologists of religion are engaged in the preservation of what they perceive as an authentic channel of contact with the donors of a priceless, though currently undervalued, bequest. Despite periodic exhortations to transcend them, the classics remain a remarkably integral part of the sociology of religion.

CLASSICAL INFLUENCES ON THE SOCIOLOGY OF RELIGION IN CANADA

It is possible, of course, to compile a list indicating the classic inspiration underlying a wide variety of works representative of the sociological study of religion in Canada. Such a compilation would undoubtedly underscore the debt to Weber — and of course to the more recent work of Ernst Troeltsch (1931) and H. Richard Niebuhr (1957) — owed by the pioneering "church-sect" studies of S.D. Clark, W.E. Mann and David Millett, and might conceivably trace the joint influence of Durkheim and Weber in the theoretical contribution of Hans Mol (Clark 1948; Mann 1955; Millett 1969; Mol 1976a, 1985). It might note the influence of Marx in R.J. Sacouman's investigation of Nova Scotian cooperatives and the Weberian rationale behind both W.E. Hewitt's work on Brazilian religious communities and Michael A. Cuneo's examination of Canadian anti-abortion organizations (Sacouman 1977; Hewitt 1991; Cuneo 1989). It could hardly overlook the explicitly Durkheimian impetus behind William Stahl's depiction of a now defunct Canadian "civil religion" or Frances Westley's research into the "cult of man" in new religious movements (Stahl 1981; Westley 1978). Finally, delineation of the Weberian and Durkheimian roots of Tom Sinclair-Faulkner's lighthearted analysis of the national sport of ice-hockey as a version of "invisible religion" might well be complemented by exploration of the urgent atmosphere of Weberian "disenchantment" that pervades Reginald W. Bibby's rumination on the decline and fragmentation of Canadian religious life (Sinclair-Faulkner 1977; Luckmann 1967; Bibby 1987).

The ubiquitous influence of the classics is, however, perhaps best appreciated by specific consideration of the theme that permeates both the background and foreground of current research within the subdiscipline: secularization. It is, either explicitly or implicitly, the overriding concern of all Canadian sociologists of religion, whatever their precise research interests (O'Toole 1984b, 1985; O'Toole et al. 1991; Wilson 1969; Martin 1978). This concern is undeniably classic in character with origins in the Marxist, Durkheimian and Weberian visions of society (Marx and Engels 1958; Durkheim 1976; Weber 1963; Gerth and Mills 1948). Even where it is far from being the focus of research, secularization constitutes an unavoidable scholarly hidden agenda whether sociological inquiry is directed towards traditionally hallowed religious phenomena or less familiar, non-institutionalized forms of religiosity. This, it must be emphasized, is no peculiar Canadian obsession but, rather, an appropriate expression of the dominant intellectual preoccupation of the worldwide subdisciplinary community.

The Sacred in a Secular Age: Toward Revision in the Scientific Study of Religion, a collection of essays by an international gathering of authors, exemplifies this widespread preoccupation (Hammond 1985). Though concerned specifically with the persistence of the sacred in secular society, this volume has proven singularly unsuccessful in its editorial efforts to displace and transcend the basic tenets of the classically derived "secularization paradigm." Rather than demonstrating that the sociology of religion stands on the threshold of a new scientific paradigm, this collection indicates the continued pertinence of classically inspired modes of thought (O'Toole 1988). While the secularization thesis has its critics in Canada as elsewhere (Martin 1965; Greeley 1972b; Greeley and Baum 1973), there is no doubt of its resilience. Its tenacious presence at the centre of Canadian subdisciplinary concern represents an eloquent subtextual tribute to the vitality of the classics as well as an enduring intellectual and experiential bridge between the "two solitudes" of national scholarly life in English Canada and Quebec.

The eminent British sociologist, Bryan Wilson has observed that in the debate over secularization, the insights of the classics are aligned with the common-sense knowledge of ordinary people (Wilson 1975). The denial of the process by some scholars thus constitutes a counterintuitive dissent from "what everybody knows." Such denials are undoubtedly in a minority among French and English Canadian sociologists of religion. Reginald Bibby's investigation of the "fragmentation" of religion on a national scale over the past four decades begins from the premise of a nearly universal public perception of religion's precipitous decline and marginalization (Bibby 1987). Similarly, a confused but acute public awareness of the Roman Catholic church's abdication of its pivotal role as the axis of social life in Quebec is the underlying presupposition of the sociological examination of contemporary religiosity in that province. The same presupposition informs not only direct assessments of the "end of religion" in Quebec, but also the various reports of religious revival. More specifically, the "return of the sacred" in the form of an exotic variety of new religious movements is interpreted as a somewhat frantic attempt to fill the vacuum created by the sudden retreat of institutionalized religion to the outskirts of Quebec's social, political and economic life (Ralston 1988; Moreux 1973; Baum 1991a; Chagnon 1985, 1986a; Courcy 1985; Zylberberg and Rouleau 1984).

The notion of the "disenchantment of the world" does not preclude musings on the possible rebirth of the gods within the context of highly rationalized societies (Weber 1958a; Wallis 1978). Thus, many scholars who endorse the essential outline of the secularization thesis also applaud the prescience of classic speculations regarding religious regeneration. Paradoxically, it is also the case that those who perceive a "return of the sacred" in any form as a fundamental challenge to the paradigm of secularization are highly disposed to invocation of the classics in pleading their case (Bell 1977; Wilson 1979). Furthermore, even those who discern in the phenomenon of "secular society" nothing more than an unfortunate contradiction in terms are likely to acknowledge the definitional breadth of the Durkheimian and Weberian theoretical legacies as the ultimate source of their own conception of the universality and ubiquity of religion (Luckmann 1967).

For both its defenders and detractors within the subdiscipline, the concept of secularization dominates discussion both of religion in general and of its particular variants, whether traditional or novel. Though the secularization thesis has encountered intense criticism in recent years, it remains the pivotal theme of scholarly discourse among Canadian sociologists of religion. On all sides, the debate over secularization is conducted within the broad boundaries mapped by the founders. In this context, the intellectual presence of the classical canon is inescapable, for its foes no less than its friends.

THE SUBDISCIPLINARY RELIANCE ON THE CLASSICS: AN ASSESSMENT

Is it desirable for a discipline or subdiscipline to function so decidedly in the shadow of the classics? Some scholars, impatient to loosen the grip of the founders, echo Alfred North Whitehead's renowned pronouncement that a "science which hesitates to forget its founders is lost." In its extreme form, this perspective is simply an expression of that generalized contempt for "the wrong ideas of dead men" especially characteristic of those forms of modern scholarship that place a premium on technical expertise. In its more moderate form, it rests upon a rudimentary cumulative or natural-science model of sociological accomplishment that assumes, somewhat naively, that in general "later means better."[2]

It is possible to applaud Whitehead's dictum, to view sociology in essentially cumulative terms, and yet to deny that a continuing concern with the classics is a symptom of intellectual inertia. This is the strategy adopted by the late Alvin W. Gouldner, a thinker whose impeccable radical credentials immediately discredit any suggestion of conservatism, traditionalism or reaction. Pondering Whitehead's words, Gouldner observes that it is impossible to forget something unless it is really known in the first place. Furthermore, it is by no means apparent that the ideas of the founders are yet really "known" in the sense of having been fully interpreted, appreciated, exploited and exhausted by subsequent thinkers. In Gouldner's view, "a science *ignorant* of its founders does not know how far it has travelled nor in what direction; it too is lost" (1958, vi). In this context, the assertion that the present generation of sociologists is "still living off" the work of the founders is no cause for shame or regret.

If, on the other hand, one rejects the cumulative model as inappropriate to the sphere of social knowledge, an obvious explanation for the persistence of the classics follows. The distinguished British sociologist and philosopher, Ernest Gellner, suggests that, in contrast to the world of natural science, the realm of social thought is characteristically static or cyclical:

> The number of available ideas seems limited rather than infinite. If there is one well-established law in the field known as the History of Ideas, it is that whatever has been said has also been said by someone else on an earlier occasion. Although a certain relative originality is

possible, it is largely a matter of the combination of primary ideas and of context (1985, 9).

For Gellner, social ideas are "finite in number, ever-present and doomed or destined to an eternal return" (1985, 10); the task of their historian is, therefore, to understand why certain ideas exert a special appeal at some particular time. From this point of view, persistent rereading and reinterpretation of the classics is unavoidable and inevitable.[3] Further, if it is accepted that the classic writings of sociology are indeed the richest veins of social knowledge, it is to be expected that they will continue to be mined selectively for ideas just as the works of Plato and Aristotle still inspire scholarly insight in diverse fields of inquiry (Eliot 1945; Bloom 1987).

For some observers, contemporary sociology in general and the sociology of religion in particular appear mired in a "pre-paradigmatic" scientific stalemate of contending visions. It is not necessary to accept the Kuhnian evolutionary and revolutionary framework, however, to appreciate that nothing resembling theoretical consensus exists at this time among professional sociologists. Whether this is a *consequence* of the persistence of the classics in the subdiscipline or conversely, as Becker implies, the *cause* of their persistence, the impact on scholarship is the same. The practising sociologist must be alert to the conflicting claims of a variety of theoretical perspectives while simultaneously being aware of their classical lineage (Kuhn 1962; Ritzer 1975; Becker 1979). As Sherman observes: "To know fully what I am doing, I need to know what I am *not* doing that I *could* be doing ... And, for that, I must read the Masters" (1974, 181).

Retaining a dominant role for the classics within the sociology of religion could have no worse result, however, than spawning a sterile scholasticism rooted in ritualistic, nostalgic reverence for academic ancestry. Appreciation and use of the masters must constitute an impetus to creativity rather than a snare of stagnant traditionalism. This view finds no more eloquent proponent than sociologist C. Wright Mills who discerns in the "classic tradition" all that is best in contemporary sociology (Mills 1960). In Mills' judgement, the standards that ought to be upheld in current sociological research are "those that have slowly accumulated in the classic tradition" and are best represented in the contributions of Marx, Durkheim and Weber. Mills urges contemporary sociologists to seek involvement in, and inspiration from, a vibrant intellectual tradition that is defined, animated and challenged by the perceptions of its progenitors:

> The classic tradition ... may not be defined by any one specific method, certainly not by the acceptance of any one theory of society, history or human nature ... [It] is most readily defined by the character of the questions that have guided and do now guide those who are part of it. These questions are generally of wide scope: they concern total societies, their transformations, and the varieties of individual men and women that inhabit them. The answers given by classic sociologists provide conceptions about society, about history and about biography, and in their work these three are usually linked closely together (1960, 4).

If we follow Mills, then, the work of those who preserve and perpetuate the classic tradition is "soaked in history" and at the same time "relevant to the public issues of their times, and to the private troubles of individual men and women" (1960, 4). Their efforts, moreover, help to define and clarify such issues and troubles and the intimate relations that unite people in society.

Prolonged exposure to the classics in the way that Mills advocates can be regarded as hazardous to the health of the sociology of religion. Indeed, more meditation of this sort might well expand the intellectual vision and research potential of the subdiscipline to a notable degree. More specifically, conscious commitment to the classic tradition on the part of Canadian scholars seems likely to yield significant gains that merit brief consideration.

Among these, an enhanced appreciation of the richness of their nation's religious history might prove of immense immediate and long-term benefit. It could be argued that the best Canadian sociology has long been marked by an acute and sustained sense of the past. Indeed, a staunch minority conviction that the study of sociology entails the study of history has outlasted the protracted influence of those orthodoxies that would have sociology concern itself with only the present (O'Toole 1985; Clark 1968). Increasing interdisciplinary awareness of the mutual profit derivable from a sociology "soaked in history" and a history sensitized to sociological insight deserves encouragement within the sociology of religion (Burke 1980; Tilly 1981). If sociologists deserve some of the credit for historians' belated but rapidly growing recognition of the central role played by religion in Canadian life, they also stand to benefit considerably from such recognition (Grant 1955; Moir 1983; McGowan 1990). They have the opportunity to turn to their own advantage the theoretical, methodological and empirical labours of those professional historians who share their curiosity concerning Canadian religion (McGowan 1990; McGowan and Marshall 1992).

A historically informed sociology of religion would be an inestimable asset within and beyond the ranks of sociologists and historians. As the great French historian Fernand Braudel observes:

> I should be happy if [social scientists could] see history as an exceptional means of discovery and research. Is not the present after all in large measure the prisoner of a past that obstinately survives, and the past with its rules, its differences and its similarities, the indispensable key to any serious understanding of the present? (1984, 20)

Reaffirmation of the role of the classics in the sociological investigation of religion is likely to have another beneficial result. The breadth of scope, emphasis on social transformation and concern with the intersection of biography and history that are characteristic of the classics are all conducive to an expanded awareness of the innumerable varieties of religious experience (James 1960; Sharpe 1986). In supplying stark, salutary reminders that the phenomenon of religion transcends the parochial, official and institutional, the classical perspective underscores the absolute necessity of examining extraordinary, popular, minority, implicit and invisible expressions of religiosity along with more familiar traditional, mainline or canonical forms (Long 1967; Nesti 1990; Bailey 1990a; Luckmann 1967; Lemert 1975; McGuire 1992).

A final positive consequence of heightened subdisciplinary preoccupation with the classic legacy should be an increasing attunement of Canadian sociologists of religion to current developments in the realm of sociological theory. If religion is undoubtedly a social phenomenon, society is arguably a religious phenomenon when discerned from certain classical standpoints. This insight implies not only that religion must be interpreted within the wide framework of sociological theory, but also that sociological theorizing ignores the vital topic of religion at its peril (Robertson 1977; Turner 1983). Reassertion and elaboration of the affinity between classical theory and religion represents the most direct route by which religion may attain its rightful place as a central concern of contemporary Canadian sociology.

Far from being a burden, the tenacious influence of the classic inheritance is an intellectual boon to Canadian sociologists of religion. In bracing themselves to explore the religious manifestations of a new millennium, these scholars can have no better place to stand than on the shoulders of those giants whose insights, both right and wrong, have inspired so many of the accomplishments of twentieth century sociology. The slogan *"je me souviens"* might appropriately express such a subdisciplinary strategy for the conscription of the past in the service of both the present and future.

Notes

[1]The concept of a "paradigm" that dominates conceptualization and research within a science was stated by Thomas S. Kuhn (1962) in his important book on scientific revolutions.

[2]Mark Blaug has recently used the term "cliophobia" to indicate distaste for historical antecedents in academic disciplines (Blaug 1990, 27; Moggridge 1992, xvi).

[3]The reading and interpretation of classic texts is, of course, a problematic issue in a postmodern intellectual climate (Rorty 1984; Skinner 1978; Tully 1988; Blaug 1990).

For Further Reading

Bibby, Reginald W. 1987. *Fragmented Gods: The Poverty and Potential of Religion in Canada.* Toronto: Irwin Publishing.

Clark, S.D. 1948. *Church and Sect in Canada.* Toronto: University of Toronto Press.

Crysdale, Stewart, and Les Wheatcroft (eds.). 1976. *Religion in Canadian Society.* Toronto: Macmillan.

Mann, W.E. 1955. *Sect, Cult and Church in Alberta.* Toronto: University of Toronto Press.

Mol, Hans. 1985. *Faith and Fragility: Religion and Identity in Canada.* Burlington, ON: Trinity Press.

Chapter 3

The Organization of Religious Life in Canada

David A. Nock

A RELIGIOUS TYPOLOGY: CHURCHES, DENOMINATIONS, SECTS, CULTS

In any society many different religious points of view exist. Some societies are "monopolistic" and allow for only one established or official religion. But even in such monopolistic societies as medieval Europe or present-day Iran there are religious ideas in tension with the established currents of thought. Modern Western societies are "pluralistic" in that many religious orientations are permitted and tolerated. Choice of religion is largely a personal matter.

Sociologists, who must study hundreds of religious movements, apply principles of classification in order to compare and contrast religious bodies and to follow their evolution. Some of the earliest attempts at such classification were developed by Ernst Troeltsch (1931). Troeltsch conceived a rather useful classificatory scheme, focusing for the most part on the distinction between the ideal types "church" and "sect" in Christian societies. As religious organizations, churches, for Troeltsch, tend to be universal; possess a definable organizational structure with a paid ministry; maintain set prescriptions for attaining salvation (life after death); practice infant baptism; largely accept the dominant social and political order; are generally conservative in political orientation; and are predominantly middle- and upper-class. By contrast, sects are typically small; are run organizationally by their own members (having no paid ministry, for example); practice baptism of adults who join voluntarily; stress the acquisition of inward perfection as the means to salvation; are hostile in political orientation or at least indifferent to the secular world; and are predominantly lower-class. Building on these distinctions, H. Richard Niebuhr (1957) examined the process by which churches spawn sects through their own internal doctrinal and other divisions, and by which these sects subsequently mature into church-like religious organizations known as "denominations." Other authors such as J. Milton Yinger (1970) and Bryan Wilson (1970) have also attempted models of church organization.

With the changes in society and the growth in diversity of religious organizations that has occurred since Troeltsch and Niebuhr wrote, such classifications have lost some of their currency. What is required today, then, is a classificatory scheme that fits the reality of present religious markets. Here we devise one such scheme especially suited to the Canadian situation based on the categories "church," "denomination," "sect" and "cult."

We may define a church as the religious body in a monopolistic society that is recognized by the state as representing the authorized religion. This often means economic and social support for the church (for example, land, tithes, seats in parliamentary bodies) and official discouragement of other religions by the state. In Canada there were a number of efforts to implement churches of this sort. For example, one-seventh of Ontario's land was initially set aside for the Anglican church. (After much protest in the 1840s and 1850s this advantage was extended to other churches and then was finally abolished after a financial settlement was made.) In the Quebec Act of 1774, the British conquerors allowed the Roman Catholic church recognition by permitting the collecting of tithes from the population for its maintenance. In Britain to this day, twenty-six of the bishops of the Church of England are entitled to sit in the House of Lords so that "Lords spiritual" hold a measure of political power, a relic of an older church pattern (Moir 1959, 1967).

This pattern of selecting a church for official recognition and preferment will seem quite foreign to most Canadians today as Canada is now a pluralistic society. Nevertheless, efforts to introduce the old established church pattern to parts of Canada extended from the founding of Quebec in the seventeenth century to 1854 when the Clergy Reserves in Ontario were secularized. In its full ideal-typical form, such a church pattern is only possible in a society that holds to an objective notion of religious knowledge — that is, that only one religious perspective holds valid truth and that it is sacrilegious to tolerate any other. Most such established churches have existed in pre-industrial agrarian societies marked by gross inequalities in

income and education, factors that make it possible for a hierarchical-
ly organized clergy to claim objective knowledge denied to a poorly
educated peasantry (Lenski 1966).

The modern age, beginning with the French Revolution in 1789,
has seen tremendous changes: democracy has become an accepted
value; education has become pervasive and clergy can no longer claim
to be the only educated persons; few people still work on the land
and fewer still work the land of hereditary land-owning aristocrats.

Modern Western society mirrors the economic system that it
glorifies: competition among a wide range of tolerated products
available for consumer choice. The denomination, which coexists
easily with other religious bodies, is the type of religious organization
most at home in modern industrial-democratic societies. Typically, the
denomination shares in the core values of the state (pluralism,
tolerance, relativism and competition), and thus belonging to a
denomination implies little tension with the wider society.

Some denominations are former established churches that have lost
their privileged status over the course of the modern age. For
example, the Anglican church in Canada, which was a partly established church in the first half of the nineteenth century, has
become a denomination in the twentieth century. Such cases of
transition are rarely complete. Thus the Anglican church retains its
highly elaborate hierarchical system and, at least in theory, doctrines
such as that of apostolic succession, which sets out forms of authority
for the clergy, that were more at home in a pre-industrial hierarchical
agrarian society. However, such "traditional" vestiges are often
significantly altered. For example, in a National Film Board film
Challenge to the Church made in the 1970s, a Roman Catholic
bishop explains that a bishop today must be more of an elder-brother
figure and less of an authoritarian old-style patriarch. In a number of
the older churches that have evolved into denominations, there is
much more effort to involve the lay people instead of, as formerly,
reserving all sacerdotal functions for the clerical hierarchy. A sign of
this change of attitude is that clergy celebrating the Mass-Communion
Eucharist today usually do so facing the congregation rather than with
their backs to the people as used to be the case. The symbolism of
hierarchy is downplayed. In many Anglican churches lay people are
permitted to administer the sacraments alongside clergy.

Other denominations are derived from what started as sect

movements (movements of religious protest) that were "cooled down" and that lost much of the enthusiasm of the typical sect. An example of this would be the Canadian Methodists who joined the newly created United Church of Canada in 1925. The Methodists had started in the 1730s in England inspired by John Wesley, a Church of England priest. Most Methodists were religious enthusiasts who accepted little of the ceremonial and hierarchy of the established church. It became clear by the 1780s that Methodism could not be contained in the Church of England and so it became a separate and independent sect. As decades and then generations went by, the Methodists prospered and their religious enthusiasm waned. By the 1990s the United Church of Canada had become one of the most liberal and undemanding of churches in Canada, with a wide variation in belief and practice — characteristics that are not typical of the sect (in the U.S. context, see Roof and McKinney 1987, 108; for Canada, see Westfall 1989, 50-81).

A sect, as an ideal type, is a new religious movement in a state of tension with the wider society and the dominant churches and denominations. Normally, involvement in a sect becomes the "key status" of a person's life, overshadowing such important definers of the self as gender, class and occupation. Members of a sect tend to be judgemental towards non-members whom they often see as "sinners" and among the damned. Ecumenicalism is not usually encouraged among members of a sect since a sect discounts such values as tolerance, relativism and pluralism in favour of a divinely ordained truth delivered once unto the saints. A good example of a sect would be the Hutterites who believe that those who do not live in a colony such as theirs and share all productive economic property are doomed. In a metaphorical comparison, they see themselves as equivalent to Noah's Ark with everyone on the outside as abandoned by God (Hostetler 1974). Another good example of a sect in Canada would be the Old Believers, an offshoot of Russian Orthodoxy now living in northern Alberta. Their beginning as a sect in the seventeenth century was precipitated by a number of innovations promoted by the Russian patriarch to accept more Greek and Western religious practices. Even such innocuous-sounding innovations as whether to sign the cross with three fingers or two and styles of painting the icons convinced the emerging Old Believers that the Patriarch Nikkon had been corrupted by Satan (Scheffel 1991).

Whether to classify most Evangelicals and Fundamentalists (often referred to as Conservative Christians) as members of a sect is a controversial decision. Rodney Stark and William Bainbridge chose to do so in their text *The Future of Religion* (1985). Conservative Christians believe Christian status is only achieved by a dramatic "crisis conversion" when the individual accepts Christ as lord of his or her life. It is expected that the "before" and the "after" will be quite different. An Evangelical biography will tend to dwell on the experience of conversion.

Those who have not undergone such a "crisis conversion" are often looked upon as not real Christians, even if they have been baptized, confirmed and attend church. At least in the past, Evangelical Anglicans would celebrate the "conversion" of a minister to their ranks as if all the person's previous experience as a Christian minister did not count.

Moreover, many Conservative Christians accept a theory of the Bible as divinely inspired. By this they mean that the human writers of the biblical books were writing exactly what was intended by God and that it is true for all time. Most academic analysts now recognize the diversity of biblical authorship and the need to analyze each book in terms of the social location of its author: period, place, religion, gender, ethnic status and so on. This latter view of the Bible, widely shared in the denominations, implies that humans are developing an evolving and changing conception of God's will. Such an understanding of the Bible makes it easier for members of denominations to accept the ordination of women and other improvements in women's status. A more fundamentalistic reading of the Bible leads to difficulties on this point, as St. Paul was rather strict on women's place in church. Conservative Christians have tended to be loyal to the patriarchal family. They have developed a strongly rooted critique of the modern era, denouncing many of the changes of the last thirty years as "secular humanism."

The last category, the cult, is the most controversial. As an ideal type, a cult is a religious movement in a high state of tension with the surrounding society and its beliefs. (This does not necessarily mean sensational matters relating to sex, violence or brainwashing.) A cult proclaims something new that is not part of the conventional religious tradition. In this it is unlike a sect, which remains within the mainstream religious tradition and claims to go back to older truths that have been neglected by mainstream churches and denominations. Thus, whereas the Hutterite sect points to the Book of Acts in the Bible as warrant for their belief that ownership of the economic system should be "in common," a cult points either to entirely new revelations or to beliefs that are very hard to accommodate within the conventional religious tradition. Various cults refer to the teachings of "ascended masters" or to the messages from spirit guides or aliens. In the nineteenth century when Christianity was so much the dominant religion, few cults could have survived a clean break with Christianity; thus nineteenth-century cults often retained a Christian name — for example, "Christian Science," founded by Mary Baker Eddy. The latter's teachings about the illusory nature of matter, sickness, death and Jesus's role as a demonstrator of such doctrines rather than as a redeemer of sin mark it as a cult. Christian Science gives the lie to the media view of cults as dangerous and weird. Most Christian Scientists live quite ordinary lives and tend to be mature, middle-class females (Stark and Bainbridge 1985).

Perhaps a word should be said about what a cult is not. A major world religion is not considered a cult, even when it is found as a minority religion in an unfamiliar environment. Therefore, other world religions are not referred to as cults when they move with their adherents to new lands. Nor are indigenous Aboriginal religions (which, after all, are a special type of world religion).

A single religion can move through several categories. It could be argued that Christianity itself started as a Jewish sect conceiving of Jesus in a way that was not contrary to Jewish tradition, and that it later became a cult to both Judaism and the Roman Empire, before finally remaking itself as the new state church of the Roman Empire.

The Religious Typology in the Canadian Context

Canada has been characterized by the dominance of churches and denominations. In the eighteenth and first half of the nineteenth century, the Anglican, Presbyterian and Roman Catholic churches conformed closely to the church type. In the latter part of the last century and especially in the twentieth century, the conventional religious tradition has been that of the denomination. However, sects have always been present as a challenge to mainline bodies. The most numerous and influential have been the Conservative Protestants

Sects

comprising Evangelicals and Fundamentalists; however, many adventist groups seem to "fit" as sects, as do less-easy-to-categorize isolationist bodies such as Hutterites and Old Believers. The influence of sects seems less in Canada than in the United States.

Cults in Canada also have seemed less of a factor than in the United States where two nineteenth century religious bodies with cult-like beliefs, Christian Science and the Mormon church, have become major religious movements. In Canada their numbers still seem tiny, whereas in the United States the former numbers in the hundreds of thousands and the latter in the millions.

As the remainder of this chapter points out, the real line of cleavage in Canada seems to separate the churches and denominations on the one hand from secularization or a very privatized religious faith on the other. This seems somewhat different from the United States where the conventional religious tradition of churches and denominations seem significantly challenged by these same trends and a much larger and more vigorous sect and cult constituency.

RELIGIOUS GROUPING IN CANADA: A BRIEF HISTORY AND OVERVIEW

Mainline Protestantism

Until the end of the nineteenth century, Canada was a country with a rather homogeneous religious population: a majority of Protestants who felt and acted as a majority, and a strong minority of Catholics who were hobbled to some extent by their economic deficiencies and their over-representation among status-deficient French Canadians. Other religious groups formed a very small percentage of the population. The mainline Protestants were strong in economic power and political prominence, as well as in numbers.

Who were these mainline Protestants? Certainly they included members of what are now the Anglican, Presbyterian and United churches. The Anglican Church of Canada used to be called the Church of England in Canada until 1955; the Presbyterians were affiliated with the Church of Scotland. The Church of England and the Church of Scotland are to this day official state-supported churches, and this undoubtedly enhanced the status of their Canadian affiliates. The United Church of Canada is a result of the 1925 union of two-thirds of Canada's Presbyterians, the vast majority of its Methodists and its smaller population of Congregationalists.

The Methodists had been an important church in Canada in the nineteenth century. Originally a type of sect (as a radical religious protest movement against the lax religiosity of the Church of England), by 1925 Methodists increasingly resembled Presbyterians and Anglicans in ethnicity and social-class background, as well as denomination-style religiosity.

To the ranks of mainline Protestants might be added the Lutherans. Lutherans mainly came from countries in Europe where their churches were state-affiliated, such as Scandinavia and parts of Germany. Although they were considered respectable by other mainline Protestants, Lutherans were set apart somewhat because of their ethnicity until recent decades — especially in the context of the two world wars. Baptists are sometimes counted part of mainline Protestantism but, especially in the twentieth century, they have tended to be more evangelical and conservative in doctrine. They are treated here under the heading "Conservative Protestantism."

The former power and status of the mainline Protestant religions and their strength of numbers can be seen in the religious affiliation of Canadian prime ministers. Until 1948, the majority of prime ministers were Protestant. Since then the majority of prime ministers of Canada have been Roman Catholic. No other affiliations (for example, avowed atheists, agnostics, or members of other world religions or of cult or sect-like religions) can be discerned.

This is not to suggest, of course, that policies can be explained by religious affiliation. Still, there are some points worth noting. The mainline Protestant religions were strongly represented among Canadians of British origin. Thus, Protestant Canadians felt that they were an important part of the British Empire. In contrast, many Catholics were of French or Irish background and saw the British Empire as an agent of their colonialism. Nevertheless, other Catholics, both French and Irish, did accept the British Empire. For example, the Quebec historian Thomas Chapais lauded Quebec's place in the Empire as a shield against anti-Catholic forces that emerged in France after the French Revolution.

Religion did play a role in the political system until the 1970s. Political analysts have noticed that, beginning in the late nineteenth century, one of the strongest voting correlations was between Protestants

Table 3.1 RELIGIOUS AFFILIATION OF PRIME MINISTERS, 1867-1948

Prime Minister	Years of Office	Affiliation
John A. Macdonald	1867-1873; 1878-1891	Protestant
Alexander Mackenzie	1873-1878	Protestant
John Abbott	1891-1892	Protestant
John Thompson	1892-1894	Roman Catholic
Mackenzie Bowell	1894-1896	Protestant
Charles Tupper	1896	Protestant
Wilfred Laurier	1896-1911	Roman Catholic
Robert Borden	1911-1920	Protestant
Arthur Meighen	1920-1921; 1926	Protestant
W.L. Mackenzie King	1921-1926; 1926-1930; 1935-1948	Protestant
R.B. Bennett	1930-1935	Protestant

Total number of years: 81. Protestant tenure: 64 (79 percent). Roman Catholic tenure: 17 years (21 percent).
Source: The Canadian Encyclopedia. 2nd ed. Edmonton, AB: Hurtig, 1988.

Table 3.2 RELIGIOUS AFFILIATION OF PRIME MINISTERS, 1948-1992

Prime Minister	Years of Office	Affiliation
Louis St. Laurent	1948-1957	Roman Catholic
John Diefenbaker	1957-1963	Protestant
Lester Pearson	1963-1968	Protestant
Pierre Trudeau	1968-1979; 1980-1984	Roman Catholic
Joseph Clark	1979-1980	Roman Catholic
John Turner	1984	Roman Catholic
Brian Mulroney	1984-	Roman Catholic

Total number of years: 44. Protestant tenure: 11 (25 percent). Roman Catholic tenure: 33 years (75 percent).
Source: The Canadian Encyclopedia. 2nd ed. Edmonton, AB: Hurtig, 1988.

and Conservatives on the one hand, and Catholics and Liberals on the other (Wearing 1988, 65). This correlation can be traced to the hanging of the Métis leader Louis Riel in 1885 and the Manitoba Schools question of the 1890s. Originally, the Catholic church had favoured the Conservative party (some priests had pointed out in sermons that heaven was blue and hell was red, the party colours of Conservatives and Liberals, respectively) but for reasons of ethnic politics, French Canadian and thus Catholic voters became dis-gruntled with the Conservative party and started voting Liberal. This tendency was exacerbated in the First World War (1914-1918) when Empire-conscious Protestant Canadians supported Conservative prime minister Robert Borden's decision to introduce conscription. The Liberal party under Wilfrid Laurier opposed this policy, which led many Anglo and Protestant Canadians to bolt the party at least temporarily. In the Second World War, the Liberal government of William Lyon Mackenzie King tried to avoid conscription. Finally, when it seemed more soldiers were needed for the army, Mackenzie King called for a referendum asking for the country to release him from his promise not to impose conscription. Quebec refused to support any change in the use of a volunteer army; the rest of Canada, Protestant in majority, supported conscription. The debate was bitter and split the country.

Scholars have noted that the Catholic-Liberal correlation went beyond the French-Liberal connection. Other Catholics also had a decided tendency to vote Liberal. In 1938 the Conservative party tried to challenge this alignment when it chose a Catholic leader (Dr. Robert J. Manion of what is now Thunder Bay) with a French-Canadian spouse, but he failed to make any progress. The religious-political correlations only diminished in the 1970s and 1980s when Brian Mulroney and Joe Clark, both Catholics, were successful in making the Conservative party more attractive to French-Catholic voters. Perhaps equally important, the sense of loyalty to the British Empire that had united many Protestant Canadians dwindled in the 1950s and 1960s as the British Empire came to an end and as the Canadian population became more multicultural and pluralistic after the immigration boom of the late 1940s and 1950s.

Recent years have seen the decline of mainline Protestantism. The reasons for this include a somewhat lower birth-rate for Protestants than for members of some other religious traditions (Roof and

McKinney 1987, 161); a change in immigration patterns away from Britain and parts of central and northern Europe, which have a high percentage of Protestants; and the rising percentage of "nones" (people who report no religious affiliation). In addition, along with other mainline denominations, Protestantism appears to be experiencing a decline in the commitment of its members. It is clear that many people who report a mainline identification to census-takers or sociologists are actually members in name only. They may be conceived of as marginal or cultural affiliates of their tradition but hardly as serious or committed members. The research of Reginald W. Bibby has demonstrated that marginal affiliates have actually grown more numerous than people who define themselves as "committed" members of a religious tradition (roughly 40 percent to 50 percent [1987, 88]).

Roman Catholicism

When it comes to Catholicism, we have something of a mixed report. Catholic affiliation has been increasing in Canada, as opposed to mainline Protestantism. In sixty years, the proportion of Catholics in Canada rose from 39 percent in 1921 to 47 percent in the 1981 census population, whereas mainline Protestantism plunged to 32 percent in 1981 from 50 percent in 1901. Also positive is the fact that the Catholic population has been enjoying a process of status enhancement over the past thirty-five years or so. This process has been most noticeable among Catholics in Quebec. In the rest of Canada, this process of status enhancement has had a lot to do with the fact that a large part of the Catholic population originally came in to do hard physical labour. Many Irish came to Canada in the 1840s and 1850s in the aftermath of a widespread famine that devastated the country. In a country where Catholics were a minority (except for Quebec), where anti-Catholic feeling existed in some degree and where educational levels for Catholics tended to be lower than for mainline Protestants, it is hardly surprising that the status of Catholics tended to be somewhat depressed. In the last generation or two, however, the Catholic-affiliated population has been increasing, anti-Catholic feeling is lower than it was before the 1960s, and Catholics have increasingly taken hold of opportunities in the educational system. The result has been a marked rise in overall status (a process discussed in the context of the United States by Greeley 1976, 1981; and Roof and McKinney 1987, 110-111).

The process of status enhancement in Quebec among the French Catholic majority has been even more dramatic. But here the story is somewhat bittersweet, as it seems that a large part of the French-Canadian population felt that the dominance of Catholic institutions had helped produce a situation of status inferiority. Thus major institutions would have to be "laicized" or "secularized," that is, taken out of the hands of the church and placed under government or other secular control. Examples of this were the "classical colleges." These were the basic academic-stream secondary and undergraduate institutions in Catholic Quebec until the 1960s. They were run by the church and they required the paying of fees. Most of the instructors were clergy or monastics, and there was a strong Catholic ethos in the colleges in which the development of vocations was encouraged. The instruction tended to emphasize ancient and medieval philosophy and the study of classical languages. Many observers agree that such colleges tended to impede entry of their graduates into business, technical and scientific occupations, and thus left commerce and industry in the hands of others, mainly Anglophones (Porter 1965). (A full account of the "ethnic division of labour" may be a bit more complicated.) Many Catholic commentators themselves agreed that the aims of such schools were much more religious than economic and that the one goal was gained at the expense of the other. With the modernization of education in Quebec in the 1960s, especially the building of secular CEGEPs (general and vocational colleges) to replace the classical colleges and the introduction of "free" instruction, Catholics in Quebec have increased their salaries, owned more of their own businesses and staffed more executive posts of multinational firms. In fact, in the 1980s it seemed as if the heroes of Quebec were business people, replacing the poets and singers of the 1960s and 1970s, and the bishops and missionaries of yesteryear.

However, these gains in affiliation and status-enhancement have come about at the same time as disregard of the hierarchy has grown and affiliation has become increasingly nominal. Catholic regular attendance at mass (traditionally a requirement) has declined from close to 90 percent in the 1950s to less than half that today. Protestants have always had lower attendance figures, but the gap between Protestant and Catholic attendance has declined from a high of 50 percent to 10 percent or less.

More generally, Catholics seem to pay less attention in their attitudes and behaviour to the edicts of the hierarchy. Here, the Catholic church in Canada seems to be following the denomination pattern. This is an issue of some importance in the Catholic church, which traditionally has been a non-democratic hierarchical structure whose head, the Pope, claims to be a successor to the mighty Apostle, St. Peter, and to be infallible in pronouncements on faith and morals. The church traditionally claims that its truth is both objective and universal, and that this truth is defined at the top. This paradigm of church organization differs from some Protestant churches that accept the doctrine of the "priesthood of all believers" — that the individual believer may enjoy a direct relationship with God through personal reading, meditation and experience without the mediation of a hierarchy. To the Catholic church in theory and as reaffirmed by Pope John Paul II (after some divergence on this point by several popes), a Catholic cannot be a Catholic in good conscience without accepting the official teachings of the church. But whereas until the 1960s or so, there seemed little divergence between official attitudes and those of the lay member, today there is often a considerable gap. Polls have shown that a majority of the Catholic laity support such ideas as a married clergy, the use of artificial birth control, the granting of more power to the laity and more democracy in church administration, and the admission of women to ordination. Thus to some observers, at least, the church that claims both absolute and universal truth seems a house divided in a way that it once was not.

Conservative Protestantism   *Sects*

If mainline Protestants have been dropping in percentage of the population and prestige, and if Catholics have been gaining in marginal affiliation but losing in deeper signs of commitment, what about Conservative Protestants?

Membership in this Christian community is defined by either a dramatic "crisis" conversion that occurs at one specific point in a person's life (being "born again") or by a conscious decision as an adult (and not simply by means of infant baptism or confirmation as an adolescent); by a literal or conservative reading of the Bible as the direct record of God's messages to humankind (as opposed to more liberal readings of the Bible as the record of humankind's yearning to understand God); and by a heightened sense of supernaturalism (as evidenced by a lively belief in miracles, in the supernatural elements of the Bible and in the demonic; and by an expectation of apocalyptic events at the anticipated coming of the End Times). Although some Conservative Protestant traditions go back a long way, quite a few date back no farther than a century or so, and their growth has been, at least in part, at the expense of the mainline churches. (An example of this is the strength of the Salvation Army and Pentecostal groups in Newfoundland.)

The major Canadian Conservative Protestant groups belong to the Evangelical Fellowship of Canada (EFC). They include some Baptist and Mennonite groups, Pentecostals, the Salvation Army, Christian and Missionary Alliance churches, Christian Reformed churches, Free Methodists, the Church of the Nazarene and so on. One major difference between these groups lies in their acceptance or rejection of charismatic "gifts" such as "speaking in tongues" (glossolalia). At one time, such differences prevented alliances such as the EFC. Today, however, faced with the prevalence of what they call "secular humanism" and with what they regard as the selling out of the mainline churches to modernism and a more liberal reading of the Bible, they seem more ready to form a common front. The distinctions that these religious movements continue to draw between themselves, on the one hand, and the denominational religions and the wider society, on the other, appear to conform to the ideal type of sect.

According to Bibby (and counter to much popular media reportage) there is no evidence of a massive shift to this religious tradition (1987, 28). This is even true in the United States where the Conservative Protestant tradition is much stronger than in Canada. Using an inclusive, three-pronged definition of Evangelical, U.S. polls consistently find responses in the 18 to 22 percent range (Smith 1992, 313). In Canada, Conservative Protestant denominations account for 7 percent of the population, a figure that has been more or less stable over a number of decades. However, in a religious climate in which the mainline Protestant religions are declining in numbers (and the Catholic church is declining in influence), it may be argued that standing still is quite an achievement.

The felt presence of Conservative Protestants in Canada may be greater than their numbers would suggest. They tend to be more unified in belief, to enjoy church services more and to be greater contributors of money to the faith than mainline Protestants. And although data from the 1981 Canadian census indicated that Conservative Protestant groups tend to be below national averages in education, income and occupational prestige (Heaton 1986), U.S. studies reveal that their educational record has been rising (Roof and McKinney 1987, 111). What this means is the emergence of Conservative Protestant leaders who are better educated and more articulate, and thus better able to engage in public discourse outside their own religious tradition. In recent years, these leaders have made full use of television campaigns in pursuing an aggressive strategy of proselytizing.

With our reliance on U.S. events and television, Canadians may have an exaggerated sense of Evangelical growth because of the greater strength of the Conservative Protestant tradition in the United States. (However, this perception may have receded after the sensational failures of some television preachers.) One fact of importance to Conservative Protestant resilience in the United States is that their numbers have a higher birthrate than mainline Protestants and Catholics. In part this would seem to stem from their more articulated "ideology of the family," as opposed to a more widespread acceptance of the feminist agenda in mainline denominations. According to the hierarchy of the Catholic church, it too has such an "ideology of the family," but in practice, the laity are often at odds with their leadership over sexual and family issues.

The continued survival and even thriving of Conservative Protestant groups has amazed many observers. Many analyses of this tradition (see, for example, Hunter 1983) focus on its heightened sense of supernaturalism and see it as adverse to modern conceptions of rationality and natural science. From the time of the "Scopes monkey trial" in the 1920s, when a science teacher was tried and convicted by the State of Tennessee for teaching Darwin's theory of evolution rather than the creation account found in Genesis, it has often been said that such religious ideas are bound to decline or disappear. There is no such evidence of such a decline. On the other hand, neither is there evidence of a march to religious dominance.

What does Conservative Protestantism offer that at least prevents a decline — whether in numbers or in influence — such as we see in the various mainline Christian bodies? First, it offers a clearer sense of identity. The prevailing ethos of the society is one that Conservative Protestants refer to as "secular humanism." While that term may have many meanings, it is used broadly to refer to one element of secularization: the loss of influence of religious organizations over other institutions in society and the decrease in individual behaviour conditioned by explicit religious norms. Since Conservative Protestants maintain a sense of "we" and "they" when they look at the overall culture, their sense of identity is often stronger than that of mainline Christians who draw no such firm distinction.

Second, it can be claimed that Conservative Protestants are provided with more opportunities to experience religion as a direct and personal force. With the experience of personal conversion often comes a clear sense of a change in one's life. Some churches encourage other spiritual phenomena such as speaking in tongues. The mainline churches have made some efforts to increase lay participation (including allowing for some charismatic gifts), but many mainline services are still marked by clerical dominance.

Finally, there is the issue of authority. Many Conservative Protestants have a very clear sense that the Bible will answer any conceivable problem. Typically, they rely on a "proof-text" method of referring to specific verses without necessarily taking the entire context into account or concerning themselves with other verses that may cause conflict. Given the different ways of reading the Bible that are recognized by mainline Christians, their counselling inevitably is more complicated. For many people, the Conservative Protestants' authority is easy to accept because it removes all doubt.

Cult Religions

Much more obvious and visible today than ever before are cult-like religions, sometimes referred to as "new religious movements" or "alternative religions." (New religious movements and their nomenclature are taken up in greater detail in Chapter 5.) The term "cult" has acquired a lot of negative baggage from its use in the media, and in popular and even some academic usage. The word often denotes "clearly" evil or criminal practices involving sex, violence, fraud and mind control. Most sociologists use a definition of cult that is quite different. This definition simply refers to religious movements that are new to the conventional religious tradition of a society. Cults emerge out of the conventional religious tradition, usually in dispute with it. They may usually be identified by either "sacred" writings or special teachings that add to or replace those of the conventional religious tradition.

In the Mormon tradition, the Book of Mormon and Doctrines and Covenants are considered sacred books; in Christian Science, *Science and Health with Key to the Scriptures* is read in services alongside the Bible. Most cult religions born in this century feel less need to appear to adhere to the conventional religious tradition. For example, the writings of Scientology by L. Ron Hubbard tell us that we are all immortal "thetans," potentially superior to matter, energy, space and time. Having relinquished our supernatural powers, we now need Scientology programming to restore us to our "thetan" awareness.

There are a wide variety of cult-religions. Some of the better known are Eckankar, the Unification church ("Moonies"), and theosophy and its offshoots. More recently, one important cult-religious movement has been Wicca or witchcraft. (Wicca should not be confused with the Satanist religious movement.)

Wicca claims to be an old religion that was suppressed by Christianity. If this were so, it would not be appropriate to refer to Wicca as a new religious movement or a cult. Stark and Bainbridge (1985) have pointed out that most Wiccan groups have emerged since 1970 and virtually all since 1950. Why do Wiccans claim to be part of an ancient religion? Partly in order to create an impressive "pedigree" for their modern beliefs and practices. Because many people (mainly, but not only, women) were put to death between the fifteenth and eighteenth centuries on the charge of witchcraft and because many of the accused confessed under torture to satanic pacts, modern Wiccans often believe that the old witchcraft was a religious movement associated with the remnants of a pre-Christian Goddess-worshipping religious tradition (Rose 1962). The attempt by Wiccans to construct an ancient pedigree is a fascinating example of a religious movement constructing a myth (a story told with an inner meaning that is not strictly dependent upon historical proof). Even Margot Adler, one of the most prominent Wiccans, recognizes the unlikelihood of Wiccan claims to this ancient pedigree as "fact" (Adler 1979).

Cult-religions often emerge in part because of dissatisfaction with the conventional religious tradition. Important to the emergence of

Wicca was dissatisfaction with the political and theological roles given to women and to the feminine ideal in the Judaeo-Christian religions. Wicca proclaims a goddess (or goddesses) and gives prominence to the female cycle of fertility and birth, which contrasts with the Christian tradition. For U.S. Mormons, one appeal was a history of the Americas that continued the story of revelation on U.S. soil, at a time when the United States had already acquired the myth of being the improved successor to the Old World. This new revelation had an obvious appeal to patriotic Americans. In addition, it explained certain issues of the day, such as the origin of Native people and blacks, in a thinly disguised fashion.

Is there a chance that such new or alternative religious movements will supersede the conventional religious tradition of this society? Stark and Bainbridge (1987) go to great pains to point out that cult rates are higher on the west coast where conventional Judaeo-Christian affiliation is weakest. They show, and their evidence has been updated, that this is also true for Canada and its west coast (Nock 1987, 89). Their conclusion is that there is a societal and individual need for religion, especially its "compensators" such as explanations of death and evil and the provision of meaning; as the old religious tradition fails, a new one or new ones will take its place to fulfil this need. Thus Christianity replaced the old gods of the Roman Empire and Islam replaced the Arabian pagan pantheon.

Despite the interesting empirical finding about the west coast, their conclusion may be weak. Stark and Bainbridge are Americans and in the United States alternative religious traditions such as Christian Science and Mormonism have taken strong root. Some commentators now observe that there are more Mormons in the United States then Episcopalians (that is, Anglicans). However, this trend seems completely lacking in Canada, except in specific regions such as southern Alberta. There is no good reason to suppose that sects or cults or new religious movements are counter-balancing the weakening commitment of mainline Protestants and Catholics. Although the de-Christianization and secularization of Canada mean more visibility for cult-like religions, it would seem that the future lies more in the religious "nones" and the "Sheilas" than in a new religious organization designed to bury its predecessors.

Religious Nones and Sheilas

Religious nones, those that are unaffiliated to any religious group, seem to be the emerging trend. Up until the 1971 census, respondents were not given the option of "no religion," although they could volunteer such a response. In 1921, 0.25 percent of Canadians reported "no religion," a figure that rose to 0.52 percent by 1961. In 1971, when the category was first offered, 4.4 percent of Canadians so responded, as did 7.4 percent in 1981. In 1985, Statistics Canada conducted a General Social Survey drawing upon a very large sample of 11,100 respondents. Of people aged 15 to 64 years, 10.5 percent reported "no religion" (Veevers 1990, 79). Thus we see a rather dramatic rise in lack of religious affiliation from 4.4 percent to 10.5 percent in a period of 14 years.

However, sociologists Jean E. Veevers and Ellen M. Gee looked more closely at the data. They decided that the unaffiliated category should include not only those who disavow any religious affiliation, but also those who "report a religious identification but 'never' attend religious services except for ceremonial occasions such as weddings, funerals, and baptisms" (1988, 17). This expanded category of the unaffiliated includes about 30 percent of the entire sample. Another 28 percent of respondents are classified as "moderates" in that they claim a religious affiliation but attend church rarely — responding either "less than once a year" or "at least once a year." Only 42.5 percent of respondents were classified as "faithfuls," defined as those with a religious affiliation and who report church attendance of at least once a month. In most estimates there is a major gender difference, and this study is no different. More men than women (one in three compared to one in four) are unaffiliated. When the definition of nonaffiliates is expanded to include affiliates who attend church less than yearly, it takes in four in ten Canadian men as opposed to three in ten women. Veevers and Gee suggest that "the unaffiliated remain a minority but they have become a substantial minority" (1988, 17). In fact, if the moderates with their very low involvement were added to the ranks of the unaffiliated, then it could be argued that those "meaningfully attached" are in the minority — albeit still an important minority of more than 40 percent.

Will this trend continue to hold in the future? As Veevers and Gee acknowledge, affiliation and unaffiliation are affected by many demographic variables. People in the Atlantic provinces tend to be more affiliated than those in British Columbia and Alberta; women tend to be more affiliated than men; mature adults and the aged tend to be more attached than young adults and so on. A number of these factors cut across one another: the aging of the population (especially the increase in elderly women) and increasing immigration from non-secularized countries on the one hand; the westward shift in population and increasing education levels on the other. Because of these cross-cutting factors, Veevers and Gee are somewhat cautious in their conclusion and simply state that "the present levels of unaffiliation are likely to be maintained and may very well be expected to increase" (1988, 20). Going beyond demographic factors, organized religion faces a rough time in the future because most members of the mass media, from which an increasing number of people get their information about religion (rather than from direct involvement), tend to be critical or dismissive, highlighting dramatic but often unbalanced stories of abuse, harassment or lack of critical reason. Thus, the respect for religion in the media that existed in the 1940s and 1950s now seems to be lacking (see Medved 1992, 50-69).

What may also be significant in the future is private religious sentiment not tied to church membership or affiliation. This phenomenon may have been insufficiently studied until recently by sociologists because there has been a tendency to accept Emile Durkheim's definition of religion as a community of believers who meet regularly to reinforce collective norms and sentiments. But today organized religion as such is under a cloud, facing accusations of sexism, hypocrisy and sexual harassment, including child molestation. In addition, Bibby's surveys reveal what is perhaps the most grievous sin in a hedonistic age: only 16 percent of the national sample say that they highly enjoy attending church services (1987, 107). The idea that attending church might be a duty commanded by the Deity, no matter what degree of self-fulfilment is received, does not go down well. Nor does the argument, right or wrong, that attending church is like going to the gas station — that there you get filled up with spiritual inspiration in order to be sustained in the secular world outside.

Sheila Larson was interviewed in the prizewinning investigation of American values *Habits of the Heart* (Bellah et al. 1986). She is a young nurse who believes in God but "can't remember the last time [she] went to church" (1986, 221). Her faith includes an emphasis on the self — "love yourself and be gentle with yourself" as well as consideration for others. "Sheilaism" also includes personal, self-defined mystical experiences. She reports that God once spoke to her to reassure her when she was about to undergo major surgery; her second mystical experience occurred when taking care of a dying woman. She became convinced that "if [she] looked in the mirror [she] would see Jesus Christ" (1986, 235).

Sheilaism includes avoidance of organized religion, a stronger emphasis on the self than encouraged in traditional religion and an emphasis on personal religious experience that is lacking in most mainline churches. To this list one could probably also add a willingness to accept or at least consider eclectic beliefs such as reincarnation and a disenchantment with traditional Christian theology that emphasizes "original sin."

Most Sheilas are convinced that it is quite possible to be religious without any commitment to a specific organization. However, it is also possible that the eventual outcome may be ever-weakening levels of religious knowledge of all traditions. Thus Sheila may resemble a person who tries to be a painter without learning any of the specific techniques or traditions of art. Because of modern relativism in values, people are apt to think that any "faith" that is developed personally holds value.

THE QUIET REVOLUTION IN CANADIAN SOCIETY

Canada has been undergoing a quiet revolution in religion since about 1965. But because the revolution has been quiet and relatively slow, the enormity of the changes may not be realized by some.

Until the 1960s, the older Protestant churches (including the United Church of Canada) and the Roman Catholic church had a great deal of power and prestige in Canadian society. Since about 1965, that power and prestige have slipped away as organized religion, religious commitment and religious experience have become separable from each other, and as increased individualism and hedonism have diminished the appeal of traditional religiosity.

Many traditional organized religions have responded by incorporating modern values into their belief systems. For example, a number of churches have redefined their attitudes towards sexuality. This adaptability appears to ensure that they will not disappear from the scene. In contrast, the very rigidity of the conservative religious bodies, which allows them to fulfil deeply felt human needs — such as the needs for certainty and community — has given them increasing vigour. There is no evidence of their disappearance, either. The full effect of the revolution in Canada may only be felt when we are in a position to assess the importance of the unaffiliated, including those who exhibit eclectic personal belief systems.

For Further Reading

Hostetler, John A. 1974. *Hutterite Society*. Baltimore: Johns Hopkins University Press.

Mann, W.E. 1955. *Sect, Cult and Church in Alberta*. Toronto: University of Toronto Press.

Moir, John S. 1967. *Church and State in Canada*. Toronto: McClelland and Stewart.

Niebuhr, Richard. 1957. *The Social Sources of Denominationalism*. Cleveland: World Publishing.

Scheffel, David. 1991. *In the Shadow of the Antichrist: The Old Believers of Alberta*. Peterborough: Broadview Press.

Troeltsch, Ernst. 1931. *The Social Teaching of the Christian Churches*. Translated by Olive Wyon. London: George Allen and Unwin.

Chapter 4

Secularization and Change

Reginald W. Bibby

Religion, like the rest of life, is in constant motion. Consequently, social scientists who have studied religion have aspired not only to understand how social change has affected religion in the past and present, but how it will affect religion in the future.

Frankly, their success to date has not been overly impressive. Many early social thinkers looked at long-term patterns and declared the demise of religion. They were wrong. Some of them, along with many observers since, have maintained that religion is not disappearing — it's just that its dominant forms and expressions are constantly being replaced by new organizations and content. Unfortunately, these latter experts have also not proven to be particularly gifted social psychics.

By now it's very clear that the impact that the passage of time is having on religion is extremely complex. For starters, religion is still with us. Major world religions remain securely in place, while minor religions continue to emerge. Contrary to prediction, organizations such as the Roman Catholic church, rather than crumbling, have shown considerable resilience. Religion forecasters have been embarrassed by their inability to anticipate even the immediate future; take, for example, experts in the 1960s who were surprised by the post-hippie "Jesus movement" of less than a decade later.

Still, the attempts of social scientists to understand the impact of social change on religion have produced many important insights. Taken together, they offer considerable help in our effort to comprehend religion's present and future.

For purposes of discussion, the varied interpretations of what is happening to religion in advanced societies can be subsumed under four main categories: secularization, oscillation, stabilization and innovation. The categories are not perfectly distinct and, to make matters more confusing, their primary spokespeople have been inclined to mix and match. Nevertheless, they provide a good overview of the effort of social scientists to make sense of the impact that social change has on religion.

STEADY DECLINE: THE SECULARIZATION ARGUMENT

Many early observers of religion took the position that religion is inherently false and that in due time, it would be discarded by "thinking people." Such a "positivistic" view assumed that as societies became more advanced, greater illumination and economic well-being would relegate religion to history.

The founder of sociology, Auguste Comte (1966), maintained that civilization has been passing through three stages of thought: the theological, the metaphysical and the positive. Religion, belonging to the earliest stage of development, was gradually being abandoned. Similarly, anthropologist James Frazer (1922) saw human intellectual development evolving from magic through religion to science. Sigmund Freud (1957) predicted that religion would gradually be replaced with science, which, in his view, was a superior and far more responsible means of dealing with reality. Karl Marx (1970) likewise saw religion as a drug-like panacea that would no longer be needed once the problem of oppressive conditions was resolved.

The secularization viewpoint, however, has hardly been limited to those who have regarded religion's demise as inevitable because it is either primitive or false. A number of observers have seen religion's influence as decreasing because of the nature of advanced societies. Adam Smith (who published *The Wealth of Nations* in 1776) and Emile Durkheim (who published *The Elementary Forms of the Religious Life* in 1893) were among the earliest proponents of such a position. Since the 1960s, perhaps the most prominent and unequivocal spokesperson for the secularization thesis has been Bryan Wilson (1969, 1979, 1982, 1985), followed closely by Peter Berger (1967, 1986) and Thomas Luckmann (1967).

Secularization is seen by such thinkers as having institutional, organizational and personal components (Dobbelaere 1981, 1987). *Institutionally*, increasing specialization in advanced societies leads to a reduction in the areas of life over which religion has authority. For example, unlike the situation in less complex settings, religion no longer has control over society's political and educational spheres.

Such specialization — or social differentiation — can be seen in the loss of influence of the church in European countries since at least the Reformation. Closer to home, secularization at the institutional level has been experienced by the Roman Catholic church in Quebec since approximately 1960. Even today, a comparison of the roles of churches in Canada's rural communities and in its urban areas illustrates the same reality. In smaller places, it is still common for churches to carry out a number of social and community functions — complete with the pot-luck supper. In big cities, however, churches frequently do little more than perform rites of passage and provide a place of worship.

Organizationally, over time, religious groups move in the direction of conformity to the secular world. Max Weber (1963), for example, in discussing the movement from sect to church, has spoken of the tendency of religious groups to experience routinization. Worship becomes more formal and less spontaneous; beliefs become more structured; the religious community itself becomes more organized. Observers such as H. Richard Niebuhr (1957), drawing on the thinking of Weber and Ernst Troeltsch, have argued convincingly that the history of Christianity, for example, has been characterized by a church-sect cycle. Groups of people, concerned about the loss of original ideals, have broken away to form sects, only to evolve into formal denominations themselves, which in turn have given way to further idealistic sects. Works in the 1960s were particularly vocal about the way in which religious groups were "selling out" to secular culture (see, for example, Berger 1961; Berton 1965). The issue has been dropped, largely because by now the reality is pretty much taken for granted.

At the *personal level*, there is "a secularization of consciousness" — a change in the way in which people interpret their worlds. They no longer see what is taking place in terms of "the gods." What happens is viewed as largely the product of human and physical factors. Other-worldly ideas that once knew special veneration are forced to compete with this-worldly claims on this-worldly terms (Demerath and Williams 1992, 190).

Science and reason relentlessly move forward to respond to the questions of life's mysteries. So-called ultimate questions concerning the meaning of life and death are seen as interesting, but beyond resolution; attention is best given to more practical and pressing matters. Religion neither interprets life nor informs behaviour.

Secularization, then, is seen as a process in which religion has decreasing importance for societies, individuals and even the religious groups themselves. The territory over which religion has authority diminishes, socially and personally, while its supporting groups are co-opted by society. Put succinctly, its role is specialized, its influence marginalized, its organizations routinized.

This is not to say that supporters of the secularization thesis assume that the process is perfectly linear, without occasional disruptions. Robert Wuthnow (1976), for example, has pointed out that differences exhibited by certain age cohorts can alter the process. He writes, "At the most general level, whether the sources are generational or otherwise, discontinuities in the secularization process need to be acknowledged as the rule, not the exception, in religious change." Wuthnow cites Robert Nisbet's observation that "change in any degree of notable significance is intermittent rather than continuous, mutational, even explosive, rather than the simple accumulation of internal variations" (1976, 863).

Secularization advocates also frequently differentiate between "church religion" and religion more generally. Luckmann (1967), for example, has little doubt that religion survives beyond its traditional expressions, as "invisible religions." Berger (1969) sees an ongoing, vigorous interest in the supernatural.

But as they look at Christianity and its churches, secularization proponents see the long-term process as moving towards a decrease in the importance of at least "that kind" of religion.

DECLINE AND RESURGENCE: THE OSCILLATION ARGUMENT

According to the oscillation argument, societies swing between an emphasis on "rationality" and "irrationality," between a moving away from religion and a moving towards it. Proponents of this view include Pitirim Sorokin, Kingsley Davis and Daniel Bell.

Sorokin's (1957) well-known thesis, for example, is that history consists of a pendulum-like fluctuation between ideational and sensate cultures. The ideational period is characterized by ideals and spiritual concerns, while the sensate period is a time when a society emphasizes material values. Davis has maintained that there is "a limit to the extent to which a society can be guided by illusion"; but "there is also a limit to which a society can be guided by sheer rationality." Secularization will therefore "likely be terminated by religious revivals of one sort or another," complete with new sects (1949, 542-544). But religion is unlikely to be replaced by secular substitutes.

In like manner, Bell sees people in post-industrial societies as experiencing the limits of modernism and alternatives to religion. He writes that "a long era is coming to a close. The theme of Modernism was the world beyond ... We are now groping for a new vocabulary whose keyword seems to be limits," says Bell (1977, 448). He maintains that new religions will consequently arise in response to the core questions of existence: death, tragedy, obligation and love.

This oscillation argument has become increasingly popular in recent years. Social analyst Jeremy Rifkin (1980), for example, claims that it accounts for the emergence of the charismatic movement and the accelerated success of Evangelical Christianity. Intentionally or not, U.S. research suggesting that baby boomers are heading back to the churches in the 1990s has fed the idea that the religious pendulum is swinging once again (see, for example, Roozen et al. 1990; Brady 1991; Koop 1991). Also contributing to such an expectation for some has been the proclamation of prominent futurists John Naisbitt and Patricia Aburdene (1990) in their best-selling book, *Megatrends 2000*, that the world is on the verge of a massive return to spirituality.

No   Persistence   Talcott Parsons
LIMITED DECLINE: THE STABILIZATION ARGUMENT   Andrew Greeley

In contrast to those who see religion in advanced societies as either losing influence or vacillating between acceptance and rejection, other observers maintain that religion's place has remained fairly constant. Perhaps taking their cue from the writer of Ecclesiastes, that "there is nothing new under the sun," they have disputed the claim that religion's influence is diminishing. Two of the most prominent people who have held this viewpoint are Talcott Parsons and Andrew Greeley. In a very influential essay, Parsons (1963b) maintained that it is a mistake to equate either the decline of the church's authority over life or the individualistic approach to religion with a loss of religious influence. Christianity continues to have an important place in the present Western world, notably in the United States. While the spheres over which religion has had direct control and authority have decreased, so-called "secular conduct" knows the legacy of religion. The reason? Religious values, such as tolerance and decency, have been institutionalized. "I suggest that in a whole variety of respects modern society is more in accord with Christian values than its forebears have been," wrote Parsons, being careful to add that the difference is relative and that "the millennium definitely has not arrived" (1963b, 295). As for highly personal expressions of religion, Parsons argues that such a pattern is consistent with both "the individualistic principle inherent in Christianity" and the emphasis on differentiation in modern societies (1963b, 296). The result is that religion has become a highly "privatized," personal matter, differing from earlier expressions in being less overt and less tied to formal group involvement.

The net result for Parsons is that Christianity, rather than being in a state of decline, has been both institutionalized and privatized. Similar to the traditional family, the religious group "has lost many previous functions and has become increasingly a sphere of private sentiments." But, he insists, "it is as important as ever to the maintenance of the main patterns of the society, though operating with a minimum of direct outside control" (1963b, 296)

One might conclude from reading Parsons that all is well on the religious front. Individuals still take religion seriously, but are keeping their commitment to themselves. Religious groups have not lost influence; they have already helped to shape their cultures' values and, if anything, are in a better position than ever before to concentrate on the essence of religion itself.

Andrew Greeley (1972a) went even further than Parsons, asserting that secularization is a myth. Greeley acknowledges that religion today faces secular pressures and is not important to everyone. However, he maintains that such realities are not unique to our time. He specifically challenges six claims that are common to the secularization position, arguing that: 1) faith is not being seriously eroded by science and higher education; 2) religion is no less significant in daily life than in the alleged great ages of faith; 3) participation levels are not down relative to more than the immediate past; 4) religion continues to have a widespread impact on life, but in less obvious ways; 5) private commitment has consequences for the public sphere; and 6) the sacred remains highly visible in everyday life. According to

Greeley, religion continues to flourish, despite talk of its decline.

DECLINE AND REPLACEMENT: THE INNOVATION ARGUMENT

Still other observers of change and religion maintain that, somewhat ironically, the decline of existing forms of religion will automatically trigger the appearance of new ones. Unlike the oscillation advocates, such people are talking about a process that is taking place *now*. It's not that things will shift back to religion in the long run; things are constantly shifting. The demand for religion is constant; only the suppliers are changing.

Such an argument goes back at least as far as Durkheim. While he is typically associated with the secularization thesis, there is an important "wrinkle" to his thinking that is often not given the emphasis it deserves. While recognizing that traditional religion in Europe was in a serious state of decline in the late nineteenth century, Durkheim maintained that religion was anything but dead. Unlike Comte, he did not see the advance of science as eliminating religion. On the contrary, he pointed out that the two types of thinking had co-existed since the birth of science, and would continue to do so. Scientific thought, said Durkheim, is a more perfect form of religious thought and progressively replaces it. However, religion will always have an important speculative function because science "is fragmentary and incomplete; it advances but slowly and is never finished; but life cannot wait" (1976, 429-431). Religious explanations may be forced to retreat, reformulate and give ground in the face of the steady advance of science. But religion never surrenders.

Moreover, because, according to Durkheim, religion has its very source in social life and is responsible for an array of important collective and individual functions, it will survive. "The old gods are growing old or are already dead, and others are not yet born," he wrote. However, while noting that "there are no gospels which are immortal," he added, "but neither is there any reason for believing that humanity is incapable of inventing new ones" (1976, 428).

In a stimulating contemporary update, Rodney Stark and William Bainbridge (1985) have maintained that religion is guaranteed an indispensable role in humanity's quest for meaning. Only references to supernaturally grounded ideas, they say, can provide plausible answers to the so-called "ultimate questions" pertaining to the meaning of life and death. As carriers of explanations based on such supernatural assumptions, religion plays a unique and irreplaceable role in human affairs.

Viewing religious activity as dynamic and ever-changing, Stark and Bainbridge make extensive use of a market analogy. Secularization, they say, is a process that is found in all "religious economies." Some religions and some groups are always losing ground. But because the market for religion remains, the activity only increases and the competition intensifies as old groups and new groups struggle to gain, retain and enlarge market shares.

Such activity sees breakaway sects attempt to rejuvenate fading traditions, while new groups — which Stark and Bainbridge call cults — attempt to bring consumers something new. Revival and innovation are consequently central features of the religion marketplace. Precisely in the geographical areas where conventional religion is weakest, cults will be strongest, vying for the chance to seize the market opportunity.

Secularization, in the minds of Stark and Bainbridge, is therefore a process that stimulates religion, rather than extinguishes it. The never-ending human quest for meaning ensures religion's viability.

SECULARIZATION AND CHANGE: SOME BLIND ALLEYS

Some facts about religion are readily apparent in the advanced societies of the Western world in the 1990s.

First, contrary to the expectations of the early secularization advocates such as Comte, Frazer, Freud and Marx, religion is hardly in its death throes. Updated proclamations of religion's imminent demise, such as those of the "death of God" movement of the 1960s, have also proven to be inaccurate. Even observers like Luckmann and Berger have underestimated the resilience of existing church religions. Established groups haven't just rolled over and died. The Roman Catholic church is a powerful, long-established multinational corporation. The same can be said for the Anglican, Presbyterian, Lutheran and Baptist churches — not to mention three or four other major world religions. A few upstarts, such as the Mormons and Jehovah's Witnesses, have also been involved in global expansion programs. Religious groups do not readily die. They retreat, retrench, revamp and resurface. Religion on a personal and organizational level is certainly far from extinct in Western nations.

Second, despite the predictions of the likes of Sorokin, Davis and Bell, talk of baby boomer returns, and *Megatrend* prophecies, it is not clear that there is anything resembling a massive switch taking place in the religious habits of North Americans and Europeans. Attendance levels remain low; interest levels do not appear to be changing very much; the major institutional carriers of culture, including the media, give little indication of becoming noticeably more (or less) oriented towards the mysterious or the spiritual. Religious groups themselves remain highly secularized. The pendulum has yet to swing.

What's more, at the individual level, there's good reason to believe that interest in supernatural and spiritual matters more generally has remained fairly constant for some time — perhaps not only from the time our records begin but since the beginning of time itself. What "swings" is not the receptivity to the things that religion has been about, but the extent to which specific religions and religious groups succeed in responding to that ongoing interest in mystery and meaning (Bibby and Weaver 1985).

Third, it's true that identification with religious traditions remains high and that allegiances to specific religious groups are fairly stable over time. Parsons' observation that the importance of the family will ensure that the overwhelming majority will accept the religious affiliation of their parents — "unless the whole society is drastically disorganized" — has proven sound (1963b, 294). However, it's difficult to find support for the assertion of Parsons and Greeley that individuals are privately as devout as their predecessors. Extensive research in North America and Europe has consistently found that levels of commitment by any number of measures has been dropping during this century (see, for example, Martin 1978; Stark and Bainbridge 1985; Hill and Bowman 1985; McCallum 1986; Roof and McKinney 1987; Bibby 1987; Holm 1989; Chaves 1989; Hamberg 1991). Further, rarely have researchers been able to link commitment in a clear-cut way to attitudes and behaviour for the vast majority of those people who do exhibit either private or public commitment. Put bluntly, if people are "just as religious" as they were in the past, they neither know it nor show it.

While cultures undoubtedly know the legacy of days when religion was more important individually and societally, by now, existing values are largely independent of their religious roots. The same values are now promoted by functional alternatives to the churches. Religion can ask for a footnote, but if religion is no longer recognized by the public as a major source of those values, extending such a credit becomes little more than a technical courtesy.

Fourth, while Durkheim, followed by Stark and Bainbridge, saw new gods coming into being that would replace the old, in actual fact the old religions that have dominated the stages of the Western world for centuries — namely, Protestant and Roman Catholic variations of Christianity — remain the dominant religions in Europe and North America. In the 1970s, considerable sociological effort was given to understanding new religious movements in a wide variety of Western countries. It is now very apparent that such movements were on the periphery of religious life more generally, embracing relatively small numbers of people (see, for example, Robbins and Anthony 1981). In the 1980s, Stark and Bainbridge's (1985) extensive research in the United States, Canada and Europe produced data showing that cult centres are most numerous in areas where conventional religion is weakest. However, they never demonstrated that new religious groups were succeeding in recruiting large numbers of people who are presumably disenchanted with the established religious groups (see Wallis and Bruce 1984; Bibby and Weaver 1985).

Interest in new religious offerings, including most recently the New Age movement, exists. Yet, the net result today is that the majority of the people in virtually every nation studied continue to identify with the well-entrenched Christian groups — or, to a lesser extent, with no group at all.

RE-EXAMINING THE PROBLEM: SOME HELPFUL INSIGHTS

The secularization advocates, such as Wilson, Berger and Luckmann, have accurately observed the decline of historical Christianity's impact on individuals, cultures and religious groups themselves. As we've seen, things are not the same as they once were.

While Greeley has a valid point in noting that attendance patterns are difficult to document, records that are available in countries such as England, the United States and Canada point to clear decreases in attendance at religious services for the periods they cover. Significantly, the years involved deal with periods of accelerated industrialization and post-industrialization.

For example, an English city like Liverpool has experienced a drop from 70 percent regular attendance in 1831 through 30 percent in 1891 to a current level of less than 10 percent (computed from Martin 1967, 44). Regular attendance in the United States has slipped from about 75 percent in 1958 to a current 45 percent (Gallup Report 1992). In Canada, the proportion of people attending services weekly has dropped from 65 percent in 1945 to a level today of 35 percent (Gallup Report 1992; Bibby 1987, 17). Further, regular service attendance levels in such countries as Britain, France, Belgium, Holland, Italy, Greece and the Scandinavian countries are estimated to be no higher than 5 percent to 10 percent, and only slightly higher in Australia and New Zealand (see, for example, Hill and Bowman 1985; McCallum 1986). It is generally conceded that such extremely low levels represent a drop from both the immediate and distant past.

Beyond attendance, even when individuals claim to be committed, they exhibit a "religion à la carte" pattern, picking and choosing those aspects of the faith that they want, while rejecting others. Faith has been highly marginalized. Undoubtedly, there has always been a tendency to be somewhat selective. Given today's consumer-driven society, where the name of the game is choice in all of life, it's difficult to imagine a time when people were more inclined to approach religion with a personal consumption mentality.

If we look at religion in a societal context, it is difficult to dispute Wilson's conclusion that traditional religion "has succumbed to the transformation of social organization" to the extent that nowhere "in the modern world does traditional faith influence more than residually and incidentally the operation of society" (1982, 170). The gods may be permanent but they are peripheral to the major events that characterize the daily developments in Western societies.

And from an organizational point of view, while variations certainly exist — notably in the Roman Catholic and Conservative Protestant instances — religious groups have frequently downplayed the supernatural aspects of their traditions, embraced societal issues, and in more than a few instances been solidly co-opted by secular culture.

Regional and local variations notwithstanding, secularization — seen as the loss of influence of religion at the societal, personal and organizational levels — is widespread in North America and Europe. Further, to date at least, the prophecies of cultural swings in the direction of spirituality and of the response to new religions by people in the market for meaning have not been fulfilled.

But as Stark and Bainbridge (1985) remind us, life is still moving. The religious situation is ever-changing. There's more to be said.

A POSSIBLE SYNTHESIS: FRAGMENTATION

If North Americans and Europeans are not particularly in the market for large amounts of religion, a great many — perhaps the vast majority — show a decided reluctance to reject organized religion altogether. Such a clue should not be ignored.

It may well be that the most important religious development associated with modern times is not the abandonment of religion. Rather, it's the growing inclination of people to reject Christianity and any other formal religions as authoritative meaning systems, in favour of drawing upon fragments of those traditions in a highly selective, consumer-like fashion.

Advanced societies provide many choices — entertainment, clothing, food, family, sexuality, education, politics, morality, lifestyle, religion. However, there is only so much money and time. The net result? Selective consumption. Religion receives no exemption.

Research indicates that Stark and Bainbridge are right: people continue to raise questions for which the gods alone seem to have adequate answers. Many also feel the need to have the gods present during life's pivotal passages: birth, marriage, death. They are intrigued with the supernatural realm, and large numbers find themselves experiencing spiritual needs.

But the customers are fussy and restrained. They want specific things and are prepared to expend only so much time and money. They also have psychological limits. Faced with the difficulty of playing out a wide variety of roles, many frequently find it easier to compartmentalize at least some parts of life, rather than to thread them together using something like a life-integrating religious faith.

Modern women and men continue to identify with established religious traditions, selectively adopt certain beliefs, practices and teachings, and occasionally turn to groups for specialized professional services — a baptism, a wedding, a funeral. Consumer-oriented as they are, many supplement the items available from their core religious traditions with fragments from other systems. They read their horoscopes, give credibility to psychic phenomena, think they might be reincarnated, don't rule out the existence of a spirit world. They are into fragments, not systems, into consumption rather than commitment. Canada is no exception (see Table 4.1)

Table 4.1 FRAGMENTATION, CANADIAN-STYLE (in percentages)

	Teens	*Adults*
Involvement and Commitment		
Attend weekly	18	23
Receive high level of enjoyment	15	32
View self as committed	24	26
Identify with a group	79	90
Rites performed or anticipated re:		
Birth	75	85
Marriage	83	86
Death	87	91
Beliefs		
God exists.	81	83
Jesus was divine.	80	75
Some people have psychic powers.	69	59
The claims of astrology are true.	53	34
Spirit world contact is possible.	44	39
I have experienced God.	34	46
I will be reincarnated.	32	27

Sources: Reginald Bibby, Project Canada, youth surveys, 1988 and 1992; adult survey, 1990.

Describing Europe and beyond, British sociologists Roy Wallis and Steve Bruce have come to a similar conclusion. They have written that people both inside and outside of religious groups "synthesize various selections to suit their own tastes. New ideas are simply added to the sum total of legitimate ideas; there is no possibility of producing a neat, coherent set of dogmas" (1984, 22). Similarly, James Beckford comments, "It is nowadays better to conceptualize religion as a cultural resource than as a social institution" (1989, 171).

Such fragment adoption appears to suit the style of today's pervasive individualism, allowing people to retain their core identification with the faith of their parents and grandparents, while at the same time "fashioning a faith" that seems "right" for them. Further, in opting for fragments over entire religious systems — be those systems Presbyterian or Roman Catholic or Anglican or Hindu — they are able to have the leeway they want in dealing with such matters as ethics in business or sexual behaviour. Many people prefer fragments to religious systems for a simple reason: they work.

For all the talk about abandoning religion, the truth is that, in practical terms, it doesn't make much sense for people to opt out of religion altogether and become members of the bland "nones." Just as it's handy to have access to a good lawyer, doctor or plumber, so it's wise to have access to a minister, priest or rabbi. It also doesn't make much sense to switch to another group, given family background and all, since it's possible to get most things by staying put.

Further, the fact that most people choose fragments over commitment hardly means that they are receptive to new religions. Quite the opposite. To venture into a strange new religious group is not only to run the risk of being stigmatized, it's also to run the risk of being asked to adopt a life-embracing system that is just as oppressive and emotionally dysfunctional as the old one.

More typically, the established religions seem to serve as "the identification nucleus" around which an array of fragments are gathered, including newer entries into the religious marketplace. The appearance of these new entries signals the opportunity to adopt a part rather than a whole. Offerings such as astrology, psychic phenomena, New Age thought and Eastern religions are literally "consumer cults."

Contrary to the assertion of Stark and Bainbridge (1985), religious markets in most countries in the Western world are extremely tight. If people want full-fledged meaning systems, they don't have to turn to cults. Total commitment to any number of versions of the Christian faith and other established world religions is already one of the offerings that they have before them. Most choose to pass.

Table 4.2 IDENTIFICATION WITH THE FRAGMENT THESIS: CANADIANS
WHO DO NOT ATTEND SERVICES REGULARLY (in percentages)

"Some observers maintain that few people are actually abandoning their religious traditions. Rather, they draw selective beliefs and practices, even if they do not attend services frequently. They are not about to be recruited by other religious groups. Their identification with their religious tradition is fairly solidly fixed, and it is to these groups that they will turn when confronted with marriage, death and, frequently, birth."

How well would you say this observation describes you?

	Accurate	Somewhat accurate	Not very accurate	Not at all accurate	Totals
Nationally	48	33	9	10	100
Roman Catholic	61	31	4	4	100
Protestant	49	40	7	4	100
Other religions	37	34	10	19	100
No religion	12	22	29	37	100
18–34	43	32	11	14	100
35–50	50	34	9	7	100
55+	53	33	5	9	100

The approximate religious composition of the Canadian population is: Roman Catholic 45%, Protestant 40%, Other 5%, None 10%.

Ironically, although religious groups typically decry such selective consumption, over time most have adjusted to such a consumer mentality. Their "religious menus" have become highly diversified to the point that the spiritually inclined through to the social activist to the person requiring a wedding or a sentimental Christmas service can be easily accommodated.

Societies are quite willing to allow religion to have its rightful, specialized place, as long as it follows the pluralistic rules and doesn't try to be overly aggressive or excessively dogmatic. Coexistence is preferable to expansion, tolerance to truth. Variety and vagueness are virtues.

Fragments work these days for individuals, groups and societies. Religion, even of the church variety, is not disappearing. An imminent swing back to faith is not on the horizon. The new gods are not yet born. But things have definitely been changing. Religion, like so many other products in the information age, has come to have a highly specific role in the lives of societies and the lives of individuals. Custom-made by religious groups for both cultures and consumers, it remains important in its own specialized way. To the extent that some would maintain that faith is supposed to address all of life, the problem religions face is not that individuals want so much. It's rather that they want so little.

For Further Reading

Beckford, James A. 1989. *Religion and Advanced Industrial Society*. London: Unwin Hyman.

Bibby, Reginald W. 1987. *Fragmented Gods: The Poverty and Potential of Religion in Canada*. Toronto: Irwin Publishing.

Freud, Sigmund. 1957. *The Future of an Illusion*. Garden City: Doubleday.

Graham, Ron. 1990. *God's Dominion: A Sceptic's Quest*. Toronto: McClelland and Stewart.

Martin, David. 1979. *A General Theory of Secularization*. London: Harper and Row.

Stark, Rodney, and William S. Bainbridge. 1985. *The Future of Religion*. Berkeley: University of California Press.

Chapter 5

New Religious Movements

Stephen A. Kent

New Religions and the Sociology of Ideology

Sociologists of religion have used some variation of the term "new religious movement" for well over twenty years. However, persistent problems exist with the term. Central to these problems is specifying the relationships between this label and the more sociologically traditional terms "sects" and "cults." Furthermore, no clear guidelines exist that allow researchers to determine in what historical period "new" (as opposed to established or old) religious movements operate (see Melton 1987). To further complicate matters, a new religious movement may practice religious expressions that are relatively new in a particular country but claim precedent for those expressions in a home country (see Bird and Reimer 1976, 313-314). Consequently, "new" occasionally may refer to the relatively recent discovery of a group or even of a religion by researchers (see, for example, Oliphant 1991) instead of the actual date of an organization's initial appearance in a local, national or international location.

By "new religious *movements*" sociologists of religion are usually referring to individual groups or organizations rather than to the larger movements or social currents in which these singular groups operate. (Take, for example, the Eastern religious movement of the early 1970s, when tens of thousands of North Americans and Europeans became involved in religious organizations or groups such as Hare Krishna, Transcendental Meditation, Sri Chinmoy and Swami Muktananda.) Unfortunately, sociologists of religion might refer to any one of these groups as new religious movements when, in fact, they are organizations or groups inside a broad religio-social movement involving Eastern spirituality. (The terms "organizations" and "groups" are used interchangeably in this chapter. Note that groups may lack the formal internal structures that characterize modern organizations.)

To clarify what researchers frequently call new religious movements, it is useful to identify these groups simply as "ideological organizations or groups" or "religiously ideological groups" and avoid both the artificiality of "newness" and the unnecessary restriction of viewing a large number of groups merely as "religious." The new religions are ideological because their members collectively do not question the primary assumptions about their groups' fundamental doctrines (Kent 1990, 394).

On a social-psychological level, the individuals who make up these groups can in practice treat issues that involve religion, politics, psychotherapy, economics, health and medicine, or family as ideological issues. Because members often hold ideological beliefs about these issues, religious ideology can have ramifications for political, medical and family life. For religiously ideological groups, theology contains elements of social control that inhibit the cultivation of negative thoughts about the organization, its leadership and its teachings.

On a sociological level, these groups prevent individuals from publicly expressing doubts or questions that they might have concerning doctrines that are fundamental to their self-legitimacy. For religiously ideological groups, these core doctrines address their collective claims to a link with the supernatural, which they use to justify the array of rewards and punishments they offer to adherents and others with whom they come in contact (Kent 1990, 394). In private, members of these organizations may have personal doubts, but in group settings they do not express them partly because they are aware that their groups would impose (often powerful) punishments upon them if they were to do so. Suppressing fundamental challenges to their basic assumptions is a characteristic that new religions share with older and more established ideologically religious counterparts.

Emphasis on the religiously ideological nature of groups such as the Unification Church/Moonies, Scientology, the International Society for Krishna Consciousness (ISKCON or Hare Krishna), and Transcendental Meditation allows researchers to recognize their similarities to groups with other ideological persuasions. For example, in a study of politically ideological Marxist sects in Toronto, Roger O'Toole (1975, 1977) used essentially the same theoretical models that sociologists of religion were using at the time. Likewise, an examination of the psychotherapeutic ideology called "est" (from Erhard Seminars Training) identified similarities with religion, even though there was little scientific value in calling it religious (Pelletier 1986). In the economic field, a former salesperson in the product marketing company, Amway (which has a production facility in London, Ontario), refers to its ideology as "the cult of free enterprise" (Butterfield 1986). Therefore, in terms of sociological analysis, Marxist sects, some psychotherapies and a few businesses share with religious groups the phenomenon of belief and behaviour systems that are ideological at core, even though the content of those ideologies differs markedly.

A historical perspective has also proved useful. Many religious traditions that are now mainstream or old were as poorly received by segments of their respective societies as are many new ideological groups or religions today. Using concepts acquired by reading contemporary attacks against Reverend Moon's Unification Church, Peter Masefield identified passages in the earliest Buddhist literature that led him to conclude that Buddha's disciples "were in their day received with as little enthusiasm – and for much the same reasons – as modern religious movements such as the Moonies" (1985, 144). Likewise, Stephen A. Kent (1982b) analyzed the emergence and development of Mahayana Buddhism in India by borrowing concepts from contemporary examinations of new religious and religiously ideological groups. Finally, anthropological material about recent expressions of religious millenarianism among South Pacific Islanders has shed light on the development of early Christianity (Gager 1975).

Focus on new religiously ideological organizations, therefore, must not obscure the fact that many older religious organizations once were new ideological groups in their respective settings. A primary reason that some social scientists study groups that are either new discoveries or proponents of new theologies is that contemporary analyses often help us to understand the early days of the now-established organizations. The term "new," therefore, is relative to the historical and cultural eras in which researchers work and live.

THE TOPOLOGICAL TRADITION OF CULTS AND SECTS

Most sociologists of new religions limit themselves to the study of groups that make supernatural ideological claims, and among these groups, to those that many people call "sects" or "cults." The term "new religious movement" is often used in the place of "sects" and "cults." However, these terms are not necessarily limited to organizations that are either of recent origin or in some sense "new" to researchers (Yinger 1970, 266-272).

Sectarian studies have appeared in the sociological literature since Max Weber (1904) sparked his friend, Ernst Troeltsch (1931), to write on the nature of religious sects (see Weber 1958a). Refinements and elaborations on their early observations provided the springboard for important Canadian work on what, for their respective historical periods, were new religions. Among the pioneers of Canadian sociology was Samuel D. Clark, whose study of Canadian Protestant sectarianism from 1760 to 1900 remains a classic in historical sociology.

Claiming that "the sect has been a product of what might be called frontier conditions of social life" (1948, xii), Clark traced the struggles that resulted as mainstream denominations confronted sectarian upsurges in the Maritimes and Ontario. From a social-psychological point of view, he argued, the sect "gains its following because it meets certain basic social needs of people which are not being met by the church or by secular agencies in the community" (1948, 432-433). Among the most prominent of these needs was the "feeling of fellowship and status on the part of people who had lost a sense of belonging to any organized society ... Today, as in the past, the support of the religious sect comes from that section of the population which has lost a sense of belonging to any settled society" (1948, 433, 434).

Clark asserted that as an institution, "the new religious movement, the sect, offered an important means of securing the adjustment of the religious institution to new social conditions. It served to maintain the religious interest as an effective basis of social organization in areas of change where traditional systems of social control, including that of the church, were breaking down" (1948, 433). In sum, sectarianism gave people fellowship and status as it allowed individuals to voice their dissatisfaction with the status quo through religious structures and expressions.

Similar themes of the integrative functions of sectarianism appeared in W.E. Mann's study of sects, cults and churches in Alberta (1955). Again, his basic characterizations of sects resembled ones put forward by both Troeltsch and Weber, although Mann himself developed them from the work of Joachim Wach (1944, 196-205). Mann's descriptive definition of a sect included reputed qualities that had woven through many sectarian typologies for nearly three-quarters of a century, and he, like Clark, used the terms "sects" and "new religious movements" interchangeably (see Mann 1955, 154). He claimed that sects practiced "ascetic morality," contained "a vigorous protest against formality and conventionality in religious procedures," attempted "to recover the original and unadulterated essence of religion," and maintained "a high degree of equality and fraternity among the members along with an unusual degree of lay participation in worship and organizational activities." In addition, they also were "usually exclusive and selective in membership and hence tend[ed] to be small and homogeneous." Many sects "tend[ed] to show great respect for leaders with charismatic powers and a casual indifference to, or an energetic protest against, the professionalization or hierarchization of the clergy." Also worth noting is that sects placed "an emphasis upon individual religious experience, a requirement that generally limits full membership to adults" (1955, 5).

As socially produced institutions, sects (according to Mann) were "institutions of social and religious protest [that were] bulwarks of certain disadvantaged social groups in their struggle against the social power, moral conventions, and ethos of the middle classes, and against institutionalized and formalized religion" (1955, 5).

> [Social conditions involving] rapid social change usually produce new sects. In such periods, settled relationships between classes and institutions are greatly disturbed, social integration is threatened, and ultimately a portion of the population finds itself on the fringe of the organized social structure ... Thus it is that sects may emerge, having as their social purpose the defence of the interests and needs of marginal sections of the population (1955, 5-6).

The basic characteristics that Mann highlighted also appeared in numerous sociological studies of nontraditional, religiously ideological groups that were published throughout the mid-twentieth century. By 1946, thirty-five groups in Alberta met Mann's sectarian criteria (1955, 27, 30). This impressive number allowed him to claim that Alberta was uniquely worthy of a focused study since it had an "exceptional history of religious non-conformity, a history without contemporary parallel among the provinces of Canada" (1955, 3).

Mann also discussed groups that he called "cults" and found ten of them in Alberta by 1946 (1955, 39). Their essential characteristic was their "syncretic feature," by which they "tend to blend alien religious or psychological notions with Christian doctrine with a view of obtaining a more 'adequate' or 'modern' faith. For this reason they are labelled heresies by both the churches and the sects and especially denounced by the latter" (1955, 6-7). Moreover, "their services are generally lacking in stirring emotional manifestations; ... most cults accept the validity of modern science ... [but] represent a protest against purely physical science and all forms of crass materialism." Cults "are adjusted to the secular culture and are therefore utilitarian and this-worldly in outlook. Their attitude to the established churches is generally one of condescension or enlightened superiority." Finally, in contrast to sects, cults seldom "take a strong ascetic stand or press upon their followers a programme of strict self-denial ... In membership regulations they are less rigid and exclusive than sects," and "women predominate among cult leaders" (1955, 7, 8).

By the late 1970s, the sect/cult and church typologies that Mann and Clark used to frame their studies had receded in importance. Too many exceptions existed both to assessments of their causes and to the content of their descriptive categories for them to remain as rigorous scientific concepts. In assessing, for example, Clark's work, Harry Hiller acknowledged "there is no question that Clark's interpretation is useful as it pertains to a particular period in Canadian development," yet he added that "we now know that sectarian forms of religion have their roots in processes far more complex than merely social disorganization, new frontiers of economic exploitation, or 'footloose' lower-class persons" (1982, 84, 85). Despite elaborate efforts by Bryan Wilson (1973, 11-30) to sustain the utility of the sectarian typology, scholars were seeing how varied these phenomena actually were.

For example, a challenge to the long-honoured belief in the exclusivity of sectarian membership illustrates one of many problems faced by sect and cult typologists. A researcher who was examining a Hebrew Christian group in Ontario realized that dual membership provided it with recruitment and resource-acquisition opportunities that would have been unavailable had the group insisted on exclusive allegiance (Kohn 1983, 162-163; 1985; see Heirich 1977, 663; Zald and McCarthy 1980, 5-6; Kent 1982b, 326). Countless other exceptions to these sectarian topological characteristics appeared with the explosion of nontraditional religions in Canada and elsewhere in the early 1970s, so scholars began developing classification categories that seemed to have greater research utility.

One study developed a new, threefold sectarian typology based on the way that groups "foster among their participants reduced feelings of moral accountability or put another way, enhanced feelings of innocence" (Bird 1979, 343). This typology emerged out of a study conducted by Fred Bird and William Reimer from the fall of 1973 to the spring of 1978 (Westley 1983, 21) on "new religious and para-religious" groups in Montreal. Bird found that devotees "of a sacred lord or lordly truth" function in such groups as Divine Light Mission, ISKCON, Christian Charismatic groups and Sri Chinmoy. They "ultimately surrender themselves to a holy master or ultimate reality to whom they attribute superhuman powers and consciousness" (Bird 1979, 336). By surrendering in this manner, devotees "allow these associations [with others in the group] to become their dominant reference group. Other moral expectations, related to worldly success in career or personal relationships, are relativized in relation to the demands and expectations of these groups" (Bird 1979, 342).

Second, disciples "progressively seek to master spiritual and/or physical disciplines in order to achieve a state of enlightenment and self-harmony, often following the example of a revered teacher" (Bird 1979, 336). Discipleship groups such as Zen and Dharmadhatu frequently reduce "secular goals and expectations" in relation "to the pursuit of this sense of balance and equanimity" (1979, 343).

Finally, Bird identified apprenticeship groups as those whose adherents "seek to master particular psychic, shamanic, and therapeutic skills in order to tap and realize sacred powers within themselves" (1979, 336). Apprenticeship groups such as est, Transcendental Meditation and Scientology reduce the moral accountability of their adherents in two ways. First, they instruct apprentices "that they are the arbiters of their own destiny and [control] how to utilize the techniques and processes learned in these groups." Second, they counsel apprentices "to relativize or discount other standards of achievement in comparison to their own sense of accomplishment with the techniques acquired in their initiatory ordeal" (1979, 342).

In sum, Bird's typology attributed to each of devoteeship, discipleship and apprenticeship its own ways of reducing feelings of moral accountability among its adherents. These are, respectively, "(a) by relativizing or diminishing the extent to which participants feel *morally answerable to others*, (b) by decreasing adherents' own feeling of *self-accountability*, and (c) by supporting moral models which reduce the *sense of difference between actual behaviour and moral expectations*" (1979, 341).

Bird's analysis of techniques that diminish adherents' feelings of moral accountability was an innovative development in the topological tradition, partly because it identified overarching similarities among different religiously ideological organizations while still recognizing significant differences in training and doctrines.

The most successful attempt to define *sect* and *cult* in sociological terms led, paradoxically, into a new debate about the origins of sectarianism and the significance of sects in Canadian secular life. Rodney Stark and William Bainbridge argued that both sects and cults functioned "in a high state of tension with their surrounding sociocultural environment" (1985, 24), yet that they differed in the extent to which they had historical precedent within that environment. "Sects have a prior tie with another religious organization" while for the most part cults "do not have a prior tie with another established religious body in the society in question" (1985, 25).

When they asserted, however, that in both Canada and the United States "cults abound where the churches are weak" (1985, 471), they initiated a conflict with Canadian sociologist Reginald Bibby over the appearance and significance of new religions in Canadian life. Stark and Bainbridge used Canadian data to show that secularization was a self-regulating process with sects and cults constantly appearing to fill voids caused by churches that lose the ability to provide people with meaning and order. "Secularization," which is the diminishing role of religion in modern life, "prompts cult formation," they claimed (1985, 457).

In contrast to Stark and Bainbridge's findings, Bibby's survey research indicated "that religiosity in Canada has been adversely influenced by modern industrialization and that ... it will continue to experience dissipation in the foreseeable future" (1979, 15). His 1980-81 Canadian national mail survey indicated that "contrary to popular belief, relatively few Canadians are turning to the so-called new religions. Only about 1% claim to be strongly interested in activities and groups such as [Transcendental Meditation], Hare Krishna, the Moonies, Eckankar, and Scientology. The most popular of these is [Transcendental Meditation], which many of the interested view more as a meditation practice than as religion" (1983a, 8).

According to Bibby, sectarian involvement is extremely small in Canada, and sects are not likely to escape the inevitable push towards secularization that is affecting Canadian religiosity (1983a, 1987; Bibby and Weaver 1985). He concluded that "Canadians who seem to have abandoned their own religious groups have shown little inclination to adopt the new religions, no matter how plentiful or active the groups may be" (1987, 39). Estimates of membership among some of the more notable groups in the late 1970s (when numbers were at their peak) state that there were "450 Hare Krishna members; 350-650 Unification Church members; 250 Children of God; about 700 full-time Scientologists and 15,000 taking Scientology courses; and over 200,000 who had been initiated into Transcendental Meditation" (Hexham, Currie, and Townsend 1988, 1479).[1] A 1984 representative telephone sample (2,014 persons) of the Quebec population indicated that 5.4 percent of the people either were in or had been involved in Eastern meditation groups (such as Transcendental Meditation, Eckankar, Divine Light Mission, etc.), while 19.9 percent of the people had read works of Eastern spirituality (Chagnon 1985b, 329-330). In an earlier Montreal survey, probably 18 percent to 22 percent of the adult population had participated in various new religious movements (Bird and Reimer 1982, 4). Another study — which does not, however, cite concrete data — says that Canadian evidence suggests that "nine out of ten children who make radical departures [from their families to join religiously ideological groups] return within several years or less to pick up the threads of their lives" (Levine 1984, 168).

THE ORIGINS AND ATTRACTION OF RELIGIOUSLY IDEOLOGICAL GROUPS

However disputable Stark and Bainbridge's analysis of sect and cult formation may be, it nevertheless implies both a *social-psychological* and a *social-structural* explanation of why religiously ideological groups appear and flourish. On a social-psychological level, Stark and

Bainbridge assume, religions offer to people desirable "compensators" (that is, the *"belief that ... reward[s] will be obtained in the distant future or in some other context which cannot be immediately verified"* [1985, 6]). Typical religious compensators include heaven, nirvana, enlightenment or a higher rebirth. Periodically, established religious bodies such as churches and denominations become so associated with secular issues that they harm their ability to offer these compensators to believers. New sects and some cults, however, emerge in the social structure to fulfil (what almost appears to be for some researchers) a basic human need for compensatory meaning and order (see Stark and Bainbridge 1985, 5-6; also Chagnon 1983, 431; O'Toole 1984, 21-23, 92) when mainstream religions fail to provide them (see Stark and Bainbridge 1985, 99). Such an interpretation aligns well with a long sociological tradition of viewing all forms of religion within a functionalist perspective that emphasizes what religion does or how it functions for individuals and the societies in which they live (see McGuire 1992, 13-15). It may even align with the conclusions of other researchers who claim "that the new religions are expressions of cultural hysteria. They amplify hysterical tendencies at the same time that they 'cure' them ... they are sought out by Westerners who display a Western form of hysterical personality" (Hexham and Poewe 1986, 162-163).

Québécois authors, however, are divided over the positive or negative functions of these religiously ideological groups in their province. The late Roland Chagnon insisted that "the new religions respond to the profoundly felt needs on the part of Québécois today of attaining a coherent and satisfying image of themselves" (1985b, 321 [my translation]). The groups "try, not only to change in a radical manner the identity of people, but also to foster a new integration of all the dimensions of their personalities" (1985b, 322 [my translation]; see Chagnon 1986b). This change is so important and meaningful for many Québécois because a series of events — the October crisis (1970); the oil crisis (1973); the federal-provincial struggle; the constitutional crisis following the May 1980 referendum; and the growth of the New Right — has resulted in a moroseness perhaps best called a *"tranquil disillusionment"* (Chagnon 1985a, 230). Arguing more broadly, a Quebec Anglophone, Frances Westley, concluded that "members of these groups themselves claim that the transformation of society depends upon the transformation of the individual in it" (1983, 172) and they represent contemporary examples of Emile Durkheim's "cult of man" by their belief in "the sacredness of the ideal human" (1983, 9).

Francophone Marxists have many of the same social and political crises in mind as Chagnon did when they lament that all of these new sects "express a lack of confidence in the capacity of [humanity] to construct a world of peace and of harmony, while at the same time [express] a fundamental pessimism about all that is the fruit of action and human will" (Gosselin and Monière 1978, 10 [my translation]). More damningly, "the sects reveal themselves as an efficacious agent of disarticulating conflicts. They isolate the individual, they marginalize the person from the system, they disengage the person from collective responsibilities by reducing responsibilities with respect to oneself" (Gosselin and Monière 1978, 153 [my translation]).

Still another Québécois author, Richard Bergeron (1982), analyzes approximately 300 newer and somewhat older religious groups in the context of their theological beliefs and their deviations from Christianity, or more particularly Catholicism, thereby minimizing their political or social significance. "The phenomenon of the new religions," Bergeron writes, "constitutes an emergence of the eternal gnosis into our contemporary world, given that gnosis is not a Christian heresy but a particular and original phenomenon of the history of religions" (1983, 76). Nevertheless, he insists that "it would be easy to show that contemporary gnoses discredit the sacramental, historical and dogmatic principles, which constitute the fundamental axes of the Christian type and define its spirituality and hermeneutics" (1983, 78).

In contrast to functionalist and theological explanations, more traditional social-psychological explanations of sectarian origins argued that religiously ideological groups (or "sects" and "cults" as they were usually called) arose out of people's collective feelings of relative deprivation. Technically defined as "the discrepancy between an individual's or group's self-perceived 'legitimate' wants and the opportunities to acquire them," relative deprivation was an implicit explanation in many older discussions of the appearance of sects (see Yinger 1970, 419-425; Hannigan 1991, 318).

Since the late 1970s, however, social-psychological arguments about sectarian origins have been giving way to a social-structural orientation, instructed primarily by the resource mobilization perspective

(McCarthy and Zald 1977; Zald and McCarthy 1980). Briefly stated, the resource mobilization approach:

> ... emphasizes organizational analysis both as internal processes within the group and as external processes in relation to society. Special attention is paid to the methods by which a group procures money and labour. Likewise, care is given to identify both the assistance and the obstructions provided by non-members and their organizations. The level of discontent among members toward a given issue is no longer presumed to be the primary motivation for either the membership or sympathetic non-members (Kent 1982a, 530).

Rather than looking at individual motivations for group-joining behaviour, then, resource mobilization focuses instead on the organization itself, and its ability to attract and maintain new members — who, in turn, themselves subsequently become important resources for achieving group goals.

To some extent, this approach is not incompatible with relative deprivation theory (Kent 1982a). Yet most researchers who use mobilization arguments do so at the expense of deprivation arguments. Moreover, the social-structural orientation of the resource mobilization perspective allows researchers to apply insights and concepts from such fields as political economy and organizational analysis to their examinations of religiously ideological movements.

Concerns, for example, about the practical, resource issue of fundraising lay behind Bird and Westley's (1985) analysis of "the economic strategies of new religious movements." Using data from the Montreal study of new religious and para-religious groups, they made three general arguments. First, "the economic strategies of all religious groups, including new religious movements, correspond to the overall policies of these groups. These strategies are rarely accidental." Second, "with some exceptions, these new religious movements have not developed on-going constituencies of committed lay members who make regular financial contributions by means of tithes, dues, and pledges." Third, the (at least partial) reliance of some groups on begging and commercial property income "indirectly reflect[s] failure of these groups to develop constituencies of committed lay members" (1985, 158).

RESOURCE MOBILIZATION AND DEVIANCE LABELLING STRATEGIES

The success of ideological groups at raising funds may be the result of their portraying themselves convincingly to society as legitimate organizations that merit public or private support. Finances are only one example of the resources they seek, however. In the societal marketplace, both opponents and competitors strive to divert resources of all kinds from these groups while at the same time attempting to acquire the same or similar resources themselves. Resource mobilization theory, therefore, allowed Kent (1990) to develop a deviance model that identified techniques and strategies that Canadian ideological groups and their opponents use in their struggle for legitimacy and the resources that flow from it.

Most religiously ideological groups want other social institutions and the public to see them either as morally normative — that is, as adhering to "the community standard against which other groups or behaviours are judged" (Kent 1990, 397) — or as tolerably deviant. Morally normative groups have the greatest access to societal resources, which include such benefits as non-profit registration, the right to issue tax receipts to contributors, social prestige for their leaders and the right to make moral pronouncements along with such established Canadian groups as the Roman Catholic, Anglican and United churches.

Occasionally, an ideological group will attempt to gain normative status by denying its religious nature (as does Transcendental Meditation) and instead insist that its teachings are scientific (Kent 1990).

[More common is the practice of ideological groups] *attempt[ing] to control the terms by which crucial sectors of society define them.* In essence, groups can attempt to shape public opinion by both continually stressing those aspects of their operations that are religious in nature, and downplaying or neglecting to discuss other aspects of their operations that are more obviously related to business, politics, psychotherapy, medicine, or economics (Kent 1990, 401).

To ensure that society will view them as normative or tolerantly deviant, these groups follow a strategic policy of "attempt[ing] to impose a *'demanded [deviance] designation'* upon society" (Kent 1990, 401).

In democratic societies such as Canada where freedom of religion is a guaranteed right, even the designation of being tolerably deviant on religious issues still allows ideological groups limited to high access to societal resources. Therefore, opponents of these ideological organizations attempt to have the groups labelled as intolerably deviant and nonreligious.

Groups or their behaviours are *legitimately tolerable* when society perceives that they are protected by law and are not threatening to society (Kent 1990, 397). For example, members of groups have the legally protected right to hold unorthodox theological beliefs. Opponents, however, may attempt to portray groups' doctrines as *intolerable* although *legitimate* (that is, protected by law) by insisting that the theology poses a dire public threat. These groups, opponents claim, are not new religions but cults, which in popular (as opposed to sociological) parlance means that they exploit their members and deceive the public about their true, devious nature (see Robbins 1988, 150-152).

Alternatively, society may view groups or their behaviours as *non-criminally tolerable* when their actions are not illegal and are not threatening to society. These behaviours typically include such things as the days or times that groups worship, peculiarities of dress and speech, and certain dietary restrictions. Again, however, opponents will attempt to portray some of these behaviours as *non-criminally intolerable* by insisting that they are repellent, disgusting, offensive or degrading. For example, while people may argue whether or not the knowing transmission of the HIV virus is a criminal act, almost everyone would agree that the leader of Halifax's Vajradhatu Buddhist group acted intolerably when he probably infected a large number of people in his organization with the precursor of AIDS (Myrden 1989).

Finally, society may view some groups or behaviours as *criminally tolerable*, which means that they are illegal but still considered acceptable. For example, at times over the past two decades opponents of various religiously ideological groups have kidnapped or forcibly confined members and tried to get them to renounce their new religious involvement through a process popularly known as "deprogramming." No accurate figures exist about how many deprogrammings have taken place in Canada, but there have been at least eight documented "successes" and five "unsuccessful" efforts (see Kent 1990, 404 n. 14; *Hamilton Spectator* 1985). Undoubtedly Canada's most famous deprogramming was carried out upon Montreal's Benji Carroll. Successful efforts to remove him from the Unification church became the basis of the popular book, *Moonwebs* (Freed 1980), and the film, *Ticket to Heaven* (*Montreal Calendar Magazine* 1981).

The people who attempt such actions (and who call themselves "deprogrammers") justify the commission of probable crimes by insisting that they do their activities in an effort to free people from even more fundamental violations of their rights as "brainwashed cult members." To support their efforts, deprogrammers cite instances in which members of cults have been convicted of crimes in Canada. Hare Krishna members have been convicted for solicitation fraud (*Hamilton Spectator* 1976; *Express* 1978), false representation of art (*Alaska Highway News* 1981; *Montreal Gazette* 1985), a school teacher's sexual assault against two devotee children (British Columbia Provincial Court 1987-1989). Scientologists have been convicted for possession of lock-picking tools (Marshall 1975), possession of stolen goods (Campbell 1985), immigration violations (Nova Scotia Provincial Court 1983a, 1983b; see *Scotia Sun* 1983) and breach of trust (Dunphy 1992b). Indeed, the Church of Scientology of Toronto is the only religious organization in Canadian history to be convicted of a criminal offence — two counts of breach of trust for the operation of a spy ring in the mid-1970s that targeted the Ontario Provincial Police and the Ontario Attorney General's office (Dunphy 1992b). Naturally, the ideological groups themselves portray all deprogramming activities as criminally intolerable behaviours, labelling them "kidnappings," "faithbreaking" and "vigilantism" (Kent 1990, 406). In sum, Kent's research showed how ideological groups use normative and deviance labelling strategies in efforts to acquire resources for themselves and restrict their opponents' access to resources. The determination of tolerable versus intolerable groups, therefore, is an ongoing process of struggle by competitors for society's resources.

RESOURCE MOBILIZATION AND TRANSNATIONALISM

The struggles over resources in any one country are frequently connected to activities in others (Wuthnow 1978; 1980). Just like many business corporations, ideological organizations that operate in Canada frequently behave like transnationals (that is, businesses that operate across national borders [see Shankar 1980, 26]).

> Many new religious movements in the west can be compared with multi- or transnational corporations in so far as they operate in different countries without apparent detriment to either their unity or their standardization. They are all controlled to varying degrees by a single leader or a centralized leadership. And there is evidence to suggest that, although the boundaries of nation states are normally adopted as bases for the movements' administrative divisions, resources are often trans- ferred between countries in accordance with international strategies for development ... The rate of their membership growth, the value of their property holdings, their economic viability, and their public prestige all vary with factors transcending the boundaries of any particular country. It is important never to lose sight of the fact that these movements appear to be deliberately managed by leaders seeking maximal effec- tiveness in the largest possible market (Beckford 1985, 219).

Classifications of religious transnationals are varied. One analysis (Kent 1991b) indicates that researchers can study them from the perspective of organizational or management enterprises in terms of possible liberal benefits to involved countries; neo-mercantilist costs, especially to host countries; and imperialist costs to weak host states.

Transnational religiously ideological organizations that operate in Canada most frequently move personnel and resources across the U.S. border, since international or North American headquarters of several groups are in the United States. Such groups include the Unification Church (Barrytown, New York), Scientology (Los Angeles and Clearwater, Florida) and ISKCON (whose major publishing facilities operate out of Los Angeles). The Unification Church (or at least some of its members) operated an interrelated art business (Creative Designs) in both San Francisco and Calgary (Bromley 1985, 257 n. 4). Canadian Scientologists routinely take upper-level courses in both Los Angeles and Clearwater, and Transcendental Meditation's Maharishi International University in Fairfield, Iowa, contains Canadians in the student population. Elizabeth Clare Prophet's Grand Teton ranch in Montana, which serves as the headquarters for Church Universal and Triumphant, contains a number of Canadians (for example, see Ouston 1989, 28c). Likewise, one of the Unification

Church's most prominent lawyers, John Biermans, grew up in Ontario (see Biermans 1988, 80).

Also worth mentioning is the apparent flow of Scientologists between Great Britain and Canada. This pattern of personnel movement became apparent from comments made by crown attorney James Stewart in the Toronto trial of the Church of Scientology of Toronto and five of its members on charges of criminal breach of trust. Stewart told the jury that "Scientology officials — some trained in a 'spy school' in England — ran a network of plants that obtained jobs with the RCMP, the OPP, Metro Police and the A-G's [Attorney General's] office" (Dunphy 1992a, 23; see DeMara 1992).

Among the many strategies that the Unification Church uses on a global scale to attract resources is sponsorship of academic conferences that cover the travel and hotel costs of the attendees. Marlene Mackie and Merlin B. Brinkerhoff observe that aside from theological justifications that supposedly foster world unity through international discussion, "the phenomenon of Moonie-initiated contacts with intellectuals deserves analysis as one of the cleverest tactics ever devised by a social movement" (1983, 22). Pondering this tactic, they insist that "whatever else they may be, the conferences represent a legitimation-seeking strategy" (1983, 35). At least one of these conferences, the New Ecumenical Research Association, met in Quebec City from July 27 to August 3, 1985.

MAINTAINING MEMBERS AND SUPPORT

Resource mobilization theory also studies the substantial resources (including inexpensive labour) that come to organizations from adherents, members or insiders. Membership issues, therefore, are fundamental for understanding group operations, but these issues are also crucial for appreciating the social psychology of adherents. In accordance with functionalism, many theorists extend their emphases on religion's meaning-giving function by arguing that sects thrive by providing communities for otherwise marginal and uprooted individuals. Mann, for example, concluded that "the sects and cults addressed themselves to the interests of those groups of the population not clearly integrated into the community structure" (1955, 154). These groups included various ethnic populations as well as recently urbanized people from rural backgrounds (1955, 154). Mann's comments suggested that sects provided otherwise unattached citizens with small communities, and presumably people stayed in them because they felt woven into their groups' social fabric (see also Bird 1977, 458). Along these same lines, many people stay in ideological groups (if not join them in the first place) because they find in them substitute, surrogate or fictive families (see Robbins 1988, 46).

During the 1980s "a new focus in the sociology of religion has been that which conceptualizes religious participation in terms of personal and collective experiences of power" (Hannigan 1991, 324). These experiences in and of themselves may be reason enough for people to remain members. As John Hannigan insists, "the concept of empowerment suggests that the collective achievements of movements in themselves constitute a major incentive to join and participate" (1991, 325).

Precisely the opposite argument, however, has also been used to explain why people remain in religiously ideological groups. Robert H. Cartwright and Stephen A. Kent developed this argument after interviewing a half-dozen former members of a Transcendental Meditation schismatic organization and personality group that operated in Victoria, B.C. These authors concurred with a newspaper account about the group (whose members followed a leader named Robin Carlsen) that concluded that "ex-members say Carlsen has a chameleon-like ability to meet the emotional and spiritual needs of group members — while at the same time manipulating them for his own purpose" (Hume 1987, A6).

Taking their cues from family violence literature, Cartwright and Kent argued that:

> Alternative religious organizations provide a unique environment for examination of the same linkages between affective bonding and coercive control that develop in the family. Few other social settings exist that involve the immersion of the "total" person within an environment of minimal external social control and intense group control ... elements of "voluntary" personal commitment ("internalized" control) frequently enmesh individuals even further within abusive family or abusive "cult" affiliations (1993, 35).

In sum, perspectives emphasizing the sense of power that people may feel from involvement in religiously ideological organizations must be balanced with the realization that members may operate under regimes of control in which compliance feels voluntary but in which they are in fact disempowered. Such organizations operate like totalistic social systems.

STUDIES OF RELIGIOUSLY IDEOLOGICAL GROUPS IN CANADA

Few, if any, of the countless religiously ideological groups operating in Canada have received ethnographic attention, and two of Canada's indigenous religiously ideological groups, the Kabalarians (Todd 1984) in Vancouver and I AM in Ottawa (*Saint John's Edmonton Report* 1978) have not received any scholarly attention. Nor has the Catholic schismatic group, The Apostles of Infinite Love, whose power base shifted from France to Quebec in the late 1960s (Beirne with Carlyle-Gordge 1982, 45).

Glimpses into other organizations and the lives of their members appear in various academic publications. Bainbridge's 1978 study of the Process Church briefly mentions the group's Toronto operations from late 1970 to early 1975, and his explanation of the group's ideology (involving the worship of Jehovah, Christ and Satan) is particularly informative. Stanley R. Barrett's exploration of Canada's religiously flavoured, right-wing racist groups led him to realize "that anti-Semitism constituted the radical right's theoretical system or paradigm" at the same time that "it enhances emotional commitment" for members of these groups (1987, 339). Rare insight into the emotionally and physically abusive child-rearing practices of Alpha and Omega Order of Melchizedek, whose Canadian counterpart began in Creston, British Columbia in 1969 (*Alberta Law Reports* 1979, 221), appears in a twenty-six page court report submitted by the judge in a child custody case. McNicoll's (1982) study of "Catholic cults" examines Opus Dei, Marriage Encounter, Cursillo, the Catholic Charismatic Renewal and Neo-Catechumen. One of these movements, Opus Dei, has attracted considerable attention because of its contested efforts to have the Canadian Senate incorporate its Regional Vicar, thereby giving him responsibility "for the management and control of the property, affairs and interests" of the group (Government of Canada, Senate Debates 1987, 853; see Government of Canada, The Senate of Canada 1986-87; Weatherbe 1987). A group with an anti-Catholic flavour, the French-based Raelians, has had its extra-terrestrial and sexually expressive ideology explored by Alain Bouchard (1990). Reporter Kevin Marron (1989) provides considerable insight into Canada's pagan and "magick" communities in his survey of contemporary Wiccans and witches.

One researcher, Susan Palmer (1976), who had worked with Bird and Reimer on their Montreal project, has produced a number of sectarian studies, including a Master's thesis on a group in Montreal known as "shakti, The Spiritual Science of DNA" that followed the teachings of Californian E.J. Gold. She also published a study on the "outer-directed, social ends" of ostensibly inner-directed meditation rituals that she "witnessed as a participating member of four new religious movements in Montreal." These social ends included "courtship displays, ... the formation of cliques, and the jostling between rivals for power positions" (1980, 403). Her study of ritual mirrored Bird's own interest on the topic, to which he devoted some attention (Bird 1978; 1980). Finally, Palmer's participant observation of the Montreal Rajneesh community resulted in two articles: one on commitment mechanisms (1986), the other on Rajneesh's leadership style (1988). Mann's (1991) recent study of the Rajneeshis provides rich insight into the group's operations and the social psychology of its members. Another rare glimpse into the life of a group occurs in the National Film Board movie, *Les Adeptes/The Followers*, which documented the life of Montreal Krishna devotees in the early 1980s (McAteer 1981).

THE STATE OF RESEARCH ON CANADIAN SECTS, CULTS AND RELIGIOUSLY IDEOLOGICAL GROUPS

A wealth of material on religiously ideological groups exists in collections around the country. Scholars have barely begun to mine its riches. Montreal may contain the most significant collections, with large amounts of material on hundreds of groups on file in as many as five locations: at Info-Cult (a "counter-cult" organization formerly known as the Cult Information Service and the Cult Project); at the Catholic-influenced Centre d'Information sur les Nouvelles Religions; at Concordia University (where the field research information from

Bird and Reimer's research project is stored on computer tape [Westley 1983, 22]); and at the Université de Montréal and Université Laval, where several academics maintain ongoing research interest on religious ideologies. In Toronto, the Council on Mind Abuse (COMA, a "counter-cult" organization) had extensive files, but its recent closure (primarily on account of financial pressures) has jeopardized the availability of its material to scholars. In Alberta, two universities have large collections. The recently formed Centre for the Study of North American Religions at the University of Lethbridge has scholars from a number of disciplines who are gathering materials and writing on both indigenous North American groups or groups that underwent mutations on North American soil. At the University of Alberta, two scholars (Stephen A. Kent and Gordon Drever) have amassed in the neighbourhood of ten thousand files and several thousand books and pamphlets on and by religiously and politically ideological groups throughout North America, and the University of Alberta Library has placed approximately five thousand of Kent's files on microfiche in an effort to preserve the information for researchers.

Valuable information on groups in Canada appears throughout Gordon J. Melton's *Encyclopedia of American Religions* (1987) and the companion compilation of religious creeds (1988). Also worth examining are Diane Choquette's (1985) annotated bibliography of U.S. and Canadian scholarship on new religious movements, and Camilla Thumbadoo's (1979) "Directory of Religious/Spiritual Cults and Sects in Canada." For historical research, the *Spiritual Community Guide* series (for example, *Spiritual Community* 1972, 1974, 1978) provides addresses of groups current during the 1970s, as does the directory of groups compiled by Armand Biteaux (1975). Sketchy histories of the appearance and development in Toronto of Scientology, ISKCON, and the North American Sikh group, 3H0, appear in Margaret Lindsay Holton's book *Spirit of Toronto* (1983). An overview of Canadian scholarship on Canadian religious movements appears in Helen Ralston's article, "Strands of Research on Religious Movements in Canada" (1988).

The Ontario government commissioned a study on "the healing arts" that published its findings in 1970. The report included a discussion on Scientology, Concept-Therapy, Christian Science and Ontology (that is, the Emissaries of Divine Light) (Committee on the Healing Arts 1970, 489-514). In addition to these groups, the

Committee received additional information about these groups (along with occult healing, hypnosis, spiritualism, faith healing and electro-psychometry) from John Lee's (1970) companion study. Further information about the Emissaries appeared in two investigations of its Ontario camp, Twin Valleys (Blair 1977; Wilkes 1982). The broadest study of ideological groups in the country was the report presented to the Ontario government by Daniel Hill (1980), although it is of limited use to scholars since it did not specify the groups upon which it based specific examples and conclusions.

FUTURE ISSUES FOR SCHOLARS

The most controversial topic that scholars of religious ideologies will debate in the immediate future involves allegations that inter-generational satanic groups have existed for decades whose rituals involve sexual violence, animal and human sacrifice, and cannibalism (Fraser 1990; Pazder with Smith 1980; Tucker 1992, 186-188). Therapists are hearing such allegations from clients throughout the country. Without definitive external evidence (of ritual paraphernalia, corpses, pictures, etc.) beyond the accounts themselves, many social scientists will continue to believe that the accounts are inaccurate and at most represent either social constructions of evil or demonized representations of victimizers by their victims (Hicks 1991; Lippert 1990; 1992; Richardson, Best, and Bromley 1991). Other researchers remain open to the possible accuracy of many accounts. Kent (1992), for example, highlighted some of the sacrificial and sexual rites that more than twenty-five alleged ritual survivors recounted to him, and located the same themes within scriptures and readings in Judaism, Christianity, Masonry and Mormonism. In essence, he attempted to support the accounts of "survivors" by providing a cultural context in which their stories might be believed.

Specifically regarding allegations of satanic practices involving children, Kevin Marron concluded:

> ... I do not accept the theory that child care workers have invented the concept of ritual abuse or that the child victims have imagined or fabricated their allegations — but I do not know what it all means. Rather than accept the idea of a network of cults, for which there is

little evidence, I am more inclined to believe that this kind of abuse is perpetrated by disturbed individuals who have been influenced by satanism or some other similar beliefs. I think it is also possible that people are using the trappings of satanism either as a theme for sadistic pornography or as a means of frightening children into complying with sexual abuse (1989, 204).

Often, however, researchers who examine the same allegations of satanism come to different conclusions about their veracity. This is what happened when two authors who attended a Hamilton, Ontario, child custody case in 1987 in which children spoke about graveyard rituals, cannibalism and infanticide (Marron 1988; Kendrick 1988).

More research needs to be done into this complicated and disturbing subject. In general, studies should be done on a wide range of topics and groups. More organizational studies must examine groups at both micro and macro levels, and macro analysis must address important issues of transnationalism. Moreover, because the impact of religious ideologies on Canada is poorly understood, analyses must be undertaken of their effects on legal decisions, law enforcement policies and cultural tolerance. For the sake of the sociological discipline, however, researchers must strive to integrate their studies of ideological groups into mainstream scholarship on belief systems, social movements, social psychology and social structure. Only by doing so will scholars ensure that their work does not become as marginalized in the social-scientific disciplines as many of the groups they study are in Canadian society. Academic marginalization of this type is a very real problem, even though few topics in the social sciences are as dramatic or as demanding as the study of people whose lives seem driven by religious fervour.

Notes

[1]From *The Canadian Encyclopedia*, New Religious Movements pages 1479-1481, by Hurtig Publishers A McClelland & Stewart Co. Used by permission of the Canadian Publishers, McClelland & Stewart, Toronto.

For Further Reading

Bainbridge, William S. 1978. *Satan's Power: A Deviant Psychotherapy Cult.* Berkeley, CA: University of California Press.

Beckford, James A. 1985. *Cult Controversies.* London: Tavistock.

Choquette, Diane. 1985. *New Religious Movements in the United States and Canada.* Westport, CT: Greenwood Press.

Freed, Josh. 1980. *Moonwebs.* Toronto: Virgo Press.

Hexham, Irving, and Karla Poewe. 1986. *Understanding Cults and New Religions.* Grand Rapids, MI: Eerdmans.

Westley, Frances. 1983. *The Complex Forms of the Religious Life: A Durkheimian View of New Religious Movements.* Chico, CA: Scholars Press.

PART II

RELIGIOUS MANIFESTATIONS IN CONTEMPORARY CANADIAN SOCIETY

Chapter 6

Nonbelief in Canada: Characteristics and Origins of Religious Nones

Merlin Brinkerhoff and Marlene Mackie

When asked by a census taker or sociologist, nine out of ten Canadians will claim affiliation with a religious denomination. The labels we give ourselves — Roman Catholic, Anglican, Seventh Day Adventist and so on — constitute a significant dimension of our identities. That is, denomination influences our views of ourselves. Church membership also affects our attitudes towards other people. Canadians feel comfortable around United Church members or Catholics, for example, but may wish to maintain social distance from religious outsiders, such as members of new religious movements — Moonies, Hare Krishna devotees and so on (Brinkerhoff and Mackie 1986).

When Canadians think about their history, it is difficult "to imagine Quebec with no Roman Catholics, Ontario with no Anglicans or Presbyterians, the Prairies with no Evangelical Protestants, and British Columbia and the Atlantic region without the Church of England" (Bibby 1987, 4). Although church membership no longer means what it once did, Canadians still tend to be baptized, married and buried under church auspices.

Despite the traditional centrality of religion in the lives of Canadians, a small but growing portion of the population claims no formal church affiliation. What do social scientists have to say about the unchurched? Glenn Vernon, who in 1968 called to the attention of sociologists a neglected category he termed "religious nones," argued that a complete understanding of religious behaviour required study of these religious independents. It was 1980, however, before Canadian social scientists adopted Vernon's proposal. Beginning in that year, Jean Veevers and her colleagues pioneered a series of demographic analyses of religious nones (see, for example, Veevers and Cousineau 1980; Gee and Veevers 1989; Veevers 1990).

As more contemporary scholars heed Vernon's message, religious nones are no longer a neglected category. Nevertheless, they continue to be misunderstood. That is the underlying theme of this chapter. Scholars often assume that religious nones are also nonbelievers, atheists or agnostics; further, they expect those who claim no church membership to be nonparticipants who never attend church, pray or engage in other sacred rituals. These assumptions need to be examined in the light of the evidence. Whether or not religious nones believe or behave religiously is an empirical research question, rather than a matter of definition.

THE INCIDENCE OF RELIGIOUS NONES IN CANADA

National censuses and surveys are useful in establishing the changing incidence of religious nones in this country. In Canada, it has always been permissible for authorities to ask citizens about their religious denomination. Unlike census takers in the United States, Census Canada has gathered information on denominational affiliation during decennial censuses. For this reason, Canadian social scientists have been "the envy" of those U.S. demographers who are interested in religion (see Heaton 1986, for example, who analyzes Canadian census data because of this inclusion).

Table 6.1 presents information about the percentage of unaffiliated in Canada from 1961 to 1990. On the surface, these data suggest that the proportion of those claiming no denomination has increased by 2,000 percent over this thirty-year period. However, these data must be interpreted with extreme caution.

Census Canada has consistently asked the question: "What is your religion?" Nevertheless, until the 1971 census, the answer options presented to respondents did not include "no religion." Thus, before 1971, some people who did not feel as if they belonged to a church undoubtedly checked a denominational category. This methodology might bring into question the reported increase in the incidence of the unaffiliated from 0.5 percent to 4.4 percent over the ten-year period 1961-1971. However, that result is supported by census data that indicate a fairly significant increase in the unchurched from 1971 to 1981, as well. During this decade, the unaffiliated went from 4.4 percent to 7.4 percent of respondents, an increase of nearly 70 percent. (At the time of writing this chapter census data for 1991 was not available.)

Table 6.1 THE UNAFFILIATED IN CANADA FROM 1961 TO 1990: SELECTED SOURCES (in percentages)

Year	Source	Percent
1961	Census[1]	0.5
1971	Census — redefined[2]	4.4
1975	Project Canada Survey[3]	8.3
1980	Project Canada Survey	10.0
1981	Census	7.4
1985	General Social Survey[4]	10.5
1985	Project Canada Survey	10.4
1990	General Social Survey[4]	12.1
1990	Project Canada Survey	10.2

[1]Census Canada, in 1961, asked "What is your religion?" but had no category to indicate "no religion."
[2]Census Canada, in 1971, included the category "no religion" as a response to "what is your religion?"
[3]Reginald Bibby conducted national surveys in 1975 (n=1,917), 1980 (n=1,482), 1985 (n=1,630) and 1990 (n=1,432), asking "Would you please indicate your religious preference?," with "none" (n) as one of the optimal response categories.
[4]The General Social Survey, conducted in 1985 by Statistics Canada, asked, "What, if any, is your religion?" The 11,100 respondents were provided with the option of "no religion." The 1990 survey was based on approximately 10,000 respondents.

Reginald Bibby, a protégé of the pioneering American sociologist of religion C.Y. Glock, began a series of national surveys on religion in Canada on Glock's advice. In 1975, he conducted the initial Project Canada survey and reported 8.3 percent of his sample to be unaffiliated. This increased to 10.0 percent in 1980 and to 10.4 percent in 1985. However, in 1990, 10.2 percent reported "no religion," suggesting a slight decrease in the unaffiliated over the five-year period.

Both the manner in which a question is asked and the response categories that are provided affect the nature of the responses. The response category of "no religion" seems to have made a real difference (compare the Census Canada 1961 and 1971 percentages). Sociologists refer to the method of establishing a measure for a variable as "operationalization." As we compare the 1980 Bibby Project Canada findings to those of the 1981 Canada census — 10 percent as compared to 7.4 percent, respectively — we may want to question the operationalization used by Bibby. Where Census Canada asks respondents "What is your religion?," Bibby is asking for religious preference (see footnote 3 to Table 6.1). Are these two questions equivalent? Might a person be one thing and "prefer" something else? Or is this considerable difference between Bibby and Census Canada due to some other error?

A comparison of Bibby's results with results from another national survey reported in Table 6.1 suggests some answers and in turn raises new questions. Since 1985, Statistics Canada has conducted a large annual study, the General Social Survey, which asks a question similar to that asked by Census Canada: "What, if any, is your religion?" The 1985 General Social Survey result of 10.5 percent unaffiliated is very close to Bibby's 10.4 percent for the same year. However, the 10.2 percent reported in 1990 by Project Canada is significantly lower than the General Social Survey's 12.1 percent for that year. Perhaps the addition of the phrase "if any" in the General Social Survey question stimulated a response set that differed from Bibby's.

Brinkerhoff and Mackie (1992) found a much higher incidence of unaffiliated in a local survey by operationalizing it differently. In a study of religious change, they asked a random sample of 928 adults in Calgary "In what religion were you raised?," followed by "Do you presently feel a part of some religious group? If yes, which religious group?" About 4.0 percent were religious nones during childhood; however, fully 51.9 percent did not identify with a denomination. This example underscores the importance of the operationalization factor.

What generalizations can be made from the national survey findings shown in Table 6.1? First, it appears that about one in ten people in Canada have no religious affiliation at present. (Again, it cannot be assumed that religious nones are also irreligious. They may still believe in a deity, have a personal kind of religion and even attend a church from time to time.) Second, there is a decrease in the percentage of unaffiliates between the 1985 Project Canada survey and the latest one, recorded in 1990. The General Social Survey indicates no such decrease between the years 1985 and 1990;

however, the General Social Survey's 1990 figure is smaller than the 13.1 percent unaffiliated it reported in 1989. Are these latest surveys true reflections of a reversal in the trend, or statistical or measurement artifacts? In a recent U.S. study, Glenn, comparing the results from 110 surveys over a thirty-year period, concludes:

> ... the conservative reaction that began in this country in the late 1970s has weakened or offset the influences that produced the steady increase of "no religion" responses during the previous 15 to 20 years. This indicates that some aspects of secularization in modern societies can be stopped and perhaps reversed, at least temporarily (1987, 302).

We can only speculate about whether or not this same "conservative reaction" is occurring in Canadian society. There is not enough data to deny or confirm such a conclusion.

THE RELIGIOUSLY UNAFFILIATED IN CANADA AS MEASURED BY ATTENDANCE

As stated before, people identifying themselves as religious nones may still attend religious services, may be believers in the supernatural or may have an alternative, personal religious belief system. Gee and Veevers (1989) argue that an individual may claim a nominal religious denomination but never attend its services except perhaps on ceremonial occasions such as weddings or funerals. Are such nominal members really affiliates? Gee and Veevers redefine the religious nones to include this group as well as those who never attend. They report that this redefinition increases the percentage of unaffiliated in Canada to nearly 30 percent. (This finding is based on the General Social Survey conducted in 1985.) Furthermore, if we are even more inclusive — and they argue we should be — and add to those claiming no religion those who attend services less than yearly, fully 38.6 percent of Canadians would be considered unaffiliates. That is, nearly 40 percent of Canada's population claim no affiliation and/or attend religious services less than once a year.

Attendance at religious services is often employed as an indicator of religiosity and commitment. Principally a measure of behaviour, survey researchers use it in lieu of better measures of religiosity because of its "ease of measurement." Some scholars of religion would argue that attendance may be an indicator of *extrinsic* religiosity; that is, people may go to church for social reasons, to be seen or to network. Analyses based on attendance, they say, may not adequately "tap" *intrinsic* religiosity — its spiritual or devotional dimension. Nevertheless, some of the national trends in religiosity can be captured using polls undertaken by organizations such as Gallup Canada. Each year, Gallup provides data on religious attendance based on representative samples. Recently, from May 6 to May 9, 1992, Gallup asked 1,032 respondents during personal interviews: "Did you, yourself, happen to attend a church, synagogue or other place of worship in the last seven days?"

Table 6.2 selects Gallup's results for those years that correspond as closely as possible with the years recorded in Table 6.1 (Bozinoff and MacIntosh 1992, 1-2). It also presents the most current 1992 data. It notes that in 1960 fully 56 percent of Canadians attended a service at least weekly. This fell to less than half that, 27 percent, by 1990. However, it shows a fairly dramatic reversal in 1992, when the percentage stood a full six points higher, at 33 percent. What broad conclusions might be drawn from these attendance data? First, the trend from 1960 onwards approximates the trend found for "religious nones" reported above; both indicators — identification and attendance — show a dramatic decrease in affiliation over this period. (Attendance figures on their own cannot substitute for identification data: they reflect affiliation but not unaffiliation.) Second, the Gallup data suggest that recently we have been experiencing a "return to religion." Just as the 1990 Project Canada data showed a slight decrease in the percentages reporting "no religion," the 1992 Gallup findings show an increase in attendance. The reversal in attendance figures may furnish support for Glenn's (1987) conclusion that we are undergoing a "conservative reaction."

Lorne Bozinoff and Peter MacIntosh (1992), analysts for the Gallup organization, also present their findings by age and region. A summary of their findings contained in Table 6.2 presents attendance data by age and region for 1992 only; however, the patterns appear consistent over time. It is not surprising that the youngest set of adults attend least frequently. Most studies report that as people grow older they attend religious services more often (see, for example, Gee and Veevers 1989). Note that those respondents older than sixty-five were two times more likely to have attended church than those younger than thirty. Bibby and Donald Posterski (1985) have been conducting an ongoing national study of teenagers in Canada. In a personal consultation, Bibby reports that 20 percent of Canadian teenagers between the ages of fifteen and nineteen who are still attending school report "no religious affiliation."

Table 6.2 AFFILIATION IN CANADA AS REPORTED BY GALLUP
(in percentages)*

Year	Attendance	Age	Attendance	Region	Attendance
1960	56	18–29	24	Atlantic	35
1970	44	30-39	27	Quebec	36
1975	41	40-49	30	Ontario	35
1980	35	50-64	45	Prairies	35
1985	32	65+	48	B.C.	21
1990	27				
1992	33				

*On May 6-9, 1992, personal interviews were conducted where 1,032 adults were asked, "Did you, yourself, happen to attend a church, synagogue or other place of worship in the last seven days?" The same question was posed at each of the other selected years.

The data in Table 6.2 illustrate that British Columbians attend religious services less often than people in other regions of the country. Interestingly, there is little regional variation in 1992, with the exception of British Columbia. Most other years, however, the Gallup data have found the Prairies second to British Columbia in non-attendance. For example, in 1989 British Columbia reported 18 percent attending weekly, the Prairies 23 percent, Ontario 30 percent, and both Quebec and the Atlantic region 34 percent. This pattern is consistent with other measures of religious involvement reported by Bibby (1987) and Gee and Veevers (1989). That is, as we traverse the country from east to west, the percentage of religious nones appears to increase, whether measured by identification or attendance.

MACRO-SOCIOLOGICAL CHARACTERISTICS OF UNAFFILIATES

Broad demographic differences distinguish "religious affiliates" from "religious nones." The following summarizes the findings on three of these demographic characteristics: gender, age and region.

Gender

Regardless of whether we are looking at denominational identification or church attendance or some combination of both, men are more often found among the unaffiliated than women. Gee and Veevers report: "The over-representation of women among the religiously devout has been noted in terms of their affiliation with organized religion, their church attendance, and the orthodoxy of their belief systems ... Regardless of the criterion selected, women of all ages are less likely than men to be unaffiliated with organized religion" (1989, 617). The 1991 Gallup release (Bozinoff and MacIntosh 1991, 2) illustrates this. Attendance can be used as the operational definition for affiliation. During the week of the study, 25 percent of the males compared to 36 percent of the females attended a worship service. Bibby (1987), in his 1985 national study found, on most indicators, that women are more involved religiously than men. However, he argues that a different national profile is emerging for the twentieth century. Bibby writes: "In allowing for both age and education, I have found that gender differences persist, though only slightly. Young women with university degrees, for example, score marginally higher on these measures than young men who are university graduates" (1987, 100). His survey data show that 89 percent of both males and females claim religious affiliation; however, only 31 percent of the males as compared to 38 percent of the females report actual membership (yet another indicator of affiliation). Furthermore, females are more likely to attend church (27 percent versus 23 percent [Bibby 1987, 102]).

Age

According to the findings of the General Social Survey, the twenty-five to thirty-four age category contains the highest number of unaffiliates. Nearly 20 percent of the males in this category responded "no religion" when asked. This compares to 10.8 percent of the females of the same age. When we adopt the operational definition used by Gee and Veevers (1989) and add those who never attend to those claiming unaffiliation, the proportion of unaffiliated males increases to 43.7 percent and that of unaffiliated females to 32.4 percent for those aged twenty-five to thirty-four. From this age on, however, the percentages decrease to where only 4.7 percent of males aged fifty-five to sixty-four and 2.3 percent of women aged sixty-five to seventy-four identify themselves as religious nones. From those ages on, unaffiliation increases slightly for both sexes. Generally, this pattern is consistent with the 1992 Gallup data presented in Table 6.2 that showed weekly attendance increasing from a low of 24 percent for the eighteen to twenty-nine year olds to 48 percent for those aged sixty-five and over. Bibby (1987), although he concurs with this finding, urges some caution in such generalizations. Because age is also related to education, differences in educational level might confound the relationship between affiliation, attendance and age. (Those adults in the younger age groups tend to have more education, and people with higher levels of education are less likely to be affiliates.) However, Bibby finds that those Canadians who have high-school or more advanced degrees attend religious services more often than high-school dropouts, regardless of age category (1987, 99).

Region

As already noted, people in British Columbia seem to attend church less often than other Canadians (see Table 6.2). Gee and Veevers (1989, 620-622) report very dramatic differences on unaffiliation by region. When they include as unaffiliates both those who report "no religion" and those who report "never attend," they find that fully 52.2 percent of the adults in British Columbia are considered "unchurched." This compares to 18.2 percent in Atlantic Canada, 22.5

percent in Quebec, 28.9 percent in Ontario, and 33.6 percent in the Prairies. Bibby's (1987, 87) national survey of beliefs and behaviours indicates the same basic pattern. "In the case of Judaeo-Christian practice, experience, and knowledge, the 'Atlantic High, Pacific Low' pattern continues with minor exceptions."

BECOMING A RELIGIOUS NONE

The relatively small number of Canadians whom sociologists of religion label "religious nones" arrive there by at least seven different routes. The description of these ideal-typical paths should be read with two important points in mind. First, the term "religious nones" refers to people who are religious independents. Although unaffiliated with formal religious groups, they may or may not be irreligious. Second, the paths outlined below focus on the experiences of individuals. This social-psychological perspective must be understood as operating within the macro-sociological context of secularization — the declining significance of religion in our society (see Chapter 4).

Primary Socialization

The stability of religious ties between generations is well documented. Research shows that the emphasis placed on religion in the childhood home, especially by the mother, is one of the best predictors of later religiosity (Hunsberger and Brown 1984). Children growing up without church affiliation are likely to become religious nones as adults. Sandomirsky and Wilson (1990, 1214) suggest a less straightforward socialization possibility: parents who belong to two different religious traditions during the child's formative years send mixed messages to their offspring, weakening the influence of either religion.

Early Adult Rebellion

Scholars such as Bibby (1987) and Caplovitz and Sherrow (1977) argue that for a sizeable proportion of religious nones, their independent unchurched status is a temporary experience of early adulthood. For many, dropping out of church is an act of rebellion against family authority. Hadaway (1989) found a predominant reason to be rejection of family pressure to attend services and to identify with a given religious group after they were old enough to have some say in the matter.

Idiosyncratic Reasons

An individual may be religiously unaffiliated for a variety of personal reasons not directly linked to family orientation. For instance, someone brought up in a given church may, as an adult, move to a community where that particular church is unrepresented. Rather than making overtures to another denomination, the person may remain detached from formal religion. Just as geographical mobility may produce isolation leading to religious disaffiliation, so may social mobility. People who are upwardly or downwardly mobile may disengage from their previous churches where they no longer feel socially and/or intellectually comfortable (Sandomirsky and Wilson 1990, 1216). Or, for a final example, two people from different religious backgrounds may marry, and, rather than confront their differences, one or both may drop their affiliation.

Ideological Involvement

Social scientists have long observed that people sometimes follow political paths to religious unaffiliation. For example, Marxism teaches that religion is both an illusion and an instrument of oppression. Working-class eyes fixated on "pie in the sky" are deflected from revolution on earth. "The abolition of religion as the illusory happiness of the people is required for their real happiness ... Religion is the sign of the oppressed creatures, the heart of a heartless world, just as it is the spirit of a spiritless situation. It is the opium of the people" (Marx and Engels 1958, quoted in Crysdale and Wheatcroft 1976, 26). Subscribing to these views, militant workers have, in the past, rejected churches as pro-management (Condron and Tamney 1985, 419). Similarly, religious drop-outs among university students in the 1970s seemed to have been motivated, in part, by the connections to political movements of the left (Bruce and Sims 1975). Finally, many contemporary feminists view traditional churches as patriarchal institutions and turn away from them.

Drift

A less dramatic but probably more common route to religious nonehood than those discussed so far is simple indifference. Individuals with no particular reason for rebellion may casually drift away from organized religion.

Expulsion

In contrast to the voluntary leave-taking assumed above, members who for one reason or another have offended church authorities may be expelled from religious fellowship. Although expulsions, where church leaders initiate disaffiliation, are much less frequent than voluntary disaffiliation (Richardson et al. 1986, 101), they do happen. See, for example, James Penton's book, *Jehovah's Witnesses in Canada* (1976).

Apostasy

Religious affiliation (and unaffiliation) involves two dimensions: religiosity (beliefs, rituals) and communality (belongingness, identity). That is, conversion to a religion means both an adoption of a set of beliefs and a prescribed way of worshipping, and a sense of belonging to that church. To this point, nothing has been stated about whether or not those people who become religious nones, that is, those who drop their affiliation with a given religious community, retain their religiosity. For instance, it is theoretically possible, though empirically unlikely, that people who drift away from their denomination may remain devout believers who regularly perform private devotions.

Apostasy, however, is a process of disengagement from both major elements of religion — religiosity and communality. In the words of Caplovitz and Sherrow (1977, 31), apostasy involves "not only a loss of religious belief, but rejection of a particular ascriptive community as a basis for self-identification." Although some apostates may cast off beliefs and community ties without feeling deep loss, many religious leave-takers experience great pain (see Ebaugh 1988). Apostasy is more apt to be dramatic and painful when members leave religious sects such as the Mormons and the Jehovah's Witnesses (which establish clear boundaries and expectations for their members), than when they turn their backs on mainstream denominations such as the Anglican or Presbyterian churches.

As sociologists of religion emphasize, the majority of religious nones eventually find paths back to organized religion. Bibby says of his Project Canada sample members:

> Most of the non-affiliated were found to be under the age of forty. Within ten years, almost half of those we have been able to follow left the None category and adopted a Protestant or Catholic affiliation — usually that of their parents (1987, 44).

Looking at why these religious nones turned again to organized religion, Bibby concludes that their affiliation "appears to be associated not with spiritual urgency but with the need for rites of passage pertaining to marriage, baptism of children, and, in some cases, death" (1987, 44).

APOSTASY: CASTING OFF THE BONDS OF ORGANIZED RELIGION

Students of religion have, in the past, devoted disproportionate attention to church involvement, commitment and conversion. Only twenty years ago, Mauss noted that the literature contained hardly more than "an occasional oblique mention of religious defection" (1969, 128). Nevertheless, as James Richardson et al. point out, many people who join religious groups "drop out voluntarily sooner or later or change groups" (1986, 97). Fortunately, religious leave-taking (disengagement, disaffiliation and apostasy) has recently begun to capture the attention it deserves from social scientists (Brinkerhoff and Burke 1980; Bromley 1988; Caplovitz and Sherrow 1977; Hadaway 1989). The literature now contains a number of fascinating studies of defection from such specific groups as the Mormons (Bahr and Albrecht 1989); the Catholics (Hoge 1988); the Hutterites (Mackie 1975; Peter et al. 1982) and the Hare Krishna movement (Rochford 1989). Although work by Brinkerhoff and Burke (1980) and Ebaugh (1988) offers insight into the processes through which individuals engage and disaffiliate, social scientists still have a great deal to learn about the matter.

The heretofore neglected topic of leaving behind organized religion has important implications for both church organizations and individual members (Bromley 1988, 11). So far as the churches are concerned, it is impossible to predict the fate of organized religion in postmodern society without an understanding of those who turn their backs on the church. The *fin de siècle* church with declining membership and weaker voice in public affairs is no longer the social and cultural force it once was. Although the status of religion in Canada is an enormously complicated, multifaceted problem, it can be argued that one of the foremost tasks of sociologists of religion is to identify those factors within organized religion against which people react when they abandon their religion.

So far as the individual apostate is concerned, the experience of leave-taking varies from casual disengagement to a momentous turning point. Many important questions about the dynamics of falling from the faith require answers. This section confines itself to two problems: What are the origins of apostates? What kinds of doubt undermined their faith? These questions were explored with questionnaire data provided by Western region undergraduate students (N = 631) and a representative adult sample from a Western Canadian city (N = 928). (See Brinkerhoff and Mackie 1992, and Brinkerhoff and Lupri 1978 for detailed information concerning methodology.)

Apostates' Origins

Changes in the respondents' religious identification can be assessed from the first two columns of Table 6.3 denoting childhood and current denominational identification. So far as the student sample is concerned, religious nones have increased by more than 300 percent. All other broad groupings of religious denomination show decreases. Of the original 252 mainline Protestants (that is, Anglicans, United Church members, Presbyterians, Lutherans, etc.) 99 (or 39.3 percent) no longer identify with any denomination. (As with other denominations, some of those who have left mainline Protestant denominations have not apostatized, but have joined another denomination.) Roman Catholics are least likely to have apostatized. In the student sample, of the original 569 students who identified with a denomination, 198 no longer do so, an apostasy rate of 34.8 percent. (These rates are somewhat lower than Wuthnow and Glock [1973] report, ranging from 47 percent among first-year students to 52 percent for fourth-year students, but higher than Hunsberger [1980] who classifies only 8.5 percent as apostates. Brinkerhoff and Mackie (1992) hypothesize that such large differences are almost certainly functions of [1] measurements or the wording of questions and [2] historical change.)

Since universities have been referred to as "breeding grounds for apostasy" (Hunsberger 1980, 159), the community sample, shown in the lower half of Table 6.3, provides a very useful comparison. Here the percentage increase for those not identifying with a denomination is over 1,200 percent. Over half (50.6 percent) of those who previously felt themselves to be "part of a denomination" are now apostates. In short, the increase in apostasy rates is not merely a function of a university student sample. Although the percentages are higher, the patterns for the community respondents follow closely those of the student sample. That is, for those who identified with one of the "major" religious groupings, Roman Catholics are least likely, followed by Conservative Protestant groups (for example, Pentecostals, Alliance, Nazarene) with mainline Protestants being most likely to apostatize.

Sources of Doubt

How does one become an apostate? Why do people drop out? Respondents were asked about their religious doubts, followed by, "What was the source of this doubt (if there was any at all)? (Check as many as apply.)" Table 6.4 attempts to group the sources of doubt according to D. Roozen's (1980) dichotomy, "Cognitive Conflicts" and "Interpersonal Discords." Not all responses fit well. Two additional categories are added: "Influence of Nonbelieving Others" and "A Gradual Drift into Nonbelief." Overall, those sources of doubt somewhat arbitrarily grouped under "Cognitive Conflicts" appear to be most common; especially common are respondents who report "experiencing problems in my life that my religion just didn't seem to help." The most common source of doubt is hypocrisy among church members, which is reluctantly classified under "Interpersonal Discords." Over a third of the apostates fall into this category, reporting "seeing behaviour of church members that contradicted my beliefs." Peers present more sources of doubt than adult friends, relatives or teachers. The "gradual drift" hypothesis is less frequently mentioned.

Table 6.3 CHILDHOOD AND CURRENT DENOMINATIONAL IDENTIFICATION OF APOSTATES FOR STUDENT AND ADULT SAMPLES PERCENTAGE CHANGE

Denominational Identification[a]	Point in Time				Percentage Change[b]	Religious Origins of Apostates[c]	
	Childhood		Current				
	N[e]	%	N[e]	%		N[e]	%
Student Sample							
Religious Nones	62	9.8	252	39.9	+306.5	–	–
Non-Christian	23	3.6	12	1.9	-47.8	12	52.2
Catholic	208	33.0	164	26.0	-21.2	48	23.1
Conservative Protestant	34	5.4	26	4.1	-23.5	9	26.5
Mainline Protestant	252	39.9	142	22.5	-43.7	99	39.3
Christian – uncategorized	37	5.9	25	4.0	-32.4	25	67.6
Nonresponse	15	2.4	10	1.6	-33.3	5	33.3
TOTAL	631	100.0	631	100.0		198	34.8[d]
Representative Community Sample of Adults							
Religious Nones	36	3.9	482	51.9	+1238.8	d	d
Non-Christian	17	1.8	11	1.2	-35.3	9	52.9
Catholic	216	23.3	131	14.1	-39.4	91	42.3
Conservative Protestant	79	8.5	54	5.8	-31.6	38	48.1
Mainline Protestant	541	58.3	215	23.2	-60.3	295	54.5
Christian – uncategorized	12	1.3	14	1.5	+16.7	5	41.7
Nonresponse	27	2.9	21	2.3	-22.2	13	48.1
TOTAL	928	100.0	928	100.0		451	50.6[d]

NOTES

[a]Non-Christian includes Jews, Hindus, Buddhists and others. Conservative and mainline Protestant categories are based on mean denominational responses to a Fundamentalism scale. Christian — uncategorized includes Interdenominational, Christian, Protestant and other similar responses that cannot be categorized. Nonresponse category differs from religious nones because it includes those who refused to respond or gave double responses.

[b]Calculated by subtracting the number of those who identify currently from the number of those who identified in childhood. Percentage change is the resulting number (that is, the number of those who no longer have that identification) as a percentage of those who had that identification in childhood.

[c]Apostates, by definition, report "no religious identification" currently. Numbers of apostates represents apostates who identified in childhood with the religion in the leftmost column. The Percentages column shows the percentage of those who identified in childhocd with that religion who are now apostates. (Because of movement from one denomination to another, numbers of apostates who originally identified with a given religion do not necessarily correspond with numbers of people who have left that religion.

[d]Percentage of all who identified with any denomination in childhood (and nonresponses) who are now apostates.

[e]The "N" refers to the total number of student respondents participating in the study.

Table 6.4 SOURCES OF RELIGIOUS DOUBT EXPRESSED BY STUDENT
APOSTATES

Sources of Doubt	Apostates Expressing Doubt (%)[*]	Students Expressing Doubt (%)[*]
Cognitive Conflict		
Books contradicting beliefs	26.8	16.3
School contradicting beliefs	30.5	19.2
Inconsistency between life demands/beliefs	24.4	17.1
Religion no solution to problems	36.4	24.2
Interpersonal Discords		
Disapproval of ministers	15.2	12.2
Church members' hypocrisy	38.6	26.0
Intolerance among believers	16.3	8.6
Influence of Nonbelieving Others		
Peers	13.7	14.0
Adult friends/relatives	12.7	7.6
Teachers	5.6	3.2
Gradual drift into nonbelief	16.3	8.6
Other, not specified	15.8	11.8

[*]Percentage totals exceed 100% because respondents may have given more than one answer.

In summary, most of these sources of doubt are cognitive since doubt, by definition, concerns beliefs. Some are clearly interpersonal (and hence probably communal) as well. Because selected sources of doubt may arise frequently but may not be considered very important, while others may arise infrequently but be more meaningful, respondents were also asked to indicate the "one most important source of doubt" from those listed in Table 6.4. Interestingly, apostates find "gradual drift into nonbelief" followed closely by hypocrisy to be the most important sources. Clearly, doubts about church teaching are central to the process of apostasy. Indeed, the apostates in the student sample report experiencing doubts as early as ages thirteen to fourteen. A likely hypothesis is that doubts precede leave-taking and that doubting members continue to participate in their denominations for some time as ritualists (Brinkerhoff and Burke 1980). Unfortunately, the cross-sectional data cannot address this question directly. However, case studies such as Ebaugh's analysis of nuns leaving Catholic convents find that "the first stage in the process of exiting is that of initial questioning" (1988, 105).

SOCIAL-PSYCHOLOGICAL CONSEQUENCES OF RELIGIOUS NONEHOOD

What difference does religious affiliation make in the lives of church members? Are church members happier and more satisfied with their lives than religious nones? From the beginning, sociologists of religion have asked what benefits people derive from their religion and what costs are incurred (Mackie and Brinkerhoff 1986). Vernon recommended that scholars attend to these old questions from the perspective of denominational outsiders. Accordingly, this section compares the happiness and life satisfaction reported by both religious affiliates and unaffiliates.

Two Methodological Caveats

It must be emphasized that although our ultimate goal is to understand what consequences accrue to the individual from being churched as opposed to unchurched, the data at our disposal are such that we must settle for statistical correlates. The available studies used questionnaires or interviews that asked respondents about their religious affiliation in one segment and inquired into their happiness and life satisfaction in another. Therefore, the resulting data establish statistical connections rather than cause-effect relations. This section also .draws broad comparisons between religious affiliates and religious nones. However, the consequences of organized religion for an individual really depend upon such variables as the salience of denominational commitment ("Does the person attend weekly or turn up once a year at Christmas?") and the particular denomination involved ("Is the individual a member of a mainline Protestant church such as the United Church, or a Conservative group, such as the Pentecostals?"). People who do not belong to a church are no more homogeneous than those who do. So far as religious beliefs are concerned, religious nones vary from devout believers to atheists; their private rituals run the gamut from frequent observances of prayer to none at all. In short, our discussion of the social-psychological consequences for religious nones (that is, the correlates that distinguish them from church-involved people) are generalizations that necessarily overlook many fine points and exceptions.

Rewards of Religious Affiliation

What do church members get out of their religion that unaffiliates receive in smaller measure or lack altogether? Religion provides meaning to life as it gives answers to existential questions. Churches make available to their members organized world views that explain the world's origin and life's purpose, and make day-to-day existence, as well as injustice, suffering and death, ultimately meaningful (Roberts 1984, 56). Religion may also provide normative closure, that is, socially supported standards of right and wrong. Interpersonal rewards also flow from religious affiliation. That is, social bonds with other religious affiliates constitute another significant reward for members. Indeed, Kelly (1978, 171) described the typical mainline Protestant church as a "clubhouse-with-a-steeple." For some, affiliation brings organizational positions of status and power. For example, a member may be a church treasurer or a lay reader of scriptures. Church membership frequently offers an outlet for expression of feelings. For instance, confession serves important psychological needs for Roman Catholics. Religious music, architecture and ceremony provide members with aesthetic satisfaction. In addition, organized religion provides an anchor for the self-concept, a sense of identity (Robbins and Anthony 1979, 80). Western-Canadian university student sample members were asked to choose, among the following five social identities, the "most important aspect" of themselves: myself as a male or female person; myself as an ethnic person; myself as a religious person; myself as a citizen of this country; myself as a resident of this province. In decreasing order, the responses were: gender, 62.3 percent; citizenship, 17.1 percent; religion, 12.5 percent; ethnicity, 4.4 percent; provincial residence, 3.7 percent (Mackie and Brinkerhoff 1984). Religious identity stood third among the responses, not very far behind citizenship. Finally, many churches present themselves as the pathway to heaven, and therefore offer the ultimate reward of immortality to their members, while denying it to outsiders.

The Costs of Religious Affiliation

What are the costs of church membership that religious nones avoid? The kinds and extent of costs (as well as rewards) vary with denomination and involvement. Nevertheless, members are invariably expected to provide their church with financial support. Money must be placed in collection plates, donations given to building funds, etc. In addition, membership costs time and energy, as individuals attend services, assume committee responsibilities, sing in choirs. Members who are expected to eschew independent thinking and to reject alternative world views pay the price of conformity to church teachings. In the case of the smaller, marginalized sects, members must assume stigmatized identities.

How do religious nones, who reap fewer rewards but pay fewer costs, come out in this religious calculus? Religious nones should be less happy, less satisfied with life and have lower self-esteem than church members. Is this, in fact, so?

Correlates of Affiliation

Happiness — Sociologists typically measure happiness, which focuses on the short term and is defined as the presence of positive feelings and the absence of negative feelings, by asking the following question: "In general, how happy would you say you are?" (Brinkerhoff and

Mackie 1992; Mackie and Brinkerhoff 1986). In general, the literature reports a modest relationship between religiosity and happiness (Hadaway 1978). When the self-reported happiness of 631 college and university students in the western region was examined, mainline Protestants, Conservative Christians and Mormons scored relatively high, while Roman Catholics and religious nones scored somewhat lower (by 0.05 percent). Indeed, religion was a stronger predictor of happiness than the demographic variables of socio-economic status and gender.

Life Satisfaction — Although empirically related to happiness, life satisfaction has a somewhat different meaning. Life satisfaction implies a cognitive or judgemental assessment of the quality of life over the long term (Campbell et al. 1976, 8). When Gee and Veevers (1990) analyzed a national sample of 6,621 Canadians (from the Canadian General Social Survey), they found that statistically larger numbers of religiously affiliated people reported themselves to be "very satisfied" with life, compared with those who described themselves as having "no religion."

Brinkerhoff and Mackie examined the relationship between life satisfaction and religious denomination for the student sample described above (1992; 1986). They found that Mormons and mainline Christians scored highest and Conservative Christians and religious nones the lowest, with Roman Catholics in between.

In summary, the religiously affiliated tend to be somewhat happier and satisfied with their lives than the unchurched. However, more research is badly needed to establish that these modest statistical correlations do, in fact, represent the rewards and costs that flow directly from being connected to religious organizations.

CONCLUSION

Religious nones are unchurched, but not necessarily irreligious people. Although approximately 10 percent of Canadians may be without a connection to formal religion at any given time, particular individuals move in and out of that category at different points in their lives (Bibby 1987), and for different motives. Religious nones are more likely to be male than female; to be young than elderly; to be from western than eastern regions of Canada. They appear to be somewhat less happy and satisfied with their lives than the religiously affiliated. Nevertheless, generalizations about the unchurched in this country should be made very cautiously.

Further research is needed in order to replicate sociologists' conclusions about demographic distributions of religious nones and to test empirically their speculations about the social psychology of unaffiliation. In particular, future studies need to carefully establish their operational definitions and invest in longitudinal designs that follow the religious careers of sample members as they pursue their lives.

For Further Reading

Bibby, Reginald W., and Donald C. Posterski. 1985. *The Emerging Genera-tions: An Inside Look at Canada's Teenagers.* Toronto: Irwin.

Bromley, David G. 1988. *Falling from the Faith: Causes and Consequences of Religious Apostasy.* Newbury Park, CA: Sage Publications.

Caplovitz, D., and F. Sherrow. 1977. *The Religious Drop-outs: Apostasy among College Graduates.* Beverly Hills, CA: Sage Publications.

Ebaugh, Helen Rose Fuchs. 1988. *Becoming an Ex: The Process of Role Exit.* Chicago and London: University of Chicago Press.

Chapter 7

Roman Catholicism in Contemporary Quebec: The Ghosts of Religion Past?

Peter Beyer

What is the status of religion in Quebec today? A casual trip through the province's countryside would show countless villages and towns named after Roman Catholic saints; prominent at the centre of many villages is a large, often impressive church, seemingly out of all proportion to the number of people living in the area. On top of Mount Royal, a huge cross stands lit like a beacon in the night sky, hovering over the modern buildings of downtown Montreal. In the heart of that city, amid the towers of corporate capitalism, is the archbishop's basilica, a scaled-down replica of St. Peter's in Rome. From such impressions, it would seem that Roman Catholicism is a powerful and even determinative force in Quebec society.

As many Canadians know, this impression is largely incorrect. Yet a main problem with trying to understand the status of religion in contemporary Quebec is that, in less obvious ways, it may not be *entirely* incorrect.

In the mid-1960s, almost 90 percent of Québécois identified themselves as Roman Catholic, and almost 90 percent of these said they attended church regularly, usually weekly. By 1985, the weekly attendance figure had dropped to around 30 percent, yet 90 percent still said they were Catholics (Kalbach and McVey 1971; Mol 1976b; Bibby 1987; 1990). In 1990, the level of regular participation was even lower (Bibby 1991). Given the importance the Roman Catholic church officially puts on attendance at mass, these figures are significant. Similarly, when asked their opinion on key moral issues, contemporary Québécois tend not to follow the teachings of the church. The vast majority would allow legal abortion if the mother's health was jeopardized, if the pregnancy was the result of rape or if the baby had a serious defect; a large majority would have birth control information available to adolescents; and well over half have no objection to premarital sex (Bibby 1987; 1990). Looking at the ranks of religious professionals, we see that since the mid-1960s, there has been a steady decline in the number of priests and members of religious orders. With the exception of some female orders that have lost members, this decline is less the result of people leaving the priesthood and religious orders as it is of failure to attract new members. Moreover, those who do leave tend to be the younger members. In consequence, the Quebec church has both a diminishing and an aging professional corps (Hamelin 1984, 308ff; Roy 1982). These facts would indicate that the influence of Roman Catholicism in Quebec society is currently low and that it has been declining for almost three decades. Evidence, however, points in a different direction. Most Québécois still consider themselves to be Roman Catholics; the vast majority claim belief in God and the divinity of Jesus; most pray at least occasionally (Bibby 1987). When the pope visited Quebec in 1984, the crowds were massive. For a whole week the media seemed to talk of little else. According to polls conducted at the time, the majority of Québécois were impressed by what the pope said, almost half of those surveyed stating that they would now reflect seriously on his moral admonitions (Lemieux 1987; Turcotte 1990, 235). In addition, according to Raymond Courcy (1988), the domain of private charitable works in Quebec is still heavily dominated by religious and parish groups, or at least ones that started out as such; and most activists in secular charitable organizations are also members of explicitly Catholic associations. Finally, even though the Quebec state took over responsibility for education in the 1960s, largely removing it from church control, schools in Quebec are still structured along confessional lines. Not only do most Québécois send their children to Catholic schools, but the vast majority of these — 92 percent in 1986 — also enrol them in Catholic religion courses, even though they have the alternative of religiously neutral moral education classes (Lemieux 1990). In some fashion, then, religion remains a salient factor for most Québécois, although quite obviously not in the same way as it used to.

The ambiguity outlined here is neither unique to Quebec nor to Roman Catholic societies. It is rather one instance of a broader question that has been at the heart of much sociology of religion since the nineteenth century: secularization. The assumption that thinkers from Auguste Comte to Peter Berger have made is that, over the last few centuries, Western society has undergone radical transformations that have led to a dramatic decline in the social influence of religion. Their observations have led them to the same conclusion. What precisely we mean by secularization and whether or not the thesis is true have been and still are disputed questions. This chapter will adapt a three-dimensional model of secularization suggested by Karel Dobbelaere (1981) and John Simpson (1988), one that is both useful for understanding what has been happening in Quebec and flexible enough to allow for different ideas about the concept. Accordingly, secularization can refer to three somewhat independent developments. First, individuals can become less religious, especially in that they cease to engage in religious practice or rituals. The figures for attendance at mass cited are one important indicator for this dimension. Second, religious institutions can become weaker, not so much in the sense that people stop participating in them and obeying their authority (that would be another instance of individual secularization) as in the sense that what they do is less and less religious. They may, for instance, worry less about maintaining and expanding religious practice and more about gaining wealth or political power. Finally, secularization can be systemic: it can mean that religion becomes a restricted area of human concern, removed from influence on other domains such as politics, the economy, art and education. The degree to which successive Quebec governments have succeeded in secularizing the Quebec educational system is a question that falls primarily under this dimension.

Movement along one dimension does not necessarily imply motion along the other two. The religious institution can, for instance, remain quite focused on religious matters even though many people cease their involvement. Then again, believing that religion should stay out of politics or the economy does not by itself mean that people will cease to consider religious questions as important. Nonetheless, the three dimensions can also be closely related. Religion in Quebec has undergone significant secularization on the first and third dimensions, but not on the second. This combination has meant important changes in the way the Roman Catholic church operates in Quebec, both internally and with respect to the surrounding society. The rapid transition from a highly religious society to a very secularized one — along the personal and systemic dimensions — is at the root of the ambiguities that we have already seen. Like the place names and church steeples that dot the countryside, the past has left echoes in the present.

HISTORICAL OVERVIEW: RELIGION, NATION AND SOCIAL INFLUENCE

When New France was ceded to the British in 1763, it came under the rule of an ardently Protestant imperial power. Under different historical circumstances, this would not have augured well for the Roman Catholic church in the newly conquered colony. That the church survived and eventually thrived under these conditions is due in large measure to the consequences of two revolutions: the American in 1776 and the French in 1789. In light of the first, the British adopted a colonial policy that tolerated the Catholic church in Canada under the expectation that the Roman Catholic clerics would keep the new French-speaking subjects away from the temptations of republicanism and loyal to the British crown. This the church did, in large measure. The influence of the second revolution was less direct but probably just as significant. For the Roman Catholic church of the time, the French Revolution was a disaster. The revolutionaries were not only decidedly anticlerical, they also espoused liberal and rationalist ideals that church leaders considered antithetical to good social order and religious authority. During the earlier decades of the nineteenth century, therefore, the Roman Catholic church became a centre of reaction against what its hierarchy perceived as the modern apostasy of liberalism. That distrust of things modern became firmly implanted among the French-speaking Roman Catholic clergy of Canada. For them, the religious crusade against liberal modernity became synonymous with assuring the survival of French Canada.

The revolutionary era was also the time when modern nationalism became a dominant force in Western society. Essentially, the idea was that an ethnic group, in order to thrive, must have its own territorially bounded state in a system of such nation-states. The notion found fertile ground among the French-Canadian elite of the early nineteenth century, especially in the nationalist patriote movement. Led by Louis-Joseph Papineau, the patriote agitation culminated in the unsuccessful Lower Canadian rebellions of 1837-38, whose defeat effectively eliminated this more or less liberal and secular elite from contention as leaders of the French Canadians. Those who took their place were both more conservative and less secular: they included an increasingly confident Roman Catholic hierarchy, one by now imbued with the anti-modern spirit that held sway in Rome.

In the decades after 1840, the clerical leaders managed to gain increasing acceptance for their own vision of the French-Canadian nation. Michel Brunet (1964) has characterized the dominant features of this vision as agriculturalism, anti-statism and messianism. Economically, the French Canadians were a nation rooted in rural farm life; modern capitalism and urban industry were the suspect occupations of others, Anglo-Canadians and Americans in particular. Moreover, the survival of this nation did not depend on the establishment of a strong and sovereign French-Canadian state. Government had a role in ensuring an environment of peace and security and in guarding against the assimilationist designs of the dominant Anglo-Protestants of North America. But politics was also a morally dangerous realm, a dirty business whose leaders ought not to be entrusted with the welfare of the nation and its mission. That mission in turn, the reason for the nation's existence, was not political and secular, but essentially religious. It was the divine task of the French Canadians to preserve and expand the Roman Catholic faith in North America. If they failed, the result would be assimilation and loss of identity. The survival of the nation and the Catholic battle against an irreligious modernity were thus one and the same.

Accordingly, the church, along with the family and the farm, was the core institution of the nation. It was here that the true leaders of the nation were to be found. It was to them that the nation should look for guidance. The process of institutionalizing this religio-national ideology, of making it a reality in the day-to-day lives of French Canadians, took some time and had a number of aspects. Only some of the more critical ones are mentioned here. Until the twentieth century, most French Canadians lived in rural areas. Communication with the outside world was limited. The parish was the most important administrative unit, and the parish priest was an important community leader. The clergy certainly did not exercise total control over the population, but the church was nonetheless a regular and significant part of people's lives. It did more than supply religion.

Instrumental in enhancing this general social presence of the church were the bishops. From around 1840 onwards, spurred especially by the bishop of Montreal, Ignace Bourget, they oversaw the gradual expansion of church resources, above all the number of priests and members of religious orders. Aside from purely religious duties, this growing corps supplied personnel for many charitable and social welfare services, and perhaps most importantly, for the French-Canadian schools. By the end of the nineteenth century, the Catholic church had almost complete control over French education in Quebec; fully half of the teachers were priests or members of religious orders.

This degree of religious presence was, of course, not unique to Quebec or to Roman Catholicism. What gives it added significance here, however, is that we are also dealing with a very conscious nationalism, one that, in contrast to the dominant pattern, did not see the modern state as the primary instrument for furthering the interests of the nation. The state, in this view of the world, is a tool more proper to foreigners and anticlerical liberals. Along with industrial capitalism and the modern city, it should be looked upon with a certain amount of suspicion, as somewhat antithetical to the fundamental character of the French-Canadian nation.

To be sure, not all French Canadians shared this attitude to the same degree, and the distrust of modern economic and political forms usually did not extend to their outright rejection. In fact, politics in Quebec was as lively and passionate as it was anywhere else in Canada at the time. The industrialization of the Quebec economy proceeded only slightly less rapidly than did that of Ontario. The Roman Catholic church had an important and expanding presence in Quebec society. Its religio-national ideology had a fair amount of purchase among elites and non-elites alike, at least to the point of considering Roman Catholic religion a necessary feature of French-Canadian national identity. The church's prominence in society and its ideology did not isolate Quebec from modernizing developments in twentieth-century Western society so much as they influenced the precise form that these developments took.

The late nineteenth century saw the beginning of significant transformations in Canadian society. Two changes stand out. In the West, eastern-Canadian settlers and a wave of European immigrants extended the agricultural frontier into the prairies. In central Canada, the rapid industrialization of the economy changed the way a great many people earned their living and brought in its wake the gradual urbanization of the population. By 1931 well over half the people in both Ontario and Quebec lived in cities (see Linteau et al. 1983). Increasingly, therefore, the lives that most Québécois led diverged from the rural ideal of the religio-national vision. The response of the Catholic church in Quebec is instructive.

Just as the transformations in Quebec were but a local manifestation of changes that were happening across Canada, so was the Canadian case but a regional variation on what was happening in most areas of Western society, including Europe. There, also in the later nineteenth century, the Roman Catholic hierarchy began to develop a concerted strategy to deal with the new situation, one that more or less accepted that society had changed and sought to establish church influence in the expanding urban and industrial milieux. Not surprisingly, it was this approach that significantly informed the response of the Quebec church.

In Quebec, the strategy consisted in trying to duplicate within the urban milieux the church's everyday social presence in the rural areas. Here are a few of the more important examples. Church leaders successfully established the parish structure in the cities in a way that made urban parishes significant social institutions rather than just religious districts. Since the church already had substantial control over education, health and social welfare services, expanding these functions in the growing urban areas was also relatively straightforward and, given the prevalence of the religio-national view, not seriously opposed (cf. Vigod 1986). Various other organizations and strategies addressed some of the unique features of the new environment. Church leaders helped organize and promote Catholic labour unions in an attempt to keep French-Canadian and Catholic workers from joining religiously neutral and therefore suspect international unions. Beginning in the 1930s, Catholic priests founded various youth groups whose avowed purpose was not only to bring religious influence to bear on new generations, but also to enlist these young people in actively spreading the church's social message. The clergy and their elite allies founded various cooperatives for consumption, marketing and banking, all with the intent of giving Québécois ways of dealing with the expanding capitalist economy through institutions that they controlled. On an entirely different front, the religio-nationalists spearheaded efforts to open up new agricultural areas in Quebec's portion of the Canadian Shield. The goal of such colonization programs was to give French Canadians a morally and religiously preferable alternative to urban life.

In certain respects, this overall strategy proved to be quite successful. Above all, it allowed the church to maintain and even expand its presence in the everyday lives of Québécois, whether they lived in the city or the countryside. That achievement, however, came at a substantial cost. Essentially, the response of the religio-national elite to the industrialization and urbanization of Quebec society was to try to insulate the Catholic Québécois as much as possible from the new economy, even while they worked in it. To a large extent, the dominant ideology in Quebec identified industrial capitalism with liberalism and English speakers. If French-Canadian Catholics immersed themselves too much in this order, they thereby risked assimilation and the betrayal of their collective mission. That distrust of modern structures as a danger to the nation contributed substantially to the marginalization of Québécois in the very industrial economy the strategy was supposed to address. The French-Canadian masses worked in the factories, but their elites did not run them. American, English-Canadian and British people did. The Québécois lived in an industrial economy, but they were not masters in their own economic house.

At the middle of the twentieth century, therefore, the Roman Catholic church was a very strong institution in Quebec society. Its leaders and its ideological outlook did not dictate everything that happened in Quebec; nevertheless, it had substantial influence in the lives of French Canadians, a fact reflected in the physical preponderance of ecclesiastical buildings and monuments, and the high level of religious practice. Here was a decidedly unsecularized situation in all three dimensions. This situation did not last.

The Quiet Revolution and the Second Vatican Council

The changes that began in Quebec in the early 1960s were of sufficient scope to warrant being called a revolution. They happened peacefully and without significant polarization among different segments of the population: hence the Quiet Revolution. In the religious context, the most striking change was that the Roman

Catholic church lost the larger part of its influence. Many of the areas of social activity that it had controlled came under the primary direction of the Quebec state, the most notable being education and social welfare. In addition, increasingly large numbers of Québécois began, not so much to attack or even harshly criticize the church, as to ignore it. In the process, the old religio-national ideology lost its hold over the minds of the majority. More and more, Québécois turned to the state as the premier institution responsible for the progress of the nation. They differentiated, perhaps for the first time in their history, religion and the nation. Indeed, as religious influence waned, explicitly political and secular Quebec nationalism grew. Today, the latter stands as the dominant ideology among Québécois.

The forces behind these changes include both internal and external developments, above all the growth of secular institutions in Quebec and the Second Vatican Council. We have already seen that traditional distrust of modern structures, especially industrial capitalism and the state, did not prevent or even greatly slow down their progress in Quebec. The one possible exception to this progress was in education. In the first half of the twentieth century, French speakers in Quebec attained significantly lower levels of schooling than their English-speaking counterparts, and relatively few received the kind of technical, scientific or commercial training appropriate for elite positions in the industrial economy. The Québécois educational system did show important growth, however, which was in large measure related to the Catholic church's expanding urban presence. What eventually upset the coexistence of the system's traditional outlook and its modern structural growth was the even greater acceleration of its growth after the Second World War.

During the war, for the first time in the province's history, the Quebec legislature made education compulsory to age fourteen. The resulting growth in the school system after the war put severe strain on the church's capacity to control it: most of the new teachers were secular and most of the new money came from the Quebec government. That government, in turn, grew significantly to meet these demands and to meet new obligations in areas such as social welfare. The federal government was busily expanding into these areas; to prevent federal encroachment, the Quebec government had to follow suit. The general post-war atmosphere in Canada was one of economic growth, optimism and greater awareness of the larger world, a result of both the war and technological developments like regular air travel and television. In Quebec this gave rise to groups of artists and intellectuals, including some members of the clergy, who embraced modern and more secular world views unequivocally, while at the same time decrying the timid and narrow provincialism of traditional religio-national outlook (see Bélanger 1977; Trofimenkoff 1982; Behiels 1985). All three of these developments exemplify how post-war institutional growth in Quebec largely escaped the controlling mechanisms of the Catholic church. One might say that Quebec grew away from the church rather than abandoning it. The Quiet Revolution of the 1960s formalized this trend, leaving the once-omnipresent institution in charge of purely religious functions and little else (cf. McRoberts and Postgate 1988; Beyer 1989).

Just as the urbanization and industrialization of Quebec in the early twentieth century was but a local version of a much broader tendency in Western society, so were Quebec's changes after the Second World War reflections of similar global change. In the earlier phase, the response of the Catholic church in Rome to the changing circumstances provided the Canadian church with models of action. In the 1960s, the larger church again set the pattern, this time in the form of a worldwide meeting of the bishops in Rome, a pivotal event known as the Second Vatican Council. In this case, however, the overall message was much more favourably disposed towards the changed social climate. For John XXIII, the pope who called the council, its purpose was to bring the church up to date. From the perspective of the church, the world around it was one where the most powerful domains were secular. It was also both a culturally and religiously pluralistic world imbued with egalitarian and progressive values. Rather than take up a defensive posture vis-à-vis this world or try to "re-Christianize" it, the council moved the Roman Catholic church towards greater collaboration and involvement in it. Internally, this meant a stress on greater lay participation in the church, thereby de-emphasizing the mediating authority of the clergy. The council sought to tone down the hierarchical nature of ecclesiastical decision making, shifting more of the responsibility to the local, regional or national levels. The general tone of the Council's concluding documents revealed a church that had abandoned its militant, triumphalist and fortress mentality in favour of greater openness and tolerance. This new liberality was nowhere more evident than in the

council's attitude to other Christian denominations and other religions: dialogue and cooperation were henceforth to mark such
relations, not distance and suspicion.

The impact of the Second Vatican Council in Quebec, as in
Canada as a whole, was profound. The council had not changed
anything fundamental about Roman Catholicism: the doctrines and
ecclesiastical structures were recognizably the same; ritual reforms
were only such as would permit greater lay involvement. Yet, in
opening the church to modern influences, church leaders were in
effect asking Catholics to re-examine virtually everything about the
way they practiced their religion. The result was a prolonged period
of fluidity and uncertainty that provided an opportunity for
questioning old priorities and trying out new approaches. In this
atmosphere, for instance, an ever-growing number of Québécois
decided to reduce their level of ritual participation without thereby
ceasing to consider themselves Catholics; hence the declining
mass-attendance figures combined with the high level of continued
affiliation. Parallel to such individual secularization, however, the
1970s and 1980s in Quebec — as elsewhere in the Catholic world —
also saw the rise of new movements within the Catholic church. These
displayed considerable variety. They ranged from Catholic Pentecostalism to feminist movements, from politicized youth groups to
"marriage encounter" groups. Viewed as a whole, they amount to a
significant reorientation of Quebec Catholicism.

Significant as the Second Vatican Council was for the Catholic
church around the world, in Quebec it took on an added dimension
because it coincided with the onset of the Quiet Revolution. The two
developments sprang out of the same post-war social context and thus
reinforced each other. In the form of the Quiet Revolution,
Québécois questioned the inherited ways of thinking and acting, and
removed the church from its omnipresent and pivotal position. The
Second Vatican Council encouraged them to go even further, to
change how one went about being a Roman Catholic. The doubling
effect manifested itself in various ways. For example, comparing
mass-attendance figures for Quebec and the rest of Canada, one of
the more striking contrasts is that, in 1965, 88 percent of Quebec
Catholics attended regularly while only 69 percent did so outside the
province. By 1975, the Quebec figure had dropped to 46 percent,
whereas the rate for non-Quebecker Catholics had only sunk to 55

percent. That gap has not narrowed since (Bibby 1987; 1991). The intensifying effect of the Quiet Revolution appears to be responsible for a good portion of the disparity. More qualitative evidence points in the same direction. In another time, the Roman Catholic hierarchy in Quebec would almost certainly have responded with vigorous opposition when faced with the prospect of losing control in any domain, such as education or social welfare, that it considered the proper sphere of the church. In the 1960s, the bishops acquiesced rather meekly, even cooperatively. Whether they felt the battle was hopeless or largely agreed with the directions matters were taking, the result was the same. From the mid-1960s to the late 1970s, the Catholic hierarchy in Quebec was, if not invisible, then certainly discrete in its interventions (cf. Denault 1986; Hegy 1987). Like the Vatican Council, the response of the Quebec bishops to the new social context was a combination of openness and questioning uncertainty — not retrenchment and resistance.

CONTEMPORARY TRENDS IN QUEBEC CATHOLICISM

In the wake of the Quiet Revolution, Quebec experienced significant secularization along two dimensions, but not the third. In the aggregate, Québécois have become less religious as individuals, perhaps, as Bibby argues, picking and choosing from among religious fragments but abandoning the sort of commitment that touches all aspects of life. In addition, there has been some systemic secularization. With some exceptions, the major institutions of Quebec society are now secularized, more or less devoid of religious tutelage or legitimation. The Roman Catholic church itself, however, has proven remarkably resilient, in effect using the loss of its old omnipresence as an opportunity to go in new directions.

Catholic Charismatic Renewal

As well as any other movement, Catholic Charismatic Renewal illustrates the main features of the post-Second Vatican Council climate in the Quebec church. Here we have experimentation, ecumenism, lay involvement, challenge to established authority, but eventually also the reassertion of traditional structures. With its origins in the United States in the late 1960s, the Charismatic movement is a Catholic version of Protestant Pentecostalism. Although they have to some extent developed different vocabulary and emphases, the essentials are the same in both: the core religious event is the experience of being possessed by the Holy Spirit, a fact that manifests itself in recognizable ways such as speaking in tongues (glossolalia), prophecy, discernment of spirits and healing. Pentecostalism is a style of Christianity that emphasizes direct and individual religious experience: it puts correspondingly less emphasis on structured ritual and collective religious authority. Divine communication is direct and largely unmediated (see Chagnon 1979; McGuire 1982; Poloma 1989). While these features accord relatively well with most forms of Protestantism, they present a definite challenge to the Roman Catholic stress on religion as participation in a mediating and authoritative collectivity. That seeming lack of fit makes the rise of Catholic Charismatic Renewal of special interest in the present context.

The Charismatic movement came to Quebec from the United States in the very early 1970s through the efforts of certain priests, above all, Jean-Paul Régimbal of Granby. During the next few years, it spread rapidly among Québécois to include from 60,000 to 70,000 followers in about 700 prayer groups by the end of the decade. In addition to the emotional and individualistic nature of their religious expression, Charismatic prayer groups were not organized along parish or diocesan lines. Instead, they formed independently of the regular church structures. A good portion of the early support came from members of female religious orders, which were losing many of their functions and members in the wake of the Quiet Revolution. In fact, the Charismatic movement consists predominantly of older, mostly married, women and members of female religious orders. The majority of these are middle-class and well-educated, but not politically or economically active. They dominate in the middle- and lower-level leadership of the movement, although lay people and women are underrepresented among its elite (Reny and Rouleau 1978; Zylberberg and Montminy 1981; Côté 1988).

Growing out of a deliberate "dialogue" with Protestant Pentecostalism, Catholic Charismatic Renewal is a phenomenon that sprang from the margins of the Roman Catholic church's power structure: lower-ranking clergy, women, lay people. The individualistic and relatively undomesticated religious style contrasts with the triumphal power and patriarchal control of the bygone era. Here was an innovative import that took full advantage of a period of uncertainty and openness in the church. It presented a double challenge to the Catholic hierarchy. On the one hand, it represented a genuine movement of religious renewal that sought to give the church new life in an era of perceived decline. On the other hand, with their Protestantizing bent, these Catholic Pentecostals expanded around Charismatic leaders of the lower clergy (male and female) and without the support of the bishops. They were little concerned about following parish or diocesan lines, and they emphasized individual and direct religious experience over institutional authority.

Catholic Charismatic Renewal reached its peak in Quebec during the late 1970s. It still survives, albeit in a more domesticated form under the firm control of the Catholic hierarchy. As in the rest of Canada, the most influential leaders are now no longer Charismatic figures, but appointed delegates of the bishops. By 1980, the prayer groups were organized along parish and diocesan lines; the hierarchy had taken measures to ensure that religious experience and scriptural interpretation among Charismatics stayed within the bounds of official orthodoxy. The postconciliar church was evidently open to this pious renewal, but only if it did not threaten traditional ecclesiastical structures and authorities.

Women in the Contemporary Church

The high proportion of women in Catholic Charismatic Renewal is indicative of a broader trend within the Quebec church. Women make up the majority of those who are still highly involved in the church; estimates range from 60 percent to 80 percent (Bibby 1990, 136; Roy 1990, 100). Of much greater importance, with the decline in the number of priests and members of religious orders, the Quebec church has come to rely more and more on women to fill an array of vital administrative and pastoral functions. These range from preparing parishioners for receiving the sacraments to religious education in the schools; from managing the affairs of pious associations to carrying out the charitable work of the church (see Hamelin 1984, 368; Bélanger 1988). In addition, women now constitute the majority of students in the province's theological schools, while there has been a decline in priestly ordinations. As a result, the Catholic hierarchy now finds that most of the people who have the proper training for the church's key positions are lay and/or female (Roy 1990).

The feminization of certain portions of the church organization may have been of more limited importance had it not coincided with the rise of the secular women's movement. In Quebec as elsewhere in Western society, many women have been seeking the removal of economic, political, occupational and other forms of social discrimination based on gender. The women's movement arose in the same historical context as the Quiet Revolution and the Second Vatican Council. Not surprisingly, therefore, a significant number of religiously involved women in Quebec have in recent years sought to change the organizational and theological status of women within the Catholic church; the aim has been to transform the church from a highly patriarchal institution into one that embodies the equality of the sexes. Issues that have informed the debate include the ordination of women, abortion, contraception, inclusive religious language and the working conditions of female church employees. Much as in the case of Catholic Charismatic Renewal, the response of the Quebec hierarchy to women's concerns has been positive, but only to the extent that changes did not threaten the fundamental authority structure of the church.

A few examples can serve to illustrate the church's ambiguous posture. In the early 1980s, the Canadian Conference of Catholic Bishops (CCCB), of which the Quebec bishops are members, formed a committee to look at the situation of women in the church. The committee, headed by the Quebec theologian Elisabeth Lacelle, gave its report in 1984: it recommended substantial change in women's position in the church. The bishops revised the report and published a final document, *Women in the Church* (CCCB 1985), the next year. This official version, while accepting that women had legitimate concerns and that things should change, altered the report in such a way as to leave the nature, extent and pace of change firmly in the hands of the bishops: the received authority structure of the church itself was not to be challenged (see Roy 1990).

The same pattern has been evident in a variety of specific issues as well. When Pope Paul VI's 1968 encyclical, Humanae Vitae, condemned artificial contraception, the Quebec bishops along with the Canadian hierarchy accepted the statement as an authoritative pronouncement of the church, but also more or less accepted that most Catholics would ignore it. In a somewhat similar vein, the clear opposition of the bishops to abortion has not prevented them from acquiescing in the liberalization of Canada's abortion laws (cf. Cuneo 1989, 26-39). The Canadian hierarchy has generally been hesitant about even raising the issue of ordination of women, given Rome's well-known intransigence, but the CCCB has openly advocated that women be allowed access to the recently revived minor orders of lector and acolyte (Hamelin 1984, 366-368).

Are the attitudes of the Quebec bishops towards women's concerns any different than those of their English-Canadian counterparts? There is reason to think that the answer may be "yes." Some Quebec bishops, notably Bishop Robert Lebel of Valleyfield, do discuss the ordination of women openly, although they do not go so far as to contradict official Vatican policy. Lebel is also one of those who permits women to serve mass in his diocese. He has his Anglophone counterparts. As a group, however, the Quebec bishops do have a reputation for being more progressive on women's issues. Perhaps the best example is what happened after the 1985 CCCB statement. The Quebec bishops began separate consultation with Quebec women's groups; in late 1989, the Social Affairs Committee of the Assembly of Quebec Bishops (AEQ) issued a statement entitled *A Heritage of Violence?*, which went much farther than any previous Canadian episcopal statement in questioning and even condemning patriarchal attitudes and structures. Nonetheless, in spite of its progressive stand, the document deals only with violence against women in society, thereby avoiding any discussion of what the analysis implies for power structures within the contemporary church. The difference between the Quebec bishops and those in the rest of Canada is evidently not that great, even if we admit divergent emphases in certain cases.

THE QUEBEC BISHOPS AND CONTEMPORARY QUEBEC NATIONALISM

Given both traditional and recent Quebec nationalism, what is the relation of the Quebec bishops to the Canadian episcopacy as a whole? The Quebec bishops have had some form of collegial structure since the nineteenth century. Until well into the twentieth century, French-speaking bishops were also the dominant force in the Canadian Catholic church, just as Francophones were and still are the majority of the Canadian Catholic population. Only with the formation in 1948 of a national episcopal body, the Canadian Catholic Conference (CCC), did it become important to decide the precise status of the distinct organization for Quebec bishops. They did not want to separate from the CCC for the sake of church unity and because of the numerous French Catholics outside Quebec; but language, history, culture and the geographical concentration of French Catholics in Quebec pointed to the continuation of a largely autonomous grouping for that province. In 1973, the CCC (today the Canadian Conference of Catholic Bishops) restructured itself along regional lines, primarily to accommodate the existence of the Assembly of Quebec Bishops (AEQ) (Hamelin 1984). The coexistence of the CCC/CCCB and the AEQ raises the question of the Quebec bishops' position on Quebec nationalism.

Inasmuch as the hierarchy did not seriously resist the broad secularization of Quebec society with the Quiet Revolution, it also did not mourn the passing of the traditional identification of religion and nation. Contemporary secular nationalism does not have a religious component in its ideology, and the Catholic church has not offered one. Although there are without doubt Quebec sovereigntists among the bishops, their official position is one of benign neutrality. Perhaps the best illustration is a public statement by the AEQ in 1979, before the 1980 referendum on sovereignty-association. Here the bishops assiduously avoided taking sides, but did unequivocally support the right of Québécois to determine their own future (see Williams 1984, 181-188).

Social-Justice Catholicism and Christian Socialists

The attention to women's concerns and the support of Quebec self-determination are both aspects of a wider social-justice orientation on the part of the Quebec episcopacy (see Baum 1991a, 159-170), and indeed the CCCB as a whole. Since the early 1970s, the bishops have been adopting fairly radical and sometimes controversial positions on a whole range of issues, including Aboriginal rights, northern development, economic policy, nuclear power and Canadian foreign policy (see Baum and Cameron 1984; Williams 1984; Sheridan

1987). In these "leftist" stands, they have the support of a not insignificant but still minority section of the church's lay and clerical elite. This social-justice Catholicism illustrates how the challenge of a secularized society has brought in its wake new religious forms and not just a decline of the old.

The leadership of the Catholic church in Quebec did not start paying attention to social issues only after the Second Vatican Council. What changed in the 1960s was that the bishops no longer equated the solution to social problems with the preservation or reassertion of ecclesiastical influence: they accepted the secularization of Quebec society. Although many of the central themes of their social critique continued, especially the concern about the deleterious effects of modern, industrial society, the solutions now envisaged a progressive, egalitarian society rather than some idealized and simpler past. A certain number of Quebec Catholics, however, went much farther than the bishops. Inspired largely by the Latin American liberation theology that was rising to prominence, these predominantly elite Catholics have advocated radical social change in Quebec society. For them, the Christian message is for the sake of the marginalized and oppressed people of this world. Christians must therefore see the liberation of such people as central to their faith and practice. What has distinguished this social-justice stand from that of the bishops is its use of Marxist analysis to understand the problem and its vision of socialism as the solution.

When the Christian socialist movement first arose in the late 1960s, conflict with the hierarchy seemed a definite possibility. After all, these Catholics wanted to change not only society, but also the church. By the mid-1970s, however, a number of developments within the church, including the more leftist public positions taken by the bishops themselves, convinced most within the movement to concentrate their energies on societal injustices rather than on setting up a parallel church. To that end, they formed numerous organizations and networks, some of which still survive. Attempts to set up Latin American-style grassroots or basic Christian communities among the poor and to marginalize themselves met with only limited success; they have for the most part disappeared. More important has been the revival of various Catholic action groups, such as the Young Christian Workers (JOC) and the Christian Student Movement of Quebec (MECQ). These are resurrected versions of organizations that were prominent in the Catholic response to the urban and industrial Quebec of the 1930 to 1960 period. They are more leftist in their orientation and more independent of hierarchical control. Between 1972 and 1982, Quebec had its own branch of the international organization, Christians for Socialism, the *Réseau des Politisés Chrétiens* (Network of Politicized Christians). Of particular note has been the key role that important segments of certain religious orders have played in supporting the movement, above all the Jesuits, the Oblates (OMI) and the Dominicans. The most important publications of the movement have been centred in these orders, specifically *Relations* (Jesuit) and *Vie Ouvrière.*

These manifestations of more socialist Catholicism in Quebec are selections from among many. The movement is still alive and well today, although, like Catholic Charismatic Renewal, its peak of growth and visibility may be in the past. In both these cases, as with others discussed here, developments after the Second Vatican Council in the Quebec Roman Catholic church have had their parallels in the rest of Canada and indeed around the world. The differences are matters of degree, not substance. Where the Quebec church does differ from its counterpart in the rest of Canada is of course in the powerful role that it used to have before the Quiet Revolution. That history carries echoes into the present; this is no more evident than in the Quebec school system.

THE PECULIAR CASE OF THE QUEBEC SCHOOL SYSTEM

In 1964, for the first time in its history, the Quebec government successfully set up a Ministry of Education charged with the task of directing education throughout the province. The loss of erstwhile ecclesiastical power and prestige was perhaps clearest in this event. From having more or less complete control over most aspects of French education, the bishops were effectively reduced to jurisdiction over religious instruction alone (Magnuson 1980, 102ff). The system as a whole, however, continued to be structured along confessional, Protestant/Catholic lines. In 1977, the Parti Québécois government passed its omnibus language law, Bill 101. It required that a great many children from English-speaking families be educated in French. Henceforth, the Protestant and Catholic school boards would both have French and English schools under their jurisdiction. In the eyes of the government and many Quebec citizens, this amounted to unnecessary duplication because the confessional difference was no longer of real importance.

For the next decade, the government sought to restructure the system along linguistic lines, but without success. The reasons for the failure are instructive.

Until the Quiet Revolution, Quebec's educational system was perhaps the principal "secular" institution through which the church brought its social influence to bear on the French majority. Thus, it should surprise no one that those who oppose secularization have often chosen the schools as their battleground. A second direct result is that, for most Québécois, Catholic religion is still a meaningful, if somewhat nostalgic, element in their cultural identity. Most parents still wish their children to receive Catholic religious instruction in the school system.

Ultimately, the Quebec government failed to deconfessionalize the school system because Section 93 of the British North America Act, now part of the 1982 Constitution Act, guarantees Catholic and Protestant schools in Quebec. Those interested in defeating the legislation appealed to the courts and won on that basis. Although some representatives of the Protestant schools supported the challenge because they saw in the confessional structure protection for schools under the control of the English-speaking minority, the main defenders of confessionality were conservative Catholics. Most visible in the Catholic Parents' Association of Quebec (APCQ), these activists gained control over several local Catholic school commissions, including that of Montreal, the largest in the province. Their aim is not merely to maintain some sort of nominal confessionality. Beyond that, they wish to see all aspects of instruction in Catholic schools imbued with Catholic principles and reflective of Catholic values (see Milner 1986). Along with a certain number of supportive bishops and teachers, they represent that portion of the Quebec population still genuinely attached, if not to the old religio-nationalism, then at least to the old religious culture.

The attitude of most Québécois, however, seems to be more equivocal. The same parents who do not practice their nominal religion in any regular or consistent way are also those who believe that their children ought to learn about the Roman Catholic faith in school, if only to decide for themselves. Thus, in the mid-1980s, only about 30 percent of adult Québécois attended mass regularly (a figure that now stands at below 25 percent; see Baril and Mori 1991), but Quebec parents sent 92 percent of their primary school children to religious education classes (Lemieux 1990, 160). As if to underscore the ambiguity and the complexity of attitudes, a 1981 poll showed that fully 40 percent of Québécois preferred for their children "a Catholic school where the religious dimension covers all aspects of school life" (Palard 1988, 99). Quite evidently, individual and, in the case of the school system, systemic secularization have not been as thorough in Quebec as one might suppose: the church spires and the saintly place names are as yet something more than anachronistic echoes of a bygone era.

Conclusion: A Cultural Catholicism?

Raymond Lemieux is one Quebec scholar who has attempted to characterize this ambiguous status of the Roman Catholic religion among Québécois. In a recent article (1990), he suggests that Québécois now practice a "popular Catholicism," one centred on diffuse spiritual quest, emotion and largely unorganized or even haphazard practice. Catholicism in Quebec, he argues, is no longer a clerical affair: it is a Catholicism without church. To defend his position, Lemieux discusses many of the things mentioned at the outset: decrease in church-centred practice, the support of religious instruction in schools, the fascination with the pope and a number of other things like the continued popularity of Quebec's major religious pilgrimage sites. Indeed, as further support, even the movements for renewal within the church, such as those examined above, are largely of a marginal character: they involve a minority and enjoy the sponsorship of the hierarchy only to a limited extent.

There is an appealing logic to Lemieux's interpretation. In Quebec during the last few decades, it is the religious institution itself, the Roman Catholic church, that has lost most of its former social power. That is the result of systemic secularization. Individual secularization, while extensive, affects above all official practice like attendance at mass and confession. The renewal movements for the most part seek to "democratize" the church, to make it, like other voluntary associations, the creature of its members. That is, the belief and practice of Roman Catholicism in Quebec no longer has a consistent and recognizable from controlled by the religious authorities; distinct patterns of belief and practice only appear at the individual level. Religion, as a mode of human action and a sphere of social meaning, is becoming or already has become publicly diffuse and only privately specific. Lemieux even speaks of Quebec Catholicism as having become a "civil religion," a kind of inclusive and anodyne culture of citizenship. As the title of his work proclaims, Catholicism in Quebec is now a matter of culture.

This analysis does have some merit; it also begs the question that has informed the entire presentation of this chapter. If cultural Catholicism is indeed the form religion takes in contemporary Quebec, does this not amount to the fairly radical secularization of that society? In terms of the theoretical model this chapter uses, Lemieux is arguing that individual and systemic secularization together amount to institutional secularization, or at least make the question of institutional secularization irrelevant: what does it matter if the bishops still claim to mediate salvation when few are listening? This argument can be misleading.

As the various sections of this chapter have attempted to show, the Roman Catholic church has undergone significant transformations since the onset of the Quiet Revolution and the Second Vatican Council. It has lost most of its adherents as regular and devoted participants. It has seen its social power pass largely to the Quebec state. Internally, new movements and directions have challenged the inherited structures — to some extent successfully, to some extent not. Yet the church as an organization and as a social system with its own particular style of social action and meaningful interpretation of the world survives. More importantly, all those contemporary manifestations that we can justifiably call "Catholicism" are still run and controlled by the church. The church through its organization, its professionals, its authorities controls Catholic religious instruction in the schools; it controls the pilgrimage sites; that popular globetrotter, the pope, is its head; social-justice Catholics, like Charismatics, value their official legitimacy; Catholic feminists want equal treatment within the church; Catholic rituals are performed under the auspices of the church. Without the institution, all this would disappear or cease to be Catholic in any real sense of the word. Québécois, like most Canadians, and indeed like most North Americans, may have a fairly loose attitude to their religious affiliation. They may, as Bibby (1987; 1990) claims, be taking their religion à la carte, but the dominant menu is still the old one. In the case of Québécois, it is the one offered by the Catholic church.

For Further Reading

Baum, Gregory. 1991. *The Church in Quebec.* Montreal: Novalis.

Linteau, Paul-André, René Durocher, and Jean-Claude Robert. 1983. *Quebec: A History, 1867-1929.* Toronto: Lorimer.

Magnuson, Roger. 1980. *A Brief History of Quebec Education: From New France to Parti Québécois.* Montreal: Harvest House.

McRoberts, Kenneth, and Dale Postgate. 1988. *Quebec: Social Change and Political Crisis.* 3rd ed. Toronto: McClelland and Stewart.

Trofimenkoff, Susan Mann. 1982. *The Dream of Nation: A Social and Intellectual History of Quebec.* Toronto: Macmillan.

Chapter 8

In Quest of Hidden Gods in Canadian Literature

Roger O'Toole

IMPLICIT RELIGION AS A CONCEPT

The concept of "implicit religion" has recently begun to achieve wider currency within the fields of sociology and religious studies (see Nesti 1990; Bailey 1990a; 1990b; Weibe 1989). Although its exponents have energetically attempted to list the attributes and define the boundaries of "implicit religion," its contents remain nebulous and its provenance unclear. In what might be regarded as a "charter document," Edward Bailey has identified implicit religion primarily with "commitments," "personal depths," "integrating foci," and "intensive concerns." He has also stressed, and attempted to clarify, its affinity with such more familiar concepts as "folk religion," "popular religion," "common religion," "civil religion" and "invisible religion." Despite these formulations, however, implicit religion retains its analytically untidy character (Bailey 1983; 1984; 1986; 1987).

Though the concept will continue to repel those who identify vagueness solely with vacuousness, it may generate more scholarly light if it is theoretically located in a broader definitional context. From this standpoint, implicit religion may simply be viewed as an aspect of broad functional and substantive conceptions of religion that are long established in sociological literature and are of acknowledged use in research in the sociology of religion.[1] The roots of the concept of implicit religion are thus, on the one hand, embedded in functional definitions that depict religion in terms of "ultimate concerns," "grounds of meaning," "identity-formation" and "moral community." On the other hand, they may be unearthed in substantive definitions characterized by such inclusive notions as "the sacred," "the supernatural" or "the superempirical."

Further, within all of these overlapping and highly inclusive cognitive, emotional, psychological and social domains, the distinction between explicit and implicit religion may be theoretically linked to a dichotomy or continuum between *manifest* and *latent* poles, respectively. Concerned essentially with distinguishing manifest and latent *forms* (rather than mere functions) of religion, the explicit-implicit distinction attempts to combine the utility of inclusive *sociological* definitions of religion in general with *societal* conceptions of religious phenomena in specific social, cultural and historical circumstances.[2]

This fusing of scholarly, generic definitions and conventional definitions may draw on ample precedent in its defence. In particular, leading exponents of various functional definitions have proven willing, rightly or wrongly, to alternate or conflate dissonant conceptions in their efforts to penetrate "a night in which all cats are grey" (see Berger 1974). In this manner, *explicit* religion is identified with those institutionalized beliefs and practices that are conventionally termed "religious" by participants in a given social context. Such religion is clearly manifest in form. In contrast, *implicit* religion refers to beliefs and practices not conventionally designated as "religious" by social actors in a given social context. These are deemed "religious" on the basis of the inclusive definition of a scholarly observer. Such religion is clearly latent in form, being essentially invisible *as religion* to any but the sociological eye (see Luckmann 1967).

A scholarly definition of religion that moves beyond conventional societal usage has the advantage of metaphorically prising religion from the monopolistic grip of the churches. Expressing a prejudice that might be summarized as "religion is too important to be left to its official practitioners," such a conception inspires a search for religion in places far removed from its traditionally hallowed locations. The concept of implicit religion is untidy and indistinct in the tradition of Max Weber's (1963) infamous implicit definition of religion, well known for its lack of clarity. It is, however, hardly less tidy or distinct than those widely revered and firmly established definitional traditions from which it originates. Similarly, while the defects and dangers of broadly inclusive definitions of religion have been amply recorded, their undoubted merits cannot be overlooked. Implicit religion has emerged as a crude but useful "catch-all" device for exploring "religious" phenomena in contexts far removed from mainstream Christian organizations and well beyond the realms of the traditional world religions.

THE SEARCH FOR IDENTITY

Like other modern cultures, Canada is characterized by an uneasy *détente* between science and religion (Weibe 1989).[3] While the imprint of secularization is evident, the resilience of religion, in many forms, is equally pronounced. Though Canadian institutionalized religion has, by all accounts, declined significantly from its Victorian heyday, the popular search for ultimate answers and moral community proceeds unabated (Bibby 1987). Thus, it is not difficult to discern in Canada those informal intimations of the sacred that have already been investigated through parallel cases in other national contexts. While local employment of foreign insights into implicit religion might, accordingly, illuminate unfamiliar aspects of Canadian folk, popular, common and even invisible religion, such ethnographic cataloguing is not attempted here (see Graham 1990). The mandate of this chapter is both more restricted and more original. Using the notion of "identity" as its threshold, it explores common literary themes and images of the artist — subjects not previously examined within the context of implicit religion. By indicating a new direction for studies of implicit religion, it thus contributes more than mere Canadian variations on familiar themes.

The concept of "identity" is an important element in so many sociological interpretations of religion that its use in studies of implicit religion is hardly surprising under any circumstances (Mol 1976a; Robertson and Holzner 1979). In a Canadian context, however, it represents the single most promising point of departure for any significant exploration of implicitly religious phenomena. To the extent that implicit religion incorporates such themes as commitment, integration, personal depths, individuation, ultimacy, meaning and community, its affinity with what is frequently perceived as a national cultural obsession is profound. Indeed, it may be suggested that much of the agonized self-examination and soul-searching that constitutes the perennial pursuit of an elusive "Canadian Identity" bears the unmistakable mark of an implicitly religious quest.[4]

To a striking degree, public discussion of Canadian national identity has been dominated by pronouncements from the humanities rather than the social sciences. Though there is, for example, a significant sociological literature pertaining to the topic, the extent to which it addresses literary and historical agenda is noteworthy. Thus, the most provocative and influential sociological exponent of a *cultural* interpretation of Canadian-American differences begins a recent stock-taking by focusing on literature as a means of understanding Canadian values (Lipset 1985; 1991; Cappon 1978).

Given the foregoing apparent connections among identity, values, implicit religion and literature, it appears appropriate to investigate these connections in more detail. If Canadian literature is a suitable source for derivation of distinctive national values, its preoccupation with the problem of identity provides *a fortiori* a proper focus for research into distinctly Canadian forms of implicit religion.

THE HIDDEN GODS OF CANADIAN LITERATURE[5]

Whether or not there exists an "obvious and unquenchable desire of the Canadian public to identify itself through its literature," there appears to be a persistent compulsion on the part of writers and critics to regard literature as a major vehicle for the expression of national identity (Frye 1971).[6] Few writers would quarrel with Lipset's assertion that of all cultural artifacts "the art and literature of a nation should most reflect *as well as establish* her basic myths and values" (1985, 119 [my emphasis]). In fact, declining to consider their creations as mere epiphenomenal *reflections* of the Canadian "soul," many writers self-consciously perceive their work as a contribution to the *formation* of national identity and values. Whereas Lipset's intention is to infer evidence of national identity from literary content and form, however, the present investigation simply uses the notion of identity as a strategic portal into a broader exploration of implicitly religious concerns.

Though its influence has frequently been underestimated, religion in its orthodox focus has been accurately described as "a major — perhaps the major — cultural force in Canada, at least down to the last generation or two." It is, therefore, unthinkable that it should not have left its imprint on the national literature as well as on the national consciousness (Frye 1971; see also Grant 1976). Latent

Judaeo-Christian themes may be divulged, therefore, in manifestly unlikely surroundings; however, it is clear that Jehovah and Jesus are not the only hidden gods awaiting disclosure by literary detection.

No survey of strange gods in Canadian fiction or poetry can ignore the work of Northrop Frye, so much of whose work is permeated by the religious impulse. Long intrigued by the "relations between a culture and the social conditions under which it is produced," Frye regards Canadian literature as an "indispensable aid to the knowledge of Canada [which] records what the Canadian imagination has reacted to and ... tells us things about this environment that nothing else will tell us" (Frye 1982, 15; see also 1971, 163, 215). Preferring to study the literary imagination as "a force and function of life" rather than as a part of an autonomous, rarefied realm of words, he employs the concept of "myth" both as the purest form of metaphor and the shaping principle of poetry. More precisely, his search for the "qualities in Canadian poetry that illustrate the poet's response to the specific environment that we call approximately Canada" is identified with pursuit of the literary imagination's mythopoeic character. In its mythological preoccupation, Frye's examination of the theme of identity in Canadian poetry and prose is irresistibly enticing and ingeniously provocative when appraised in a context of implicit religion (Frye 1971, 177-179, 232-241; 1982, 72-78).

Frye's pursuit of national identity is less concerned with a political state than with imaginative states of mind. Exploring psychological rather than geographical frontiers, it refutes the notion of Canada as "a country without mythology"[7] populated solely by practitioners of a bland, unadventurous materialism (Frye 1971, 238; 1977, 28; see also Kenner in Ross 1954). In his literary investigations, which link history, landscape, communications, culture, psychology and spirituality, Frye presents insightful, sweeping and controversial analyses of commitments, concerns, foci and, most significantly, personal depths that he perceives as characteristically Canadian.

While acknowledging the profound impact on Canadian writers of a "garrison mentality," which is the inevitable ideological product of prolonged counter-revolutionary colonialism, Frye's exploration of the national literary and artistic "soul" is decidedly elemental and preternatural in its focus. According to Frye, the question of identity ("Who am I?") must be translated, in a Canadian context, into a sense of place ("Where is here?"), and the answer to either query may be found only in the fundamental confrontation of the human with the forces of nature. In discussions evocative of the works of Max Müller, Andrew Lang, Sir James Frazer, Claude Lévi-Strauss and Mircea Eliade among others, Frye depicts this confrontation as it is experienced and described by Canadian writers and artists of the greatest sensitivity. His account is both morally disturbing and existentially chilling: a frightening encounter with the numinous, the ultimate and the eternal.[8]

Beneath a lyrical chorus of "maple-leaf" exuberance over sunsets, waterfalls, the challenges of a new land, and the destiny of dominion and empire, Frye discerns a more sombre elegiac note in Canadian poetry. Intimating that pastoral and patriotic versifiers alike are whistling in the dark, he discovers the unique, elegiac theme of Canadian poetry and painting in the primeval inscrutability of a land that God gave to Cain.

The poets depicted by Frye are strangers in a strange land that confronts them with bleak indifference. Meditating on the awesome isolation, desolation and menace of inhumanized landscape, they experience confusion, guilt, loneliness, alienation and sheer terror. Such circumstances undoubtedly fuel religious speculation in the most general sense, for they provoke intense ruminations on the purpose of existence, the meaning of life and death, and the problem of evil. Faced by overwhelming natural forces that are simultaneously indifferent and brutally red in tooth and claw, the poetic imagination strives for sanity through a quest for ultimate meaning, an encounter with the transcendent, or both. To gaze upon the blank, vast coldness of the Canadian landscape is to glimpse intuitively "a frozen hell of moral nihilism" and to ponder riddles of experience entirely alien to human or social values. By this "shutting out of the whole of moral creation," the Canadian landscape suggests tragic themes of inexplicable death and inexplicable evil that are threateningly chaotic in the most profound sense. Thus, according to Frye, the source of a distinctly Canadian mythopoeic imagination in its various manifestations lies in the literary or artistic encounter with a completely unconscious nature whose horrors coincide with those of the subconscious human mind. To contemplate such silent, sinister scenery is also to survey "the cruelty and subconscious stampeding" of the human mind. To envision the taming or domination of nature is thereby to anticipate the subjugation and ordering of human passions, a task to be accomplished by the mythical fusion of humanity and its natural environment. Through mythology, the poet or painter domesticates the mysterious. Myth facilitates exploration of the farthest reaches of the cosmos while simultaneously promoting examination of the depths of the human soul. It enables a sense of place to be transformed into a conception of personal identity and allows the transcendence of meaninglessness by morality.

In their quest for appropriate mythologies, Canadian writers and artists have been driven by a conviction of *not belonging* in an inhospitable land that even the gods have abandoned. Haunted by "lack of ghosts" in a "country without a mythology," such strangers can find no mythical signposts to guide them. Bereft of monuments and landmarks, they can apprehend nothing more than "environment as object." The process of humanizing the environment through mythology involves both the rehabilitation of archaic Native myths and the "idealization of memory" through innovative pastoral myths. Both these forms of the invention of tradition generate a sense of belonging, and thereby a sense of identity in their creators (Frye 1971; see also Hobsbawm 1983; Schmitt 1969; Tanner 1987).

This dual identity, deriving from the "primitive" and the pastoral, is presumably transmitted to, and shared by, appreciative audiences of those works of art that seek to express it. Widespread appropriation of Canadian Native mythology doubtless derives "from an unconscious feeling that the primitive myth expressed the imaginative impact of this country" in ways that prove impossible for the intellectual creations of an intruding civilization. Nonetheless, it also represents a conscious effort to revive or reanimate indigenous, slumbering sacred forces. This neo-primitivism inevitably leads to quasi-totemism — the search for heroic ancestors or ancient symbols of the nation — in the attempt to reproduce a supposed Native rapport with nature. At the same time, various forms of pastoral myth emerge to express a growing sense of safety, security and satisfaction in an environment previously perceived as shapeless, soulless and sinister. Whether this new sense of belongingness is articulated in imagery derived from Natives as the "true forbears" of the land's contemporary inhabitants or in modern, flag-waving political mythologies of nation and empire, it represents a significant transformation in both Canadian consciousness and unconsciousness. The rebirth of mythological imagination signifies the end-of-exile of a people now indigenous to its vast, bleak environment. Formed "in the belly of a mindless emptiness," this poetic, literary and artistic consciousness, for better or worse, belongs within the leviathan of Canadian nature. The leviathan in which it lives is no more alien to it than those inner depths of the human mind into which it anxiously descends (Frye 1977, 39-43; 1982, 69-70; see also Woodcock 1977).

Frye is not alone in his exploration of implicitly religious themes in his depiction of the mythopoeic character of Canadian literacy and artistic endeavour. Other writers and critics both detect and create mythology in literary and artistic contexts. Their writings examine concerns and commitments linking the personal depths of human individuality with the communal heights of human imagination. Chronicling various pilgrimages to the sources of identity and ultimate meaning, they test the tensions between the individual and society while explicating the dialectic between humanity and its natural environment. The image of Canada and Canadians that is manifested in this diversity of creative conceptions is greatly at odds with familiar and boring stereotype; this is no "dull place, devoid of romantic interest" inhabited by "a dull people without charm or ideas." Canada's artists, writers and critics appear to exhibit "a sense of the unfathomable wonder of the invisible world," demonstrating "a readiness to see daemons where nowadays we see neuroses and to see the hand of a guardian angel in what we are apt to shrug off ungratefully as a 'stroke of luck.'" If this is an implicit religion, it is "a religion with a thousand gods, none of them all-powerful and most of them ambiguous in their attitude toward men" (Atwood 1977; Davies 1975).[9]

By peering beyond the "solidly social-realistic mainstream" of Canadian fiction, Margaret Atwood demonstrates that there is "more to Canada than meets the eye." Her perusal of supernatural themes discloses a literary world of wonders in which unpredictable, invisible forces lurk behind the mundane routines of everyday reality. Like Robertson Davies, she perceives that the "cold and cautious" Canadian exterior conceals an inner realm of "intuition and dark intimations" whose seething contours are best apprehended through the medium of literary and artistic creativity.

The fictional land charted by Atwood is, in many respects, "a polar night of icy darkness and hardness," though it is far from the disenchanted domain envisioned in Max Weber's Formulation (see Gerth and Mills 1948, 28; Weber 1958a, 181-182). This terrifying, icy wilderness of mountains, forests and bottomless lakes is also a magical, enchanted world inhabited by primeval beings whose existence is undreamed of in a rational world of regimented routine. Within its borders, reborn and mutated monsters of Native and Inuit myth combine with modern manifestations of the mysterious in invoking a mood of horror punctuated by dazzling glimpses of exotic beauty. Dispelling any notion that Canadian culture is really as "flat and lacking in resonance" as it appears, these creatures confront the sterile world of orderly common sense with supernatural visions of unreason, chaos, ecstasy and evil. The hybrid monsters, subhumans, demigods, vampires, clairvoyants, succubi and sorcerers that populate the pages of Canadian fiction are modern mythical creations whose bridge-building is by no means restricted to the linking of the natural with the supernatural. Part animal-part human, part myth-part reality, part Native-part white, part individual-part collectivity, part self-part other, part internal-part external, these creatures range from incarnations of a hostile external universe through embodiments of human inner evil to chameleon-like nonpersons without any central core of identity.

In her literary criticism as well as her poetry and fiction, Atwood is an intrepid explorer of "Canada as a state of mind," a mysterious land in which many are lost. To survey this territory is to plumb the depths of the Canadian soul and then surface with a mythological map indispensable to survival (Atwood 1972a, 18-19; see also 1972b; 1991; Frye 1977, 42-43).[10] With an "instinct for what is imaginatively central in Canadian sensibility," Atwood's descent into the personal depths and collective wellsprings of national identity is a mythopoeic quest for those meanings, integrative symbols, commitments and concerns that characterize implicit religion. Observing that the critic is "a kind of magician," she unveils a vision of enchantment and mystery that was once the privileged possession of the priest but is now perceptible through the attuned literary or artistic imagination (1977, 121-122).

The mysterious forces revealed by Frye and Atwood are by no means the only hidden gods of Canadian art and literature. So profoundly have Christian myths and symbols infused Canadian culture that, even in the secular climate of the twentieth century, such themes as sacrifice, salvation, sin and redemption still supply a recognizable, if sometimes disguised, religious dimension to much contemporary creativity. Thus, a number of sociological, theological and literary investigators have recently detected and elucidated the sometimes obscure Christian communications that are implicit in many works of Canadian fiction.

Hans Mol investigates the transmission of the traditional Christian message through the medium of the modern popular novel. Asserting that biblical archetypes and religious symbols permeate some of the best-known works of Canadian fiction, he describes a "growing understanding of the Christian view of salvation, sin, crucifixion and resurrection" promoted through the narration of imaginary individual life histories (Mol 1985, 271-283). Using a somewhat broader bibliography than Mol, Louis MacKendrick also explores "some fictional relationships of individuals to the divine, or to divinity, in a selective survey of some modern and contemporary English-Canadian fiction." Analyzing variations in the relationship "between God and His people," however, MacKendrick fails to detect any single "unifying perspective or theme" common to them. In a conclusion highly pertinent to the notions of implicit or invisible religion, he observes that the God of Canadian fiction is "not a consistency but a diversity, a multifaceted deity" who differs according to each individual's needs and concerns (1986, 30-46). This is a personal God formed and transformed in the eye of the beholder, a projection of the self no longer confined to the traditional symbolic forms of the Judaeo-Christian heritage. The archetypes that dominate the "secular scripture" of modern literature appear to be diverse, amorphous and transitory reflections of the confusion, complexity, differentiation and privatization of the secular world.

Such co-existence and synthesis of traditional religious elements with more exotic and novel mythological creations has been noted by a number of other scholarly investigators, among them William C. James, Elizabeth Waterston and Dennis Duffy. Guided by the insights of Rudolph Otto, Mircea Eliade, Peter L. Berger and Joseph Campbell, James examines "the representation of this-worldly transcendence" as it occurs in Canadian fiction of recent decades. He traces, in the development of the Canadian novel, a "passage from the depiction of eternity as the backdrop to the temporal world to the representation of life as an interplay between everyday reality and transcendence." Using Berger's minimalist conception of the super-natural as "*an other reality*, and one of the ultimate significance ...

which transcends the reality within which our everyday experience unfolds," James suggests that the signals of transcendence transmitted through current fiction are unlikely to derive from, or refer to, eternal or extra-terrestrial entities. It is rather through "an intensification of ordinary experience" that the transcendent is to be glimpsed — not in some distant external realm but within the personal depths of everyday reality. The hero or heroine of modern fiction "may be transported beyond the usual realm of ordinary experience by an experience of the numinous or the uncanny, of death or madness, of nothingness or non-being." For James, therefore, the transcendent depicted in recent Canadian writing resembles "the Holy" characterized by Rudolph Otto. It is a "negative horizon of ultimacy" from which may emerge "a new identity of ultimate integration and well-being." As "a void which must be filled up with some positive meaning," it is the focus of the transformation from chaotic plight to ultimate meaning, from anguish and despair to fulfilment and redemption (James 1985, 256-259; see also Berger 1969).

The theme of life as "interplay between everyday reality and transcendence" is explored in Elizabeth Waterston's case study of the work of Rudy Wiebe. Tracing Wiebe's spiritual journey from the rigidities of his Mennonite roots to his obsession with the religion of Native people, she recounts his struggle to recapture the Canadian past, to forge a genuine Canadian identity and to rediscover an ancient route to personal salvation. Less interested in mythological and ritual revival than in restoring essential contact with the sacred, Wiebe seeks spiritual insight by entering the Native world of the "dark other." His Mennonite conviction of God's role in human destiny is thereby transformed into a "new and larger vision" of an immanent deity. Like his Métis hero Louis Riel, Wiebe has "made a crucial, difficult and radically important shift" from inherited communal beliefs "to a renewed sense of the divine." Comprising nothing less than a realization of his own direct access to the will of God, Wiebe's revised faith is rooted in a radically revised sense of reality that obliterates the division between "we" and "other." This "undifferentiated unity of the mystical experience" constitutes the spiritual prerequisite for hearing that "almighty voice" of God, which has spoken, over the centuries, to shamans, prophets, hermits, rebels, innovators and charismatics of all kinds. Most significantly, however, this hidden faceless God now reveals himself primarily in the "inner voice" of the artist, writer or poet. As a "vessel" whose direct contact with the supernatural occurs within the mysterious personal depths of individual identity, the creative writer mediates between the sacred and profane by interpreting contemporary signals of transcendence, ultimate meaning and spiritual redemption (Waterston 1986, 21-29).

Observing that the "search for a new form of godhead to replace the old has haunted our culture since its beginnings in the Industrial Revolution," Dennis Duffy describes the most recent phase of this quest as manifested in contemporary Canadian literature. Despite the Dionysian element injected into Canadian writing during the 1960s counterculture, Duffy detects no subsequent dilution of the "strong moral tone" of the Canadian novel. In his view, "a greater degree of aberrant and anti-social behaviour" on the part of fictional characters by no means precludes their participation in a moral or transcendental quest. Indeed, they are still essentially involved in the plight "of the romantic hero or heroine seeking to find in this world hints of a better one elsewhere" so familiar to Berger, James and others.

For Duffy, the model of "the new religious quest in Canadian fiction" involves escape from the dehumanized, technological culture of modernity followed by pilgrimage through "the dark forest of demented rationality" in search of the "dark gods of Paganism." No longer, in his assessment, do Canadian writers experience revelation of the "ground of being" in the encounter with nature, in secularized versions of ancient myths, rituals or theodicies, in the merging of self and community, or in "veiled, ambiguous hints" of transcendence. Rather, their insight into the "grace and mystery" that underlies and sustains the cosmos is achieved "in a personal release from the bonds of modern culture" that segregates the rational from the moral and emotional. The rejection of modern culture by contemporary Canadian writers thus implies a "search for some ground of transcendence" solely in the context of a struggle for personal salvation. Confined to the form, if not the content, of classic Protestantism, this privatized pursuit fails "to locate a new grounding for the self that is more than an individual refuge" and, accordingly, furnishes the individual with "no genuine alternative to that of solitude." The pursuit of loneliness becomes the price of salvation (Duffy 1985, 260-273).

As Duffy demonstrates, some writers experience an estrangement so profound that they pursue "union with natural forces whose strength and creativity lie beneath the arid superficialities of human culture." Fuelled by the clichés of cultural despair, their desperate quest for incarnate authenticity propels them even into the (sometimes literal) embrace of the animal kingdom. Rejecting the possibility that human communities or social institutions can, any longer, supply individuals with a "coherent vision" of their role in the universe, they regard "personal revelations confined to individuals" as the sole "alternative to the cultural rot that obsesses them."

If, as Duffy asserts, the yearning for a coherent vision of the world is implicitly "religious in nature," its expression is the prerogative of visionaries within the worlds of serious art and literature. In the contemporary, secular world the gift of grace in all its mystical, ascetic and prophetic focus has been "farmed out" to this new clerisy where it has not already been appropriated. Its fate, in the custody of such isolated and "crisis-prone individuals" is precarious indeed (Duffy 1985).

CONCLUSION

It is unnecessary to believe that literary or artistic creativity is *in itself* religious in order to appreciate the pervading implicitly religious character of much past and present Canadian writing.[11] In directing attention to art and literature as repositories or vehicles for religion, however, the sociological analyst is compelled to contemplate the artist or writer as an inherently religious figure. From the foregoing discussion, it is apparent that influential Canadian writers and critics explicitly define the serious literary *virtuoso* in the inspirational, visionary, charismatic, prophetic, mystical and ascetic terms usually identified with a romantic conception of individual creative genius (see Kermode 1957, 13-42).[12] It seems reasonable to suppose, furthermore, that this conception is shared by a significant section of the educated reading public. Whether this is an accurate depiction of the Canadian writer is of less consequence than an underlying assumption that the creative aesthete is the legitimate contemporary instrument of redemption and salvation. The notion of the aesthetic or intellectual cultural hero as the rightful heir to the religious legacy of the past is, of course, far from novel (see Woolfolk 1986; Brenner 1990). Yet, within the current context of sociological research into implicit religion, it represents a provocative and plausible hypothesis.

Despite distinguished precedent, contemporary sociological pre-occupation with signs of the sacred in secular society appears singularly insensitive to the possible religious significance of aesthetes and intellectuals in an increasingly disenchanted world. Such manipulators of symbols and architects of meaning are by no means the inevitable agents of religious revitalization (see Weber in Gerth and Mills 1948, 154-155, 342-343).[13] They are, nonetheless, undoubtedly worthy of greater scrutiny by scholars pursuing the hidden gods of modern life. If the Canadian national "soul" can be sought in the domain of literature, religious leadership may well be discovered in unfamiliar realms previously the preserve of sociologists of knowledge.[14] After all, strange terrain is, by definition, the natural habitat of the implicitly religious.

Notes

[1]For a review of such definitional strategies, see O'Toole (1984a, 10-51).

[2]Though not identical to it, our discussion parallels, in some respects, that of Greil and Rudy (1990).

[3]It should be noted that, although the present discussion is restricted to English Canada, a similar exploration of French Canada would prove equally interesting. Comparison of the role of implicit religion within these "two solitudes" would, in fact, be particularly intriguing.

[4]The literature on this topic is immense. See, for example, W.L. Morton (1972), Robin Mathews (1988), Blair Fraser (1967) and Malcom Ross (1954).

[5]In order to provide a better sense of the tone of these works, short quotations from a variety of literary sources have been interspersed throughout the text in this section. To preserve the integrity and flow of the argument, page numbers have been omitted. The precise location of the material in question is, however, available from the author upon request.

[6]This compulsion was recently applauded by Keith Spicer, chair of the official Citizens' Forum on Canada's Future, who announced that he was taking literally his search for the poetry in the Canadian soul. See Robert Matas (1990). In a similar vein, novelist Matt Cohen perceives English Canada as "engaged in a desperate search for its lost soul" and depicts artists and writers as "the only people left able to apply the intensive national therapy Canada needs." See "O Canada" (1990).

[7]"A Country without a Mythology" is the title of a poem by Douglas LePan; the phrase "haunted by lack of ghosts" is derived from Earle Birney's poem "Can. Lit."

[8]The parallel in this regard between Canadian poetry and painting (especially the works of the Group of Seven and Emily Carr) is appropriately underlined by Frye. See Frye (1971, 138-143, 146-154, 164-166, 170-172, 224-226, 236-238, 243, 200; 1977, 26-39). See also George Grant (1969, 17), Margaret Atwood (1972a) and Hugh Kenner (in Ross 1954).

[9]Davies explores the Magian world view of Spengler in other novels, as well; see also Davies (1987) and Gollnick (1990).

[10]Frye and Atwood have forged a widely held view of the Canadian imagination. For an alternative vision, see Arnold Harrichaud Itwaru (1990).

[11]On the necessary connections between literary creativity and religion, see, for example, John Simons (1986), Nathan Scott (1958), Jefferson Humphries (1983), William C. James (1985), George Steiner (1989), and, most compellingly, Salmon Rushdie (1990). Various writings of Rudolph Otto, Paul Tillich, Mircea Eliade and Peter Berger are also pertinent.

[12]On the origins of the ideology of individual artistic and literary genius, see Francis Haskell (1959, 444-445), and Robertson Davies (1985, 272-273). The rise of this ideology may be viewed as both a cause and consequence of the process of secularization.

[13]It should be stressed that the "implicit religion" of an intellectual or aesthetic elite is culturally very distinct from "popular," "folk" or "common" religiosity.

[14]Deriving initially from the works of Max Scheler and Karl Mannheim, the sociology of knowledge has long exhibited a particular (even inordinate) interest in the role of intellectuals, artists and aesthetes (see Karl Mannheim [1936]).

For Further Reading

Cappon, Paul (ed.). 1978. *In Our Own House: Social Perspectives on Canadian Literature.* Toronto: McClelland and Stewart.

MacKendrick, L. (ed.). 1986. *God and Man in Modern Literature.* Windsor, ON: Canterbury College.

Mathews, Robin. 1988. *Canadian Identity.* Ottawa: Steel Rail Publishing.

Ross, Malcolm (ed.). 1954. *Our Sense of Identity.* Toronto: Ryerson Press.

Staines, David (ed.). 1977. *The Canadian Imagination.* Cambridge, MA: Harvard University Press.

Chapter 9

Canadian Civil Religion

Robert Blumstock

A little more than thirty years ago "the end of ideology" was proclaimed (Bell 1961). The euphoria that greeted the end of the Second World War and the destruction of Nazi Germany led many people to believe that all that remained for Western societies was to find the appropriate techniques to create a better life for all. The ends of political action were clear; only the means to achieve these ends differed.

Now with the demise of the Soviet Union, new seers are claiming that "the end of history" has arrived (Fukuyama 1991). Although the argument is more sophisticated now than in the past, the prediction that only liberal democratic systems can provide the base upon which a better life can be constructed for humankind remains much the same. In this view of the future, the ideological divisions of the past are irrelevant and justly deserve to be cast into the dustbin of history.

This hope is predicated on the triumph of process and procedure over belief and sentiment. In this future scenario the differences between the past, present and future are obliterated for the sake of practicality, cost effectiveness and utility. The responses to issues will assume a high degree of consensus.

For many, this very reductionism, in which moral arguments based on cultural traditions will play a limited or non-existent role, has been the source of what has been termed "the moral crisis of modernity." Max Weber noted this pattern and the potential responses to it when he argued:

> The tension between religion and intellectual knowledge definitely comes to the fore wherever rational, empirical knowledge has consistently worked through to the disenchantment of the world and its transformation into a causal mechanism. For then science encounters

the ethical postulate that the world is a God-ordained, and hence somehow *meaningfully* and ethically oriented, cosmos (1958a, 350-351).

This quest for meaning finds its clearest exposition in those arguments that set the stage for history as drama, assigning roles to the leadership elite and the chosen class, and preparing for the historical culmination (Feuer 1975, 4).

The identity of those who resurrect these arguments may well be as important as why they arise. Here it is suggested that the social sources of this reaction may lie in the way different generations[1] confront their past, challenge the present and attempt to justify their own roles in the future. If this is the case, ideologies will probably never "fade away," but will always be with us in one form or another, as generations replace each other.

Ideological arguments are never dispassionate analyses deriving from a disinterested class with nothing to gain or to lose.[2] They may rather be seen as the arena in which representatives of different generations attempt to "re-enchant" the world in conformity with their own professional and personal interests.[3] Ideology is in these terms a technique by which those threatened with displacement or irrelevance will defend themselves by assuming a mantle of righteousness, which defines their role as unique, deserving and unchallengeable. It is a "marketing" strategy in the marketplace of ideas. The moral arguments that Robert Bellah first put forth in "Civil Religion in America" (1967) and similar Canadian responses to "the crisis of modernity" appear to be ideological arguments of this type. They perform the same functions for their proponents, as well.

CIVIL RELIGION IN AMERICA

Is "civil religion" really a religion, or is it simply an ideology that finds resonance within a broad sector of American society (Gehrig 1979)? For many sociologists of religion, the distinction between religions and secular ideologies remains crucial.[4] Robert Bellah, however, who originated the concept of "civil religion" (1967), pays little attention to this distinction. Instead, with a bold stroke he defines a uniquely American creed whose beliefs, rites and rituals affirm the existence of, and provide a rationale for, the continual renewal of the meaning of the nation.

What Bellah has done (and he is certainly not the first to do so) is to impute meaning to political and historical events by placing them within a religious framework (Aron 1957). By drawing on a religious paradigm in which the future will follow a "divine" plan, Bellah has defined his analysis so that it cannot be effectively challenged with arguments. It can only be flatly denied or confirmed. Bellah does not deny his reliance on the biblical archetypes that underlie his thesis: "Exodus, Chosen People, Promised Land, New Jerusalem, Sacrificial Death and Rebirth" (1967, 18). Moreover, his concern with the current "time of trial" is apparently the source of his need to articulate the dimensions of American civil religion.

Times of trial play an important role in Bellah's argument, as the very substance of civil religion has been forged from the crucible of their resolution. The first two times of trial he discusses are the Revolutionary War and the Civil War. The current time of trial, he states, involves "the problem of responsible action in a revolutionary world, a world seeking to obtain many of the things, material and spiritual, that we have already attained" (1967, 16). Writing in 1967, Bellah was clearly concerned with the civil rights movement, opposition to the Vietnam War, and other challenges to the status quo in the United States.

The enthusiasm of relatively privileged American youth, who saw their life chances threatened by a war whose goals were unclear and the obvious injustices that characterized the situation of black Americans, developed into a moral crusade that sought to bring American reality into line with its ideals. Bellah's response was to call attention to the underlying unity that Americans shared and to the virtues embedded in the substance of American society, that for the moment were obscured by the rush of events in which confrontation replaced understanding. In a sentence all too reminiscent of Durkheim's definition of religion, Bellah states that the American civil religion "provides a collection of beliefs, symbols and rituals with respect to sacred things and institutionalized in a collectivity" (1967, 8). To Bellah, civil religion is more than simply an affirmation of the American way of life: "civil religion at its best is a genuine apprehension of universal and transcendent religious reality as seen in or, one could almost say, as revealed through the experience of the American people" (1967, 12). The pervasive theme is the hope that the United States will "be a society as perfectly in accord with the will of God as man can make it, and a light to all nations" (1967, 18).

If this faith is accepted and understood, the result will be "a new vision of man, a new sense of human possibility and a new conception of the ordering of liberty, the constitution of freedom" (1975, 162).

Civil religion, according to Bellah, provides both a means of understanding and a source of motivation that links the individual to broader national and political goals. It is the ultimate source of inspiration for the re-attainment of a morally based society that could play a major role in providing "for some kind of viable and coherent world order ..." (Bellah 1967, 18).

Who is to lead this "revival"? Who has the appropriate knowledge to re-establish the basis of the re-invigorated moral order? This "awakening" to recover what has been lost will probably be led by what Bellah calls "core groups [or] those actually trying to live a new vision, [who] give hope that they are actually working out a new balance of impulse and control, energy and discipline, rather than abandoning all control and discipline" (1975, 159).

After defining these positive attributes of civil religion, Bellah then questions the capacities of a technically based liberal democracy to sustain itself. "I am convinced that the continual and increased dominance of the complex of capitalism, utilitarianism and the belief that the only road to truth is science will rapidly lead to the destruction of American society, or possibly in an effort to stave off destruction, to a technical tyranny of the brave new world variety" (1975, iv).

In essence we are presented with the portrait of an American polity that has an explicit sacralized quality in its mission to define and "save" a new world order. Americans are a chosen people who have surmounted previous trials, but who have now fallen from grace by worshipping the golden calf of material success. This lusting after the good life has caused them to lose sight of their role in the eternal plan. However, there are stirrings that give signs of a rebirth among a new elect who will lead their people out of the wilderness of moral decay back to the path of righteousness.

The one notable weakness in Bellah's arguments resides in the fact that it involves a myth, which, he admits, "may be true or false, but the test of truth or falsehood is different" (1975, 3). The test of this myth is unstated; as a result, civil religion cannot be challenged, only confirmed or denied (Fenn 1976, 160-166; Bellah 1976, 167-168). It awaits amplification (Bellah 1976, 167-168; Gehrig 1979, viii).

BELLAH'S MORAL PRESCRIPTIONS

In continuing his quest to define exactly what is entailed in a revitalized America, Bellah, now aided by several colleagues, attempts two things: first, to specify the vocabulary that Americans use to define their lives, and second, to present a design by which the institutional structure of the country may be reconstructed, both to enhance personal fulfilment and to create "The Good Society." In *Habits of the Heart*, Bellah interprets the major elements of American culture, which consist of three strands: the biblical, the republican and the modern, individualistic strand. He finds fault with America's overemphasis on the language of individualism and neglect of the older biblical and republican traditions. He does, however, find two organizations that come close to recognizing the importance of the distinctions he is making. One of the groups that he believes able to develop a vocabulary of the common good is the Campaign for Economic Democracy in California.[5]

Still in pursuit of a "moral order," Bellah (1991) and his colleagues offer in the follow-up volume, *The Good Society*, an analysis of the failures of American society and an exhortation to alter the nation's institutional structure in a way that will create better citizens. His ideal is citizens engaged, not with their own narrow interests, but with the broader moral condition of the society they inhabit. The core of the problem, as he states it now, is not the "cultural and personal resources for thinking about our common life," as in *Habits of the Heart*, but "the patterned ways Americans have developed for living together, what sociologists call institutions" (1991, 4). A better understanding of institutions, he suggests, will not only help to solve the problems of homelessness, poverty in the Third World, ozone depletion and the greenhouse effect (1991, 5), but also the "problems of emptiness and meaninglessness in our personal lives" (1991, 5). This far-reaching plan, whose details do not go beyond the call for discussions to examine which institutions affect our lives, how they do so and why, is broadly directed to questioning the "individualistic" ethos, which he sees as the source of the problems confronting America. This very individualism leads Bellah to question the potential corruption of "civic" politics by "claimant" politics in which private interests have come to dominate the national political arena (1991, 61).

Perhaps the most telling criticism Bellah makes of the way American society has fallen is when he argues that economic concerns have displaced civic and moral issues. Individualism and the quest for power, wealth and prestige have replaced concern for the common good. The obsession with rational economic choices, profit maximization and cost-benefit analyses has led to "savage capitalism" (1991, 91-92), in which decisions on everything from adopting babies to choosing sexual partners and committing suicide is subjected to evaluations of individual self-interest.

Max Weber, too, criticized the character of capitalist civilization. In the final pages of *The Protestant Ethic and the Spirit of Capitalism*, he gloomily proclaimed, "Specialists without spirit, sensualists without heart; this nullity imagines that it has attained a level of civilization never before achieved" (1958a, 182). Weber diagnosed the same problem that Bellah is grappling with, but he cautiously declined to offer a resolution of the problem. He argued that to go any further would "bring us to the world of judgements of value and of faith."

CHALLENGES TO THE FUNCTIONALIST CONSENSUS

It is easy to forget that at the time of Bellah's writing, several major issues were clearly threatening the broad functionalist consensus that defined much of American sociology, whose dominant figure was Talcott Parsons.

The 1960s were a time of turmoil during which the "core" values of American society, which have been termed "instrumental activism,"[6] were subjected to considerable criticism. Where Parsons stressed consensus and integration around these values, others, led by C. Wright Mills, saw power, exploitation and domination.[7]

The functionalist paradigm was first "tested" by the Civil Rights movement, in which the promise of full membership and participation in American society was found wanting. Second, the Vietnam War highlighted the schisms in society and threatened the very middle-classes who were the carriers of these "core" values. Third, the structure and organization of higher education, the major means by which this integration was to take place, was challenged by sit-ins and demonstrations. Finally, there was the widespread use of drugs by the "flower children" of the period.

Bellah's call for the rediscovery of civil religion in America was a sign that the consensus to which the functionalists were committed was threatened.[8] A new understanding was necessary, in order to overcome the immediate and long-run crisis threatening American society. He believed that "instrumental activism," with its stress on achievement, technical skill and competence, had become the source of the moral crisis, since it emphasized individualism rather than broader, selfless concerns. What would replace or modify this value consensus was obscure and unspecified, but some replacement was absolutely necessary if American society were to be redeemed.

Both *Habits of the Heart* and *The Good Society* show how deeply Bellah is concerned with the possibilities of creating the means for the moral reconstitution of America. In looking not simply at values alone, but at the institutional structure that reflects these values, he faces the problem of transcending the market economy (see 1991, 52-110). Bellah rejects the stifling consumerism that defines much of the economic activity in modern societies. He suggests an indeterminate balance that lies between individual pursuits and those broader interests that would rein in the selfishness that has diminished concerns for the common good.

It is at this point that Bellah introduces the origins of much of the disquiet with which extremes of wealth and poverty are viewed in our society. In the Western Christian tradition there has always existed a tension between worldliness, with its associated defects of luxury and greed, and a higher morality linked to poverty and abnegation. This is clear from Matthew 19:24, where Jesus is quoted as saying, "It is easier for a camel to go through the eye of a needle, than for a rich man to enter into the kingdom of God."

With the increasing importance of markets in the development of industrialization, there were numerous attempts in the nineteenth century to establish "utopian" communities in which the market was subordinated to higher goals (Kanter 1972, 75-138; Polanyi 1944, 258a). Further, Marx's early essay, "On the Jewish Question," stressed the dehumanizing character of the concern with money and profits

(1959, 38-42). Much of Marx's work may be seen as following in this long tradition of defining the virtues of the natural life of the poor and the compromised character of the wealthy.

The poverty and unemployment associated with the complex phenomenon of capitalism have generated major problems for democracies. However, the alternatives to capitalism have usually created more problems than those that they purport to solve. We need only note that the two major attempts to control economic activity in this century for the good of the "*Volk*" or for the benefit of "Workers and Peasants" have led to the horrors of the Holocaust and the degradation of the Gulag. The real issue, when confronting intemperance, greed and selfishness — which existed well before capitalism came on the scene — is not the disavowal of markets, but rather finding the means to maintain and enhance human freedom and dignity.[9]

Rather than explaining how this might be managed, Bellah suggests that we look to those who have recently been liberated from Soviet domination, such as Vaclav Havel, who might offer new insights into the nature of the trust necessary to create a viable economy linked to a democratic political order (1991, 139, 272).[10] However, few Eastern European dissidents who led the struggle against the domination of the Communist Party have been entrusted by the citizens of those lands with their future.

THE FUNCTIONALIST GENERATION

The decline of functionalism was only one of the casualties of the 1960s and 1970s. The great "youth revolt" of that period was very much a part of the search for a new framework in which the conflicts then emerging in American society could be understood. Among the academics who were involved, Herbert Marcuse was perhaps best known as the "guru" of generational revolt. He was one of many who encouraged the young to challenge accepted authority and to create a new morality that would transcend the limits provided by a "free" society. The conventional wisdom of the period held that the more free a society, the more repressive it actually was (Feuer 1975).

This "radical" approach to the seeming moral contradictions in America drew its inspiration from many sources: among them were the young Karl Marx and his discovery of alienation; George Lukács' concern with aesthetics and the higher morality of Communism; and the work of the Frankfurt School, which centred on uncovering the contradictions in capitalism. Those who were influenced by these works attempted to develop a general critique of capitalist society and to show the way to a more fulfilling, more compassionate and less technically demanding social order.

Bellah's call to moral regeneration shares much with this past generation's challenge to establish a more responsive polity and a more humane economy and social order. Even though he emphasizes the virtues of Christian piety rather than hallucinogenic drugs, there remains a wistfulness in his desire to redirect the institutional structure that is more than reminiscent of a time now long gone.

Bellah is thirty years too late to attract the kind of response that allowed Herbert Marcuse, who was one of the leading figures in the Frankfurt school (Jay 1973; Slater 1977),[11] to revitalize a career established on the study of Hegel. Marcuse became a leader to the those who sought an escape from the demands of a complex world where slogans could replace debate, and intuition excluded reason.

What motivated someone like Marcuse, with a long and established career, to seek the homage of students young enough to have been his children? There are no simple answers, but Eric Hoffer (1966, 131-132) suggests that at some point in the careers of creative people, they may sense a loss of the ability to generate new ideas, and seek adulation or involvement in a mass movement, where the pressure to continue on a creative path is minimized. Hoffer's argument suggests that those who have seen better days may seek a new audience when faced with stagnating careers.

If this is the case, then Bellah's argument can be seen in a new light, as an entreaty to a generation that initially raised the concerns with which he is currently involved. The dismay at America's failures makes his argument a more personal one than we are led to assume.

After twenty-five years of grappling with the problem, Bellah's response to the "crisis" he announced is more comprehensible when seen as an attempt on the part of a major figure in the functionalist generation to justify his past and to champion his presence to a new generation who look upon functionalism as a relic of the past.

CANADIAN RESPONSES TO THE CRISIS OF MODERNITY

In contrast to Bellah's vision of mythic proportions, Canadian efforts to define the national destiny betray a sober realism. Canadians have never been able to construct a rhetoric that defines prime ministers in the near totemic roles that Washington, Jefferson and Lincoln assume. There is little ambition in peace, order and good government, compared to life, liberty and the pursuit of happiness; the United Empire Loyalists do not cut much of a figure compared to the Sons of Liberty; the Canadian West did not generate folk heroes of the calibre of Billy the Kid or Wyatt Earp; and our pioneer mothers and fathers are anonymous carriers of a more mundane, more ordered and less romantic image of the frontier.[12]

Symbols of unity have often been imposed but not universally accepted. Confederation was hardly an overwhelming success, as evidenced by the fact that a black flag flew above the Nova Scotia legislature on the very day Canada came into existence. The emblems of nationhood and independence − the flag and the Constitution − have not been received without considerable debate and expressions of betrayal.

Where there have been attempts at defining a national society, the effects have been exclusive rather than inclusive − for example, the advocacy of separatism by those in the province of Quebec who argue that confederation has been demeaning and exploitative of the national interests of the Québécois. Defining the argument in terms of "us" versus "them" is not a tactic that is likely to develop inclusive and uniting symbols (Richler 1992).[13]

Earlier, church union, which brought together Methodists, Congregationalists and Presbyterians in 1925 under the banner of the United Church of Canada, sought a redemption and unification of Canadian society.

The key motifs of the new society were Christian democracy and equality of opportunity for all Canadians. There was to be a realignment of powers in Canada such that the dispossessed and disenfranchised of every economic, geographic and ethnic group would share equally in the benefits and responsibilities of the nation (Ross 1973, 235).

While well intentioned, the very term "Christian democracy" reflected the specific denominational character of the United Church. This would clearly limit its applicability to a multi-denominational, not to say pluralist, society, in which democracy's link to Christianity would be questioned.

The social gospel movement that influenced church union also had an impact on the development of the CCF (NDP), which sought, in its early stages, to eliminate private property and to control the depredations of capitalism (Lipset 1950). Despite the NDP's presence in Ontario and elsewhere, its strength lies mainly in western Canada. The same has been true of the Social Credit Party. Both parties were established as a result of the pervasive sentiment that western Canada's interests were not fully understood in central Canada.

More recently, the rise of the Reform Party has paralleled that of the other western parties. Whether or not it can establish itself in Ontario and the Maritimes is at this point an open question. Of course, since its platform is seen to encourage a unilingual English Canada and a separate Quebec, it has not even attempted to involve Quebec in its political formation.

This paucity of "national" symbols and issues has not meant that there have been no attempts to delimit the parameters of Canadian life. In fact, one commentator has noted that defining a national identity has become an established cottage industry (O'Toole 1984, 93). It may be that the quest for a Canadian identity parallels, in a way, Bellah's civil religion.

Identity

One emphasis in the quest for a Canadian identity has been expressed in a series of empirical, statistical studies on the more conventional aspects of Canadian life. These focus on how Canadians feel about themselves and how they compare to the Americans, the British and others on a broad range of topics.

Another emphasis is found in analyses and arguments expressing a pervasive resentment against the hiring of American and British faculty to staff Canadian universities during their period of greatest expansion, and the effects this had on Canadian culture.

The empirical studies show Canadian society to be more stolid and less litigious than U.S. society. Canadians are more prone to acquiesce to authority (Friedenberg 1980; see also Lipset 1963, 248-273), accord high prestige to public office holders (Pineo and Porter 1967), save more money and invest heavily in life insurance.[14]

These studies received a major impetus with the publication of John Porter's *The Vertical Mosaic*, in 1965. Porter's work was the starting point for a new sociological inquiry into the analysis of Canadian society. It was a benchmark in the transition from the kinds of historical analyses that had until then defined the academic interest in the social structure of Canada. Porter presented a view of Canada that argued for a major overhaul of the educational system. He viewed Canadian society as profoundly limited by structures and institutions that locked the country into a situation where it would be unable to offer its young people the kinds of occupational opportunities that modern societies had to create.

Porter's work offered a challenge to alter the character of the country. His solution was a technical and not a moral one. He simply assumed that a more open society, which encouraged mobility by expanding its educational resources, would be a better one.

Coincident with the publication of Porter's book was the major expansion of institutions of higher education in Canada. Beginning in the mid-1960s, notably in Ontario, but also in the rest of the country, many new universities were built and schools already in existence were expanded. Graduate programs were developed to cope with the expected expansion of the labour force and the expected need for more highly trained workers. Because Canadians to staff this university "gold rush" were in relatively short supply in some disciplines, the obvious solution was to recruit academics from the United States and Great Britain.

While this seemed a practical way of dealing with staffing difficulties, this practice quickly drew the ire of such critics as Robin Mathews (Mathews and Steele 1969; Mathews 1988; see also Morton 1972), who were upset that foreigners, usually Americans, were moving into positions of significant influence in such culturally sensitive areas as the humanities and social sciences. The critics were concerned that the newcomers had neither an awareness nor a sympathetic understanding of Canadian history and culture. Mathews touched a nerve with his arguments. Canadian universities have responded to the challenge by making an awareness of the country's past an important part of curriculum. This has resulted in a broad proliferation of course offerings focused directly on Canadian content in history, literature and the arts.

Along with Mathews, other literary figures, notably Northrop Frye (1971, 1982) and Margaret Atwood (1972a; see also Jones 1970), also sought to define the essence of the Canadian character within the Canadian literary tradition. While Frye and Mathews stressed the defensive collectivism of Canada, in contrast to the greater individualism of the United States, Atwood showed that a dominant theme in Canadian literature was not the surmounting of obstacles, but survival in spite of them. The resulting image of Canadians is that of an underdog, someone who manages to get by but never aspires to be more than what he or she is, and who while not content with his or her lot, is too timid to demand more.

This literary exposition of Canada and Canadians is a response to the "crisis" entailed by the expansion of opportunities, both social and educational. In this, the artist's response is as a prophet who alone is able to discover the "soul" of the nation (see Chapter 8). Those who assume this mantle are therefore in a unique leadership position in recognizing and understanding the course to be followed for the nation's destiny to be fulfilled.

It is not surprising that this Canadian response parallels Bellah's revelation of America's civil religion and his role in defining what it entails and identifying those who will lead the way. However, here the vision is more muted, which, given what we know about Canada and Canadians, is what we might expect.

Nostalgia

One variation of the identity argument focuses solely on the past. It, too, came into prominence in the 1960s, shortly after Canadian universities began their expansion.

According to this view, Canada has forsaken its commitment to the virtues of the British tradition, in seeking to adapt to the demands of the new technical dynamism exemplified by the United States. In so doing, the traditions that defined the country will be unable to compete with these newer technically defined criteria, and Canada is consequently doomed to be nothing more than a northern appendage of the United States. The character of the country is and will be increasingly determined by its "branch-plant" mentality.

This nostalgic perspective differs from the one that struggles to define Canadian identity since it assumes that a clear identity existed under British institutions, which were guided by an elite who possessed a clear conception of what the "good" society entailed.

George Grant (1965), one of the more articulate spokespeople for this position, takes the view that in the modern world technical proficiency is the only measure of whether or not any procedure, role or institution is acceptable. In applying this model to Canada, Grant sees the ultimate dissolution of Canadian values, if not the absorption of Canada into the American empire. He does not see any alternative available to compete with the blandishments of efficiency, expertise and productivity. For Grant there is no redemption from the cold, calculating future that awaits us, and he simply retreats from the battle without offering any reassurances for the future.

Grant's response may be seen as an attack on those who have benefitted most from the expansion of opportunity in Canada during the last several decades. The "good" society delimited by Grant is one of narrow scope, led by bearers of an arcane tradition whose arbitrary revelations can be justified only by those traditions that most of us are delighted are a thing of the past (Blumstock 1967).

For Grant, the closed society was a comfort; for John Porter, it limited opportunity and growth. The kind of nostalgia that Grant expresses is perhaps nothing more than rancour directed at the complexities of a modern society that rewards its football players more than its university professors. Few football players would find this argument attractive. For the less muscular, provided they have the appropriate "ethnic" ties, this argument's appeal lies in the fact that it promises to be a "saved remnant" that holds fast to a moral authority that defines what being a Canadian is really all about.

Max Weber wrote that those strata in possession of social honour and power tend to define themselves as having a special quality, based usually on their "blood," or as we might now say, their ethnicity (Gerth and Mills 1958, 276). Simply "being" is enough to define their intrinsic ability to dominate and control.

Grant's conservative reaction tells us more about the nature of wistful musings on past glories than about anything that deserves to be re-established.

Dependency, Political Economy, Radical Critiques

If "blood" defines those in possession of social honour, then "those strata whose status is negatively valued is nourished most easily on the belief that a special 'mission' is entrusted to them; their worth is guaranteed or constituted by an *ethical imperative*, or by their own functional achievement" (Gerth and Mills 1958, 276).

Instead of a displaced elite concerned about justifying their "being," new guardians of the Canadian moral order are surfacing who define their mission both in terms of their desire to eliminate past injustices and to ensure their own place in the future.

This group is most evident in those social science departments that were established or enlarged during the 1960s and 1970s. The "crisis" that has activated this cohort derives from an attempt to create a more "Canadian" emphasis in the material studied. It pits a younger group of Canadian sociologists against an older group of Americans, but also against some Canadians who came into the discipline when functionalism was in full flower. The theoretical critique developed is a consequence of a generational conflict in which a distinctively Canadian sociology is the battleground, as opposed to a definition of the discipline that transcends national boundaries.

In this critical view, Canadian sociological nationalism "is a response to past cultural, political, and economic domination of Canadian society by Great Britain and the United States" (Felt 1975, 377). This response has led to the justification of the term "political economy" as defining a theoretical approach unknown to the Americans and "uniquely" Canadian. This term has a particular relevance since it draws on the work of Harold Innis and S.D. Clark, among others (Clark 1942; 1976; Innis 1930; 1933), who were oriented to historical studies of Canadian economic and political development.

The new political economy's goal is to provide a framework that distinguishes it from its American counterparts. However, in so doing, it has come to rely more on sources from within the Marxist tradition than more traditional Canadian analyses, which were oriented to analyzing those factors within Canada that had an impact on political and economic developments.

From this new political economy perspective, Canada remains an exploitable resource-based hinterland — an economic colony used by the more developed industrial centres for their own advantage. The crisis that this emphasis defines resides in the very character of industrial development in which moral emphases are subordinated to capitalist motives.

As with the nostalgia perspective, there is an elite, but this elite is not a colonial leftover. Rather, it is a group drawn together by its awareness of the negative effects of capitalist business enterprise on the social fabric of Canada. Exponents of this perspective have shown the closed character of business elites (Clement 1975; 1978), the exploitation of the underdeveloped "hinterland" in favour of the "metropolitan core" (Cohen 1978), and the corrupting influences of capitalist enterprise in general, as well as the decline of living standards in Canada — even though objective factors would indicate that the Canadian standard of living is really improving (Johnson 1974; see also Cuneo 1980, 246).[15] Some go so far as to announce the call for the "revolution" that will slay "Capitalism, the dragon source of our alienation" (Archibald 1978, 265).

The analyses deriving from this perspective define Canada both as a victim of more mature economies and an exploiter of those who have entered later into the industrialization process. It is a relatively simple model that has the advantage of clearly defining those who undertake it as quite different from those who do not. Further, its ties to a simplistic Marxism are quite evident. It also places those doing it in a leading role, as the moral vanguard of the future who recognize the path that history will take.

This radical emphasis coming to dominate the Canadian sociological scene paralleled the transformation of the discipline in the United States, where the older functionalist paradigm was increasingly being flayed for its failure to deal with conflict and dissension. An alternative theoretical model was sought for and found in much the same Marxist formulations in both cases.

The curious thing about these analyses is that there is rarely if ever a critique offered of the socialist societies of the Soviet Union and Eastern Europe, not to mention China. The standard response when confronted with this challenge is that these socialist societies were never socialist at all. They were dismissed as varieties of "state-capitalism" and consequently there was no significant difference between them and capitalist societies of the West.

This neglect of the contradictions and discrepancies of socialism leads to the conclusion that the resurrection of the "Marxian" paradigm lies in the quest of the generation espousing it to justify their activities. They claim that their paradigm provides a better fit to the available data, and they define themselves as advocates of a higher morality.

However, it may well be that now with the collapse of the Soviet Union and the fragmentation of Eastern Europe, and the more secure status of the cohort championing this kind of inquiry, this kind of analysis has seen its peak and a new generation may be waiting in the wings to don the mantle of ideological purity.[16] However, it is not likely that the "Marxian" paradigm will fade into oblivion without a long battle. If the past is any guide, then we would expect that as with other belief systems that reality fails to support (Festinger 1964), a variety of apologies will be forthcoming to justify the commitment to a failed prophecy.

CONCLUSION

All three Canadian responses, identity, nostalgia and political economy, seek to define an image of Canadian society and correspondingly a particular group who understands the country and can protect it from the potential distortions of participation in a disenchanted and technically dominated world.

Bellah's argument shares with the nostalgia and the political economy positions a concern for the current failure of complex societies to define a coherent moral posture. The rampant individualism of a "secular" society indicates a loss of authority, meaning and cohesiveness. Bellah's hope, however, contrasts with Grant's pessimism, while the political economy argument suggests that a viable future depends on the recognition that national interests can only be protected by a moral posture derived from Marxist sources.

The concern with a distinctive Canadian identity has also had a moral quality attached to it. This search for factors that define the country's character, if such a thing can be ever defined, is never likely to end. While the search for the abstract essence of the nation continues, the more important issue of Quebec separation demands that priority be given to finding a means to coordinate the interests of Québécois and other Canadians.

In taking moral commitments as a basic priority, Bellah and his Canadian counterparts do not accept that the social sciences can play only a limited role in defining the ends of action, a limitation that Weber never forgot.

There are many ironies in the current predicament that these positions attempt to define. Pitirim Sorokin (1950) many years ago also indicated a concern with creating a better society. He was led to study the lives of Good Neighbours and Christian Saints in order to discover what influenced people to express selflessness and altruism. The assumption was that once these influences were known they could be generated in the institutional structure and, more directly, in the lives of people, to create a better society.

Sorokin's work has long been ignored, as he was superseded by Talcott Parsons as the dominant sociological theorist of the twentieth century (see Sorokin 1963, 241-251). Sorokin's emphasis on what he called the "Three Systems of Truth" — ideational, idealistic and sensate — led him to see fluctuations in a culture's dominant themes, with each system of truth being displaced by one or another of the systems in time. This patterning would suggest that the current moral crisis is a harbinger of a transition from a sensate-dominated culture to an ideational one. In time this could be tested, something that Bellah's argument cannot be.

The loss of selflessness, ironically, may well be so much a part of modernity that it has no remedy, no matter how much we may desire it (Eksteins 1989).[17] The very influences that have created the freedom of choice in our life-styles may have destroyed the possibility of creating the kind of commitments that seem so desirable.[18] This is not to suggest that a world in which human life is nasty, brutish and short is all we can look forward to. Certain moral elements in society may still await discovery. Modern society itself may not be as distraught, confused and alienated as those utopians are who search for the new bases of cohesion. Most of us may well belong to an "unfocused majority" (Bibby 1983b, 118; Greeley 1972b; Callahan 1966, 101-126, 129-144) driven by our daily involvements and yet more than able to withstand the ambiguity of uncertainty than we are given credit for.

Finally, there is a long tradition of "false messiahs" who have offered hope that the moral ambiguities of life could be resolved once and forever, to lead to humankind's redemption. Sabbatai Sevi (Scholem 1954; 1973), Jacob Frank (Mandel 1979; Plaut 1988), Karl Marx and other utopians all have proved incapable of solving the ultimate problems of humankind in this world. But they have all been able to market their messages of selflessness, while at the same time seeking to better their own situations.

There is always likely to be this continual renewal and replacement of ideologies, as new cohorts seek their entry into positions of importance and influence. These experiences ought to provide a defense against the all-too-ready acceptance of ultimate solutions offered by those who wish to take on a prophetic or messianic role. For sociologists, the question remains as to whether or not an analysis can be tested in reference to other ideologies in the marketplace.

Notes

[1]The importance of generations in the formation of ideologies is discussed in Mannheim (1952, 276).

[2]Mannheim assumes that intellectuals belong to a relatively classless stratum and that they are unattached to any particular class interests until they either choose to affiliate themselves with a particular interest or "become aware of their own social position and the mission implicit in it" (1936, 160).

[3]The political character of the challenge to paradigms (which are analogous to prevailing ideologies) is recognized in Kuhn (1970). See also Friedrichs (1970).

[4]A distinction is usually made between functional and substantive definitions of religion. Functional definitions usually define religion in terms of its consequences in delimiting a system of ultimate meaning. Substantive definitions focus on the essence of religion in which a supernatural element is crucial in the determination of an ultimate meaning system. See Spiro (1966), Berger (1967), Stark (1981), Stark and Bainbridge (1985).

[5]"Although we do not identify Economic Democracy exclusively with the position taken by the California Campaign for Economic Democracy, that position is well expressed in Tom Hayden, *The American Future: New Visions beyond Old Frontiers* (Boston: South End, 1980)" (taken from Bellah [1985, 327]).

[6]The term "instrumental activism" was used by Williams (1951). At that time, Williams devised a list of American values that stressed achievement, optimism and hard work. Its derivation from Parsons and Shil's (1965, 165-166) "instrumental action" is obvious.

[7]The contrast between the perspective of C. Wright Mills and Talcott Parsons is characterized by Mills (1959, 25-49) in *The Sociological Imagination*.

[8]The analysis of the crisis of functionalism and Bellah's response relies to a considerable extent on the discussion in Hughey (1983).

[9]B.F. Skinner, in *Beyond Freedom and Dignity* (1971), takes the contrary view. He argues that the concepts of "freedom" and "dignity" create major obstacles in the creation of a "good" society. This is an extreme statement of a technical solution.

[10]Bellah's argument on the distractions of markets is reminiscent of some of the "populist" writers in Eastern Europe during the 1930s who were searching for a "third way" or a "middle course" where the excesses of capitalism and communism could be avoided. Some of this thinking has resurfaced recently; see Schlopflin (1991).

[11]It ought to be noted that one of the major criticisms that can be directed to the Frankfurt school was that none of its members tried to come up with a radical critique of socialism.

[12]Civil religion has not found much favour in Canada except for Stahl (1979; 1984). Pierre Berton (1970; 1974) and Peter C. Newman (1985) have in recent years published a number of best-sellers that have attempted to give a more heroic tone to Canadian history.

[13]Although the Quebec press has disputed Richler's contention that Quebec nationalism excludes newcomers to Quebec and non-Francophones, Richler's commentary on the laws and his sense of exclusion seem to make his point.

[14]See Porter (1967) for a discussion of the generally conservative character of Canada.

[15]Karl Marx used much the same tactic to show that the condition of the working class was continually deteriorating under capitalism. However, it has been shown that Marx knew he was using faulty data in making this generalization. See Paul Johnson (1988, 64-65).

[16]There may well be signs of this in a competing paradigm that goes under various specialized names, such as participant observation, phenomenology and ethnomenthology. The focus of this new paradigm (actually, it is a rather old paradigm, which traces its origins to the early years of sociology at the University of Chicago) centres on the individual and his or her interactional problems rather than concerning itself with the direction of history.

[17] In the ideal moral code of the nineteenth-century middle class, the goal of individual effort was always social harmony, the commonwealth, the public good. In the end the interests of the individual, which were to be protected and furthered by the state, were nevertheless subservient to the public good; personal restraint was the hallmark of respectability; and the idea of service to the public, or duty, became the great achievement of this class (Eksteins 1989, 177).

Eksteins argues that this was the last gasp of the nineteenth-century bourgeois ethos. After the First World War, this kind of "duty" and "commitment" was no more.

[18]In seeking for a substitute for the lost nineteenth-century bourgeois family, Bellah (1991, 258) quotes a passage from Mihaly Csikszentmihalyi and Eugene Rochberg-Halton's *The Meaning of Things: Domestic Symbols and the Self* (Cambridge: Cambridge University Press, 1981), in which the bourgeois family type is rediscovered.

> For one thing, the classical bourgeois family is held together by the heavy weight of social traditions. Economic advantages, status considerations, social controls, and expectations maintain it; they provide the constriction goals that channel the psychic energy of its members. Thus it might be a closely knit unit, but it is not necessarily a warm one because the meanings that maintain it are rigid creations of social forces. By contrast, the warm families in our midst are practically *invented* by their members. Outside constraints are relatively light; the meanings that keep these families together are woven and mended by the constant attention of those who comprise them.

Csikszentmihalyi and Rochberg-Halton are really talking about the re-establishment of "bourgeois mentality," but for them this will come about as the result of discovery, rather than being limited by nature as was the older form of bourgeois existence.

For Further Reading

Bellah, Robert, et al. 1986. *Habits of the Heart: Individualism and Commitment in American Life*. New York: Harper and Row.

Gehrig, Gail. 1979. *American Civil Religion: An Assessment*. Society for the Scientific Study of Religion, Monograph Series, No. 3.

Grant, George. 1965. *Lament for a Nation: The Defeat of Canadian Nationalism*. Toronto: McClelland and Stewart.

Hughey, Michael W. 1983. *Civil Religion and Moral Order*. London: Greenwood Press.

Chapter 10

Religion and the Environment[*]

Kenneth Westhues

THE ENVIRONMENT AND THE HUMAN SPECIES

The environment is what surrounds, encircles, encloses the human species. It is the atmosphere, the layout of continents and oceans, the arrangement of mountains, rivers and plains. It is all that is inanimate on earth plus all that is animate, all flora and fauna — except one species. Everything else, so the word implies, surrounds one thing: us. Therefore, just by using the word "environment," we not only affirm a radical distinction between humanity and the rest of the universe, we even claim for our species a certain superiority, make ourselves the reference point and lump everything else together into something that lies around us.

This claim needs to be defended, since many proponents of so-called "deep ecology" reject any notion of "human exceptionalism" and insist on viewing our species as merely one of many (see Manes 1990; Catton and Dunlap 1979). They argue that over the past five hundred years, an intellectual revolution has steadily undermined the privileged position in the universe humanity once thought it had. The shift from geocentric to heliocentric astronomy a few hundred years ago was the first major step. Charles Darwin and Sigmund Freud, in their respective ways, pulled humanity farther from the centre of its pedestal. Now finally, in our generation, humanity has been toppled altogether and revealed as just one transient component of the ecosystem, destined like all other species for eventual extinction and replacement. The "human exceptionalism paradigm" must therefore be abandoned. Humanism itself must go by the board, in this view, since it similarly keeps humanity at centre stage.[1]

A far greater revolution is underway, and that is away from a narrow, one-sided, either-or, usually positivist way of thinking towards the kind of dialectical thinking that finds truth not in this or that formulation but in the interplay of opposites. For at the same time as evidence has been piling up, over these past few centuries, for the similarities between humanity and other species, and for the embeddedness of our species in the larger living organism of earth, so also has the evidence of human distinctiveness increased.

If observers from outer space had orbited the earth just twelve millennia ago, they might understandably have failed to notice anything special or distinctive about our human species. There were just ten million of us then, not many more than the population of present-day Austria. Whole continents, including North and South America, were virtually free of human habitation. Even in Africa, Europe and Asia, the human marks on the planet were as yet few and faint, dwarfed and obscured by the free proliferation of thousands of other species — trees, shrubs, mammals, fish, bugs. The control of other species by ours had scarcely begun. Tools were so primitive that alien observers could scarcely have distinguished between how humans gathered fruits and how squirrels or deer gathered them, or between the human hunt for meat and that of the wolf or owl.

By now, alien observers would have to be blind and deaf to miss the supreme fact of life on earth, namely that the human species *is* distinctive, special, exceptional, unique. Not only because it has multiplied five hundred times over, so that more than five billion specimens are now alive. Not only because it has decimated the population of most other species, compelled many species to live on small reserves called orchards, fields and gardens, while forcing many other species into eternal extinction. What would impress alien observers still more is that especially in these past few centuries, humanity has reconstructed its environment into something new: not just domesticated plants and animals but bred new, heretofore unseen varieties of them; not just mined the elements but mixed them into alloys and polymers not previously found on earth, and then shaped these into tools and machines that magnify human strength a million-fold; it has not just harnessed the energy of rivers, oil and coal but made it transmissible as electricity and even carried it around in tiny batteries. But among humans' distinctive qualities, alien observers would notice above all that humans are cultural beings, that we have done all this on purpose, creatively manipulating symbols and substances, changing not only by the slow process of natural selection evident in all species, but by the faster, more assertive, autonomous and indeterminate process of history.

Whether aliens from outer space would notice it or not, it is increasingly obvious to us humans that, especially in the dominant Western civilization, we have made a bad mistake, overemphasized the unique capabilities of our species and made our history on the basis of development plans, ideologies and systems of belief that exaggerate our ability to transform and create. Blessed with imagination, we have imagined ourselves to be more different from plants and animals than in fact we are. We know now that we have allowed ourselves to reproduce far too freely, that we are rapidly exhausting the planet's supply of fossil fuels, that we have cut down too many trees and that we have polluted the air, water and soil of the only planet available.

In the present predicament, however, it is the height of folly to ignore millennia of empirical evidence and to say, "We were wrong; humanity is just one species among many." Unamuno (1954, 78) warns that "none are so likely to believe too little as those who began by believing too much." Intellectuals who manipulate the symbols that constitute culture and underlie law and public policy cannot afford to substitute a new half-truth for an old one. Whatever we say at this critical moment must include recognition that humanity *is* the guardian of the planet, the steward of the earth, that our species and ours alone is responsible now for creatively designing ways to enhance the life of the global organism, ways to preserve and continue the enhancements our ancestors have made, ways to heal the wounds they and we have inflicted, ways to allow this old planet to flourish in all its diversity.

The word "environment" is therefore an accurate and useful word, not in spite of but because of the human exceptionalism it implies. When we speak of the political environment, we mean all that surrounds some particular actor that is the focus of concern. A student's academic environment consists of all those professors, curricula, requirements and other students that form the context of the student's work. Similarly, when we speak of the environment in its broader sense, it is everything outside the species to which we ourselves belong.

The fundamental distinction between culture and nature, as made by Hegel and many others since, including the Brazilian educator, Paulo Freire (1970), and the American biologist, Stephen Jay Gould

(1981), will be apparent by now.[2] But this distinction does not precisely coincide with that between ourselves and our environment. For nature is what lies outside the domain of our history-making, as if nothing distinctly human had ever happened. By now, having cut down 60 percent of the planet's forests, having sucked megatonnes of minerals from the planet's crust and having altered the atmosphere by the emissions from our cars and factories, we can no longer find pure nature anywhere.[3] Much that is natural remains in our environment, as also in ourselves. But there can be no question now of leaving the environment alone, or even of preserving it, as if it were still pristine and virginal. It is not. Nor could our environment possibly be returned to its natural state, even if humanity became extinct, since the marks and scars we have made would remain. The question is just what further marks we in our generation will leave, or more precisely, how we now will relate to all that is outside of us. That is the question of the environment.

RELIGION

The answer to the question of how we will behave in relation to the environment depends in part on the degree and kind of religion we practice. As a first step, we need to offer a definition of religion.

"Religion," like the word "environment," must be defined in a straightforward, empirical way — that is, in terms of what we can see and hear. A good definition should distinguish clearly between an action, an idea, a person or a society that is very religious, and one that is not religious at all.

Moreover, if our definition is to serve us well, it must not be tied too closely to any particular kind of religion. No one would define the environment simply in terms of the Alpine climate and terrain, however accurate this might be in Switzerland or Austria, since other societies face tropical, desert, maritime and other kinds of environment. Similarly, it will not do to define religion as belief in God, since recognizably religious people outside the Judaeo-Christian world believe in whole pantheons of gods or, as in the case of some forms of Buddhism, in no real deity at all. What, then, is the empirical definition of "religion"?

It is a hard question, especially because the typical social-scientific definitions have disapproval built into them. In North America, a sizeable literature in sociology measures religion in terms of dogmatic adherence to particular beliefs about God, the devil, heaven and hell. The respondent who is fixed, rigid, close-minded and dogmatic scores high, while the one who admits uncertainty and is open to new thoughts scores low. This cannot be a precise way of measuring. Is a close-minded, authoritarian politician *more* political than an open-minded one? Is a worker who thinks that his or her way is the only way *more* of an economic actor than one who admits that work can be done in many different ways? Obstinacy does not make a person political, nor economic, nor religious. Religion and dogmatism are two different concepts that sometimes overlap.

Nor should we define religion mainly in terms of bureaucratic structures and functionaries that formally serve religious purposes. Professors and students know very well how imperfectly education is measured by the accumulation of marks on transcripts. If someone asked us to point out something that captures what education really means, we would not direct the inquirer to the registrar's office or introduce the inquirer to the average university president. We would rather point to a great teacher and an ardent student engaged in the learning process, even if altogether outside the halls of academe. In the same way, it is not the pope who best illustrates what religion is, nor church attendance that best measures it. It is a woman, a man, or a group at prayer, in contemplation, or worshipping: people actively engaged in the special class of activities with which we are concerned.

Proceeding in a direct, empirical way, we cannot help but notice particular postures that distinguish religious activity in the broadest range of cultures and societies: bowing the head, kneeling, outstretching the arms, lying prostrate on the ground, keeping silent and motionless. What these postures have in common is an attitude of submission, surrender and/or acknowledgement of one's own weakness or powerlessness.

No one recognizes as religious, however, the assumption of such a posture towards another person, as when a British subject bows or curtsies to the Queen or when a graduand kneels before the university chancellor. The submission and acknowledgement of contingency or dependency reflects in these cases mere inequality among humans (and therefore offends those of us with democratic sensibilities). Similarly, the stillness of a student in a lecture hall is but a sign of deference to the very lecturer, who should reciprocate with equally deferential silence later when the student responds. Postures of surrender are recognized as religious only when the object of obeisance is outside the human domain, when the surrender is to beings or forces beyond any human power: as when Catholics genuflect towards the altar, when Muslims kneel towards Mecca, or when Quakers fall silent in the face of God.

The empirical variety of religious expression is indeed immense: icons, temples, chants, dances, costumes, scriptures, credos, liturgies and much more. But all express the same defining attitude: acquiescence to who or what is beyond the limits of human power, acceptance of the ultimate mystery of earthly life, affirmation of the fact that we are not in complete control.[4]

As history has advanced, especially in recent centuries, we have pushed back the limits on human power, drained the world of mystery (the process Max Weber called "disenchantment") and placed previously uncontrolled elements of the environment under human management. Understandably, the main ideologues of this history-making process have had little use for religion. The man who named sociology, Auguste Comte, renounced his native Catholicism at the age of thirteen, and never looked back. The so-called universal religion of humanity he invented in his later life was not a religion at all, but a set of beliefs and rituals for celebrating human achievement through its own powers. Karl Marx and Frederick Engels, the great champions of limitless human ability, condemned religion as an obstacle to self-consciousness of that ability. Emile Durkheim, for his part, overlooked the essential inner religious attitude, saw only the necessarily culture-bound outward religious expression, and therefore misdefined religion as a symbolic instrument of social integration. Weber understood religion better than Durkheim, but Weber too failed to see much room for it in the overall process of rationalization.

On the whole, sociologists have been too overwhelmed by the historical, humanly constructed character of contemporary life, and too eager to place it further under human control, to notice the contradictory evidence, much less to analyze insightfully the human response to that evidence. The handful of sociologists who have done so — Martin Buber, Thomas O'Dea, Ernest Becker, Werner Stark — have worked on the margins of the discipline.

To understand religion, we must look beyond the particular

expressions to the defining attitude. The Münster philosopher, Josef Pieper, does this in his illuminating analysis of the feast, or festival, which he rightly points out is no fun unless informed by a religious attitude. "It is certainly true," he writes, "that all festivals are in one sense man-made ... Almost everything about festivals, including the great and traditional ones, is understandably the result of human arrangements, from the fixing of a particular calendar day to the specific form of sacrifices, the ceremonies, the parades and so on. Human institutions then" (1987, 13f). But the thing celebrated, he adds, the thing that makes it a festival, is not human-made, and that is the gift of creation and the joy of accepting that gift. Pieper's definition of a festival is "to live out, for some special occasion and in an uncommon manner, the universal assent to the world as a whole" (1987, 11) — a world that we did not create and over which we have still so little control that we cannot prevent even our own impending deaths.

What then is religion? It is the acceptance of that which was, is now, and ever shall be beyond us. It is giving thanks for life — not the particular shape of life, which is our own doing and responsibility, but life itself, including the shaping ability we humans have. Religion, as Rudolf Otto has said, is standing in awe of what we did not and cannot do. It is rejoicing in the eternal sacredness of this planet, no matter how much profane knowledge about it we accumulate. Religion is a compassionate attitude towards all other beings, human and nonhuman, because however unequal we may be in our strengths, we are all equal in our weakness: in our inability to escape death, the earth or the terror of uncertainty in which we live our short lives.

RELIGION AND THE ENVIRONMENT: THE BASIC ARGUMENT

Keeping these general, empirical definitions in mind, what can be said about how religion and the environment connect? The definitions themselves imply a basic proposition: the more religious a society is, the less aggressive it is in reshaping its environment, and the more accepting of environmental constraints. The religious attitude and the economic one are opposites. The former accepts the environment as a sacred gift, a given, and counsels humility, caution and submission to the limits of human power. It tells us to live the mystery. The latter tackles the environment as an utterly profane object of human ingenuity, and calls for pride and a hands-on attitude. It invites us to push back the frontiers of our capabilities, to solve the problem.

This basic proposition, religion's stifling effect on environmental exploitation, is supported by diverse evidence. Few if any scholars who have studied economically primitive peoples — hunters and gatherers, for instance — have failed to notice how much more intense and pervasive religion is in their lives than in ours. The historical record of Western history, moreover, shows that virtually every successive step up the ladder of economic and political development was made in spite of the Church of Rome, the most influential religious organization of Western Christianity. This is true of both the scientific revolutions (remember Galileo) and the bourgeois revolutions that unleashed the human inventiveness that has so enriched humanity and impoverished the earth. Our own civilization has reached its present height of resource control and consumption by freeing the state and the economy of ecclesiastical control, so that by now almost nothing is sacred, and everyday life is sheer profanity.

During this century, especially these past fifty years, our increasingly aggressive and thorough ravaging of the environment for human purposes has coincided with declines in virtually every measure of religious practice: church membership, church attendance, meal prayers, pilgrimages and popular devotions, icons in the home, religious education of children, membership in religious orders, clerical prestige, the place of theology in universities and so on (Baril and Mori 1991; Bibby 1987).[5] Empirically, secularization has been just one facet of an overall process whose other facets include industrialization, urbanization, automation, increased longevity, health and prosperity for our species, and ever greater degradation of the planet.

Other evidence, however, seems at first glance to challenge the basic proposition that among human attitudes, religion is the environment's best friend. Max Weber (1958a) demonstrated the affinities between Protestantism and capitalism — arguing that a particular religious movement spawned the economic system that is largely responsible for our species' ruinous domination of the earth. The present environmental crisis is often attributed even more broadly to the whole Judaeo-Christian tradition, to the attitude bluntly stated in the first chapter of the first book of the Bible, where the Creator tells Adam and Eve: "Be fruitful, multiply, fill the earth, and subdue it; have dominion over the fish of the sea, the birds of the air, the domestic animals, and all the living things that crawl on the earth" (Richards 1985). From the vantage point of our generation, it seems almost as if the two main branches of Christianity — Protestantism and Catholicism — simply divided Yahweh's commandments between themselves, Protestantism emphasizing the part about subduing the earth through relentless hard work, Catholicism insisting with equal relentlessness: "Multiply, multiply!" The result has been a devastating one-two punch to the rest of creation.

Niagara Falls provides a graphic, even paradigmatic illustration of Christianity's collusion in the Western attack on the environment. The Falls are a natural wonder, a place where sight, hearing and smell are easily overwhelmed by nature's power and where a religious attitude might therefore be easily aroused. To the pre-European inhabitants of the area, Niagara was a sacred place. The name itself is said to be the last surviving word of the language of the Neutral Indian tribe, which is now extinct. Some individual Europeans also responded to the Falls in a religious way. Charles Dickens described his experience of Niagara as follows: "I seemed to be lifted from the earth and to be looking into Heaven" (Marsh 1985).[6]

In the main, however, especially after the invention of hydroelectricity, American and Canadian societies have seen in the Falls not heaven but dollars, not proof of nature's power but a chance to exercise human power. Most of the water has long been diverted into turbine generators; transforming stations loom over the gorge.[7] An expressway hugs the cliff. The tourist industry flourishes amidst observation towers, curio shops, wax museums, motels, amusement parks, video arcades, and the relics left by the death-defying daredevils who have tried to conquer the Falls in one way or another. The scene is altogether profane and secular, a jubilant celebration of capitalist culture and enterprise.

There is, however, one striking reminder of the Judaeo-Christian origins of capitalism. At the entrance to the New York State Power Authority Visitors' Center beside the gorge stands a monument, a tall slab of polished stone erected by the local churches. Carved deep and clear upon the stone are quotations from the Eighth Psalm:

O Lord, Our Lord,
How glorious is thy name in all the earth!

What is man that thou shouldst think of him,
And the son of man that thou shouldst care for him?
Yet thou hast made him but little lower than God, ...
Thou hast put all things under his feet: (Psalms I, 8:1, 4-5, 6.)

None of this evidence, however, refutes the basic argument, because every specific religious tradition, especially once routinized in creeds, rituals and bureaucracies, is a mix of religious and non-religious elements. What we have defined as the religious attitude, the surrender to all that is beyond human power, the embrace of mystery, is an integral part of Judaeo-Christian tradition, but so are other, more calculating and obtrusive attitudes. Not all religions are equally religious, and as religions go, our Western religion is among the less religious ones. Already three or four millennia ago, the Jews had located the god they would worship not in the earth but beyond the earth, thus turning all of nature, in principle, into an arena of profane, aggressive human action. Yahweh, the transcendent Jewish creator god, was not only categorically different from the immanent, cosmic gods of the Orient, Africa and the Americas, as many scholars have pointed out (see Harrington 1983, 219-221).[8] Yahweh was *less* of a god, a farther boundary, an extraterrestrial being who for this reason could authorize the human species to own and rule all others.

Christianity diminished religion still more. God remained far away in his heaven, but sent his son to be born a man, to live a fully human life, to die as a sacrifice on behalf of the human species, and then to come back to life and return to his home beyond the stars, where faithful followers could join him after their deaths. The limits implied by such a theology are few, the humility it counsels in the face of nature is slight, for death itself is now overcome. The earth is no longer even humanity's true home, just a temporary place of trial, a vale of tears, from which death provides escape. It is no wonder that under the influence of Christian teaching, humans would become like those nomadic mammals that freely foul their own habitations, since they will soon be moving on.

From this point of view — of measuring Christianity against the empirical definition of religion offered earlier — the Reformation appears as not just a change in Western religion but a further reduction of it. For as Protestantism spread through Europe and North America, the Christian god lost a public voice and could no longer inhibit human inventiveness through ecclesiastical authority, but only in the privacy of individual conscience. Every believer became a priest, able to draw whatever lessons from the Scriptures he or she decided on.

From Protestantism it appears in retrospect to have been but a short step to the birth and popularity of still newer Western religions, Mormonism most notably, where the deity is drawn into the same historical process as humanity: "As man now is, God once was; as God now is, man may become."

And from there, it is but another short step to the profane society we are now, one in which the idea of any god, of any limits that demand surrender, is openly defied. Such defiance is obvious in Marxism, but almost equally so in the liberal capitalist ideology that holds increasing sway. Jan Narveson, a liberal philosopher at the University of Waterloo, gave in 1991 a much publicized lecture in which he disputed the claim that natural resources are scarce, fixed, finite and limited, and questioned whether we face any environmental risk at all. At Disney World in Florida, an enormous sign at the Exxon pavilion proclaims, "If we can dream it, we can do it." Here at last is the utterly irreligious "religion of humanity" of which Comte dreamed, where awe is reserved for nothing but ourselves.

Truth therefore lies on both sides of the argument, both in those who say that Western religion has impeded the rapacious Western process of development, and in those who say that Western religion facilitated the process. The former are comparing the Christian churches, especially Rome, to the corporations and states of this same civilization, organizations with no religious character at all. The latter are comparing Christianity, especially Protestantism, to the cosmic, immanent, earth-centred religions of non-Western societies. We started with a permissive god, that is, a god who generally let us rampage upon the earth, and then little by little we pushed even that god aside.

RELIGION AND THE ENVIRONMENT: IMPLICATIONS FOR TODAY

Our generation has come face to face with the limits our ancestors progressively denied. The Western model of development has reached a point of consumption and waste that the planet cannot sustain.

Projections from readily available current data with respect to human population growth, air and water pollution, resource depletion, accumulation of toxic waste, the risk of nuclear accidents, and global warming all point to an ecological disaster within the next few decades — an event or series of events that will far overshadow the devastation of the Second World War (Weiner 1990). We can expect droughts, famines, epidemics, shortages, and as the necessities of our way of life become more scarce, wars and civil strife. The destruction in Iraq and Kuwait in 1991 is a portent of much more to come.

This is not a prediction of doomsday. If the impending catastrophe brought death to every living soul in Europe, and in North and South America as well, there would still be more people left alive than there were altogether in 1950. Indeed, if humanity were wiped away from all continents except Africa, the planet's remaining human population would be larger than it was when Columbus travelled to the Americas. To predict the end of the planet or of our species is not science. What lies on the near horizon is just a setback to the process of history, albeit a setback involving cruelty, suffering and death.

In the face of this impending disaster, the hypothesis that religion and respect for the environment go hand in hand would lead us to expect that the movement aimed at averting the disaster and sketching a new model of sustainable development should have religious roots. Specifically, we would expect the movement to draw its inspiration from intellectuals who recognize the limits of human power and who have surrendered to those limits in their own personal lives. This appears to be the case, though the particular forms of religious expression are varied. For good historical reasons, some environmentalists reject Judaeo-Christian traditions altogether, preferring the cosmic, immanent traditions of non-Western peoples. Others, for equally good historical reasons, remain within the Western tradition, while emphasizing its more sensual, cosmic aspects: for instance, the teachings of Francis of Assisi or Bernard of Clairvaux, or the earthy symbolism of much Catholic liturgy.

It was, after all, an English clergy, Thomas Malthus, who two hundred years ago first alerted the Western world that the size of the human population could be a problem. Generations of sociologists and economists have ridiculed Malthus, pointing out (correctly) his underestimation of the human ability to increase production. Now, however, Parson Malthus is revealed not to have been all wrong.

We might even say that the current politics of the Western world are best understood as a conflict between those who would implement further the longstanding, aggressive, secular theory of Western development (both the now-deposed communists and the uneasily ruling capitalists) and, on the other side, those who are trying to write new theories that have room for a genuine religious attitude. The conflict is between those who still believe in the old one-sided story of conquering nature and subduing the earth, and those for whom that story no longer makes sense (see Berry 1988, Chapter 10). The October, 1991, issue of the influential *National Geographic* magazine was entitled "America before Columbus," and consisted mainly of articles on the pre-European cultures of North America. This exemplified a new-found respect for Aboriginal cultures, which has also been demonstrated in the unwillingness to enforce assimilation to Western ways and the sacrifice of Western megaprojects in favour of Native land-claims. These new attitudes can be explained by the fact that a large and growing portion of the Western world has lost faith in Western ways. The most remarkable thing about the *National Geographic* issue was that Americans of Aboriginal origin were allowed to write the articles in their own poetic and religious ways.

Interestingly, E.F. Schumacher's (1973) *Small is Beautiful* contains, amidst his overtly secular proposals for economic restructuring, some footnotes to papal encyclicals. This practical-minded economist is a convert to Catholicism. His later book, *A Guide for the Perplexed* (1977), leaves no doubt of his deeply religious attitude. Similarly, Barbara Ward's (1979) *Progress for a Small Planet* appears at first glance as straightforward economic analysis, free of religious commitments. It turns out, however, that she was not only a practising Catholic and friend of Schumacher's, but also an active and influential participant in Vatican affairs. In 1988, the Sierra Club, arguably the most influential environmental organization in the United States, published a book by Thomas Berry, *The Dream of the Earth*, a scientifically informed exposition of cosmic, even pantheistic, thinking about the human situation. Nowhere in the book is Berry identified as a Catholic, yet in fact he is a priest, a member of the Passionist Order.

Just as authentically religious as the Catholicism of Schumacher, Ward or Berry is the explicitly anti-Christian surrender to mystery in *Dreaming the Dark* (1982), a book by a California woman who writes under the name of Starhawk. Starhawk is a witch, she lives in a coven, and her purpose is to destroy the ethic of "power-over" that has guided Western man's relation on the one hand to nature and on the other hand to women. In the sixteenth and seventeenth centuries, she argues, Western civilization estranged itself from nature more completely than before. The organicism of feudal society broke down, common lands were enclosed as private property, new professions undermined popular knowledge, and sensual, cosmic religious attitudes were condemned. Between the sexes, it was women who represented the values that had to be rooted out. Among the classes, it was peasants. The identification, persecution and execution of peasant women as witches was a means of ensuring the success of a more secular way of life. It is to recover the older tradition that Starhawk became a witch.

Not all of the environmentalist movement is informed by religious sensibilities. Many businesspeople support reforestation simply as a long-term investment, while deriding those with compassion for other species as "tree-huggers." But some environmentalists themselves insist on absolute secularity. The most prominent such voice in America belongs to Murray Bookchin, who wrote: "The clear-sighted *naturalism* to which ecology so vividly lends itself is now in danger of becoming supplanted by a *supernatural* outlook that is inherently alien to nature's own fecundity and self-creativity" (1989, 12). Bookchin is outraged by the contention of Swedish philosopher Arne Naess, that "the basic principles of the deep ecology movement lie in religion or philosophy." Bookchin wants to keep religion out and "to turn the world into an ever-broader domain of freedom and rationality" (1989, 204).

Thousands of people are attempting to conjure up new interpretations of the meaning of this planet and of humanity's place on it, interpretations that can guide us away from the impending ecological disaster towards the enhancement of life in all its forms. Not every new interpretation that is informed by a religious attitude is a valid one, however; Bookchin is correct in opposing dogmatism, authoritarianism and the ethic of hierarchy.

But we must not oppose on principle the use of a religious viewpoint in the writing of the new interpretations we so urgently need. Instead, we should insist on it. The evidence compels, it seems, two basic but contradictory truths about the situation of humanity on earth. One is that we humans *are* special, that we *do* reshape our environment, make history and break limits. The other truth is that, like all other species, we live within limits that we cannot break: the limits of death, of earth as a place of habitation, of dependence on other species and so on. The former truth implies the goodness of reason and the importance of an active, disciplined, economic attitude. The latter truth implies the goodness of unreason and the importance of a peaceful, compassionate religious attitude.

These two attitudes appear in different mixture across societies. The argument here has been simple and basic: Western society suffers from too little of the religious attitude; all the earth is suffering on this account; and only by reawakening our religious sensibilities can we come up with the ideas we need to ensure life and an inheritance for our children. This does not mean we can forget the economic attitude. We have to learn to embrace contradiction, because contradiction is inherent in earthly life, and to let ourselves be torn between contradictory truths as we decide what to say and how to act. This is what Albert Schweitzer (1955) meant when he described the farmer who, after a day's work mowing down thousands of plants in full bloom, nonetheless, while walking home, steps carefully around the single wildflower growing in his path. We use our environment. We must. We should. Yet as an Amerindian poet writes, "Remember that you are the universe, and the universe is you."[9]

Notes

*This chapter is a revised version of an article, entitled "Religion and the Environment," first published by Kenneth Westhues in *Geschte and Gegenwart* 2/1992, pp. 134-147.

[1]Haworth (1977, 107), for instance, rejects humanism, seeing in this concept the idea that "whatever is other than man is an object to be used, a utility." Ehrenfeld (1978) elaborates an even more extreme version of this argument. For a perceptive discussion of the issue, see Dobson (1990, 67-73). Even though his work is too unappreciative of the importance of religion, Murray Bookchin's (1989) defence of a certain anthropocentrism is quite valid.

[2]Gould (1981, 324) makes the point nicely: "We are inextricably part of nature, but human uniqueness is not negated thereby. 'Nothing but' an animal is as fallacious a statement as 'created in God's own image.'"

[3]Jesse Hardin, a radical environmentalist poet, has written: "The only problem with the Greens is that their defense of the natural world started too late, only after they no longer had anything natural to defend" (quoted in Christopher Manes [1990, 107]).

[4]For an earlier but more detailed definition and analysis of religion along these lines, see Westhues (1982, Chapter 6).

[5]Similar trends are also continuing in Europe, according to press reports of the 1990 European Values study, as analyzed by Ruud de Moor and his colleagues (*Globe and Mail*, 18 September 1991, A17).

[6]From *The Canadian Encyclopedia*, Niagara Falls pages 1257-1258, by Hurtig Publishers A McClelland & Stewart Co. Used by permission of the Canadian Publishers, McClelland & Stewart, Toronto.

[7]In *The Americanization of Edward Bok: An Autobiography* (New York: Scribner's, pocketbook edition, 1965, 254ff), the former editor of the *Ladies Home Journal* describes how Niagara Falls would now be "only a thin trickle of water crawling down its vast cliffs," had this magazine not led a massive protest against the power companies by hundreds of thousands of American and Canadian women. As a result of this protest, the American government passed the Burton Bill in 1906, restricting the diversion of water to generate hydroelectricity. Similar restrictions remain in force to this day, both by American and Canadian law and by international agreements.

[8]Harrigan (1983, 219) quotes Heraclitus for a succinct statement of cosmic religion: "This cosmos, here before us, the same for all, has not been created by one of the gods or by a man. It was always thus, it is and will be."

[9]Joy Harjo, quoted in *National Geographic* (October 1991, 14).

For Further Reading

Berry, Thomas. 1988. *The Dream of the Earth.* San Francisco: Sierra Club Books.

Ehrenfeld, David. 1978. *The Arrogance of Humanism.* New York: Oxford.

Schumacher, E.F. 1973. *Small is Beautiful.* London: Blond and Briggs.

Starhawk. 1982. *Dreaming the Dark.* Boston: Beacon Press.

Weiner, Jonathan. 1990. *The Next One Hundred Years: Shaping the Fate of Our Living Earth.* New York: Bantam.

PART III

CHALLENGE, CONTINUITY AND CHANGE WITHIN CANADIAN CHURCHES

Chapter 11

Gender Relations in Contemporary Christian Organizations[1]

Nancy Nason-Clark

Weekly they gather together to sing, pray and listen. The building is a modern structure: fan-shaped auditorium, padded pews, white stucco walls, coloured glass reflecting a hint of natural light, lush carpet, coordinated colour scheme carefully chosen to offer a warm atmosphere. Everyone appears comfortable.

Families are seated together. Older women congregate in the middle section. The young people — carefully coiffured to attract each other — sit at the front. Whispers are heard, but there is little other noise. An air of expectancy permeates the room. The 11:00 worship service is about to begin.

Outside the sanctuary it is far less serene. Women and children hurry inside after being dropped off at the entrance. Men in cars jostle for spots in a parking lot. Inside, women scurry to ensure that their little children are placed in either the nursery or the toddlers' room. Young people are hanging out, waiting for their friends to arrive. Even the washrooms are a hub of activity. Amidst the bustle, people are smiling and socializing.

Soft pre-recorded music begins. The choir files into the sanctuary; three men take their places on the platform; the female musicians appear in place. Everyone is ready.

The opening prayer invites God the Heavenly Father to come by His presence into the sanctuary. The congregation sings a couple of choruses: *He is Lord; Father I Adore You;* and *We are One in the Bond of Love.* The singing is lively and the congregation enthusiastic. The service proceeds with announcements, the singing of hymns, and prayers. Older children and several women leave the service on cue to attend Junior Church at the same time that several middle-aged men collect the offering. The service builds to the high-point: the sermon. For forty-five minutes, the senior minister preaches a sermon, based on the Bible but purposefully made specific to everyday life concerns: men in the world; women in the home.

After the closing prayer, people linger: some at the altar; some in the pew; others in the aisles chatting to one another. There is no stampede to the door. Most of the people seem at home here.

Every Sunday morning, millions of Canadians gather together in churches to worship God, learn about the Christian faith, celebrate family life and socialize with other believers. But the messages they hear extend beyond talk about a loving God and the historic Jesus. The rights and responsibilities of women and men feature prominently both in the teaching and in the general life of a typical Christian congregation. Building on the opening description of a service in a large Evangelical church in Atlantic Canada, this chapter explores the relationship between women and religion in modern society.

Throughout history (as in our contemporary example), the relationship between religion and women has been composed of a complicated set of social interactions involving teaching and practice concerning the supernatural, the essence of man and of woman, human sexuality, roles and responsibilities accorded to each sex, spiritual vocations, the power and status of ordained elders, and the weekly routine of church life. But within the last twenty-five years, much of the taken-for-granted teaching and practice within Christianity in the Western world has come under challenge.

To understand the feminist challenge to contemporary Christianity, we need to catch a glimpse of the "problem," the features of modern church life that have been criticized by people seeking reforms. Consider the opening excerpt documenting a Sunday service in a large church in eastern Canada. In this context, are men and women treated differently? What do we learn about gender from the teaching offered by this church? How does the way the message is preached reinforce the practice of church life?

THE CHALLENGE TO RE-EVALUATE THE BIBLICAL MESSAGE TO WOMEN

Confusion and controversy continue to characterize biblical teaching on the roles and status of women and men. Many women through the centuries of church history have been told that God does not want them to be teaching men spiritual truth. Just as Florence Nightingale was commanded to "go back and do crochet in [her] mother's drawing room" (Bliss 1952, 14), so scores of contemporary Christian women experience the sadness and pain of rejection when they offer their energies and abilities to the modern church. Theological teaching has been used to exclude women from full partnership with men in the life and ministry of the Christian church. Denominations differ in the degree to which they build their gender practices on scriptural teaching; yet, all brands of contemporary Christianity have been influenced by the biblical record. As a result, we need to consider what roles emerged for women in the Judaeo-Christian tradition and how these were translated into practice as the early Christian church grew in number and influence.

Four particular events encapsulate the biblical message of God's relationship with men and women: the creation story; the fall into sin; redemption through Jesus; and the consummation of God's plan for humankind in the End Times. In the beginning, we are told, God created humanity, both male and female. Sin entered the world through disobedience and the creation of God was marred. The Old Testament records the story of Israel, God's chosen people, who anticipate the coming of a Messiah to redeem the people of God. Redemption is the theme of the New Testament. God's sacrificial lamb, Jesus, is crucified, rises from the dead and ascends into heaven. Upon this message, the early church was conceived.

THE OLD TESTAMENT AND WOMEN

The Old Testament record of the status of a woman shows continued dependency on men — first on her father and later on her husband at marriage (Deuteronomy 22:13-21). Sexual purity and faithfulness to one husband were the law's demands of her, thereby protecting the patriarchal context of her main function: childbearing (Genesis 30:23; Numbers 5). A woman's identity in ancient Israel, as in other patriarchal cultures, was based solely on family membership. With respect to the laws regarding inheritance, sexual impurity and binding vows, women were considered subordinate to men. They were treated as minors for the entire duration of their lives, with either a father or husband bearing responsibility or providing consent for all actions (Numbers 30). Moreover, a woman's life was valued at less than a man's (30 versus 50 shekels; Leviticus 27:2-8) and cleanliness codes prescribing the period of impurity were twice as stringent upon the birth of a female than a male child (fourteen versus seven days; Leviticus 12:1-5). Furthermore, polygamy (one man having more than one wife) and divorce were both provisions for men exclusively. Priesthood and monarchy were outside the domain granted to women, but the charismatic office of prophetess was open to their participation. Women could be professional mourners (Jeremiah 9:17-22) and temple servers (Ezra 2:65) as well.

The Old Testament paints a picture of man-woman relationships founded upon a clear division of labour. As a result of the disobedience of Adam and Eve, a "gendered" environment was created, where the role of men primarily involved the task of conquering nature (work outside of the domestic sphere) and women's status revolved around the burdens and joys of reproduction (work within the domestic sphere). Men and women unable or unwilling to pattern their lives in this way were subject to sanctions. Within the context of the Old Testament, shame was attached to being without land or without child.

THE NEW TESTAMENT AND WOMEN

Jesus entered into a Jewish society where traditional rabbinic custom saw the Jewish man thank God daily that his birth had not been that of a woman, slave or foreigner: a society where Jews considered it better that the words of the Torah (that is, the law) be burned rather than taught to a woman. The nickname "Bleeding Pharisees" was applied to several teachers of the law because they closed their eyes at the approach of any woman, and thereby were prone to stumble. Further, a rabbi was not permitted to speak to any woman in public — not even his sister.

Few stories in the Bible are as well known or as well loved as the Christmas story. Children and adults alike are drawn to the images surrounding the birth of the baby Jesus: the crowded streets of

Bethlehem; the manger scene; the shepherds; the heavenly host; the star of the east; the gifts of the wise men. Featured prominently in the entrance of God into human history is the peasant girl Mary. In many ways, Mary was typical of many other young Jewish women, yet she was chosen for a role that was to alter God's relationship with Israel and surrounding nations. She was asked to cooperate in God's plan. In the words of Rosemary Radford Ruether (1979), she was an "active, personal agent in the drama of God's incarnation." Realizing the importance of her role, Mary exclaims: "All generations will call me blessed" (Luke 11:48).

Mary can be understood to symbolize the new Eve, as Jesus her son represents the second Adam. Just as the virgin Eve was misled by an angelic being and disobeyed the Lord God, so a second virgin Mary received graciously the Lord's message delivered by the angel Gabriel. The *sinful* Eve and the *sinless* Mary represent the two prevailing images of women, images that became enshrined in Christian myths about sexuality and spirituality as the early church became institutionalized.

Women played an important role in the life and ministry of Jesus. Both rich women and prostitutes found in Christ warmth, acceptance and friendship, much to the astonishment of even his closest disciples. Jesus permitted women both to listen and respond to his teaching, and even to accompany his travelling band. In a more intimate way, he allowed women to support him financially, and it was the tears and hair of a lowly prostitute that washed the Messiah's feet. Contrary to traditional rabbinic teaching, Jesus taught mixed audiences and the content of his messages used examples drawn from the experiences of both men and women. His actions towards women — like the Samaritan woman at the well (John 4:1-42), the woman with an issue of blood (Mark 5:21-43), or the sisters Mary and Martha (Luke 10:38-42) — confirmed the authenticity of the words he spoke. Women could find comfort in the promise of Jesus that "who-ever does God's will is my brother and sister and mother" (Mark 3:35).

Last at the cross of Jesus and first at his tomb on that historic Sunday morning was Mary Magdalene. Despite the fact that the men did not believe their report, the women with Mary were the first witnesses commissioned to spread the Good News. As we shall see, official church tradition did not favour a prominent role for this Mary.

In many ways, she was an unconventional woman. Her faithfulness at the close of Christ's earthly life reveals evidence of her love. Christ's loving call to her, when she mistook him for a gardener, signalled his recognition of her love. In many ways, she was a role model that later church leaders preferred to ignore (Ruether 1979), though she was exalted in the Gnostic traditions (Pagels 1979). On the other hand, Mary the mother of Jesus was considered a perfect role model for both the Christian virgin and the Christian mother. Her love for Jesus — a mother's love — was safe.

As the early church began to form, women played a prominent role in its life and ministry. As Constance Parvey (1974) and Dorothy Pape (1976) concluded, the early church had great success among middle- and upper-class women: they opened their homes for Christian worship; they welcomed the travelling disciples as house guests; they ministered to other women, using domestic and other talents; they were full members of the newly formed house groups; they were doers of charity and victims of persecution; they were spirit-filled prophets called to proclaim the message.

Such examples of the diversity of roles for women in the early church must be considered against the back-drop of Pauline teaching on women, with its references to the submission of wives (Ephesians 5:22-25), the silence of women in the churches (I Timothy 2:11-14) and the concept of hierarchy as it relates to man-woman relationships. These passages exhort women to submit to the authority of their husbands, forbid women to teach men and suggest a male-female hierarchy in marriage.

The testaments provide materials for debate and controversy concerning the scriptural record as it relates to the role and status of women in the familial, societal and religious spheres. Those who argue for restrictive gender relations base their position on the books of the law, the story of the fall into sin, and the Pauline instructions contained within the pastoral epistles. Others conclude their biblical search by justifying an expanded role for women in all facets of life, and root their arguments in the equality of men and women at creation, report examples of women in the Old Testament who broke through traditional moulds, view the life and teaching of Christ as exemplifying the highest esteem for women and cite Paul's openness to equal and free participation in the body of Christ for all people, regardless of sex, race or social standing.

THE CHALLENGE TO RE-EVALUATE CHURCH HISTORY

The sinfulness of Eve and the sinlessness of Mary encapsulate the prevailing themes about women as the early church became institutionalized. A similar message was conveyed by the evils attributed to sexual intercourse and the purity of virginity and celibacy. Spirituality and natural womanliness were considered incompatible. Thus, up to the time of the Reformation, women who aspired to spiritual heights were removed from home and family and placed in cloisters. The early church fathers held that every woman, because of her ultimate identification with Eve, was both a corruptor of mortal men and an angelic being. As a result, each woman must continue to bear the shame of that first sin. In an essay entitled, "On Female Dress," Tertullian (c AD 160-220) lays the responsibility for sin clearly at the feet of women.

> And do you not know that you are each an Eve? The sentence of God on this sex of yours lives in this age: the guilt must of necessity live too. You are the devil's gateway: you are the unsealer of that forbidden tree: you are the first deserter of the divine law: you are she who persuaded him whom the devil was not valiant enough to attack. You destroyed so easily God's image, man. On account of your desert — that is, death — even the Son of God had to die (1869, 304-305).

The later church fathers, Gregory of Nyssa (c. AD 330-395), Augustine of Hippo (c. AD 354-430) and Jerome (c. AD 342-420), constructed a theology of sexuality based upon the Platonic concept of a monistic spiritual reality coupled with a dualistic physical reality (Ruether 1974). By implication, neither God nor God's image implanted in man could be bisexual (having both sexes in one individual). Because God could not be both male and female, Augustine argued that both God and His image imparted to humanity must be male. By this argument, maleness was assimilated into monism — the one spiritual reality — whereas females were relegated to the lower, bodily nature. Taking this position further, Augustine concluded that the male bears the full image of the Creator, but the female only a secondary reflection. He felt that with the exception of procreation for which woman was indispensable, a male helpmate would have been more suitable for Adam. The dilemma faced by man in his relation to woman is summed up in the following statement taken from Augustine's essay entitled "Love and Hatred of Temporal Relationships":

> Thus it is characteristic of a good Christian to love in one woman the creature of God whom he desires to be transformed and renewed, but to hate corruptible and mortal intimacy and copulation — that is, to love the human being in her but to hate that which makes her a wife (1948, 51).

Finally, Jerome takes the strict Augustinian deliberations to their ultimate conclusion: a renunciation of marriage. In two of his famous letters entitled "The Virgin's Profession" and "Feminine Training," virgins are told to shun the company of married women and rather choose companions "pale and thin with fasting." As much as possible they should stay in their own room, fast, study the Scriptures and pray. Squalid dress and neglect of hygiene were recommended as they protect a woman from becoming an object of desire.

During this period, women who wished to embark on a spiritual journey needed to leave behind their sexuality. Only in a cloistered environment could a woman hope to transcend the curse laid upon her sex, only there could she please God, only there could she completely deny her sexuality. The same was true, of course, for men; but male sexuality was never viewed with as much horror as female sexuality. Virginity became the criterion for female spirituality in much the same way as circumcision had been the sign of God's elect in the Old Testament. The choice for women was thus to leave behind the authority of a father or potential husband and enter into a world that suggested and symbolized spiritual equivalence.

With the dawn of the Reformation in the sixteenth century, sparked by the nailing of Martin Luther's 95 theses to the Wittenburg door, came a new role for women supported by a reformed theology of sexuality. The abolition of monasticism and celibacy as Christian ideals paved the way for the vocational consequences of the priesthood of all believers. Rather than condemn the marriage state or condone only its procreative power, the Reformers regarded women and sexual union as fundamentally good. Domestic life was exonerated, marriage for women regarded as a Christian career and the role of clergywife placed upon a pedestal. Cloisters and virginity were symbolically replaced by parsonages populated by large families.

Thus, many happy children, a contented husband, help and hospitality for the poor and sick were the new emerging responsibilities accorded by the reformers to women. And it was their wives who set the example of godliness in character and practice through their lives in the home. Myrtle Langley (1983) and Jane Douglass (1974) both regard this change as enhancing the possibilities for women, whereas Susan Dowell and Linda Hurcombe in *Dispossessed Daughters of Eve: Faith and Feminism* claim:

> ... when the church made a place for the loyal wife by the side of its priesthood, the seeds were sown for the vulnerability of both the clergywife and the women who do not marry. The "domesticity rules" ethos of parish life, and the single woman, traditionally excluded from it, can present a depressing picture. It is as if Eve were allowed back into the garden just so long as she took the rest of those offending apples and made them into chutney for the bazaar (1981, 93).

Beginning in the eighteenth century, religious revival began to sweep England and then America, bringing with it a cleansing of hearts, levelling of social inequalities and an abandonment of ecclesiastical institutions. Focusing on the priesthood of all believers, men and women were challenged to proclaim the good news of Christ and the spirit-filled life as evidenced at Pentecost. Such preaching by lay people was accomplished amidst psychological abuse, physical hardship and even torture. The Revivals in England and the Great Awakening in America gave women the place that the Reformation had put denied. The campaign against slavery and the fight for women's suffrage went hand in hand with evangelistic and feministic proclamations.

By the end of the eighteenth century, religious women were lobbying for change in the political and social order. Seeds of unrest about the status of women had been kindled by the French Revolution; British and American churches affected by religious revival gave women a platform. For example, the Women's Rights Convention held at Seneca Falls, New York, in 1848 was conducted on the premises of a Wesleyan Chapel. Once the slaves had been freed and the vote for women won, the efforts, once so revolutionary, of women who took part in these campaigns drifted towards respectability.

Concern with the language and message of Scripture to women is not new. In 1895, Elizabeth Cady Stanton succeeded in publishing what she called *The Woman's Bible*. Based on her belief that the language and interpretation of passages dealing with women in the Bible were a major contributor to women's inferior status, she mounted an effort to write commentaries on passages from the Old and New Testaments (Stanton 1895). Today, many religious groups are attempting to re-think the language of their sacred books, their liturgy and their hymnals.

Recent years have witnessed an explosion in research attempting to understand and interpret the world from the perspective and experiences of women. With the rise of the second wave of feminism in the 1960s and the maturing of the women's movement in the decades to follow, feminist scholars have begun to revise, reformulate and reappropriate the knowledge base of the Western world. Not only has this been true in the realm of the work world, in the domestic sphere and in re-claiming of history, but it has also occurred in the religious and spiritual realms as well.

One of the first tasks of religious feminists has been to argue that religion treats women poorly and to suggest that the Judaeo-Christian tradition is sexist. For Mary Daly (1968, 1973), since God is male then the male is God. We need to move beyond the concept of God the Father, she contends. "A woman's asking for equality in the church would be comparable to a black person's demanding equality in the Ku Klux Klan" (1975, 6). Other feminist theologians disagree. Phyllis Trible (1979) and Elizabeth Fiorenza (1979) argue for the liberating potential of biblical faith: for them, the essential message is not the sanctity of patriarchy but liberation for men and women through a sense of relatedness to God. Building on the theme of the exodus of the children of Israel, the prophetic plea for justice or the concern Jesus expressed for the poor and oppressed, Fiorenza (1985) contends that feminist "herstorians" can rediscover in the Judaeo-Christian tradition the theme of liberation.

For Fiorenza and a host of other feminist theologians and other Christian writers, there is sufficient ground to hope and work for the church's repentance and reform (Christ and Plaskow 1979). From this perspective, the task of feminist theology is to "uncover Christian theological traditions and myths that perpetuate sexist ideologies, violence and alienation. A Christian feminist spirituality thus has as its theological presupposition ... the Christian community's constant need for renewal and conversion" (Fiorenza 1979). Fiorenza believes that this can be accomplished only when women are granted full spiritual, theological and ecclesiastical equality.

THE CHALLENGE TO RE-THINK THE IMAGE OF THE CLERGYMAN

The issue of women and ordained ministry continues to be contentious, even within those denominations that formally recognize women's ordination. Opposition to women's ordination persists despite the growing number of women in the labour force, changes in attitudes and behaviour towards women in secular society, and advances made by the women's movement (Nason-Clark 1987b). It is an emotional issue for those on both sides of the debate. Proponents are hurt and saddened by the churches' collective failure to recognize the gifts and calling of women, while opponents agonize over the potential upheaval should priestly doors or ministerial positions open to substantial numbers of women. There is pain on both sides. Few have taken a moderate position.

Although the struggle for admission into the ordained ministry has received the most attention, the career struggle of clergywomen continues after their ordination as they seek placement and career opportunities (Lehman 1985). Women tend to be offered junior positions, paid lower wages and deprived of career moves to more prestigious posts (Nason-Clark 1987a; Carroll et al. 1983). This tendency prevails despite evidence that calling/installing a woman brings no measurable disadvantage to the local church and, in fact, several advantages (Stevens 1989; Royle 1987; Weidman 1981).

As in other parts of the Western world, the debate on the professional ministry of women as ordained elders (priests or ministers) has been a source of contention in Canada throughout this century — even within the Catholic church, where ordination has not to date been permitted. Amongst the theologically conservative denominations (like the Baptists and holiness groups) small numbers of women have always been engaged in active ministry. When the numbers of men available to fill positions as itinerant preachers or pastors of remote churches fell short of the demand, these groups were willing to send women; this practice, of course, has occurred in the mainline denominations as well, particularly with respect to missionary service. The first woman in Canada ordained as a minister was Lydia Gruchy and that ordination took place in 1936. Today, 25 percent of ordained United Church ministers are women; that figure rises to 30 percent if those in the diaconal ministry are included (whose numbers are predominantly female). Six Canadian women were ordained to the Anglican priesthood in 1976. Today, approximately 10 percent of Anglican priests in Canada are women. Within Baptist, holiness and Pentecostal groups there are isolated cases of ordained women, but the proportion is very small indeed. In the Atlantic Baptist Convention, for example, thirteen women are ordained and serving full-time in churches (out of a total of 383 pastors). In the Atlantic District of the Wesleyan Church (a holiness group) two women are ordained and serving full-time in pastoral ministry (out of a total of 125 ministers).[2]

While the struggle for women's ordination varies from one denomination to another, several common features can be identified and discussed. In the early stages of the debate on women and ordained ministry, theological issues appear in the forefront of the discourse, followed by secular or practical reasons. Proponents tend to focus on the equality of men and women in the creation story, the examples of women in Scripture who fulfilled nontraditional roles, the life and ministry of Jesus as well as his treatment of women, the variety of roles occupied by women in the first-century church, the expressed need for women to minister to other women, women reporting a "call of God" to ministry, the examples of women who have ministered in some official capacity (as missionaries, deaconesses, nuns, etc.), the advancement of women in other professions (as physicians, professors, etc.), the complementary role women would bring to ministry and the declining number of male ordinands.

On the other hand, opponents of the ordination of women point to the creation story as teaching male leadership, the record that Jesus chose no women to be among his twelve disciples, the passages in the New Testament exhorting women to be silent, the predominant Scriptural pattern to refer to God in male language, the belief that only males can represent God to the people, the years of tradition of male-only authority, the New Testament passages referring to man as "head of woman," the issue as divisive among the clergy and laity, the impediment to unity with other denominations that do not ordain women, as well as issues related to the emotional and intellectual makeup of women, women's marital and childcare responsibilities, the perceived lack of geographical mobility for married women, the role of the clergyhusband and the response of church members.

While it is true to say that theological arguments weigh heavily in the discourse of the debate in the early stages of discussion about the ordination of women to the priesthood or ordained ministry, there is little evidence to show that theology is at the heart of the matter. Those who have considered this issue from a social-scientific point of view agree that religious beliefs alone are unable to account for the opposition to the ministry/priesthood of women (Lehman 1987; Nason-Clark 1987a; Carroll, Hargrove and Lummis 1983). Rather, an unwillingness to accept women in ordained positions has been found to emerge as a specific example of a more pervasive conservative gender-role ideology (Nason-Clark 1987a; Lehman 1985).

In a British sample of clergymen, those opposed to the ordination of women to the priesthood in the Church of England were more restrictive in their views on women's role in society and the family (Nason-Clark 1984). They were more likely to believe that a woman's place was in the home, reported less support for equality between men and women in the workplace and were less supportive of women choosing to combine motherhood and careers (Nason-Clark 1986). A study of these clergymen in 1991 revealed that factors such as working with a clergywoman, fathering a daughter or having a wife who works full-time for pay were related to changes in clergy attitudes towards the ordination of women to the priesthood (Nason-Clark 1991a).

Once denominations have exhausted the debate in theological terms, the second series of arguments tends to centre around appropriate timing: "Is the time ripe for a decision of this magnitude?" The answer is invariably "yes" for strong proponents and "not yet" for the majority who have no strong theological objections. At this stage, practical issues begin to loom large: the possibility of temporary vacancies due to pregnancy leave; geographical mobility for married clergywomen; the acceptance of young, never-married clergywomen by their parishioners; problems of placement and opportunities for advancement. In most denominations, the result of this discourse is to prolong the decision to ordain women, under the umbrella that while there are no theological reasons to prohibit women's ministry, there are practical details that must be worked out.

Once women are no longer denied access to ordination within a particular tradition, the next level of debate centres around *placement* issues. There have been contradictory reports as to the ease of placing clergywomen (Lehman 1981a, 1985; Carroll et al. 1983). The characteristics of obtaining ministerial appointments differ between denominations: some congregations are responsible for "calling" their own minister (for example, Baptists), whereas there are other denominations where a church official has responsibility to appoint an incumbent (for example, Anglicans). In both cases, women candidates are frequently passed over in the selection process. Partly this is a function of a perceived incompatibility between the image of the "minister" and the image of a "woman" in the minds of many church members and partly a concern about the organizational viability of the local church (Lehman 1981a; 1981b).

While research concerning the placement, acceptance and career opportunities of clergywomen in Canada, the United States and England is in its early days, it can be concluded tentatively that: (1) there appears to be no positive discrimination in favour of female candidates, even when churches have experienced a woman pastor (Carroll et al. 1983; Lehman 1981a); (2) women are overrepresented in the junior positions on the church staff (Nason-Clark 1984; Carroll et al. 1983; Lehman 1980); and (3) having a woman pastor does not appear to be related to either church membership or financial figures (Nason-Clark 1984; Royle 1987).

An obstacle faced by all clergywomen − in varying degrees − is resistance to their ministry by clergymen within their own denomination and by colleagues in other denominations (Nason-Clark 1987a). Although contact between clergywomen and clergymen plays a role in reducing the resistance (Nason-Clark 1991a; Lehman 1985), clergymen have few opportunities to work with female colleagues and as a result changes in their gender role ideology occur at a slower pace. Even those clergy supportive of women clergy tend to think of women incumbents in restrictive ways. For example, many clergy perceive that the single, middle-aged woman is the most appropriate type of woman to be placed as a ministerial candidate and the assistant position in a church the most favoured role for her to perform (Nason-Clark 1987a).

A further area of overlap concerns traditional masculine symbolism and liturgy. Issues here range from the language used in reference to the people of God to images of who God is. "If we do not mean that God is male when we use masculine pronouns and imagery, then why should there be any objection to using female imagery and pronouns as well?" (Gross 1979). The centrality of the *fatherhood* of God and the *brotherhood* of the people of God differ between denominations as does the call for and the opposition to the use of inclusive language. Considering God in feminine as well as masculine terms is not new (Carmody 1982; Jewett 1980; Crabtree 1970) and there is a general recognition that women have been used as symbols by Christianity and treated in a subordinate manner because of the existing symbols within the tradition (Neal 1979). Yet, there is broad disagreement on how this might be altered. Some denominations, like the United Church of Canada, have produced guidelines on the use of inclusive language;[3] there is great diversity, however, in the extent to which such guidelines have been adopted by individual ministers and congregations.

A further issue to emerge from the clergywomen research concerns the degree to which women are changing the image of ministry (Lehman 1992; Stevens 1989; Ice 1987; Nason-Clark 1987b; Carroll et al. 1983). Published personal accounts by ordained women document the variety of images through which the woman minister seeks to carve out her ministry by redefining traditional clerical roles (Weidman 1981; Doely 1970). As a group it appears that clergywomen bring enhanced sensitivity, better pastoral care, collective leadership and a wider vision of Christian ministry. Whether they embrace or challenge traditional female roles, women ministers are changing some aspects of the ministry, not least through their skills at counselling and their person-centred focus (Nason-Clark 1987b; Ice 1987; Stevens 1989).

THE CHALLENGE TO RE-THINK THE DIVISION OF LAY LABOUR

Although it is appropriate to highlight the struggle for women's recognition in official, ordained ministries of the Christian church, it is important to realize that women do not participate on an equal footing with men even as lay members of local congregations (Nason-Clark 1984). On the contrary, a sexual division of lay labour still defines the weekly routine of church life. Women polish the brass, clean the linens and fill the pews. Yet, they are less likely than men to participate in any formal, recognized way in the worship service. While women bake for church suppers and sew for bazaars, they are often powerless in determining how the money is spent. They tend the nursery and teach the children in Sunday School, but they have limited input into church policy decisions. This division of lay labour persists within a context where women are more likely than men to believe and behave in ways condoned by the community of the faithful (Harrison 1983; Martin 1967). But does this division still exist in Canadian churches?

A recent survey (1991) amongst 287 Evangelical women in Atlantic Canada suggests that it does (Nason-Clark 1992). Women reported an average of two regular responsibilities in their local church, with 33.3 percent of the respondents indicating that they hold four or more jobs in the regular routine of church life. A total of 93 different types of ministries or tasks — most of which could be considered sex-typed — were fulfilled by these church women. While it is accurate to report that the typical Christian church may be staffed by one or two male ministers, much of the work of the church is completed by an army of female volunteers. And this pattern extends beyond the Evangelical sector. In a recent study of Catholic church women in Nova Scotia, it was found that they reported an average of two church-related responsibilities (McInnis and Nason-Clark 1989), while among a small group of Newfoundland Catholic women the average number of volunteer responsibilities in their parish stood at three (Stapleton and Nason-Clark 1992).

Clearly, part of the "gendered environment" of church life is reflected in the multitude of sex-typed tasks fulfilled by women in a supportive role to men, not unlike the array of responsibilities performed by women as a "labour of love" in the home (cf. Luxton 1980). The challenge in the contemporary Canadian context is to prevail over sex-typing and to recognize and incorporate the differences amongst women by offering choices of ministries and tasks based on talent rather than gender.

What would a church look like if it took the responsibilities of Christian men and women as equal partners in sharing their faith and the responsibility for leadership? The gender breakdown of the local church board or governing council would not differ from the nursery roster; the proportion of women on the platform would approximate the proportion of women in the pew; the language and liturgy of worship and instruction would be inclusive of the diversity amongst believers; the full expanse of the church's ministry would have men and women serving as partners, on the basis of talent, willingness to serve and spiritual maturity; and the programs offered to the congregation and the local community would represent the full range of needs and experiences of ordinary women and men, boys and girls alike. The full inclusion of men and women in active lay service can only be accomplished by rethinking the power and prestige conferred by ordination.

THE CHALLENGE TO RE-THINK CLERICAL POWER AND PRESTIGE

The sex scandal that shook Newfoundland beginning in 1988, involving Roman Catholic parish priests and lay brothers, is primarily a story of broken trust. While it would be clearly erroneous and misleading to suggest that all ordained priests and ministers wield unleashed power over parishioners and the public, this sexual scandal provides a case study of the power of the "clerical collar." These crimes continued for so long partly because of the awe, respect and reverence attributed to the priesthood. And the Catholic church failed to respond quickly and decisively to curtail the abuse and support the victims partly because of its desire to protect the priesthood and the office of the parish priest.

Several factors have begun to erode the power of the priest or the minister across Canada and indeed within the Western world. First, women have been performing some clerical functions. There is a serious shortage of men entering the Roman Catholic priesthood (Hoge 1987; Wallace 1992). Catholic women have been performing some roles traditionally assigned to priests, in the community and sometimes in the religious service. At the same time, other denominations have noticed a marked increase in the number of women entering theological college and subsequently asking that their "call to ministry" be recognized. Women bring a more inclusive, less hierarchical style to the clerical profession and as a result begin to challenge the clergy/laity distinction so prevalent in the past. Second, declining church attendance in Canada (Bibby 1987) has affected the influence of the parish priest/minister in the community. Third, increased education among the general populace has produced a balance and challenge to the authority of the "all-knowing" priest/minister. As the base of information about the secular and religious world has increased amongst lay members of congregations, clerical incumbents have been forced to reassess their raison d'être. Fourth, the pluralism of modern Canadian religious life and the proliferation of secular professionals — psychologists, social workers, university professors and so on — has relegated the ordained clergy to one professional amongst others competing for the minds and hearts of a select public. Fifth, there is a growing intolerance with unchecked power in any sphere of contemporary society, accompanied by a scepticism of the integrity of the person to whom such political, religious or economic power has been given.

The challenge to rethink clerical power and prestige is not new. Within the hearts and minds of Canadians, however, the need to come to terms with the abuse of clerical power has been heightened beyond measure by the sexual scandals involving members of the clergy that have occurred in Newfoundland and elsewhere.

EQUITABLE GENDER RELATIONS AND CONTEMPORARY CHRISTIANITY: WHY IS IT SO IMPORTANT?

Embarking upon the process of equitable gender relations — understanding and acting in ways that support and celebrate equally the knowledge, experiences and religious participation at all levels of both women and men — is critical for contemporary Christianity for several reasons. First, it maintains the integrity of the message. As mentioned earlier, there are examples of challenges to patriarchal structures and power all through the biblical record and in the history of the church. The message of Christianity is not bound up in these patriarchal institutions even though patriarchal language, liturgy and symbolism have co-existed with the message. Love, freedom and release from bondage are the integral concepts in the Christian world view, however distorted they have become in the translation of the message into a particular time and space. Second, equitable gender relations in contemporary Christianity ensure that the mission of the church — to proclaim the gospel and live according to its principles — goes forward. Sexual justice within the broader Christian community equips and sends men and women together as full partners in proclaiming the gospel. Freedom from bondage, be it sexual, physical or emotional in its manifestation, is as critical a message for modern society as it has been in the past. Women will never achieve full equality in the secular society as long as a major institution like the church prevents and thwarts the development of their potential. The mission of the church is intertwined with the proclamation that all people are equal. Third, equitable gender relations enhance the viability of the local church. As a faith community, the local church is in a position to respond quickly to the needs of both the congregation and the community in which it is located. In order for its potential to be maximized, all able and willing volunteers need to have their energy and skills tapped and directed, a task more easily done in an egalitarian setting. The strength of the local church is housed in the people, not in the building or administrative structure. Once the people catch the vision, the community and its needs will no longer be the same. Was this not the message, mission and strength of the first-century church?

Notes

[1]All biblical quotations in this chapter are taken from the New International Version of the Bible.

[2]Data on women's ordination obtained by telephone interview by Nason-Clark with officials of church organizations listed.

[3]The 1986, 31st General Council of the United Church of Canada adopted "Guidelines for Inclusive Languages in all Documents, Worship and Liturgy" cf., Record of Proceedings, 87-89, 131, 647-653.

For Further Reading

Carmody, Denise Lardner. 1982. *Feminism and Christianity: A Two-Way Reflection*. Nashville: Abingdon.

Daly, Mary. 1975. *The Church and the Second Sex: With a New Feminist Post-Christian Introduction*. London: Colophon Books.

Lehman, Edward C., Jr. 1985. *Women Clergy: Breaking Through Gender Barriers*. New Brunswick: Transaction Publishers.

Ruether, Rosemary Radford (ed.). 1974. *Religion and Sexism: Images of Woman in the Jewish and Christian Traditions*. New York: Simon and Schuster.

Wallace, Ruth. 1992. *They Call Her Pastor*. Albany: State University of New York Press.

Chapter 12

Canada's Native Peoples and the Churches

David L. Lewis

Whether we like it or not, it is a historic fact that the great expansion of Christianity has coincided in time with the world-wide and
explosive expansion of Europe that followed on the Renaissance;
that the colonizing powers have been the Christian powers; that a
whole variety of compromising relationships have existed between
missionaries and governments; and that in the main Christianity has
been carried forward on the wave of Western prestige and power
(Neill 1964, 450).

The year 1992 was the 500th anniversary of Columbus's first voyage
to the Americas. Although Europeans had been in contact with this
hemisphere for centuries before Columbus — as the Norse settlement
at L'Anse aux Meadows demonstrates — Columbus's arrival was
significant in that it marked the beginning of colonization. Through
a series of wars and treaties between European powers, the New
World was parcelled out between Portugal and Spain, Britain and its
successor the United States, France and several others. Indigenous
inhabitants were subjugated or wiped out; settlers and slaves were
brought in.

Significantly, it was not until 1537 that the debate over whether the
"Indians," as they came to be called, were fully human was definitively resolved by a papal bull declaring that Native peoples had souls
and were therefore endowed with rights (Neill 1964, 459).

That declaration underscores the tension between the churches and
Native peoples. In Canada particularly, the churches have often cast
themselves in the role of advocates for and defenders of Native
interests, in keeping with the biblical parable of the shepherd and his

flock. But the churches have also been among the advance guard of Euro-Canadian society, dedicated to the destruction of Native culture and the assimilation of Native peoples. While all denominations have now renounced the attempt at cultural genocide, as it is sometimes called, the legacy of their involvement lives on.

THE PERIOD OF FIRST CONTACT

Euro-Canadians often take pride in the comparatively peaceful course of colonization in this country, at least compared to the protracted "Indian wars" that took place in the United States: "Spanish civilization," wrote Parkman (1867, 1:1), "crushed the Indian; English civilization scorned and neglected him; French civilization embraced and cherished him." In fact, Calloway adds, the British "cultivated and observed" the Native peoples too, in sharp contrast to American practice (see also Kehoe 1989; Berkhofer 1979).

However, the reasons for this difference have more to do with the general lack of interest in Canada as a place of settlement than with any enlightened attitudes on the part of the colonizers in this country.

Although French and British settlements were established on the banks of the St. Lawrence and in the Maritimes, these were sparsely populated and marginal; neither country was terribly interested in conquering Canada. Rather, the primary goal was trade (Innis 1930).

Successful traders were those who tapped into the already existing networks of exchange between different Native nations by setting up trading posts at key points throughout the north and west. The traders sought furs, especially beaver — which became the basic currency of the continent — and offered in return items like guns and steel-bladed knives, which could make hunting and other traditional Native pursuits more effective, at least for a while. Thus, while some Europeans penetrated deep into the interior seeking innocents who really would exchange pelts for "beads and trinkets," the primary arrangement involved a long sequence of transactions between Native nations, with European outposts being the anchor or endpoint. In that way, firearms (from the St. Lawrence and Hudson's Bay networks) and horses (from the Mississippi trading system) were traded throughout the continent (Calloway 1987, 25ff).

No doubt, European trade led to an intensification of this exchange network, but it did not start it. It was in the interests of the Europeans to leave Native practices as they found them. International alliances, such as that which existed between the French and the Hurons, would close off trade with whole other peoples and were therefore to be avoided; those that did form appear to have been inadvertent.

Nevertheless, the gun and the horse did alter Native life profoundly. Longstanding technical and craft skills were quickly forgotten. Nations that were in exclusive contact with Europeans could deny trade goods to their enemies and command high prices from their trading partners, so long as that exclusivity persisted. And with trapping more necessary and hunting easier, the longstanding emphasis on maintaining their nation in balance with its environment became lost (Mol 1985, 29). As a result, there appears to have been an increased dependency on Europeans as a source of now-necessary goods, a sudden flare-up and deadliness in warfare, and a decline in food stocks resulting from over-hunting (Dobyns 1984).

All of this pales to insignificance beside the introduction of diseases such as smallpox to which Native North Americans had no resistance. One after another, plagues roared through the continent, all but wiping out whole nations; in some cases, as many as 90 percent died. By the time Europeans found their way into the interior in the eighteenth century, they often confronted only the shattered remnants of bands and villages devastated by war, by illness and by starvation (Dobyns 1984). In all of these changes, religion played a small part.

Little is known for certain of First Nations religion prior to contact with Europeans (see Jenness 1976; Mol 1985, chapters 1, 2). Archaeological evidence is fragmentary and subject to hot debate (Korp 1990). Existing written accounts – such as the Jesuit *Relations* (see Kenton 1927) – derive from European Christian sources who were, at best, liable to misunderstand what they saw and were told; at worst, they might cast it in as unflattering a light as possible.

Moreover, Native cultures were not static: they changed in response to their times. As A. Hultkranz (1979, 10) points out, the very word "religion," in the few Native languages where it exists, may well have been created only after contact with European ideas, in acknowledgement of Europeans' fondness for hiving off aspects of life into discrete compartments.

The very diversity of Native groups precludes general discussion of First Nations religion: terms like "Indians" or "Natives" are categorizations that obscure the fact that each nation — and sometimes each clan (Hultkranz 1979) — had its own religious beliefs and practices. The words of Smohalla (a Native prophet) have been widely quoted and have sometimes been taken as general statements of "Native religion":

> You ask me to plow the ground. Shall I take a knife and tear my mother's breast? Then when I die, she will not take me to her bosom to rest. You ask me to dig for stone. Shall I dig under her skin for bones? Then when I die, I cannot enter her body to be born again. You ask me to cut grass and make hay and sell it, and be rich like white men. But dare I cut off my mother's hair? It is a bad law, and my people cannot obey it. I want my people to stay with me here. All the dead men will come to life again. We must wait here in the house of our fathers and be ready to meet them in the body of our mother (David 1972, 85-86).

This statement, however, cannot be taken to be definitively "Native" in tone or context. It is, for one thing, as much a rejection of Euro-Canadian culture and politics as an expression of a creed. Moreover, as Korp (1991, 18f) points out, the Six Nations were horticulturalists, and such modern staples as corn (maize), beans, tomatoes and potatoes were all introduced to Europeans by the Native peoples.

As Mol notes, the legends or myths that First Nations possessed prior to contact with Europeans probably did not serve as an account of the origins of the cosmos that tellers had to believe was literally true in the way a Fundamentalist Christian is expected to accept the historic truth of the Bible.

> [The explorer] Rasmussen tried to reason about the problem of irrationality in myths with Ikinilik, his clear-headed Utkuhikjalingmiut informant, who mixed up the tale of a girl Putilik being mated to her father's dog with the myth of Nuliajuk ... But Ikinilik made it plain that logic was not the essence of the tale and myth. What to him was important was that "Nuliajuk ... watches over all beasts, all the game of mankind, and that is enough for us. How she turned into such a dangerous and terrible spirit is surely immaterial" (Mol 1985, 17).

As in this example, the beliefs espoused by Native peoples were symbolic and allegorical. Therefore, the First Nations could readily adopt the artifacts brought by Europeans, in part because they did not challenge a deeply held world view.

Even so, it is possible that contact with Europeans, and the devastating series of changes that accompanied that contact — changes that the Native peoples were powerless to halt — led to a state of anomie, a gap between apparent reality and the norms and values that were supposed to guide behaviour. Their cosmology might have been discredited by the existence of technology and peoples for whom there was no explanation, their ethics by the intensification of warfare and the new disregard for the stewardship of the land, their theology by the inability of shamanistic medicine to cure disease or to call forth the vanishing animals.

In such conditions of anomie, it could be expected that the Native peoples would be receptive to the new cultural forms offered by missionaries, so that wholesale conversions became commonplace. This is the explanation proposed by Mooney (1896) and Wallace (1956; see also Mol 1985), and there is some evidence to support it: missionaries had been active in Canada since 1534, after all. Stories abound of the courage and dedication of these early missionaries (see Kehler 1969; Harris 1893; Devine 1923); they are as much a part of folklore as anything ever becomes in Canada. It would be surprising if their efforts were totally fruitless.

But it appears that much of the excitement over wholesale conversions in the seventeenth century (and continuing through the nineteenth century) was misplaced, perhaps because of misunderstanding over the Native peoples' practice of listening politely to the missionaries' message. In addition, many seem to have been willing to accept baptism and religious instruction, to attend church services and the like, out of a kind of religious syncretism, in which the beliefs espoused by the missionaries were incorporated into the traditional belief system (Calloway 1987, 108; Mol 1985, 52ff).

The early missionaries in New France faced an uphill battle, so long as the "heathen nations" retained their autonomy. Consequently, the policy of "Francization" was abandoned as futile (and, in any case, economically counterproductive) and efforts were made to adapt the Christian message to local conditions by, for example, translating the Bible into Native languages (Mol 1985, 48ff; Dyke 1991, 37ff).

Missionaries were often frustrated in these efforts; their listeners would generally incorporate the "Good News" of Christ and Christianity into a syncretist sort of religion that did not involve the expected rejection of their ancestral beliefs. Eminently sensible to the Native peoples, it was unacceptable to Christians, "for the Lord thy God is a jealous God."

Wholesale conversion, therefore, depended on separating the converts, forcibly if need be, from the assumptions, the beliefs and the values embedded in their language and perceptions, and imposing a new way of life and a new world view.

THE PERIOD OF CONSOLIDATION

Over time, the French metropole gave way to the British as the seat of colonial power, colonists' populations expanded and populations of Native nations' declined, Native dependency deepened and spread. The independence of the First Nations was lost, and the strength of Christianity quickly grew.

The circumstances seemed consistent with an evolutionary viewpoint, still widely held. While this can be highly sophisticated as in Karl Marx's or Emile Durkheim's theories (see Lenski 1966; Parsons 1966 for more contemporary variants), the basic view is that societies progress from small, technologically and culturally simple forms to large, complex, specialized and elaborate forms.

In this kind of thinking, then, societies would progress from savage to barbaric to civilized: Native North Americans were "savage"; Europeans were "civilized." "Savage" was not always applied pejoratively — the Native peoples were as likely to be called "noble" as "dirty" savages — but there was always the view that contact between the "civilized" European and the "savage" Native meant that the latter had to adopt European culture or die.

The ideology of progress sees the same process taking place in religion, although here the complexity of "totemism" or "animism" was taken to be an "elementary form of religious life" (Durkheim 1976), while monotheism was seen as advanced. As such, a people could not adopt monotheism until they were sufficiently "developed" to accept it (see Swanson 1960). The evolutionary view accepts that "primitives" were devastated by the effects of their contact with the "civilized" society. The process of development was a delicate one, fraught with dangers: as early as the seventeenth century, observers were already commenting on the negative effects of alcohol on the Native peoples (see Calloway 1987, 66, 154ff). This view also suggests that the "primitives" themselves recognized the superiority of outsiders' cultures as distinct from the superiority of some of their trade goods. In fact, there is little reason to suppose that Native peoples were any less proud of their own culture than British and French were of theirs (Calloway 1987, 184, 197). Out of their element, Europeans were self-evidently helpless compared to "savages," dependent on imports from their homeland, and just as unable to stop disease. There was, then, little reason for the Native peoples to share the idea of "white" superiority.

Even so, some leaders — notably the prophet Makenunatane, the "Swan Chief" of the Sekani nation in northern British Columbia in 1799 — were urging their people to adopt Christianity as a "shortcut to heaven" (Kehoe 1989, 99-100).

But, on the whole, the cultural flux of the day led to a wave of syncretism, as already mentioned; that is, it led to new religions that combined elements of Native beliefs and European ones in a decidedly non-Christian vein. Among these are the Longhouse religion propagated by the followers of Handsome Lake since 1830; the Ghost Dance religion, which originated among the Paiute in 1892, and spread to Saskatchewan at the turn of the century; and the more short-lived religions propagated by Tenskatawa, "the Shawnee Prophet," until the defeat of his cousin Tecumseh by American forces in the War of 1812, by Louis Riel during the Métis rebellions (Flanagan 1979; Müller 1968; Mol 1985, 53ff) and by a host of less well-known charismatic leaders. Each advocated a renunciation of European practices and a "revitalization" of Native culture (Kehoe 1989; see also Wallace 1956).

The missionaries, of course, believed that their dogma was the one true religion, so that syncretism was for them not acceptable. Conversion of the Native peoples to Christianity, then, when attempted using the resources of the churches alone, was singularly unsuccessful. As late as 1871, the Census noted that virtually all of the

Native inhabitants of the Prairie provinces and the Territories were pagans (Leacy 1983). In those cases where an apparently sincere and total conversion was achieved, there seems to have been widespread "backsliding" in fairly short order (Calloway 1987, 125ff).

As a result, the missionaries (Dyke 1991, 42; Calloway 1987, 125), hit on a method similar to the "reductions" employed by the Jesuits in South America. Converts were isolated in new settlements, away from their own people and from secular European influences; the missionaries undertook intensive efforts to train the young in Christian living, by which was meant formal schooling for children, the practice of agriculture by males on individual plots of land and close regulation of every element of life by the clergy (Calloway 1987, 124).

This new strategy was effective in achieving lasting conversions to Christianity. Adults might come to a mission as "belly Christians," forced there by starvation and epidemic disease or by the instability of the times; but their children were subjected to intensive acculturation quite explicitly aimed at separating them from their language, their way of life and their beliefs.

From the missionaries' point of view, this was the only course available. It appeared obvious to observers at the time that Native peoples were everywhere in decline, overwhelmed by the technology, the weight of numbers, the diseases — and the vices — of the settlers. The very survival of the Native peoples depended on their alliance with missionaries, who would protect them from the depredations of secular Europeans while training them in the arts needed to be independent members of the new society forming in Canada. The physical survival of the Native peoples depended on their cultural annihilation (McMillan 1988, 206ff). Regrettable though that was, at least the "savages" would be Christian, which the missionaries naturally saw as an unalloyed benefit.

This was the beginning of what Dyke (1991) has called "coercive tutelage." Widely imitated by Protestant missionaries in Canada, it centred more on the school than the church, because culture is a complex whole, dependent on a complex interweaving of experience and the language (or, technically, "signifiers") used to order and make sense of that experience.

In time, maintaining the Native peoples in conditions of tutelage came to be official policy in the new Dominion of Canada, embodied in the Indian Act and the vast bureaucracy established to administer it. When the churches operated mission schools, attendance was sporadic at best. Even in the 1960s, the average Native child missed 40 of 180 school days; not surprisingly, fully 94 percent did not graduate and 80 percent repeated grade one at least once (Hawthorne 1967, 130-134). Parents actively resisted the schools' efforts to make English or French the dominant language or to train students in industrial and agricultural arts. In consequence, the churches began to rely on the cooperation of the state — Mounted Police, truant officers and legislation. Constrained as are all government bureaucrats by the need to keep costs low, Indian Affairs agents found it convenient to discharge their treaty obligations regarding the provision of formal education by subsidizing schools established by religious denominations — primarily Anglican, Roman Catholic and the several denominations that later formed the United Church. There was, in essence, a deal between the state and the churches, where the latter were to provide cheap education and social welfare; in return, the churches received virtual carte blanche for religious recruitment (Hawthorne 1967, 46ff).

When the religious fervour of the missionaries was supported by the power of the state — the "coercion" in coercive tutelage — a rapid series of changes followed.

Conversion of Native peoples to Christianity involved separating them from their old beliefs by "proving" these beliefs inferior. Since religion, which is implicit even in secular society (see Chapter 8), is much more pervasive in traditional ones, this separation involved a concerted attack on every aspect of indigenous culture. Rituals like the Potlach and the Sun Dance were prohibited by statute (Dyke 1991, 76-83); artifacts with religious significance — whether real, as in the case of the calumet (often called the "peace pipe"), or only apparent, as with the totem poles of the B.C. coast — were demolished or carted off to museums (McMillan 1988, 209ff); medicine men and other elders were denied the recognition routinely afforded to Christian clergy (Vallee 1976).

In the churches and the schools, traditional beliefs were derided as superstitions or worse, as with the Inuit group described by F. Vallee (1976) who had come to understand their old practices as satanic rituals. "Civilized" dress and language were required even during free time; to minimize the possibility of other influences taking root, students were compelled to live at the school even if the campus was close to their home. Visits with family were strictly limited to as little as two hours every week (Hawthorne 1967), and punishments for infractions were severe (Carlson 1991, 82f).

> My father, who attended Alberni Indian Residential school for four years in the 'twenties, was physically tortured by his teachers for speaking Tseshaht: they pushed sewing needles through his tongue, a routine punishment for language offenders (Smith 1991, 8).

The residential school was a total institution in which students had to adjust their own needs to the demands of the facility. Some schools were badly run, and physical and sexual abuse sometimes took place (Address by Alberta Native leader 1991, 9ff; Somerville 1991). Others were better run:

> At the [residential] school, where we were, we were treated with kindness ... They taught me many things (Carlson 1991, 167).

But whether they treated students well or badly on an individual basis, the schools did, at least ostensibly, effect a dramatic transition in their world view:

> We came out of residential school and we didn't want to be Indian. We were taught Native spirituality was heathen and that the ways of the white people were superior (Carlson 1991, 83).

Thus, after a few generations of this treatment, most Native peoples now report membership in the major Christian religious denominations. The first missionaries to contact most Native peoples were Roman Catholics, Anglicans and members of the denominations that formed the United Church. As is shown in Table 12.1, close to 82 percent of Aboriginal respondents adhered in 1981 to the religions propagated by the missionaries who first contacted their ancestors. For instance, 80 percent of Inuit reported themselves to be Anglicans (Neill 1964; Mol 1985, 59).

These figures cannot be the source of much celebration, even to the most zealous Christians; for along with them came an appalling rise in the indicators of social disorganization or breakdown, the so-called "Indian problem."

Table 12.1 DISTRIBUTION OF NATIVE PEOPLES AND THE TOTAL CANADIAN POPULATION BY RELIGIOUS DENOMINATION, IN 1981 (in percentages).

	Native Peoples	Total Population
Roman Catholic	53.0	47.3
Anglican	20.3	10.1
United Church	8.6	15.6
Pentecostal	3.3	1.4
Baptist	1.3	2.9
Presbyterian	1.1	3.4
Lutheran	0.4	2.9
Other, non-Native	5.0	9.1
Native, Inuit religions	1.0	1.0
No religion	6.0	7.3

Source: Statistics Canada 1986.

THE MODERN PERIOD

Beginning in 1945, but especially during the 1960s and subsequently, relations between the churches and the Native peoples in Canada have been governed by a process of "institutional secularization," in which the longstanding alliance between the state and mainstream Christian denominations has been broken. Sociologists of religion often concern themselves with the phenomenon of secularization (see Chapter 4). Usually defined as the rise of the "nonreligious" or profane, secularization is thought to be particularly advanced in North

America: the functions of religion that Durkheim identified long ago have been largely transferred to institutions other than the churches, or lost altogether. Thus, the state provides discipline through laws and law enforcement; politics and philosophy provide meaning; "sex, drugs and rock and roll" provide euphoria; and nationalism, ethnic identifications and the like provide cohesion or a sense of belonging.

In the *Social Sources of Denominationalism*, Niebuhr (1957; see also Johnson 1963) argues that the established churches themselves accommodate to the secular world. In a secular age, then, they become "junior partners" in the preservation of societal integration by legitimizing the existing order. This works to create "moral communities" within a society; thus, research shows that cities with high church membership rates have lower rates of "social disorganization" – crime and other forms of deviance – than do other cities (Stark et al. 1980; 1983). But Native peoples have relatively high church membership rates, and also high rates of crime, suicide, alcoholism and so on. Clearly, then, the churches do not function as expected in this case.

Members of those societies for whom established churches do not fulfil the functions outlined by Durkheim – euphoric, vitalizing, disciplinary and cohesive – have two choices: they can reject religion altogether, or they can seek other religions. There is little evidence for the rejection by Native peoples of religiosity altogether. Native peoples declaring no religion – the "unchurched" – are somewhat rarer than in the total Canadian population.

This might lead us to look for evidence of sectarian religious innovation. Niebuhr (1957) roots religious and political sectarianism in disprivilege; in a sense, so does Weber (1947) in his discussion of charismatic authority, which is most likely to arise in periods of crisis. Others (for example, Troelstch 1931) suggest that sectarianism reflects social disorganization: a sect is a relatively disorganized religious denomination that is therefore sometimes at odds with the larger society, and that is also therefore shortlived in most cases (since it must either organize better and become a church, or continue on its current course, which may well lead to dissolution). Rodney Stark and William Bainbridge (1985) point out that, especially where state-provided equivalents to the functions of traditional organized religion are not fully satisfactory, sects and cults find converts among the "unchurched."

In these circumstances we should expect to see a plethora of sectarian and cultic religious innovation, especially among religious movements whose orientation to the larger society is extremely retreatist or conflictual. This ought to be all the more true given the rise in the last generation of "self-determination" movements, ranging in shape from the political advocacy groups like the Assembly of First Nations and Inuit Tapirisat to more activist or "militant" organizations like the Mohawk Warriors Society. As these political movements gained prominence, we might have expected to see a shift from involvement in sects to cults; that is, a rejection of Christianity as the "religion of the oppressor" and a corresponding rise of reborn or redirected indigenous religions. Parallel examples would be Black Muslims in the United Sates and Wicca (witchcraft) for feminists.

This has certainly been the case in the United States, where there has been an excess of religious innovations among Native peoples, some of which have spread across the 49th parallel (Kehoe 1989). It is much less true for the First Nations in Canada. There has, it is true, been some growth in sectarian groups, such as Pentacostalism. Most startling of all is how few are those who claim exclusive adherence to a Native belief system; just 4,200 people across the country do so. This is a decline of more than half the 9,000 who had made such a claim in 1971 (Grant 1984).

It seems, then, that however questionable their methods in attaining it, mainstream denominations continue to enjoy all but monopolistic control over the sacred elements of Native peoples' lives.

Religious organizations themselves are not, after all, passive in all of this; they can perceive dissatisfaction among their congregations and respond to it, perhaps by becoming less "accommodating."

That is precisely what has happened. The tendencies noted for Catholicism in Canada apply to the mainstream churches in general: confronted by their own irrelevance to the daily lives of many Canadians, these denominations have undertaken a profound self-examination (Hewitt and Lewis 1988). Each has become, in some sense, more worldly. Each is now more concerned with achieving God's kingdom on earth, and each is less willing to accept the separation of church and state that political philosophy mandates — and the marginalization and impotency of religion that this doctrine entails. In consequence, each has aligned itself with those for whom religion retains more meaning than it does for the privileged. This is the "option for the poor" that is now official Roman Catholic policy, and is echoed by the other mainstream groups as well.

The churches' newfound interest in social justice for Native peoples is therefore a response to secularization in Euro-Canadian society. It has entailed a dramatic repositioning of religious identity in Canada, so that — contrary to Niebuhr's theory — new religions (sects and cults) attract the privileged who sense a lack of religious meaning in their lives (Berger 1967). It is the sectarian bodies that are generally the most conservative, while the established denominations are, ironically, the more liberal.

First Nations concerns are only one among many social-justice initiatives: others include disarmament, advocacy on behalf of immigrants and women, and environmentalism. With all of these, but particularly with the First Nations, the churches' efforts at advocacy have also entailed an extended process of self-criticism, an effort to ensure that the churches' own house is in order so that accusations of hypocrisy cannot be levelled against them.

That process has been painful since, as already noted, proselytization was a process of working hand in hand with the state to undermine Native independence and cultural identity.

The excesses and cruelties of the residential schools have been a target for especially vehement complaint by Native leaders, notably by Phil Fontaine of the Assembly of Manitoba Chiefs. Stung by his criticisms, the Catholic church instituted a Residential Schools project in 1991, aimed at uncovering the full extent of the abuse that occurred in these institutions and the impact on Native students (Somerville 1991).

More generally, however, the churches — beginning with the Anglican church (Anglican Church of Canada 1977) — have sought to distance themselves from the actions of their agents in the past, as if it were possible to have Christianized the First Nations *without* sabotaging their society. The statement of Canadian Conference of Catholic Bishops on Residential Schools, made March 15, 1991, in Saskatoon is fairly typical:

> We are sorry and deeply regret the pain, suffering and alienation that so many experienced. We have heard their cries of distress, feel their anguish, and want to be part of the healing process (p. 10).

In keeping with the renunciation of coercive tutelage, the churches — again aided by the state — have instituted efforts to restore and revitalize a distinctive Native identity. On the churches' part, these involve programs to recruit and train more clergy or other personnel from among Native peoples themselves and the establishment of separate administrative bodies to serve Native peoples exclusively.

The syncretism once so abhorred by missionaries is now official policy among the major denominations. Typified by the Katerai Movement in Roman Catholicism, syncretism now involves incorporating traditional Native and Inuit objects, practices and beliefs into the churches' liturgy and dogma. Thus, the Anglican church provides a specific liturgy for Native peoples, while drums and sweetgrass form part of Catholic mass. Both of these churches also maintain exclusively Native parish organizations, while the United Church has fifty-five Native congregations, most organized into its "All Native Circle Conference" (Kenny 1989, 9).

These innovations have met with some resistance among the faithful (Krotz 1982, 24). The "option for the poor" in Canada is a "top-down" process, instituted by the church elite without much input from the rank-and-file (Hewitt and Lewis 1988). But to a very large extent, they merely provide official sanction for practices that have gone on informally for hundreds of years (for examples see Carlson 1991; Hummelen and Hummelen 1985).

Most surprising have been some of the new directions in theology that the social-justice initiative has produced. Catholic theologians such as Karl Rahner, for instance, declare that the faithful of other religious traditions are "anonymous Christians," who can attain salvation through adherence to the tenets of their own faiths.

The United Church's Clifford Hospital and Wilfred Cantwell Smith go even further, stating that God's revelation to humankind has been a "pluriform" one, so that Christian and non-Christian are equivalent (Hospital 1989). By implication, then, *any* effort at proselytisation, no matter how sensitive, denies the value of non-Christian world views, is culturally disruptive and therefore necessarily wrong.

The extent to which the practical policies of the churches are mere tokenism is not, at present, clear. In *Prison of Grass* (1975), Harold Adams expresses deep suspicion of such policies, equating them with the "opiate" Marx declared all religion to be. Adams asserts that support for an indigenous religious revival serves to direct attention and effort away from more practical matters like land claims. This stands in sharp contrast to Harold Cardinal's view that a distinct religion is essential to Native peoples' "rebirth" and liberation from "the stultifying, century-long hold the so-called Christian denominations have imposed on them" (1976, 222).

If what Cardinal says is true, is there any evidence for the rise of such a religion? The figures cited in Table 12.1 appear to discount this. However, these figures should be taken with a grain of salt. Mol (1985, 59), for one, questions the depth of belief of the converts and their offspring, while Kehoe (1989, 132) — despite the mere 4,200 claiming adherence to Native and Inuit religions — proclaims that indigenous and syncretistic non-Christian beliefs remain vigorous, at least on the prairies. Since these religions were suppressed until quite recently — the Ghost Dance religion, for instance, called forth military intervention leading to the massacre at Wounded Knee, South Dakota, in 1890 — it would not be surprising if adherents kept their membership to themselves (Kehoe 1989, Chapter 10).

With these cautions in mind (and although the latest census data have not yet been released), it still might be possible to speak of a resurgence of interest in Inuit and Native religion over the last decade, accompanying a sharp increase in First Nations activism. Thus, the militant American Indian Movement officially adopted the Ghost Dance religion (as portrayed in Niehardt's 1932 book *Black Elk Speaks*), and Handsome Lake's Longhouse religion played a major role in the confrontation at Oka in the summer of 1990 (Smith 1991).

Christian missionary activity has represented the extension of an essentially foreign world view to groups who are, by any measure, among this country's most deprived peoples. Following standard church-sect theory, we might have expected to find that the churches were mere agents of a triumphant state, junior partners in the annihilation of Native cultures. We might further have expected that a series of sectarian and cultist groups would have formed to help Native peoples cope with their "relative deprivation" (Aberle 1962) and to "revitalize" their culture (Wallace 1956).

The current reality, however, is a bit more complex. While some "revitalization" movements persist (strongest among them the Longhouse religion), it is hard to say whether they are growing or declining in adherents. Further, they are largely a product of the eighteenth and nineteenth centuries, and/or they are imports from the United States. All, in any case, are distinctly in the minority, if the data are to be trusted. Yet Native peoples remain rather less secularized than the Canadian population, and spirituality seems to be of central importance to Native peoples' lives. Ironically, then, First Nations cultural revitalization appears to be occurring in large part through the medium of the very churches that sought so strenuously to destroy those cultures in the past.

For Further Reading

Cardinal, Harold. 1976. *The Rebirth of Canada's Indians.* Edmonton: Hurtig.

Hultkranz, A. 1979. *The Religion of the American Indians.* Berkeley, CA: University of California Press.

Kehler, L. (ed.). 1969. *The Church and the Original Canadians.* Winnipeg: Mennonite Central Committee.

McMillan, A. 1988. *Native Peoples and Cultures of Canada.* Vancouver: Douglas and McIntyre.

Kehoe, A. 1989. *The Ghost Dance: Ethnohistory and Revitalization.* Fort Worth, TX: Holt, Rinehart and Winston.

Chapter 13

The Quest for the Just Society: Canadian Catholicism in Transition

W.E. Hewitt

Since the late nineteenth century and the relentless advance of secular ideology and practice, the Roman Catholic church as an institution has made a concerted effort to make its religious teachings speak with greater authority to the problems of an increasingly complex and divided social world. This quest for social relevance is demonstrated most recently in the documents of Rome's Second Vatican Council of Catholic bishops (1962-1965), which called for significant changes in the church's traditionally conservative social and political outlook. The Second Vatican Council effectively opened the doors to greater participation in church governance on the part of ordinary lay people and, perhaps more importantly, paved the way for direct church involvement in promoting social justice throughout the world (see Abbott 1966; MacEoin 1966).

In the sociological literature, as elsewhere, doctrinal changes on this scale have often been interpreted as having a profound effect not only on the attitudes and behaviours of individual believers, but upon the social world as a whole. In his now famous work, *The Protestant Ethic and the Spirit of Capitalism*, Max Weber (1958a) argues that the shape of the modern capitalist economic order was very much conditioned by the unique ethical prescriptions of the Protestant churches that emerged during the Reformation. There is precedent, then, to surmise that the "new" ethical doctrine of Catholicism defined by the Second Vatican Council, stressing cooperation, sharing and, above all, social justice, might also possess world-transforming potential. It might even exceed that of Protestantism, given the monolithic structure of the Catholic church, the power of its hierarchy and, not least, the church's numerical strength, estimated at over 850 million worldwide (Barrett 1982, 791).

It is in the developing world — where political oppression and inequality are often institutionalized — where the Catholic church's new social teaching has been seen as having the greatest potential for social transformation (see Gannon 1989; Levine 1980). Nevertheless, inspired by the Second Vatican Council, the experience of their sister churches in the Third World, and social and political injustice within their own societies, churches in at least a few developed nations have also attracted attention in recent years for their activities on behalf of the oppressed (Cox 1984; Hewitt and Lewis 1988; Varacalli 1983). One example of this tendency is the Catholic Church of Canada. Indeed, its commitment to improving the lives of the socially and politically marginalized, as evidenced in a variety of statements authored by the episcopate on the social-justice front since at least 1970, can be seen as a nothing less than a world-transforming ethical doctrine, designed to forge a new and socially responsible citizenry.

The institutional leadership (vested in the Canadian Conference of Catholic Bishops) seems anxious to confront the evils of an increasingly secular world through strident calls for social action on a number of specific fronts. Such calls, however, have been less than fully carried out through the development of concrete strategies and programs. Consequently, the world-transforming potential of the Canadian Catholic church has been, and is likely to remain, limited.

RELIGION AND SOCIAL CHANGE: A BRIEF OVERVIEW

Within the sociology of religion, the relationship between matters of faith and social change, in general terms, has been contentious. What we see is a very broad spectrum of opinion, from the argument that religion has little or no effect upon societal transformation to arguments suggesting that religious ideas may pave the way for entirely new forms of social organization.

One of the better known categorical statements on the matter from the "negative" end of this spectrum was voiced by Karl Marx (1958a). For Marx, religion is in essence epiphenomenal — in other words, simply a product of the broader struggle of social classes to control societal resources. Within this class struggle, religion is a form of cultural "property" that is used by the dominant classes in society to help preserve social relations of commodity production and distribution favourable to themselves. The principal use of religion lies in its ability to obscure the true nature of class dominance and conflict, and thus pacify of the propertyless. In Marx's words, religion is the "opium of the masses." Thus, in its fundamental essence, it does not so much contribute to social change as help ensure that the status quo of dominance/subordination is maintained.

Although largely opposed to Marx's conflict perspective, developmental theorists of the middle twentieth century, such as Rostow (1956) and Moore (1965), also adopt a somewhat negative view of the potential of religion for effecting change. In their examination of societies in transition to "modernity," these analysts tend to view social, economic and political development as occurring largely in conformity with patterns previously established in industrial Europe and North America. The societies of Asia and Latin America, for example, modernize as they are able to offer universal education, encourage entrepreneurship, and also − not least importantly − overcome cultural barriers to progress. Religion, for its part, represents precisely one of these cultural barriers, insofar as it may preclude participation in economic life, as would be the case of religious proscriptions against the charging of interest (usury).

More recently, however, such visions of religion's negative impact on societal change have come under challenge. Oddly enough, one challenge has come from the ranks of those adopting a Marxist perspective on society. While largely upholding Marx's interpretation of religion's narcotic effect, Italian Marxist Antonio Gramsci has suggested that religion may, under certain circumstances, play a key role in social change. In essence, this role is related to the thought and action of intellectuals in society. Under normal circumstances, Gramsci claims, intellectuals play a key role in maintaining existing social relations by articulating positions that defend the integrity of dominant institutions or classes. However, as at least some interpreters of Gramsci have argued (see Fulton 1987), some intellectuals − including those within the church − may, under specific historical circumstances, cross class lines to assist the just cause of the subordinate classes. Potentially, therefore, religion may possess revolutionary consequences.

This same argument has been developed further by contemporary liberation theology. Many of its proponents have argued that religion can and does promote change as historical and social factors forge a link between the poor and oppressed and intellectuals within the churches (see Ferm 1986; Planas 1986). For example, it has been argued that the progressivism of Latin American Catholic churches is directly attributable to popular pressure — stimulated by repressive political regimes and extreme social inequality — for the ecclesia to adopt the social-justice cause of the downtrodden.

Without question, however, the most salient and enduring interpretation of religion's complex relationship to social change has been developed by Max Weber. As part of a much larger body of work dealing with the nature of rationalization and the development of modern capitalism, Weber's *Protestant Ethic and the Spirit of Capitalism* (1958a) stands as Weber's testament to the power of religious ideas over individual lives. In the *Protestant Ethic*, Weber argues that the ethical doctrine of Protestantism, as developed and disseminated in the teachings of Martin Luther and especially John Calvin, was conducive to that spirit necessary for the successful undertaking of capitalistic enterprise. Weber claims that, following prescriptions established by Luther, the Protestant was ethically called to work in the service of God. This work, moreover, was to be conducted diligently and methodically, as a way of pleasing God. Later, under the influence of Calvin, this diligence in work became a means of relieving anxiety stirred by Calvinist ideas regarding the divine predestination of souls to heaven or hell. The relentless activity spawned by these teachings, Weber further suggests, led to the accumulation of considerable wealth among the faithful. In accordance with the dictates of the Protestant ethic, however, the profits of one's work could not be used for frivolous ends. Rather, they were to be reinvested in further productive enterprise. Thus, the modern capitalist system, with its workaholic and expansionary demands, was, in Weber's view, a product of religious exigencies.

Weber's thesis has not, of course, gone without criticism. Milton Yinger (1957), for example, has suggested that Weber essentially failed to appreciate the social and economic context of the Reformation period, and thus to fully assess the impact of secular or nonchurch developments when discussing the rise of the Protestant ethic. As a result of this omission, adds R.H. Tawney (1938), Weber may have in the end mistaken cause for effect. Rather than conditioning the economic order, Protestant teaching may have merely been a *response* to the capitalist advance in Western Europe. In light of the new economic environment, in other words, Luther and Calvin may simply have been trying to forge a new Christian ethic appropriate to the times.

Another common criticism is that Weber maintained a faulty understanding of both Catholic and Protestant doctrine, and that consequently, the unique world-transforming character of Protestantism he described may have been overstated. Critics have suggested, as well, that Weber's distinction between modern and earlier forms of capitalism is spurious, suggesting consequently that the essential features of capitalism as we know it today existed long before Protestantism, and hence the Protestant ethic, ever arose (comment by Giddens in Weber 1958a, 11-12).

Finally, there are those who argue that Weber failed in the end to make the empirical connection between the ethical doctrine of Protestantism and modern capitalism. Tawney (1938; 1957), for instance, has suggested that the teachings of Calvin himself are not necessarily the same as that body of thought that came to be known as Calvinism. Thus, the ethical doctrine of Protestantism may have been less stringently tied to Calvin's original teachings than Weber had supposed. Moreover, Tawney (1938) suggests that Protestant teaching was understood and acted upon differently among different groups in different societies, thus potentially forging a significant gap between Protestant teaching and actual social practice.

This last question, that of the relationship between religious teaching and societal practice, is especially important to an understanding of the ability of modern churches to forge social change. To be sure, the Catholic church in Canada, for example, may have laid out a very clear set of guidelines for ethical behaviour, which seek to promote a uniquely Christian ethic and banish social sin — in the form of social, economic and political inequality — from this world. Yet, in assessing the contribution of such prescriptions for social change, one must inquire as to how, and in what measure, they have been acted upon by the faithful at large.

Social Justice and the Canadian Churches

Collectively, the mainstream Christian churches in Canada have a long and noteworthy history of involvement in social-justice matters.

For the most part, this involvement can be traced to the rise of the Social Gospel Movement during the first two decades of this century. According to Crysdale (1976, 425-426) this movement embraced a wide variety of primarily Protestant clergy and active lay people, united by an emphasis on one particular Christian requirement: the "responsibility of each person for his neighbours and for the development of just social and political institutions."

At heart, the thrust of the Social Gospel movement in Canada was reformist (Crysdale 1976, 426). Nevertheless, due to the unique social and economic circumstances of the area, it attained revolutionary overtones in certain parts of the Canadian West, especially Saskatchewan. Owing in part to the "sympathy of British settlers for labour and socialism," the failure of the local wheat crop and sagging world markets for the region's agricultural products, the Social Gospel here took a radical turn to the left. Among the movement's members, calls for economic restructuring, including the transfer of property from private to public hands, were not unknown.

Whether in its reformist or revolutionary moulds, however, the movement was not overly successful, and by 1920, it began to fade. Importantly, though, it still played an influential role in legitimating socialist ideology in later years, especially during the Great Depression. This role was perhaps evidenced most clearly in the case of the Co-operative Commonwealth Federation (CCF, later the New Democratic Party or NDP), whose base and platform owed a great deal to Social Gospel thinking. The Social Gospel also lived on within formal church structures, representing an important current within mainstream Protestant groupings, and especially the United Church (Crysdale 1976, 428).

Today, certainly, the legacy of the Social Gospel lives on in a range of church activities and proclamations on social issues. These have included calls by the large Protestant churches for government negotiations on Native land claims, calls for action on unemployment and opposition to Canadian involvement in foreign wars (see Williams 1984). Within the United Church in particular, the call for social justice was dramatically and most recently expressed in the church's decision to remove barriers to the ministry on the basis of sexual orientation (see Chapter 14).

Roman Catholic involvement with social-justice matters in Canada has until very recently been somewhat limited. During the heyday and immediate aftermath of the Social Gospel period, the Catholic hierarchy voiced a deep suspicion of left-wing movements, and in some cases (especially in Quebec), explicitly denounced socialist groups — in particular, the CCF (Baum 1980, 119; Mol 1988, 253). Such tendencies were largely in keeping with the church's historic role in Canadian society, which has been described as preservationist — meaning oriented towards maintaining the social, economic and political status quo (Mol 1988).

After 1930, however, participation by ordinary Catholics in both the CCF and other socialist groups was not unknown, especially in English Canada where official hostility to the left was more muted. Moreover, within the institutional Catholic church itself, there is at least some evidence of concerns for social justice dating to the 1890s. Important Papal documents, such as Pope Leo XII's *Rerum Novarum* (1891) and Pius XI's *Quadragesimo Anno* (1931), stressed the need for social justice, and called for harmony between social classes. Such teaching helped give rise to a limited number of Catholic social-justice initiatives, such as the Antigonish movement. Spearheaded by Father Moses Coady, this movement led to the formation of a large number of consumer and producer cooperatives throughout the Maritime region during the 1930s and 1940s (see Baum 1980, 191-204). Although perhaps not directly stimulated by Papal teaching, notable as well have been the various Catholic cells in 1960s Quebec that combined nationalist zeal with the political cause of socialism.

This emphasis on social justice, especially as it manifested itself at the level of the institution, nevertheless tended to present a somewhat organic view of society, emphasizing social unity and integrity as opposed to change (Baum 1984, 22). It was only during the 1970s that the church began to adopt a more critical, conflictual approach to both Canadian society and the problems that afflicted it. This new approach, claims Baum (1984, 27-28), was influenced by a number of factors. These include the bishops' growing awareness of the Third World churches' struggle for popular liberation, the move towards consideration of social-justice issues within Canadian churches generally, and not least, Vatican teaching emerging in the wake of the Second Vatican Council, especially after 1971, and Pope Paul VI's *Justice in the World*.

THE NEW SOCIAL-ETHICAL DOCTRINE OF CANADIAN CATHOLICISM

Despite its relatively recent appearance, the shift to the left within the upper hierarchy has been a development of no small importance within Canadian society. The church is, after all, the largest single religious organization in the country. Some 12 million Canadians, nearly 50 percent of the population, identify themselves as Catholic. In terms of institutional strength, the church possesses some 120 bishops, 12,000 priests and 40,000 men and women religious, who operate from a territorial base that includes 17 archdioceses and 47 dioceses (*Canadian Catholic Church Directory* 1988). Consequently, when the leaders of the church speak, Canadians, especially Canadian Catholics, tend to at least listen; and where social-justice matters are concerned, they have spoken reams.

Even before the Second Vatican Council, in such statements as "Christian Citizenship in Practice" (1956)[1], "Collaboration between Management and Labour" (1959) and "The Social Teaching of the Church" (1961), the leadership of the church, as vested in the Canadian Conference of Catholic Bishops (CCCB), had already initiated an attempt to educate Catholics about church teaching with respect to social justice. During the 1960s, after the close of the council, these initial statements were followed by documents address-ing social and political issues even more directly, and often on a global scale. CCCB pronouncements such as "Poverty in Canada" (1966) and "On Development and Peace" (1968) outlined the nature of social problems in some detail and affirmed the church's role as a defender of the downtrodden. This tendency was further strengthened in important documents subsequently prepared by specific episcopal committees. Among the most important of these were "The Church's Solidarity with Workers and with Victims of Social Injustice" (1968) and "Liberation in a Christian Perspective" (1970) by the Episcopal Commission for Social Affairs.

It was after 1970, however, that the most strident and controversial episcopal declarations began to appear. In a string of documents produced by the CCCB or its administrative board, including "Sharing National Income" (1972), "From Words to Action: On Christian Political and Social Responsibility" (1976) and "A Society to be Transformed" (1977), the Roman Catholic church launched a frontal attack on the Canadian social, economic and political establishment. These and other statements also called, in no uncertain terms, for a fundamental restructuring of Canadian society, so as to make it more compatible with Christian ideals. As the bishops stated in their "Unemployment: The Human Costs":

> The Gospel calls us to prepare for God's Kingdom by participating in the building of a society that is truly based on justice and love. In Canada today, this vision includes a more equitable distribution of wealth and power among the people, and the development of this country's resources to serve basic human needs (CCCB 1980).

Throughout the 1980s, these trends continued, with the release of some of the most focused and explicit episcopal statements yet witnessed — most of them prepared by the CCCB's Social Affairs Commission. This commission's "Ethical Reflections on the Economic Crisis" (1982), for example, offered a stinging attack on government inaction during the economic recession of the time, and even laid out a program for social and economic reform. Still another document, "Free Trade: At What Cost?," released in 1987, decried the Canadian government's intention to remove trade barriers with the United States, citing detrimental effects the plan would have on employment and social programs.

Collectively, these various statements and documents constitute nothing less than a type of ethical doctrine — directed not only towards Catholics, but to Christians in general. In essence, the good Christian is called upon by the Canadian Catholic church to maintain a clear vision of the structure of injustice and how it is maintained; to ally himself/herself with like-minded individuals to discuss the nature and consequences of this reality; and then to work to replace unjust structures with just ones — to create, in other words, the Kingdom of Heaven on Canadian soil.

The simple existence of such a doctrine, however, does not imply acceptance or compliance by the faithful. Certainly, in their own detailed assessment of the Weberian position on religion and social change, Weber's critics were fully aware of this disjuncture. It is equally apparent in the Canadian case. In fact, there is considerable evidence suggesting that the ethical doctrine of the bishops may not have captured the hearts and minds of individual Catholics to any appreciable extent. Consequently, the potential of the doctrine to effect real change has been limited.

INSTITUTIONAL, SOCIETAL AND LAY CATHOLIC RESPONSES
TO THE BISHOPS' TEACHING

Among church-based personnel at least, the bishops' ethical teaching appears to have been received with considerable enthusiasm. As part of his study of Catholic responses to the abortion issue in Canada, Michael Cuneo argues that social progressivism has, in fact, "emerged as the elite orthodoxy of Canadian Catholicism," insofar as "its symbols, language, and presuppositions have been adopted by many religious orders, academics, and chancery officials" (1989, 157).

While somewhat sparse, research from individual dioceses confirms Cuneo's contention. A 1991 survey[2] of 243 church officials conducted in the diocese of London, Ontario, for example, which included priests, heads of religious orders, high school and university chaplains, and members of the bishop's advisory council, revealed a very high degree of conformity to the social-justice teachings of the CCCB. Ninety-four percent of these respondents, for example, agreed with the bishops' designation of social inequality as a sin; 92 percent agreed with the bishops' call for action on unemployment; 82 percent concurred in the bishops' statements on the need for settlement of Native land claims; and 86 percent believed the bishops' calls for respect for the environment to be appropriate.

Reaction to the bishops' calls for a new social order from segments of society other than Catholic lower officialdom, however, have been mixed. For their part, the Canadian media, political and business establishments have viewed church innovation on the social-justice front rather negatively. Over the years, newspaper editorials have condemned the bishops' concerns as uninformed, misplaced or misguided. Politicians have argued that the Catholic church has no place in commenting on affairs of state; business people have suggested that the bishops lack sufficient knowledge of economic matters to comment upon current or potential fiscal arrangements (see Baum 1984, 20-21; Block 1983).

Within the church's own constituency, the response to the new

Catholic social teaching among ordinary lay Catholics has been difficult to gauge. Informal lay Catholic involvement in those specific areas of social justice mentioned by the bishops is far from unknown. In the large and diverse archdiocese of Toronto, for example, lay Catholics are active in a number of groups and activities, among which are social-justice worker cells and co-op businesses that hire ex-offenders. There are also informal networks that mobilize around specific issues, such as the environment. Lay Catholics also participate in a range of inter-church organizations and committees, including the Coalition for Human Rights in Latin America, the Ecumenical Forum and GATT-Fly (formed to discuss world trade issues). Toronto is also home to *Catholic New Times*, a critical Catholic newspaper that examines issues ranging from women's rights to the fortunes of Latin-American basic Christian communities (small faith groups oriented towards social action).

Nevertheless, studies that have specifically examined the impact of episcopal statements on lay Catholics generally are rare. For the most part, though, there is a strong sense among observers of the Canadian church scene that the institution and its leaders have largely failed to reach the faithful in large numbers. Although he is a strong supporter of the bishops' social teaching, Gregory Baum (1986, 64), for example, admits that the new orientation of the Canadian episcopate has been taken up only by a minority, and thus the concrete impact of church teaching in Canadian society has been marginal. "In Canada and the U.S." states Baum (1986, 67), "the minority which permits itself to be inspired by this teaching represents largely church people; that is to say, people who have, or have had, a special relation to church organizations." If Baum's analysis is correct, it may be further observed that the body from which this "minority" is recruited is itself dwindling. As Bibby's (1987) work shows, only about 35 percent of Canadian Roman Catholics attend church regularly.

Those few social-scientific studies examining lay Catholic affinity for episcopal social teaching tend to mirror Baum's observation. In a 1985 study conducted in the Archdiocese of Toronto, few Catholics were found to have been moved to action by the bishops' episcopal teaching on social justice. Despite the rhetorical barrage in recent years, of 400 Catholics surveyed by Gallup (1985) — which conducted the poll for the local church — only 6 percent reported that receiving leadership on social and political issues from the church was impor-

264 The Sociology of Religion

tant to them. Thirty-five percent indicated that it was not important.

THE GAP BETWEEN WORDS AND ACTION

Given the organizational presence of the church, and the strength of
the bishops' rhetorical push for social justice, it is difficult to understand why the bishops' ethical doctrine appears not to have taken
hold among the laity on a broader scale. To some extent, the bishops'
negative assessment of the Canadian political and economic leadership — which some Catholics may find offensive — may play a role
here, but clearly, other factors that are much closer to home are also
at work.

One church observer who has commented on this issue is Baum,
who, while noting the strength of the bishops' rhetoric, has openly
questioned the bishops' collective base-line resolve to see changes
actually brought about. "If church leaders want to promote radical
social teaching," he states, "then this can be effective only if they are
also willing to engage themselves in constructing a new organizational
base for this" (1986, 67). The fact is, however, as Baum himself
suggests, that institutional leaders have been reluctant to place its
formidable resources at the service of the justice cause.

What we see, then, is a church leadership that, while verbally
committed to a new society in Canada, has settled into a kind of
complacency where action on social justice is concerned. As Cuneo
notes, "Social Justice Catholicism has lost much of its radical tincture
and has settled into familiar domesticity" (1989, 157). Moreover, he
states:

> As in the case of any orthodoxy, adherence to it often involves little
> more than sending out the correct signals, learning the appropriate
> terminology, and displaying good intentions. Despite its rhetoric of
> radical political engagement — to which only a virtuoso minority are
> personally committed — it has largely become a viewpoint that may be
> subscribed to without the forfeiture of middle-class comforts, career
> opportunities, or social standing.

Given this situation, the chances of motivating the laity, and thus in
turn of involving them directly in the construction of the just society,
are greatly diminished.

Upon closer examination of the bishops' social-justice program, the gap between rhetoric and world-transforming action is certainly evident. This is not to say, however, that the church has developed *no* action-oriented strategies for enhancing justice. Indeed, compared with its counterparts in Europe and North America, the Canadian episcopal conference has developed more than a few concrete initiatives. What may be called into question, however, given the pattern and depth of their implementation, are the scope and effectiveness of such programs.

One important agency established by the CCCB to promote social justice in Canada is the Canadian Catholic Organization for Development and Peace (CCODP). Mandated to promote international cooperation to fight underdevelopment, the CCODP has undertaken since its inception in 1967 to educate Canadians about the reality, causes and consequences of world poverty. With a yearly budget of some 16 million dollars, it frequently sponsors small-scale development projects in underdeveloped countries. Currently, CCODP has some 2,500 volunteer members in 278 local groups, and maintains representative bodies in 50 of the 64 Canadian dioceses (*Development and Peace* 1988, 8).

Still another vehicle supported by the church for the carrying out of its social-justice agenda has been the Social Affairs Commission of the CCCB. Having operated in various forms since the 1950s, the commission is currently formed of eight bishops, and maintains a permanent secretariat — the Social Affairs Office — to put its directives into action.

The social-justice concerns of the commission fall into three program or target areas (see ECSA 1984). The first area concerns questions of faith and justice, and the relationship in general between religion and secular practice in the social and political spheres. The second area is justice in Canada and deals with issues of regional inequality, Native people, urban poverty and so forth. The third area is justice in the Third World and involves issues such as human rights, world peace and environmental protection.

In each of these areas, the commission, through its national office, undertakes a variety of activities following a methodology that roughly resembles the "see-judge-act" strategy developed by the Catholic Action movement and later propagated by Latin American liberation theology (see Cleary 1985, 63-65). To begin with, the commission maintains a social research function, gathering information on issues of concern (for example, urban poverty). Secondly, it attempts to educate Catholics and other Canadians as to the extent to which problems exist. This is usually accomplished through the publication of statements and documents, such as "Ethical Reflections on the Economic Crisis." Finally, the commission stimulates concrete action through various social outreach strategies. For example, it seeks representation on relevant social-policy bodies or inter-church committees; it networks with various organizations and agencies already active on projects related to the commission's priority areas; and it attempts to establish and maintain communication links with popular associations such as labour unions, women's groups, ecumenical organizations and church groups[3] (ECSA 1984).

One last area where the institutionalization of social-justice concerns has been attempted by the leadership is through the promotion of small, social-action-oriented faith groups known as basic Christian communities. Indeed, in the CCCB's "From Words to Action" (1976), parish and local community groups are seen as playing a vital role in the fight for social transformation, by denouncing injustices, "speaking the truth to those in power," and directly participating in "actions to change the policies of governments, corporations, and other institutions that cause human suffering."

Sympathetic observers of the Canadian basic community phenomenon have identified lay communities in Canada existing among all social classes, and attuned to a variety of issues. According to Clarke (1981), for example, there exist, on the one hand, a number of "popular Christian communities" — composed of factory workers, Native people, the poor, refugees and immigrants — that focus on issues of immediate importance to their participants. On the other hand, Clarke has discovered a variety of "progressive Christian communities" — formed of more affluent Canadians — with an interest in more global issues, such as industrialization, food and energy production, development, regional disparities and human rights.

Viewed both individually and collectively, however, these various programs and strategies (from CCODP to the basic communities) appear to form far from a stalwart front in promoting social-justice ends. Although it has been a strong supporter of overseas development projects, CCODP has maintained only a skeletal presence where public education in Canada is concerned. In 1989-1990, public awareness programs accounted for only 14 percent of organizational disbursements, an amount only slightly greater than that used for administrative purposes ("Development and Peace worries" 1991). Moreover, CCODP maintains educational coordinators or "animators" in only nineteen of Canada's sixty-four Roman Catholic dioceses; and while it is true that these are spread out rather evenly given the distribution of the Catholic population, the ratio of dioceses to "animators" in all regions is typically above three to one.

The national Social Affairs Office, similarly, has been less than effective in engaging ordinary Catholics in social-justice activities. This is because, according to the terms of the Social Affairs Commission's mandate, it is prohibited from interfering, directly or indirectly, in local church affairs. Thus, if the bishops decide not to involve themselves or the laity in social-justice matters within their own dioceses, the Social Affairs Office has no power to circumvent diocesan authorities to stimulate or assist social-justice initiatives. As a result, the ratio of dioceses to social-justice offices in Canada has remained at approximately two to one, with over 300,000 Catholics served by each office. Outside Quebec, the ratio is much higher, at approximately five to one.

Finally, the basic Christian communities have remained largely unexploited by church leaders as a means for furthering social-justice ends. In fact, although accounts of grassroots community activity have been provided in generic form by authors such as Clarke, and occasionally appear in Catholic media sources such as *Catholic New Times*, the dimensions and scope of the phenomenon have not even been definitively established by the church.

Viewed from the subnational or diocesan level, other program weaknesses are also in evidence. As mentioned previously, church personnel in the diocese of London appear strongly committed to the social-justice ends of the national bishops' conference. Nevertheless, the local commitment to concrete social action is less than we might expect. Only about one-quarter of diocesan pastors, chaplains and organizational heads are presently involved in any social-justice and related groups. As a result, only about one-quarter of parishes in the diocese possess CCODP discussion groups, just one-third have social-justice committees and one-third have refugee assistance groups. Further, basic communities of any quality are present in only 6 percent of parishes. By contrast, almost 100 percent have local branches of the Catholic Women's League, and about three-quarters have a local Knights of Columbus or St. Vincent de Paul group, the more traditional Catholic groups.

Often as well, simply possessing a social-justice group doesn't necessarily imply a strong commitment to social-justice action. Some social-action offices are clearly more activist than others. At one end of the spectrum, there do exist "ideal-typical" social-justice offices such as those found in the dioceses of Victoria or Charlottetown. In the case of Victoria, the local justice office is run by a committee of fourteen lay people and clergy and has involved hundreds in its initiatives. Formed in 1979 to deal with issues of importance to local Catholics, the office has concerned itself with local problems of poverty, exploitation of Native people, militarization and workers' rights, but it also maintains a direct interest in the social, political and economic problems of the Third World. In order to deal with these issues head-on, the Victoria office has been involved in action on several fronts. To begin with, it has worked to establish church and ecumenical coalitions and political movements (for example, against militarization of Vancouver Island, or in favour of Native land claims) and has cooperated with others already in existence. Secondly, the office has sponsored a campaign for popular education with respect to social-justice issues. To this end, it publishes its own social-justice newsletter, *Snuwugul* (meaning "justice" in the Cowichan language), and occasional pamphlets explaining the work of the local justice committee and office and/or advocating support for existing causes. Finally, the office facilitates the discussion of social-justice matters at the parish level, by stimulating parishioners' awareness of problems that directly affect them or their neighbours, such as housing problems or discrimination against Natives. There has also been an attempt to establish local social-justice committees, which now operate in about half of Victoria's parishes.

Yet hardly all social-justice offices in Canada operate in this way. In many dioceses, the social-action "office" is not much more than a contact person, working with little or nothing in the way of material resources. In still other dioceses, there is even some question that local social-justice entities are involved at all in action on behalf of the socially disadvantaged. In Toronto, for example, there appears to be very little attempt on the part of the social-action office to stimulate any level of lay or religious involvement in attacking the root causes of social injustice. Unlike Victoria, what exists here at the level of the institutional church is really just a one-person show designed primarily to attract government funding to limited projects (primarily in the housing area) that are essentially assistive or charitable in nature.

CONCLUSION

In Weber's view, the spirit of modern capitalism was forged on the anvil of the ethical doctrine of Protestantism, which in turn emerged as a response to the corruption of medieval Catholicism. In effect, Protestantism served as an incentive to the faithful to engage in activities of a world-transforming quality.

As part of its own answer to the corruption of modern-day society, the world-transforming capabilities of Canadian Catholicism, however, can be seen as having no such parallel effect. Indeed, as student of the Canadian churches John R. Williams notes, the social-justice statements of either the Catholic or its sister churches appear in the end to have had "little success in making Canada a just society" (1984, 11).

The problem is not a lack of strident language. The bishops' statements speak with an unparalleled passion for the renewal of society and the implantation of a Kingdom of Heaven on earth. Nevertheless, the strident character of such language has not been translated into strong institutional forms, thus inducing the faithful to act. The institutional church's potential for forging the new Jerusalem is then clearly limited.

Moreover, in the years ahead, any potential the Catholic church may possess in this regard is likely to be reduced further still. The church's flirtation with social-justice issues increasingly appears to be falling prey to powerful conservative tendencies within the national and international Catholic churches. Indeed, in the final issue of the much-respected journal *Ecumenist*, Baum (1991b) laments the increasing conservatism of the Western churches in general; because of it, he believes, their concern for social justice is now at an end. "The new politico-economic situation and the corresponding cultural trends," he states, "have ... affected the life and the policies of the Christian churches. Retrenchment is the order of the day." "In the

Catholic Church," Baum continues, "the new emphasis on identity is making the hierarchy more self-involved, putting brakes on its involvement with other churches, its association with other religions, and its cooperation with secular movements. Fear is becoming the church's counsellor" (1991b, 2-3).

Evidence of this retrenchment within the Canadian Catholic church is readily at hand. In late 1989, for example, the CCCB determined that statements and documents released by the formerly outspoken Social Affairs Commission should be both fewer in number and subject to approval in principle by the CCCB's general assembly. Previously, such releases needed only the approval of the CCCB's president. In a further development, a number of social-justice offices in the dioceses have reportedly been slated for closure ("Canadian bishops renovate" 1989). One much publicized closing has been in the diocese of Victoria, where in 1991, the social-justice office director was dismissed. Ostensibly, this was due to a contract dispute. Yet, since the director's departure, the local bishop has openly questioned the need for maintaining a justice office at all. Instead, he has suggested, in rather vague tones, social-justice concerns should be incorporated into all diocesan organizations ("Szollosy Dismissal" 1991).

Does this ultimately signify the failure of Canadian Catholicism's attempt to adapt to modern times? Perhaps, but then again, perhaps not. The institutional church and its leaders may simply have misread the current milieu and the needs of the faithful. Social analysts and forecasters, for example, have pointed increasingly to the growth of not just social and economic needs among Canadians, but personal spiritual needs as well — needs that are perhaps not satisfied within the context of existing church structures. As Bibby has suggested (1987), what we may see in the years ahead, then, is an increasing emphasis within both the Catholic and other churches on providing spiritual services to the faithful, alongside a growing tendency to leave those things that are Caesar's unto Caesar.

Notes

[1]This reference and others listed on pages 260-261 are taken from Sheridan 1987.
[2]Unpublished survey conducted by W.E. Hewitt.
[3]Taken from an interview with Tony Clarke, Director of Social Affairs Office, CCCB, 30 June 1989.

For Further Reading

Baum, Gregory. 1980. *Catholics and Canadian Socialism*. Toronto: Lorimer.
Gannon, T. 1989. *World Catholicism in Transition*. New York: Macmillan.
Planas, Ricardo. 1986. *Liberation Theology*. Kansas City: Sheed and Ward.
Sheridan, Ed (ed.). 1987. *Do Justice! The Social Teaching of the Canadian Catholic Bishops*. Toronto: Editions Paulines.
Williams, John R. (ed.). 1984. *Canadian Churches and Social Justice*. Toronto: Lorimer.

Chapter 14

The United Church in Crisis[*]

Roger O'Toole, Douglas F. Campbell
John A. Hannigan, Peter Beyer
John H. Simpson[1]

INTRODUCTION

The national constitutional and social crisis facing Canada is paralleled by deep discord within its leading Protestant denomination. As in the nation as a whole, the crisis in the United Church of Canada has not yet run its course and few would wish to predict its final outcome. The crisis centres on the issue of whether professed homosexuals should be allowed ordination to the ministry (see Gault 1988; Shapiro 1990; Riordan 1990). Controversy concerning this matter has been so intense that it has threatened the denomination with the first major schism since its foundation in 1925.[2] The reasons for this are, at one level, fairly obvious and, at another, subtly profound. They may only be disentangled by careful sociological scrutiny combined with historical sensitivity.

Uncovering the roots of this specific struggle in broader intradenominational divisions and social developments may provide an instructive case study of some of the crucial tensions characterizing contemporary Christianity. Though, of necessity, homosexual ordination is thus treated purely as an aspect of "symbolic politics" (see Gusfield 1953), this in no way represents a crude reduction of theological discourse into sociological categories. Internal theological disputes may only be adequately understood, however, if they are appropriately situated in their specific denominational context.

THE ORDINATION CRISIS

On August 24, 1988, in an atmosphere charged with emotional tension, the 32nd General Council of the United Church of Canada affirmed (by a majority of three to one) the proposition that all church members, regardless of sexual orientation, should be eligible to be considered for ordination. Though this resolution was typically swathed in a cushioning compromise formula, its impact was far from blunted. In the interpretation of most observers, the council had undoubtedly voted in principle to allow the ordination of professed and sexually active homosexuals of either gender.[3]

Passage of this resolution had, not surprisingly, been preceded by the intense lobbying, mobilization, promises and threats that might have been anticipated. Indeed, the decision of General Council was, in some respects, simply the final act of a drama that began in February, 1988, with the publication of an internal report that proposed a radically neutral view of human sexual orientation, and that appeared both to depreciate and deprecate the traditionally central role of the family in a sexual context (see "Toward a Christian Understanding" 1988). Heralded on one side as a far-sighted, loving expression of a socially relevant progressive theology, it was vilified on the other as the last straw in liberal theological appeasement of the forces of sin and evil. Opponents of this report lost no time in organizing a "Community of Concern" that threatened mass congregational defections from the United Church fold if its major recommendations received General Council's approval. Though, in fact, the report as a whole was rejected, its most contentious proposal concerning homosexual eligibility for ordination received decisive approval, albeit in modified form.

DENOMINATIONALISM AND THE UNITED CHURCH

As Canada's most indigenous mainstream religious body, the United Church is frequently regarded as being "typically Canadian" not least because its origins, like those of the nation itself, lie in merger and compromise. Rooted in such stereotypical Canadian virtues, this organization stands as a shining example of a denomination in the sociological sense of the term (Martin 1962). As depicted by sociologists, the ideal-typical denomination walks the tightrope of a theological, social and political *via media* in a way that distinguishes it from both sect and church in their pure forms.[4] Making no claim to a unique and absolute truth, the denomination regards itself as merely possessing one of the keys to heaven. This tolerance towards its rivals is replicated within its own organization, where democracy, pragmatism and open-mindedness flourish. The typical denominational strategy of securing peace and harmony through location of the broadest, uncontentious common ground is, however, not without its costs. Extensive accommodation of intermediate goals and values continually provokes the charge of compromise with the secular "from disenchanted groups appealing to transcendental goals and values" (Thompson 1975, 10).

This general depiction of the denomination as a pure type applies admirably to the United Church, which has, from its very inception, witnessed clashes between the dominant forces of accommodation and conciliation on one side, and those of an increasingly frustrated minority that resists such attempts to come to terms with the world on the other. Analytically, such tension represents the conflict between the denominational and sectarian tendencies within this religious organization, a struggle in which the former has been remarkably and consistently successful.

The struggle over homosexual ordination symbolizes a contest between two fundamentally different and opposed models or paradigms of the United Church, and it may be no exaggeration to describe it as a battle for the soul of this organization. In this context, opponents of homosexual ordination tend to perceive the United Church in exclusivist terms and to regard any loss of exclusivity as surrender to the forces of secularism. By contrast, proponents of homosexual ordination are undoubtedly inspired by a goal of inclusivism that has been a dominant theme of denominational policy during most of the years of the United Church's existence. This tension between exclusivism and inclusivism is, however, far more complex than it appears at first glance. This complexity may best be revealed by close scrutiny of the balance struck by this denomination during the six decades of its history.

SECULARIZATION AND THE UNITED CHURCH

One conservative stereotype of the United Church is of an organization so obsessed with the process of secularization that it constantly succumbs to those very secular forces that it fears. From this point of view, it has followed Niebuhr's classic process (1957) of increasing compromise with (or, less kindly, "selling out" to) the world in a sisyphean quest for popularity and relevance that constitutes a religious version of the philosophy of "how to win friends and influence people." In this conception, principle constantly surrenders to pragmatism, doctrine is progressively diluted and ethics are increasingly relativized while church leaders scramble to conform to the ephemeral fads and fashions of a rapidly changing society. While there are, undoubtedly, elements of truth in this depiction, it is inaccurate in a number of important respects.

Sociologists differ widely in the meaning and importance they attach to the concept of secularization. For some, the process is glaringly manifest in its inexorable march while, for others, it is an illusion born of linguistic confusion, theoretical imprecision and rationalistic prejudice. Theologians, as divided on this matter as their sociological counterparts, debate whether the sacred should resist or embrace the secular (see especially Wilson 1987, 159-165). If any credence whatever is given to the concept of secularization, it undoubtedly makes sense to view the United Church (like other major denominations) as both responding to this process as an external phenomenon and, at the same time, being profoundly affected by it internally. But, response to secularization or even incorporation of some of its aspects cannot be reduced simply to the attempt to "move with the times" or "give people what they want" by gauging and accommodating to the prevailing shifts of public opinion. In the case of the United Church, such a portrayal would, indeed, be wide off the mark.

The broad consensus forged by this denomination over the past half-century has been built upon ethical and pastoral, rather than doctrinal, foundations. Indeed, especially in the last ecumenical quarter-century, its theology has become increasingly liberal and modernistic.[5] Henry MacLeod (1980, 103-126, 229) has described the United Church consensus as resting primarily on a theologically moderate or liberal majority comprising 60 to 70 percent of the members. This two-thirds moderate majority exists in uneasy alliance with two radically different minorities: conservatives and progressives totalling, respectively, somewhat more and somewhat less than 20 percent of the church's membership. According to MacLeod, therefore, the United Church is involved in a continuous "quest for balance, the dilemma of the denomination" that proceeds at every level "from the national office to the grass-roots." Focus on pastoral rather than doctrinal consensus, however, reveals a far less precarious state of affairs. Evidence that "social action" or "mission" in the Social Gospel tradition is the truly binding theme of this denomination may be detected in the facts that about 70 percent of members favour a "social conscience" emphasis and that over 90 percent of conservatives are not opposed to a "socially conscious" clergy. The typical United Church member, in MacLeod's view, is willing to support official policies and programs "so long as worship is satisfactory and his/her family is involved." This point is underlined by the observation that the "conservative element" within the denomination views "mission, reform and justice" in a generally favourable light. In a prescient comment of significance to the present study, MacLeod notes, however, that "the more conservative side of this otherwise liberal, ecumenical denomination" is most likely to be manifested, if anywhere, in the sphere of sexual morality (1980, 120, 220, 229-230).

In steering its moderate course, the United Church has not simply appeased majority opinion within its ranks; it has also endeavoured to live up to the terms of its founding mandate. The organizational merger that created this denomination was achieved only by theological compromise and even that could not command complete commitment. Thus, depreciation of doctrine at the expense of social concern is in full accord both with historical precedent and its founders' intentions. It should not be assumed, however, that this strategy has always been a cautious and easy option. On the contrary, it has on many occasions (including the present crisis) been pursued at considerable cost. The quest for theological and ethical middle-ground has continually and consistently annoyed, alienated and occasionally outraged those at the conservative and progressive extremes of United Church opinion. In circumstances where apparent concession to one side may entail resentment, disaffection and even defection from the other, the United Church has maintained its balance through many battles by reaffirming its primary commitment and redirecting its energies into urgent matters of social reform.

Any notion that the United Church has eluded dissent by deprecating dogma is rapidly dispelled by even the most cursory glance at the historical record. Though it has striven for internal compromise and consensus in its social ethics as much as in its theology, it has never pursued internal tranquillity at any price. Often resisting the temptation to sacrifice its social principles on the altar of organizational harmony, the United Church has usually chosen to challenge rather than comfort its flock whatever the consequences. In this regard, its recent landmark decision on homosexual ordination is only the latest in a long line of innovative and controversial rulings that refute the accusation that United Church social ethics simply bend with the breeze of secular, public taste.

INCLUSIVISM, SECULARISM AND HUMAN RIGHTS

As noted earlier, the dominant organizational and ideological tendencies of any denomination are towards inclusion rather than exclusion; such is the case *a fortiori* within the United Church. An organization whose conception of theology has been accompanied by pioneering liberal positions on sexual ethics and gender discrimination may, thus, simply be seen as pushing its organizational boundaries to their logical limits. The inclusiveness of the United Church may be interpreted in two main ways; one approach draws upon church-sect theory while the other concentrates its analysis on cultural values. While far from being mutually exclusive, these perspectives will be treated separately for analytical purposes.

It might be argued that, in the degree of inclusiveness to which it aspires, and perhaps even in the degree that it has already attained, the United Church is becoming increasingly "churchly" in character. Of course, it would be absurd to identify this organization with the ideal-typical church depicted by Max Weber and Ernst Troeltsch (see Gerth and Mills 1958, 305-306; Troeltsch 1931) for it is neither conservative nor monopolistic as required by their typologies. Nonetheless, the United Church might, with obvious reservations, be plausibly described as "a sort of trust foundation for supernatural ends, an institution necessarily including both the just and the unjust" that, in principle at least, "desires to cover the whole life of human-ity" (Weber 1958a, 144). Thus, while the United Church is the bearer of an undeniably noble legacy of toleration and ecumenism, its apparently inexorable drive for inclusivism might be interpreted as indicating an underlying self-conception as Canada's "national church." Contemporary conservatives within the United Church may accordingly regard themselves as the core of a resistance movement, defending a particularistic or sectarian conception of religion against a universalistic and churchly expansionism. From their standpoint, the battle against Canadian ecclesiasticism has not yet been won, though the form of the conflict has evolved remarkably since the nineteenth century.

Implicit within the current ordination debate lies a familiar defence of exclusivism and sectarianism against a prevailing inclusivism and ecumenism. In this respect, the debate may be interpreted as representing (in part at least) a symbolic manifestation of the central question for mainstream religion: whether success and survival in the face of secularization in the outside world may be attained by reinforcing historically sacred boundaries or by dismantling them.

This question, naturally, has ideological as well as organizational referents. While it is clear that the United Church decision regarding homosexual ordination is in keeping with its general inclusivist policy of breaking down irrelevant barriers between social categories, the ideological source of the policy itself is somewhat unclear. Though, as noted earlier, its source does not lie in prevailing public opinion, there is a more subtle sense in which it may be viewed as reflecting the *Zeitgeist*. Though the prevailing social ethics of the United Church are invariably justified and legitimated by appeals to the message and the spirit of the gospels, their general and specific indebtedness to "a global stirring of the democratic spirit" (see Hornsby-Smith 1989, 34-35) seems evident. While the United Church undoubtedly requires its social policies to be consistent with a liberal reading of scripture, these social policies appear to derive in part from the contemporary worldwide preoccupation with individual human rights.

Given the past organizational and ideological record of the United Church, its espousal of a broad global humanitarianism should come as no surprise. Its inclusivist and ecumenical momentum has led logically, and perhaps inevitably, in this direction to the dismay of conservatives within its ranks. The matter may be put in perspective, however, if it is remembered that the United Church is by no means unique among mainstream Christian denominations in its apparent embrace of ethicalism and humanism (see Glock and Stark 1965, 217-220). Commentators on Roman Catholicism, for example, have detected similar developments since the Second Vatican Council. In a highly pertinent observation, Michael Hornsby-Smith asserts:

> ... the struggle to be free and to participate meaningfully in all
> decisions which significantly affect the lives of individuals is ubiquitous
> and continually being reinterpreted and negotiated. Given this fact and
> its articulation in the post-war world, it is only to be expected that
> similar stirrings will emerge in the Church ... (1989, 35).

Perhaps even more noteworthy, in this context, is the cultural
transformation of Catholicism discerned by Danièle Hervieu-Léger
(1985) towards a "transcendent humanism" that offers an "ethico-
effective" this-worldly conception of salvation.

Like other mainstream religious organizations, the United Church
has chosen accommodation rather than defensiveness or intransigence
in its effort to cope with the realities of the modern world. This
choice, like the Catholic policy of heeding the "signs of the times,"
has inevitably entailed the absorption of prevailing progressive ideas
grounded in secular humanism (Hornsby-Smith 1989, 210-211). The
affinity of the United Church for the prevailing "progressive" values
of secular society is rooted in far more than the obvious Judaeo-
Christian ancestry of these values. Far from being merely an oppor-
tunistic attempt to combat irrelevance and "move with the times," the
dominant tolerant inclusivism of the United Church's theology is
central to its development as a denomination. Heeding the "signs of
the times" for the United Church is part of a systematization and
demystification set in motion at the denomination's foundation.
Whether the inner logic of this process leads inexorably to secularism
or whether, on the contrary, it affords the means of revitalizing
religion is the fundamental dilemma lying deep within the rhetoric of
the ordination debate.

DENOMINATIONAL INNER DYNAMICS

The discussion so far has of necessity dealt with the context of the
ordination debate in a rather abstract manner. Closer analysis of the
inner dynamics of the denomination, however, reveals in more specific
terms the origins of its policy of systematic pastoral progressivism.

The most crucial determinant in the formulation of United Church policy is, arguably, a characteristic consequence of the process of rationalization — the existence of a full-time staff of professional administrators employed in its central headquarters. This is a fact of unique significance for the investigation of the origins and nature of this denomination's world view. In this regard, the United Church is by no means unusual among religious organizations with a democratic ethos.[6] It faces a familiar sociological dilemma in its attempt to balance the benefits of democratic representation of its membership against the need for efficiency and decisive action. The emergence and growth of professional bureaucracy within voluntary, democratic organizations has intrigued sociologists for generations, provoking promulgation both of an "iron law of oligarchy" and a rival "iron law of democracy" (see Michels 1962; Gouldner 1955; Lipset 1956). Without espousing either law, the present discussion considers the impact of professional administrators employed within the United Church National Office on the form and content of policy.

As MacLeod (1980) notes in the best investigation of this matter, the elusive nature of appropriate evidence means that only tentative conclusions may be drawn. Despite this limitation, however, he makes a convincing case for a striking disparity between theory and practice in the United Church conception of the distribution of power and authority within its ranks. Identifying, in this Canadian denomination, a process observed by P.M. Harrison in his classic study of the American Baptist Convention, MacLeod (1980, 188-193; see also Harrison 1959) depicts a growth in the power, authority and influence of professional administrators while noting the specific possibility that "national staff members of the United Church, who theoretically are confined to the implementation of policy, will tend to become the initiators of policy."

Theoretically, the United Church is a constitutional democracy employing an administrative staff to carry out its directives. In practice, matters are more complex due mainly to the unwieldy nature of this denomination's representational structure. While conscientious efforts are made to ensure the expression of the full range of rank-and-file opinion through formal democratic channels, this process culminates in the intense deliberations of the church's General Council, which assembles every two or three years. In this highest court, nearly 500 delegates struggle intermittently to give voice to the collective will of more than 800,000 members. Apart from the inherently daunting nature of this task, it is clear that this body faces formidable difficulties from a sociological point of view. Noting that the assemblies of many other denominations are hampered both by their size and infrequency, Macleod depicts the General Council of the United Church as a quintessential case in point: a body that finds it "increasingly difficult ... to exercise its legal authority to set policy because of a number of vital factors" (1980, 181).

Among these factors is that the General Council is an amateur elected body too large to be intimate and too diverse to preclude factionalism. It lacks the continuity of a "collective memory" due to rotation of official duties and limitations on terms of service; at any time it includes many novices who are learning its procedures "on the job." Furthermore, its members are confronted increasingly with indigestible agenda and documentation to be dealt with in a severely restricted timeframe. These familiar constraints on modern democracy have, within the United Church, engendered a typical and predictable response: a growth in the power of the denomination's permanent administrative body. The rise of bureaucracy as a means of facilitating the transaction of business within democratic assemblies is a familiar theme. So also is the consequent shifting of the balance of power away from elected legislators and towards professional administrators. Thus, while the United Church clearly makes a conscientious effort to strike the right balance between bureaucratic efficiency and effective representation, there is little doubt that it has taken the typical evolutionary path of modern complex organizations in its increased reliance on professional expertise and bureaucratic initiative (Blau and Meyer 1971). Some idea of the constraints imposed on members of General Council is provided by MacLeod:

> ... even though the council may approve, affirm or adopt reports, its policy-making consists mainly of amendments that introduce word changes into the recommendations of a specific report (1980, 183).

Thus, though in theory accountable to General Council, the full-time professional staff of the United Church seems to exert a growing influence over policy-making. Not surprisingly, increasing awareness of this state of affairs among rank-and-file members has engendered frequent and repeated expressions of concern. Deciding where such discontent may profitably be directed is also a problem.

Nonetheless, committed to a progressive vision of social justice, and correctly perceiving such a vision to be the essential core of the evolving United Church consensus, full-time officials attempt to expedite fulfilment of their church's mission by challenging its elected representatives with radical and avant-garde proposals that expand the limits of the Christian conscience. The stereotype of the inherent conservatism of bureaucracies is considerably undermined by this evidence (MacLeod 1980, 222-223).

With this in mind, it may be inferred with some justification that informal assumption of the prerogative of policy initiation by the professional staff of the United Church has played its part in the current ordination crisis as it has in earlier policy proposals concerning human sexuality. To affirm this is simply to recognize that "the permanence of officials in a church of constantly changing legislators gives them a measure of power that need not be attributed to any sinister intent on their part" (Grant 1988, 12).

In the ecclesiastical politics of the ordination case, full-time church officials appear to have made common cause with delegate ministers, whose opinions are, for the most part, more liberal than those of their congregations, as well as with laity representing what MacLeod calls "an educated membership of urban and suburban sophisticates with middle-class prejudices ... characterized by a liberal humanistic outlook" (1980, 219). But, in what precise way were such delegates open to persuasion in the delicate and provocative matter of allowing homosexual ordination? It must be remembered, after all, that the majorities that endorsed and subsequently reaffirmed this policy at General Council were significantly at odds with the apparent state of public opinion in the denomination as a whole (Bibby 1987, 155-158).[7] The answer to this question is to be found in the context in which the issue has been framed: a context calculated to win the support, however grudging, of the moderate majority of delegates. For such delegates to endorse it, it was vital that homosexual ordination be defined, not as a purely *doctrinal* matter, but as a case of fundamental *human rights* and *social justice* in keeping with the dominant ideological orientation of the United Church. If the moderate conscience had concerns about the morality of homosexual practices (in line with the view of a majority of church members), these were overridden by concern for the greater goals of minority rights and nondiscrimination.

No analysis of the current debate in the United Church would be complete without some attempt to sketch the character of the opposition to homosexual ordination. From the vantage point of full-time officials and theological "progressives," active opponents of homosexual ordination represent an obstacle to the predominant ecumenical and inclusivist model of the church so that, paradoxically, an inclusivist church may require their exclusion. The minority that threatens the denomination with its first major schism is both new and old, more and less representative than it appears, and better and worse equipped to resist the apparently inexorable evolution of the United Church towards humanism and ethicalism.

Though the rapid mobilization, in recent years, of "Community of Concern" and affiliated groups deserves a separate study, its major significance is clear. The forces resisting the ordination of professed homosexuals are fighting possibly the last battle in a long war of attrition in which they have already suffered many defeats. They are struggling to defend an exclusivist or sectarian model of religious organization against an increasingly inclusivist or churchly one. By stressing scripture, traditional morality and a necessary connection between them, the "conservative" wing of the United Church erects a barricade against theological liberalism, ethicalism, humanism and pragmatism. Their struggle is a symbolic one in two senses. First, it is simply the specific occasion of a more diffused conflict between two fundamentally opposed models of religious organization. Second, it is a crusade of principle rather than practice, since official approval of homosexual ordination in no way affects each congregation's right or ability to choose its own pastor.

Naturally, those opposed to the new ordination proposals are not entirely homogeneous in their attitudes. They range from highly committed theological conservatives to those who simply resent what they perceive as the anti-democratic manner in which this recommendation (among others) was "steam-rolled" through General Council. They also include those who simply seek a spiritual anchor and feel increasingly unhappy in an organization apparently dedicated to the pursuit of relevance.[8] Nonetheless, the "hard-core" opposition to homosexual ordination derives from a theologically conservative minority that can trace its roots back to the very foundation of the denomination and that clings to an intransigent scriptural absolutism. Its essentially sectarian conception of religious doctrine and organization distinguishes this faction within the United Church from those who merely sympathize with some of its views. Clearly, many members of this denomination share at least some of the views on sexual ethics expressed by conservatives. When confronted by the inclusivist rhetoric of human rights and social justice, however, they are willing to concede the point. The tolerance that they show is anathema to the conservative sense of scriptural and moral truth opposed to sin and evil.

CONCLUSION

Exploration of the current crisis in the United Church of Canada sheds light on many of the dilemmas faced by mainstream Christianity in post-industrial societies. Like many others, this denomination is a predominantly progressive or liberal organization that embraces a conservative minority. Its internal power struggle over homosexual ordination may be viewed as a symbolic confrontation between the forces of religious accommodation and intransigence in the face of a perceived ubiquitous secularization. In the attempt to outline the dilemma of the United Church, a varied sociological literature has been employed ranging from analyses of secularization through studies of complex organizations to (currently less fashionable) theories of church and sect. This clarifies a process by which a United Church aspiration to inclusiveness impels it simultaneously in "churchly" and "secular" directions while it also elucidates the "cognitive deviance" (Berger 1969, 19) of a minority that rejects both these destinations. In its continuing attempt to bridge the sacred and secular, principle and practicality, democracy and efficiency, comfort and challenge, and its sacred mission on earth and maintenance as an institution, the United Church epitomizes the tensions that pervade mainstream denominations. It does so, however, while retaining its identity as a uniquely Canadian organization with a distinctive agenda forged through the resolution of many crises. In seeking clues to the religion of the twenty-first century, many sociologists have misdirected their curiosity. Sensitive investigation of the United Church of Canada might well furnish them with more reliable hints of the future than may be derived from exploration of more exotic contemporary religious movements.

Notes

*This chapter is a revised version of an article first published by Roger O'Toole, Douglas Campbell, John Hannigan, Peter Beyer and John Simpson, "The United Church in Crisis: A sociological perspective on the dilemmas of a mainstream denomination," *Studies in Religion/Sciences Religieuses* 20, 2 (1991):151-163. Permission has been granted by the "Canadian Corporation for Studies in Religion," which holds the copyright.

[1] Though incorporating information obtained through informal interviews and context analysis, this chapter is less concerned with the provision of data than with the application and fusion of sociological insights in a United Church context.

[2] For general overviews of United Church history see Silcox (1933) and Grant (1967).

[3] Some observers took the view that no significant shift in policy had occurred. In any case, the proposition was a matter of exhortation rather than regulation (see McAteer 1988).

[4] Originating in the work of Weber and Troeltsch, the "church-sect" dichotomy has spawned a vast topological literature. For a useful review see Robertson (1970).

[5] The United Church's theology is modernistic in the sense that "modernism names an openness to the various discoveries, sciences, and criteria that have arisen with modernity and to the task of making positive use of these in the interpretation and understanding of the Christian gospel" (Farley 1990, 135).

[6] The classic study is P.M. Harrison (1959). While democratic in spirit and structure, the United Church maintains a special constitutional status for its clergy. Thus, all ordained ministers are *de facto* members of presbytery and conference, while General Council has an equal number of clerical and lay representatives.

[7] Of 360 letters to the editor of the *United Church Observer*, opponents of the church outnumbered its supporters by approximately a six to one ratio (see *United Church Observer* June 1988, 10). For a brief discussion of the difficulties associated with the use of such letters as sociological data, see Plummer (1983, 21-24).

[8]This range of opinion was apparent from our content analysis of letters to the *Observer* (see Perman 1977).

For Further Reading

Grant, John Webster. 1967. *The Canadian Experience of Church Union.* London: Lutterworth Press.

Hornsby-Smith, Michael P. 1989. *The Changing Parish.* London and New York: Routledge.

Perman, David. 1977. *Changes and the Churches.* Oxford: Bodley Head.

Silcox, C.E. 1933. *Church Union in Canada.* New York: Institute of Social and Religious Research.

Chapter 15

Canadian Evangelicals: Facing the Critics

Irving Hexham

INTRODUCTION

Theologically conservative churches and interdenominational para-church organizations (such as Campus Crusade for Christ), sometimes called Fundamentalists, Born Again Christians or even Charismatics, usually prefer to be called Evangelicals. (Sociologists often call them "Conservative Christians.") Therefore, this chapter will use the generic term Evangelical to encompass a wide range of denominational and interdenominational groups that share a common core theology, basic Christian world view and similar perceptions of reality.[1]

Since the mid-1970s, Evangelical groups have regularly been in the news, first as a result of the claims of various celebrities, such as Watergate convict Charles Colson and Bob Dylan, to be "born again," and later through the success and excesses of American television evangelists (see *Newsweek*, 25 October 1976; *The Wall Street Journal*, 19 May 1978; *New Internationalist*, August 1990). It comes as a surprise, therefore, to discover there is no serious book written by a historian, sociologist, theologian or other scholar that gives an overview of Evangelical Christianity in Canada.

The only book that makes an attempt is Judith Haiven's (1984) highly critical *Faith, Hope, No Charity: An Inside Look At the Born Again Movement in Canada and the United States*. The tone of the book is set by Charles Templeton in his "Introduction" when he says:

> I have had considerable experience with evangelists ... Most of them were ignorant men with narrow minds and circumscribed interests ... These are potentially dangerous men ... [because] most evangelicals no longer take Jesus seriously (1984, 10).

Following these highly prejudicial statements, Haiven suggests that Evangelical Christianity can be described as "myopic, intolerant, right-wing, fascist, even anti-Semitic ..." (1984, 22). Supporting this stinging incitement, Haiven cites numerous books, press, radio and television reports that regularly portray Evangelical Christianity in a highly negative light (cf. Conway and Siegelman 1984; Barr 1977).

It may come as a surprise, therefore, to discover there is another side to the story. Many scholarly books, especially those written in other countries, give sympathetic accounts of Evangelical Christianity (cf. Marsden 1980; Bebbington 1989; Bruce 1984). This chapter attempts to correct the imbalance in Canadian coverage of Evangelical Christianity by presenting an overview of Evangelicals as they see themselves.

WHO ARE EVANGELICALS?

Considerable confusion exists about who Evangelical Christians really are and what they believe. Radio and television news programs often refer to Evangelicals "as being more a cult than a religion" (Haiven 1984, 22). Sociologists reject this simplistic categorization. In sociological terms, Evangelicals are considered sectarian because they are exclusive in their membership: they insist on a profession of faith, conversion or a "living relationship with Jesus Christ the Lord" as the basis for full church membership. Since Max Weber and Ernst Troeltsch, the term "sect" has signified any religious group that is exclusive in its membership. In theology, however, sect has a different meaning that should not be confused with its sociological meaning. The theological use of the term implies deviation from Christian orthodoxy. Evangelical Christians are proud that they uphold theological orthodoxy and reject the liberal or modernist theological views that triumphed in academic theology during the nineteenth century.

Evangelicals are found in a wide spectrum of Protestant churches including many mainline denominations, such as the Anglicans, Presbyterians and the United Church of Canada, which are dominated by liberal theology. In mainline churches they usually form a vocal minority that protests such theological fads as Death of God Theology and criticizes the various forms of modern spirituality that negate traditional Christian beliefs as well as the replacement of personal faith by social commitments. Outside of Canada the one mainline exception is the Church of England where the majority of ministers, including Archbishop George Carey, are Evangelicals. In Canada most Evangelicals are found in Baptist, Pentecostal and similar churches.

EVANGELICAL THEOLOGY AND WORLD VIEW

The world view of Evangelical Christians is that of historic Christianity, by which they mean a faith based on the Bible, the Ecumenical Creeds and the Protestant Reformation (Carnell 1961; Griffith-Thomas 1930). Evangelicals begin by presupposing, although many also argue for the rationality of belief in, the real existence of a personal God who is both the creator and sustainer of the universe (cf. Plantinga 1967).

They explain the human predicament, in a world where evil is a reality, in terms of a primordial human rebellion against God. Subsequently, God's love was revealed through His actions in history and incarnation in the person of Jesus who died on the cross to redeem us from sin. The ultimate triumph of good over evil and evidence of the truth of the gospel is seen in the resurrection of Jesus.

Accepting the original goodness of creation and God's continuing providence, Evangelicals have no difficulty believing in the reality of miracles, because the laws of nature originate with God. They also accept the Bible as "the Word of God" through which the Creator reveals Himself to His creatures. The presence and continued activity of the Holy Spirit, the third person in the Godhead or Trinity – who guides the church today – is also important in understanding Evangelical religion as a living faith (cf. Orr 1948, 32-36; Pinnock 1985).

Evangelicals claim to be orthodox in their acceptance of historic Christianity. The core beliefs of Evangelical Christians are thus identical with those of Roman Catholicism and traditional Anglicanism. This can be seen by comparing standard statements of Anglican beliefs (see also Griffith-Thomas 1930) with the doctrinal statement of any major Evangelical denomination, independent congregation or para-church organization. Evangelicals believe in the trinity, the incarnation of Christ, His bodily resurrection, the activity of the Holy Spirit, and original sin. The key doctrine on which both traditional Anglicans and Evangelicals separate themselves from Roman Catholicism is, like the Protestant Reformers, salvation understood as Martin Luther's justification by faith alone.

Among themselves, Evangelicals divide over the mode of Baptism. Anglicans, Presbyterians, Methodists and other members of mainline groups favour infant baptism, while Mennonites and most Pentecostals, Baptists, independent churches and para-church groups insist on adult or "believers'" baptism. Like all Protestant groups there are various forms of church government among Evangelical denominations, although most North American churches lean towards some form of congregationalism, where each congregation governs itself.

The expression "born again" is used among Evangelicals to refer to the conversion process by which nonbelievers become Christians. Popularized in the 1950s by Billy Graham (1955, 133) and later in the 1970s by Charles Colson (1977), it is often regarded as a mark of Evangelical oddity. Yet Jesus first used the term (John:3.3), and it became a favourite theme of many great preachers including John Wesley and Charles Spurgeon (Toon 1987).

EVANGELICALS IN CANADA

Reginald Bibby estimates that "Conservative Protestant groups currently form about 6 percent of the nation ..." (Bibby 1987, 27). Other writers give a slightly higher figure of 7 percent (Motz 1990, 43; see also Jacquet and Jones 1992). By comparison, the percentage of the population identifying as Evangelical in the United States ranges from 22 to 44 percent (Gallup and Castelli 1989, 3).

It is tempting for politicians and social scientists to dismiss such a small group of people as irrelevant. However, when we turn from repeated affiliation to actual attendance and measurable commitment a completely different picture emerges. Motz (1990, 65) estimates that on a normal Sunday 810,000 Canadians attend mainline churches. At the same time another 1,016,000 Canadians attend churches belonging to Evangelical denominations. This figure is supported, in a very imprecise way, by the fact that during an inter-faith week of prayer in 1992, involving all Calgary churches, Evangelical denominations gave out about a third more advertising leaflets than those belonging to mainline Protestant denominations.

Another indicator of Evangelical vitality and real influence comes from financial statistics. Compare the per capita giving to religious causes for the denominations listed in Table 15.1. It must also be noted that even between the mainline denominations giving increases in proportion to the number of Evangelical congregations within the denomination.

Table 15.1   PER CAPITA DONATIONS TO RELIGIOUS CAUSES FOR SELECTED DENOMINATIONS IN CANADA (in Canadian dollars)

Mainline Denominations	
United Church of Canada	$283.04
Anglicans	$299.92
Presbyterians	$350.00
Evangelical Denominations	
Associated Gospel Churches	$993.86
Baptist Union of Western Canada	$1,100.57
Christian and Missionary Alliance	$1,891.22

Source: Jacquet and Jones 1992, 278-279.

To put these figures in perspective, in 1991 one large Baptist church in a western Canadian city employing five clergy had $105 more in its annual budget than the entire Anglican diocese consisting of 92 clergy and over 100 congregations. Comparable figures can almost certainly be found in the annual reports of churches across Canada. They show the reality of religious commitment in Canada.[2]

Other measures of religious commitment, such as time spent in devotional or church-related pastimes, involvement in the community, etc., also confirm that Evangelicals are far more committed than either mainline Protestants or Roman Catholics (Mackie and Brinkerhoff 1986). It is clear that when Canadian religiosity is measured in terms of actual involvement, Evangelicals represent the core religious group in Canadian society. Remove Evangelicals and 2

Christian presence in Canada would be noticeably reduced.

EVANGELICALS AND SOCIAL ISSUES

Many mainline church members will argue that Evangelicals represent a narrow, ingrown group emphasizing "spiritual things" at the expense of Christian charity. This argument is used by Haiven who says:

> ... born agains are mysteriously silent on love or charity ... They were sceptical of and angered by mainline churches' aid to developing countries, their speaking out on Canadian social issues, and their allying their church and their membership with popular struggles against oppressive regimes in, for example, South Africa ... (1984, 18).

Therefore, secular critics and many mainline Christians argue, mainline denominations make a far greater social contribution to Canadian society than Evangelicals.

Plausible as this argument seems, the facts do not support it. Many Evangelicals have a lively interest in world affairs and the plight of the poor both in Canada and overseas. They are also very involved in a wide range of social initiatives.

Evangelical denominational journals and the two national Evangelical interdenominational journals, *Christian Week* and *Faith Today*, do take an interest in social issues and do support the poor and oppressed. These publications show how Evangelicals support foreign aid; are involved with child poverty and sexual abuse; support a multicultural society and seek acceptance for refugees and minority groups; are deeply concerned about poverty in Canada; and are aware of the injustice done to Native peoples. Finally, the picture that Evangelicals' own publications give is that they decidedly *do not* support apartheid or the South African Government, nor are they anti-semitic.[3]

More significant in giving the lie to claims that Evangelicals do not support charitable causes are the financial statistics issued by individual congregations. A comparison of data from churches belonging to mainline and Evangelical denominations shows that in general Evangelical churches devote more of their budgets to charitable causes than mainline churches.

Even allowing that most members of mainline churches make their charitable donations to secular rather than religious agencies, the average charitable giving of Canadian taxpayers is only $215 per annum. This figure *includes* all money given to churches. Thus, on the unlikely assumption that Evangelical donors give absolutely nothing to secular causes, the amount they give to their churches, a proportion of which always goes to charity, indicates that, on average, Evangelicals give more to charity than members of mainline churches. Further, a complex network of social programs originate within the Evangelical community, demonstrating practical commitment of Evangelists to charity.[4]

EVANGELICAL SOCIAL PROGRAMS

Most Germans happily pay church tax, although very few actually go to church. When asked why so many people are willing to pay a percentage of their income to the churches the usual reply is that while personally they no longer attend church, they recognize that the churches run many social welfare programs far better and for much less cost than similar government programs. Therefore, supporting the church actually saves taxes because if the government took over church activities there would be a dramatic rise in taxation.[5]

Canadians rarely think in this way because they fail to recognize the extent of church-related welfare programs. Consequently, many Canadians resent the tax-exempt status of churches not realizing that churches actually provide a secondary social safety net. If it disappeared, either taxation or suffering would greatly increase in Canada.

Regular articles in Evangelical publications such as *Christian Week* and *Faith Today* show that individual Evangelicals, congregations and denominations are involved in a wide variety of social programs that benefit the entire community. A dramatic instance of such action is the free Christmas dinner offered by First Baptist Church in Calgary to anyone who requests it. The church has fed more than seven hundred people at a time. Throughout Canada many other Evangelical churches offer free Christmas dinners to the needy.

Nor is feeding the needy at Christmas an isolated event. The same church provides a free weekly dinner for poor children, various activities for pensioners, support groups for the unemployed, and a major outreach to street people that involves counselling and the provision of food and shelter. These are in addition to other programs that the church runs, such as youth group and Bible studies and prayer groups.

Churches in other Canadian cities run equally impressive programs. The Burnaby Christian Fellowship has among its many social programs one for people on probation plus a highly professional counselling service. The Langley (B.C.) Vineyard Church runs a second-hand clothes shop and a work training program, which includes providing daycare for single mothers.

Evangelical churches also support interfaith food banks and similar programs in addition to their own food programs, as well as shelters for the homeless. They assist battered women by providing houses of refuge and run old peoples' homes, camps for poor children and a host of other activities (cf. *The Alberta Report*, 2 March, pp. 38-39).

In addition to social programs that are open to all, Evangelical churches run a variety of specifically religious programs that have important social implications. These include weekly Sunday schools for children, youth groups, vacation Bible schools, summer camps, men's and women's fellowships, and weekly Bible studies.

A seemingly sexist businessmen's Prayer Fellowship group functions at least as well as many secular support groups intended to help men cope with their problems. Similarly, the prayer requests of Women Aglow meetings reveal real needs that could otherwise drive people to despair. Once a rapport develops between members of such groups they freely discuss acute marital and work problems. Positive suggestions are made and, very often, wisdom is gained in a uniquely sympathetic atmosphere where people feel they can be completely open because they trust one another. Although they are too often ignored by social scientists, Christian support groups like these play an important and underestimated role in society.[6]

EVANGELICALS, SCHOLARSHIP AND THE ARTS

Acceptance of the Evangelical world view and theology is entirely compatible with intellectual and artistic endeavour. Since the 1960s there has been a renaissance of Evangelical scholarship, especially among philosophers, as the journal *Faith and Philosophy* shows.[7]

Evangelicals support Christian schools across the nation. Some of these, particularly those started by Dutch Christians, maintain a very high academic standard, although others are embarrassingly poor. The same fluctuation in academic standards is found in the many Bible colleges across Canada. Some, like Ontario Bible College, are excellent; others are narrow and parochial. Evangelical liberal arts colleges (including the King's College, Edmonton; Trinity Western University, Langley, B.C.; Providence College, Manitoba; and Redeemer College, Ancaster, Ontario) generally promote undergraduate education of a high calibre.

The flagship Canadian Evangelical educational institutions are Regent College, Vancouver, a first-class graduate school of theology that specializes in teaching lay students; the Institute for Christian Scholarship (ICS), Toronto, which offers graduate education in philosophy; and Ontario Theological Seminary (OTS), the largest seminary in Canada. What makes Regent College and the ICS particularly interesting is that both have produced a significant number of academics who have gone on to teach in secular institutions.

Canadian Evangelical religion has an impact on cultures around the world; its contact with other cultures affects Canadian society as well. Evangelical organizations like the Mennonite Economic Development Agency (MEDA), World Vision, Youth With a Mission, and a host of smaller mission and development agencies bring a Canadian presence to many parts of the world. In turn, Canadians who serve overseas with such organizations return to Canada with new perspectives and cultural understanding.

In addition, various action groups like the Evangelical Fellowship of Canada, Citizens for Public Justice and MEDA express Evangelical social and political concerns while the Canadian Scientific Affiliation seeks to bring together Christians working in the sciences.

ARE EVANGELICAL CHURCHES GROWING?

Various American writers, such as George Gallup and Dean Kelly, claim that conservative Evangelical churches are more successful than mainline churches in attracting and maintaining new members (Gallup and Castelli 1989; Kelly 1986). In Canada, Reginald Bibby has disputed these claims, arguing that "it has never been demonstrated

that Conservatives have actually been successful in reaching unaffiliated or inactive Americans ..." (1987, 27).

Bibby says: "Some theologically conservative Protestant groups,
such as the Pentecostals, the Christian and Missionary Alliance and
the Salvation Army, have grown faster than the population during this
century. Others, however, including the Baptists and Mennonites,
have not ..." (1987, 27). To back up this claim, Bibby cites his and
Merlin Brinkerhoff's Calgary study, which seemed to show that "for
all their efforts, 70 percent of the new additions come from other
evangelical churches ... Another 20 percent were the children of
evangelicals. Only about 10 percent of the new members had come
from outside the evangelical community ..." (1987, 29).

Before it is possible to conclude that Bibby is correct, far more
research needs doing. The basic weakness of his study lies in its
methodology and definition of "new additions." For his primary data
about church growth, Bibby relies on interviews with church leaders,
not the new members themselves. Therefore, a considerable margin
of error may have crept into the data through the failure of his
informants to really know their own congregations. Further, because
Bibby relies on a random sample of churches, he missed some highly
transient churches and para-church groups that are able to make but
not retain converts, who go on to join other Evangelical churches.

Using the anthropological technique of in-depth life history
interviews, professor Karla Poewe has established that at least some
transfer growth, correctly identified by Bibby, came from new converts
made by churches like the Calgary Christian Centre and the para-
church Full Gospel Businessmen's Fellowship International.[8] The role
of such institutions in making converts who then quickly move on to
more stable churches needs careful investigation.

THE GLOBAL IMPACT OF CANADIAN EVANGELICAL CHRISTIANITY

Canadian Evangelicals have a considerable impact on other Christians
worldwide. Internationally known evangelists like Aimee Semple
McPherson (1890-1944) and devotional writer Oswald J. Smith (1889-
1986) and others made significant contributions to the international
Evangelical movement. Similarly, Canadian theologians W.H. Griffith-
Thomas (1861-1924), A.B. Winchester (1858-1943), John McNicol

(1869-1956), Dyson Hague (1857-1935), William Cavan (1830-1904) and T.T. Shields (1873-1955) made significant contributions to the formation and growth of the Fundamentalist movement in its initial, more intellectual, stage (Marsden 1980; Rawlyk 1990a, 158-171).

Canadians founded the fast-growing Christian and Missionary Alliance (A.B. Simpson, 1843-1919), and the Sudan Interior Mission (R.V. Bingham, 1872-1942), while the Charismatic/Pentecostal Movement received a major boost by the Latter Rain Movement that originated in North Battleford, Saskatchewan, in 1948 (Riss 1987).

Today, two uniquely Canadian educational institutions — Regent College, Vancouver, and the Institute for Christian Studies, Toronto — draw a sizeable proportion of their students from around the world. Even more significant is the fact that in Australia, Austria, Britain, New Zealand, South Africa, Singapore, the United States and several other countries there are now similar institutions explicitly modelled on the Canadian originals.

Other lesser-known institutions, like Prairie Bible Institute in Alberta and Briarcrest Bible College in Saskatchewan, have a global impact in that they draw large numbers of students from overseas and send many Canadians to other nations as missionaries. The impact of these schools on American Fundamentalism also should be recognized because many best-selling American authors and preachers, like Don Richardson (1974), trained in Canada.

CONCLUSION

The academic climate in Canadian universities does not encourage the study of Evangelical Christianity (Rawlyk 1990b, 4-5). Religious studies departments, in particular, tend to attract disillusioned theologians, often from lower-class or rural Fundamentalist homes. Many of them exhibit a sense of cynicism deriving from an academic rejection of their own social and religious heritage. In this situation, the biblically based language used in Conservative Christian circles is easy to ridicule. It is also very easy to doubt the sincerity of Evangelicals and look askance at what are genuine concerns about religious truth.

Political prejudice also plays a role in this disparagement of Evangelicals. Although Conservative Christians are theologically orthodox, many are politically liberal and sometimes quite radical. They do not conform to academic fashion. Therefore, while there have been politically radical Evangelicals who were at least as critical of Canadian social policies as members of the New Democratic Party, the same people were far more critical of communist regimes. This anti-communism, based on the experience of fellow believers, often made them look reactionary. For example, a book like Richard Wurmbrand's *Tortured for Christ* (1967) sounded like pure fiction when it first appeared. Since the fall of East European communism, we know that what once could be dismissed as "wild exaggeration" was really an understatement.[9] Academics ought to be careful in dismissing Evangelical views of world affairs too easily. Sometimes grassroots contacts are better informed than academic analysts.

Very little has been written about Evangelical Christianity in Canada, and much of what has appeared is very biased. Solid sociological and anthropological studies that recognize the need for empathy and a thorough understanding of theological issues are needed. However, they must be done in a comparative perspective if Evangelicals are not to appear alien. Only when viewed within the historic Christian tradition and seen in relation to other Christian and religious groups in Canada can the significance, strengths and weaknesses of Canadian Evangelical Christianity be appreciated.

Notes

[1]Probably the best short introduction to Evangelical religion is John Stott's *Basic Christianity* (1958). A short but valuable systematic presentation of Evangelical theology is T.C. Hammond's *In Understanding Be Men* (1960), while David Fuller's *Valiant for the Truth* (1961) provides an excellent introduction to the way Evangelicals see the historic Christian tradition. John Stott's *Issues Facing Christians Today* (1984), Gerald Vandezande's *Christians in Crisis* (1983) and Brian Stiller's *Critical Options for Evangelicals* (1992) give an overview of Evangelical responses to social issues.

[2]Data obtained from interviews with Revenue Canada personnel, Calgary, Alberta.

[3]Note, for example, the following: *Faith Today's* regular column "World Relief and Canada"; *Christian Week,* "Hurting people find church offering real help" (5 November 1991:1); *Christian Week,* "A drastic re-ordering of our national priorities" (4 February 1992:6); *Christian Week,* "Native justice advocates see role for Christian churches" (2 December 1991:2); *Christian Week,* "Glimmer of hope for apartheid's peaceful end" (20 March 1990:5); *Faith Today* (November/December 1989).

[4]Data obtained from interviews with Revenue Canada personnel, Calgary, Alberta.

[5]Based on interviews taken by Hexham in Germany, 1991.

[6]There are no national registers or similar sources providing a comprehensive overview of Evangelical social programs. The nearest thing to a general source is the outdated *Christian Resources Handbook: A Dictionary of Christian Organizations in Canada* (Scott 1986). While it is helpful, it only hints at the full range of Evangelical activity, for it concentrates on specific national and regional organizations, overlooking local interchurch initiatives and individual congregations.

[7]Well-recognized scholars like Alvin Plantinga (philosophy), Nathan Hatch (history), James Davidson Hunter (sociology), Donald Guthrie (New Testament studies), G.C. Berkouwer (theology), Bob Goudzwaard (economics), Paul Marshall (politics), Richard Bube (engineering), Elaine Storkey (feminism), Elaine Botha (philosophy of science) and John Polkinghorne (physics) all identify with Evangelicals.

Canadian Evangelical scholars include Larry Hurtado and Richard Longnecker (New Testament), R.K. Harrision and the late Peter Craigie

(Old Testament), J.I. Packer and Clark Pinnock (theology), Phillip Wiebe and Henk Hart (philosophy), David Jeffery (English), John Toewes and Ian Rennie (history), Walter Thorson (physics), and Peter Krüger (chemistry).

Rudy Wiebe and Janette Oke (literature), Margaret Avison (poetry), Rex Deverell and Bruce Stacey (playwrights), John Innis (acting), Peter and Patricia Gerretsen (film-making), Wayne Eastcott (print-making) and Tim Denbok (painting) are only a few successful Canadian artists (cf. *Faith Today*, November/December 1988).

The Rosebud School of the Arts (Alberta Report 23, December 1991) in Drumheller, Brookstone Productions in Toronto and the Pacific Theatre in Vancouver are just a few of many Evangelical initiatives in theatre. Canadian Evangelicals benefit from the Mennonite and German tradition of classical music. Rock groups, like Vancouver-based Rise Up, have not attained the status of American Evangelical groups like the internationally famous Petra and the heavy metal Stryper. Nevertheless, the Canadian contribution to the large, and increasingly mature, Christian music market is growing.

[8]Unpublished data.

[9]On the recent exposure of the harsh realities of these communist regimes, see *Die Zeit*, 11-13 March 1992, pp. 11-12; 7-14 February 1992, pp. 4-5; *Der Spiegel*, 10, 1992, pp. 28-37; 11, 1991, pp. 41-46.

For Further Reading

Barr, James. 1977. *Fundamentalism.* London: SCM.

Bebbington, D.W. 1989. *Evangelicalism in Modern Britain: A History from the 1730's to the 1980's.* London: Unwin Hyman.

Haiven, Judith. 1984. *Faith, Hope, No Charity: An Inside Look At the Born Again Movement in Canada and the United States.* Vancouver: New Star.

Marsden, George M. 1980. *Fundamentalism and American Culture: The Shaping of Twentieth-Century Evangelicalism, 1870-1925.* Oxford: Oxford University Press.

Rawlyk, G.A. 1990. *Champions of the Truth: Fundamentalism, Modernism and the Maritime Baptists.* Kingston, ON: Queen's University Press.

Conclusion

Religion and Social Change: An Agenda for Further Research

W.E. Hewitt

If there is one constant within the sociological study of religion, it is change. Over the centuries, religion and the wider societal structure of which it is a part have unquestionably changed. Today this process continues, as each reacts not only to change in the other, but also to the host of ideological and material forces common to both.

This dynamism is perhaps most clearly evident in Part III of this book, "Challenge, Continuity and Change Within the Canadian Churches." Here, we see how change and adaptation has occurred within the established mainline churches in response to Canadians' desires for the entrenchment of basic human and civil rights. Chapter 11, for example, discusses the ways in which the churches have attempted to meet the challenges posed by women, especially their demands for equal treatment within the traditionally male-dominated structures of religious organizations. Chapter 12 shows us how the churches have attempted to respond to the "errors" of past Evangelization of Native peoples and to the growing militancy of Native groups. Chapter 13 considers the Canadian Catholic church's "preferential option for the poor" as a recent response to domestic and international treatment of the oppressed generally. Chapter 14 analyzes the United Church as an institution in light of its leadership's decision to allow the ordination of homosexuals. In Chapter 15, the examination of the evolution and orientation of Evangelical Protestant groups, chiefly outside of the mainline denominations, offers us a glimpse of change in another direction. It describes these religious groups as providing their followers with traditional forms of dogma and personal devotion at the same time as they turn their attention to Canadian society and the world.

Part II of the book, "Religious Manifestations in Contemporary

Canadian Society," adopts a similar theme, albeit touching on the relationship between religion and social change in a more generic fashion. Chapter 6, for instance, examines the changes that have led some Canadians to turn away from any and all forms of religious belief and practice in recent years. Chapter 7 explores the process of secularization within the context of Quebec, where formerly dominant Roman Catholicism has come to assume a more modest role in society. At the other end of the scale, religious resurgence, of a sort, is the subject of Chapters 8, 9 and 10, each of which explores the increasing visibility of religious phenomenon in places where we might least expect to find them within Canadian society: in the first case, within the sphere of Canadian literature; in the second, within ideas about the core of national identity; and in the third, within the sphere of current widespread concern with the environment.

Clearly, as we have seen from Part I, "The Sociological Study of Religion," theory itself has changed over the years. As Chapter 2 shows, Canadian sociology of religion, while rooted in the classics, nevertheless has evolved at its own pace and in accordance with its own unique concerns. As a concrete example of this tendency, Chapter 3 moves beyond classical conceptions of religious organizations to present a typology of religious forms more relevant to the sociological study of "denominational" life in Canada. In Chapter 4, Reginald Bibby challenges the secularization thesis by pointing to the new ways in which Canadians have come to participate in religious life in this country. Their new "consumer oriented" approach to religion, Bibby further shows, reflects broader changes in Canadians' attitudes towards the use of goods and services generally in our society. Chapter 5 undertakes a task similar to Chapter 3, re-examining time-honoured terms such as "cult" and "new religious movement." Taking another look at some of the recent tendencies noted by Reginald Bibby, Stephen Kent argues for a new way to conceive of and study religious innovation that reflects the goals and patterns of organization or "alternative" religious groups.

All of the examinations presented here do not, and cannot, of course, represent the final word in the study of religion and social change in Canada. Whether in its theoretical or empirical dimensions, the sociological study of religion in this country is far from complete. In many respects, it is still in its infancy.

The question remains open as to the subject matter that may

interest Canadian sociologists of religion most in the days ahead. A number of possibilities are suggested by the material in this book.

Within the theoretical realm alone, there are no shortage of avenues for exploration. Using Chapter 2 as a starting point, we may wish to further illuminate the unique qualities of a Canadian sociology of religion through comparative analysis of similar study in other countries. In this regard, we may inquire how the sociological study of religion in Canada is different from that of England, France, India or Australia. What, for example, are the major theoretical orientations and assumptions of researchers in these societies and how, in comparison to Canada, has this instructed the lines of research they have adopted?

In a comparative theoretical vein, there is much to be done even within Canada. Sociology in English and French Canada largely conforms to the reality of the "two solitudes," with surprisingly little interaction between academics in both parts of the country. This is also true of the sociology of religion. The similarities and differences between English and French Canada in terms of the way sociologists of religion approach their subject matter theoretically are worth examining. To the extent that differences do exist, why is this so?

The academic marginalization of the sociology of religion in Canada, discussed in the Introduction, also calls for explanation. In Canadian university departments of sociology, the employment of academics with expertise in religion is far from a priority. Few, if any, jobs that specifically require expertise in this area are advertised, and departments rarely staff more than one full-time religionist. Indeed, many departments have no sociologists of religion who publish regularly in their field. Compare this state of affairs with the United States, where it is not uncommon for even smaller departments (fifteen full-time faculty or less) to employ two or even three sociologists interested in religion. In a similar vein, Canadian sociologists of religion are provided with few venues for publication of their research. Canada's two principal sociology journals, *The Canadian Review of Sociology and Anthropology* and *The Canadian Journal of Sociology*, have largely serviced other, perhaps more fashionable areas; those journals that do focus on religion originate within other disciplines. This has left most Canadian-based sociologists of religion with little choice but to search out publication venues in other parts of the world, especially the United States. Why is this so?

Beyond these broad questions from within what we might call "the sociology of sociology of religion," there is certainly plenty of room for further investigation using the theoretical assumptions and categories presented in this book. Is the process of religious change and fragmentation described in Chapter 4 occurring uniformly throughout the country, or might there be regional or other variations at play? What is the ultimate course that these developments are likely to take? Similarly, over time, how may the religious typologies developed by Chapter 3 and Chapter 5 help us to understand changes in the present and future organizational compartmentalization of the religious market?

In terms of the changing nature of religious manifestations in Canadian society, a number of studies also suggest themselves. Using Chapter 6 as a starting point, we may wish to further investigate irreligion in terms of its ethnic or gender dimensions. Where is irreligion growing fastest in Canadian society and why? Turning the question around, we may wish to follow up on the commentary in Chapter 7 regarding the tentative resurgence of religion in Quebec. If, indeed, some Québécois are reviving an interest in things religious in what has been seen as the most secular of Canadian provinces, what are the social sources of this revitalization, in terms of gender, age group, ethnicity and so forth? What is the role of the established churches in this development, if any, and what are its likely social and religious consequences?

With regard to religious manifestations in other areas, the work of Roger O'Toole (literature), Robert Blumstock (nationalism) and Kenneth Westhues (environment) open the door to a world of opportunity. To what extent is the growth of informal religion in other areas, such as sport and business, apparent? Existing religious groups – especially Evangelical Protestants – are already active in both of these areas, but how so, and what effect has their presence had on these and other spheres of human interaction? We also might inquire as to the success of recent attempts on the part of religious entrepreneurs to move beyond places of formal worship, and into the sphere of day-to-day life in Canada. Increasingly, we hear about "shopping mall ministries," and even mobile churches operating from tents, buses or tractor-trailers. There is also a growing move in this country towards a broader range of religious television and radio programming than now exists, through the establishment of broadcasting facilities dedicated wholly to delivering religious messages. How are these attempts organized, and how will Canadians respond to them?

The present and likely future state of Canadian church institutions also provides fertile ground for analysis. Nancy Nason-Clark (women), David Lewis (Native people), W.E. Hewitt (Catholicism and the "option for the poor"), and Roger O'Toole, Douglas Campbell, John Hannigan, Peter Beyer and John Simpson (the ordination of homosexuals in the United Church) all point to onging tensions within the mainline churches as they attempt to deal with the fundamental social-justice concerns facing the wider society. How much success are they achieving on these fronts? Will the churches continue to move to address these issues, or will conservative pressures from the laity force a return to the basics of devotionalism? How have these divisions affected the outward perception of these religious bodies, and thus their ability to attract new members? Will young people and those disillusioned by their own churches' liberal stance eventually move to the more religiously conservative organizations described in Chapter 15?

Certainly, as well, there are other institutional pressures to explore beyond those cited here. For example, the Catholic church has grown considerably in recent years, owing primarily to recent immigration from southern and eastern Europe and Latin America. In fact, now accounting for some 47 percent of the Canadian population (Bibby 1987, 47), Roman Catholicism is poised to become the religion of the majority in this country. Yet, such growth has undoubtedly created some strains within the institution, as the church attempts to incorporate a growing body of members with very diverse cultural roots. Will the ethnic conflict afflicting the homelands of some of these newcomers transpose itself to Canadian Catholicism? How will church norms, including those related to governance, be affected by the influx? How well will the institution deal with the special needs of its new members, not only in terms of language, but also in social and counselling services?

It is also a fact that in its treatment of Canadian religious organizations, this book has primarily considered the Christian religion. While this does indeed reflect the reality of the Canadian religious market (close to 90 percent of Canadians identify with one Christian denomination or another), other religions are growing in adherents — many of which are relatively new to Canada, such as Hinduism and

Islam (Bibby 1987, 27). What factors condition — and threaten — the growth and maintenance of these religions? Perhaps more importantly, we may inquire as to the tensions that such newly transplanted faiths (and indeed their members) experience in the largely Christian (and often hostile) Canadian environment.

While these suggestions for further research in the sociology of religion represent a broad range of subject areas, they are certainly not the only possibilities. Without question, these are turbulent and challenging times for Canadian religion; therefore, researchers today are provided with an almost unlimited array of opportunities to ply their craft. This book is more than an attempt to inform. It is also intended to serve as an incentive to both neophyte academics and "old pros" alike to step forward and avail themselves of these opportunities, thus contributing further to knowledge within this most fascinating sub-area of sociological enquiry.

Works Cited

Abbott, W. 1966. *Documents of Vatican II.* New York: American Press.

Aberle, D. 1962. "A Note on Relative Deprivation Theory..." In S. Thrupp (ed.), *Millennial Dreams in Action.* The Hague: Mouton.

Adams, H. 1975. *Prison of Grass.* Toronto: New Press.

"Address by Alberta native leader Harold Cardinal." *Catholic New Times* (31 March 1991):9, 13.

Adler, Margot. 1979. *Drawing Down the Moon: Witches, Druids, Goddess-Worshipping and Other Pagans.* Boston: Beacon Press.

Alaska Highway News. 1981. "Krishna paintings scam was to further God consciousness" (May 11, Fort St. John, BC).

Alberta Law Reports. 1979. Juvenile Court. "Re M. (L. and K.)." 7:220-246.

Altizer, Thomas J.J., and William Hamilton. 1966. *Radical Theology and the Death of God.* New York: Bobbs-Merrill.

Anglican Church of Canada. General Synod. 1977. *A Transforming Influence.* Toronto: Anglican Book Centre.

Archibald, Peter. 1978. *Social Psychology as Political Economy.* Toronto: McGraw-Hill Ryerson.

Aron, Raymond. 1957. *The Opium of the Intellectuals.* Translated by Terence Kilmartin. New York: Doubleday.

Assembly of Quebec Bishops. Social Affairs Committee. 1989. *A Heritage of Violence? A Pastoral Reflection on Conjugal Violence.* Translated by Antoinette Kinlough. Montreal: Social Affairs Commission of the Assembly of Quebec Bishops.

Atwood, Margaret. 1972a. *Survival: A Thematic Guide to Canadian Literature.* Toronto: Anansi.

————. 1972b. *Surfacing.* Toronto: Anansi.

————. 1977. "Canadian Monsters: Some Aspects of the Supernatural in Canadian Fiction." In David Staines (ed.), *The Canadian Imagination.* Cambridge, MA: Harvard University Press.

————. 1991. "Concerning Franklin and his Gallant Crew." *Books in Canada* 20(4):20-26.

Bahr, Howard M., and Stan L. Albrecht. 1989. "Strangers Once More: Patterns of Disaffiliation from Mormonism." *Journal for the Scientific Study of Religion* 28:180-200.

Bailey, Edward. 1983. "The Implicit Religion of Contemporary

Society: An Orientation and Plea for its Study." *Religion* 13(1):69-83.
———. 1984. "Civil Religion, Common Religion and Folk Religion." In J. Bowden (ed.), *A Dictionary of Religious Education.* London: SCM Press.
———. (ed.). 1986. *A Workbook in Popular Religion.* Dorchester: Partners Publications.
———. 1987. "The Folk Religion of the English People." In Paul Badham (ed.), *Religion, State and Society in Modern Britain.* London: Macmillan.
———. 1990a. "The Implicit Religion of Contemporary Society: Some Studies and Reflections." *Social Compass* 37(4):483-497.
———. 1990b. "Implicit Religion: A Bibliographical Introduction." *Social Compass* 37(4):499-509.
Bainbridge, William Sims. 1978. *Satan's Power: A Deviant Psycho-theraphy Cult.* Berkeley: University of California Press.
Bainbridge, William Sims, and Rodney Stark. 1982. "Church and Cult in Canada." *Canadian Journal of Sociology* 7(4):351-366.
Banks, Olive. 1986. *Faces of Feminism.* Oxford: Basil Blackwells.
Baril, Alain, and George A. Mori. 1991. "Leaving the Fold: Declining Church Attendance." *Canadian Social Trends* (Autumn):21-24.
Barr, James. 1977. *Fundamentalism.* London: SCM.
Barrett, David (ed.). 1982. *World Christian Encyclopedia.* New York: Oxford.
Barrett, Stanley R. 1987. *Is God a Racist? The Right Wing in Canada.* Toronto: University of Toronto Press.
Baum, Gregory. 1980. *Catholics and Canadian Socialism.* Toronto: Lorimer.
———. 1984. "The Shift in Catholic Social Teaching." In Gregory Baum and Duncan Cameron (eds.), *Ethics and Economics.* Toronto: Lorimer.
———. 1986. "Recent Roman Catholic Social Teaching: A Shift to the Left." In Walter Block and Irving Hexham (eds.), *Religion, Economics, and Social Thought.* Vancouver: Fraser Institute.
———. 1987. *Compassion and Solidarity: The Church for Others.* Toronto: CBC Enterprises.
———. 1991a. *The Church in Quebec.* Ottawa: Novalis.
———. 1991b. "Good-Bye to the Ecumenist." *The Ecumenist* 29 (Spring):1-3.
Baum, Gregory, and Duncan Cameron. 1984. *Ethics and Economics:*

Canada's Catholic Bishops on the Economic Crisis. Toronto: Lorimer.

Bebbington, D.W. 1989. *Evangelicalism in Modern Britain: A History from the 1730's to the 1980's.* London: Unwin Hyman.

Becker, Howard S. 1979. "What's Happening to Sociology?" *Society* 16(5):19-24.

Beckford, James A. 1985. *Cult Controversies.* London: Tavistock.

————. 1989. *Religion and Advanced Industrial Society.* London: Unwin Hyman.

————. 1991. "Quasi-Marxisms and the Sociology of Religion." In David G. Bromley (ed.), *Religion and the Social Order: New Developments in Theory and Research.* Greenwich, CT: JAI Press.

Behiels, Michael D. 1985. *Prelude to Quebec's Quiet Revolution: Liberalism versus Neo-Nationalism, 1945-1960.* Kingston and Montreal: McGill-Queen's.

Beirne, Anne, with Cathy Carlyle-Gordge. 1982. "The sackcloth adversity." *Macleans* (6 September):44-45.

Bélanger, André J. 1977. *Ruptures et constantes: Quatre idéologies du Québec en éclatment: La Relève, la JEC, Cité Libre, Parti Pris.* Montreal: Hurtubise HMH.

Bélanger, Sarah. 1988. *Les soutanes roses. Portrait du personnel pastoral féminin au Québec.* Montreal: Bellarmin.

Bell, Daniel. 1961. *The End of Ideology.* New York: Collier Books.

————. 1977. "The Return of the Sacred? The Argument on the Future of Religion." *British Journal of Sociology* 28:419-449.

Bellah, Robert N. 1967. "Civil Religion in America." *Daedalus* 96(1):1-21.

————. 1970. "Christianity and Symbolic Realism." *Journal for the Scientific Study of Religion* 9:89-96.

———— (ed.). 1973. *Emile Durkheim: On Morality and Society.* Chicago: University of Chicago Press.

————. 1975. *The Broken Covenant: American Civil Religion in Time of Trial.* New York: Seabury Press.

————. 1976. "Comment of 'Bellah and the New Orthodoxy.'" *Sociological Analysis* 37(2):167-168.

Bellah, Robert et al. 1986. *Habits of the Heart: Individualism and Commitment in American Life.* New York: Harper and Row.

————. 1991. *The Good Society.* New York: Alfred A. Knopf.

Berger, Peter L. 1961. *The Noise of Solemn Assemblies.* Garden City, NY: Doubleday.

———. 1967. *The Sacred Canopy.* Garden City, NY: Doubleday.

———. 1969. *A Rumour of Angels.* Garden City, NY: Doubleday.

———. 1974. "Some Second Thoughts on Substantive Versus Functional Definitions of Religion." *Journal for the Scientific Study of Religion* 13(2):125-133.

———. 1986. "Religion in Post-Protestant America." Commentary 81:41-46.

Bergeron, Richard. 1982. *Le Cortege des fous de Dieu ... Un Chretien scrute les nouvelles religions.* Montreal: Editions Paulines & Apostolat des Editions.

———. 1983. "Towards a Theological Interpretation of the New Religions." In John Coleman and Gregory Baum (eds.), *New Religious Movements.* New York: The Seabury Press.

Berkhofer, R. 1979. *The White Man's Indian.* New York: Vintage.

Berry, Thomas. 1988. *The Dream of the Earth.* San Francisco: Sierra Club Books.

Berton, Pierre. 1965. *The Comfortable Pew.* Toronto: McClelland and Stewart.

———. 1970. *The National Dream: The Great Railway, 1871-1881.* Toronto: McClelland and Stewart.

———. 1974. *The National Dream: The Last Spike.* Toronto: McClelland and Stewart.

Beyer, Peter. 1989. "The Evolution of Roman Catholicism in Quebec: A Luhmannian Neo-Functionalist Interpretation." In Roger O'Toole (ed.), *Sociological Studies in Roman Catholicism.* Lewiston, NY, and Queenston, ON: Mellen.

Bibby, Reginald W. 1979. "Religion and Modernity: The Canadian Case." *Journal for the Scientific Study of Religion* 18(1):1-17.

———. 1983a. "Religionless Christianity: A Profile of Religion and Covergence in the Canadian 80s." *Social Indicators Research* 2:169-181.

———. 1983b. "Searching for Invisible Thread: Meaning Systems in Contemporary Canada." *Journal for the Scientific Study of Religion* 22(2):118.

———. 1987. *Fragmented Gods: the Poverty and Potential of Religion in Canada.* Toronto: Irwin Publishing.

———. 1990. "La religion à la carte au Québec: une analyse de tendances." *Sociologie et sociétés* 22(2):133-144.

———. 1991. "Religion Facing Serious Credibility Crisis." *Project Can90,* Release #11.

———. 1992. Personal communication to authors re: Project Canada unpublished results.

Bibby, Reginald W., and Donald C. Posterski. 1985. *The Emerging Generation: An Inside Look at Canada's Teenagers.* Toronto: Irwin Publishing.

———. 1992. *Teen Trends: A Nation in Motion.* Toronto: Stoddart.

Bibby, Reginald W., and Harold R. Weaver. 1985. "Cult Consumption in Canada: A Further Critique of Stark and Bainbridge." *Sociological Analysis* 46:445-460.

Biermans, John T. 1988. *The Odyssey of the New Religions Today: A Case Study of the Unification Church.* Lewiston, NY: Edwin Mellen Press.

Bird, Frederick. 1977. "A Comparative Analysis of the Rituals Used by Some Contemporary 'New' Religious and Para-Religious Movements." In Peter Slater (ed.), *Religion and Culture in Canada.* Canadian Corporation for Studies in Religion.

———. 1978. "Charisma and Ritual in New Religious Movements." In Jacob Needleman and George Baker (eds.), *Understanding the New Religions.* New York: The Seabury Press.

———. 1979. "The Pursuit of Innocence: New Religious Movements and Moral Accountability." *Sociological Analysis* 40(4):335-346.

———. 1980. "The Nature and Function of Ritual Forms: A Sociological Discussion." *Studies in Religion* 9(4):387-402.

Bird, Frederick, and William Reimer. 1976. "New Religious and Para-Religious Movements in Montreal." In Stewart Crysdale and Les Wheatcroft (eds.), *Religion in Canadian Society.* Toronto: Macmillan.

———. 1982. "Participation Rates in New Religious Movements." *Journal for the Scientific Study of Religion.* 21(1):1-14.

Bird, Frederick B., and Frances Westley. 1985. "The Economic Strategies of New Religious Movements." *Sociological Analysis* 46(2):157-170.

Biteaux, Armand. 1975. *The New Consciousness.* Willits, CA: Oliver Press.

Blair, S.R. 1977. "An Investigative Report on Twin Valleys Requested by the Minister." [Ontario] Ministry of Colleges and Universities.

(December).

Blau, Peter M., and Marshall W. Meyer. 1971. *Bureaucracy in Modern Society.* New York: Random House.

Blaug, Mark. 1990. "On the Historiography of Economics." *Journal of the History of Economic Thought* 12:27-37.

Bliss, Kathleen. 1952. *The Service and Status of Women in the Churches.* London: SCM Press Ltd.

Block, Walter. 1983. "On Economics and the Canadian Bishops." *Focus* 3:1-76.

Bloom, Allan. 1987. *The Closing of the American Mind.* New York: Simon and Schuster.

Blumstock, Robert. 1967. "Anglo-Saxon Lament." *Canadian Review of Sociology and Anthropology* 4(2):98-105.

Bookchin, Murray. 1989. *Remaking Society.* Montreal: Black Rose.

Bottomore, Tom. 1981. "A Marxist Consideration of Durkheim." *Social Forces* 59:902-917.

Bouchard, Alain. 1990. "La Bible et la Sensualite. Reevaluation du concept de syncretisme par l'etude d'une nouvelle religion: le Mouvement raelien." Paper presented at the Canadian Society for the Study of Religion, May 21-24, Victoria, BC.

Bozinoff, Lorne, and Peter MacIntosh. 1991. "Church Attendance Rebounds Slightly to 31%." *The Gallup Report.* Toronto: Gallup Canada (June 22):1-2.

————. 1992. "Church Attendance Highest in Five Years." *The Gallup Report.* Toronto: Gallup Canada (June 6):1-2.

Brady, Diane. 1991. "Saving the Boomers." *Maclean's* (June 3):50-51.

Braudel, Fernand. 1984. *The Perspective of the World.* Translated by S. Reynolds. New York: Harper and Row.

Brenner, Rachel Feldhay. 1990. "A.M. Klein and Mordechai Richler: The Poetics of the Search for Providence in the Post-Holocaust World." *Studies in Religion/Sciences Religieuses* 19(2).

Brierley, Peter. 1991. *"Christian England": What the English Church Census Reveals.* London: Marc Europe.

Brinkerhoff, Merlin B., and Kathryn L. Burke. 1980. "Disaffiliation: Some Notes on 'Falling from the Faith.'" *Sociological Analysis* 41:41-54.

Brinkerhoff, Merlin B., and Eugen Lupri. 1978. "Theoretical and Methodological Issues in the Use of Decision-Making as an Indicator of Conjugal Power: Some Canadian Observations."

Canadian Journal of Sociology 3:1-20.

Brinkerhoff, Merlin B., and Marlene M. Mackie. 1984. "Religious Denominations' Impact upon Gender Attitudes: Some Methodological Implications." *Review of Religious Research* 25:365-378.

———. 1986. "The Applicability of Social Distance for Religious Research: An Exploration." *Review of Religious Research* 28:151-167.

———. 1992 "Casting Off the Bonds of Organized Religion: A Religious-Careers Approach to the Study of Apostasy." *Review of Religious Research* (forthcoming).

British Columbia Provincial Court. 1987-1989. "Information on Stephen Phillip Kapitany." Court File Number 32840C F.

Bromley, David. 1985. "Financing the Millennium: The Economic Structure of the Unificationist Movement." *Journal for the Scientific Study of Religion* 24(3):253-274.

———. 1988. "Religious Disaffiliation: Analytical Social Process." In David G. Bromley (ed.), *Falling from the Faith: Causes and Consequences of Religious Apostasy.* Newbury Park, CA: Sage.

Bruce, Steve. 1984. *Firm in the Faith.* Chippenham: Gower.

Bruce, William E., and John H. Sims. 1975. "Religious Apostasy and Political Radicalism." *Journal of Youth and Adolescence* 4:207-214.

Brunet, Michel. 1964. "Trois dominantes de la pensée canadienne-française: l'agriculturisme, l'anti-étatisme et le messianisme." In Michel Brunet (ed.), *La présence anglaise et les Canadiens: Etudes sur l'histoire de la pensée des deux Canadas.* Montreal: Beauchemin.

Burke, Peter. 1980. *Sociology and History.* London: Allen and Unwin.

Butterfield, Steve. 1986. *Amway: The Cult of Free Enterprise.* Montreal: Black Rose Books.

Callahan, Daniel (ed.). 1966. *The Secular City Debate.* New York: Macmillan.

Calloway, C. 1987. *Crown and Calumet.* Norman: University of Oklahoma Press.

Campbell, Angus, Philip E. Converse, and Willard L. Rodgers. 1976. *The Quality of American Life.* New York: Russell Sages Foundation.

Campbell, Murray. 1985. "OPP scientology raid finally nets guilty plea." *Globe and Mail* (14 December):A19.

Canada (Statistics Canada). 1986. *Census of Canada, 1981.* Ottawa: Department of Supply and Services.

"Canadian Bishops 'renovate' their corporate house." 1989. *Catholic New Times* (17 December): 8-9.

Canadian Conference of Catholic Bishops. 1985. *Women in the Church: Discussion Papers.* Ottawa: Canadian Conference of Catholic Bishops.

Canadian Conference of Catholic Bishops (CCCB). 1980. *Unemployment: The Human Costs.* Ottawa: CCCB.

Caplovitz, D., and F. Sherrow. 1977. *The Religious Drop-outs: Apostasy among College Graduates.* Beverly Hills, CA: Sage Publications.

Cappon, Paul (ed.). 1978. *In Our Own House: Social Perspectives on Canadian Literature.* Toronto: McClelland and Stewart.

Cardinal, Harold. 1976. *The Rebirth of Canada's Indians.* Edmonton: Hurtig.

Carlson, J. (ed.). 1991. *The Journey.* Toronto: Anglican Book Centre.

Carmody, Denise Lardner. 1982. *Feminism and Christianity: A Two-way Reflection.* Nashville: Abingdon.

Carnell, Edward John. 1961. *The Case for Orthodox Theology.* London: Marshal, Morgan and Scott.

Carroll, Jackson, Barbara Hargrove, and Adair Lummis. 1983. *Women of the Cloth: A New Opportunity for the Churches.* San Francisco: Harper and Row.

Cartwright, Robert H., and Stephen A. Kent. 1993. "Social Control in Alternative Religions: A Familial Perspective." *Sociological Analysis* (forthcoming).

Catton, William R. and Riley E. Dunlap. 1979. "Environmental Sociology: A New Paradigm." In S.G. McNall (ed.), *Theoretical Perspectives in Sociology.* New York: St. Martin's.

Chagnon, Roland. 1979. *Les charismatiques au Québec.* Montreal: Québec/Amérique.

———. 1983. "Nouvelles religions et quête d'identite: Le cas de l'Eglise de Scientologie de Montreal." *Studies in Religion* 12(4):407-432.

———. 1985a. *La Scientologie: une nouvelle religion de la puissance.* Montreal: Hurtubise.

———. 1985b. *Trois nouvelles religions de la lumiere et du son: La*

Science de la Spiritualite, Eckankar, La Mission de la Lumiere Divine. Montreal: Editions Paulines and Mediaspaul.

———. 1985c. "Les nouvelles religions dans la dynamique socio-culturelle recente au Quebec." *Canadian Issues* 7:118-151.

———. 1986a. "Religion, secularisation et deplacements du sacre." In Yvon Desrosiers (ed.), *Religion et culture au Quebec.* Montreal: Fides.

———. 1986b. "Les nouvelles religions d'inspiration orientale au Quebec." In Yvon Desrosiers (ed.), *Religion et Culture au Quebec.* Montreal: Fides.

Chaves, Mark. 1989. "Secularization and Religious Revival: Evidence from U.S. Church Attendance Rates, 1972-1986." *Journal for the Scientific Study of Religion* 28:464-477.

Choquette, Diane. 1985. *New Religious Movements in the United States and Canada.* Westport, CT: Greenwood Press.

Christ, Carol, and Judith Plaskow (eds.). 1979. *Womanspirit Rising.* San Francisco: Harper and Row.

Clark, S.D. 1942. *The Social Development of Canada.* Toronto: University of Toronto Press.

———. 1948. *Church and Sect in Canada.* Toronto: University of Toronto Press.

———. 1968. *The Developing Canadian Community.* Toronto: University of Toronto Press.

———. 1976. *Canadian Society in Historical Perspective.* Toronto: McGraw-Hill Ryerson.

Clarke, Tony. 1981. "Communities for Justice." *Ecumenist* 19 (January-February):17-25.

Cleary, Edward. 1985. *Crisis and Change: The Church in Latin America Today.* Maryknoll, NY: Orbis.

Clement, Wallace. 1975. *The Canadian Corporate Elite.* Toronto: McClelland and Stewart.

———. 1978. *Continental Corporate Power.* Toronto: McClelland and Stewart.

Cohen, Ronald. 1978. "Modernism and the Hinterland: The Canadian Example." In D. Glenday, H. Guindon, A. Turowetz (eds.), *Modernization and the Canadian State.* Toronto: Macmillan of Canada.

Collins, Randall. 1985. *Three Sociological Traditions.* New York: Oxford University Press.

Colson, Charles W. 1977. *Born Again.* Old Tappen: Fleming H. Revell.

Committee on the Healing Arts. 1970. *Report of the Committee on the Healing Arts,* vol. 2. Toronto: The Queen's Printer.

Comte, Auguste. 1966. *System of Positive Polity.* New York: Burt Franklin Research and Source Works Series.

Condron, John G., and Joseph B. Tamney. 1985. "Religious 'Nones': 1957 to 1982." *Sociological Analysis* 46:415-423.

Conway, Flo, and Jim Siegelman. 1984. *Holy Terror: The Fundamentalist War on America's Freedoms in Religion, Politics and Our Private Lives.* New York: Dell.

Coser, Lewis A. 1981. "The Uses of Classical Sociological Theory." In Buford Rhea (ed.), *The Future of the Sociological Classics.* London: George Allen and Unwin.

Côté, Pauline. 1988. "Socialisations sacrales, acteurs féminins, post-modernité: les femmes dans le Renouveau charismatique canadien francophone." *Studies in Religion/Sciences religieuses* 17:329-346.

Courcy, Raymond. 1985. "L'Eglise catholique au Québec: de la fin d'un monopole au redéploiment dans une société plurielle." *Canadian Issues* 7:86-98.

————. 1988. "L'Eglise catholique au Québec: de la fin d'un monopole au redéploiement dans une société plurielle." *L'Année sociologique* 38:109-133.

Cox, Harvey. 1984. *Religion in the Secular City.* New York: Simon and Schuster.

Crabtree, Davida F. 1970. "Women's Liberation and the Church." In S.B. Doely (ed.), *Women's Liberation and the Church.* New York: Association Press.

Craven, Wesley Frank. 1956. *The Legend of the Founding Fathers.* Ithaca, NY: Cornell University Press.

Crysdale, Stewart. 1976. "The Sociology of the Social Gospel: Quest for a Modern Ideology." In Stewart Crysdale and Les Wheatcroft (eds.), *Religion in Canadian Society.* Toronto: Macmillan.

Crysdale, Stewart, and Les Wheatcroft. 1976. "The Analysis of Religion." In Stewart Crysdale and Les Wheatcroft (eds.), *Religion in Canadian Society.* Toronto: Macmillan.

Cuneo, C. 1980. "Class, Stratification and Mobility." In R. Hagedorn (ed.), *Sociology.* Toronto: Holt, Rinehart and Winston.

————. 1989. *Catholics Against the Church: Anti-Abortion Protest in Toronto, 1969-1985.* Toronto: University of Toronto Press.

Daly, Mary. 1968. *The Church and the Second Sex.* London: Harper and Row.

————. 1973. *Beyond God the Father: Toward a Philosophy of Women's Liberation.* Boston: Beacon Press.

————. 1975. *The Church and the Second Sex: With a New Feminist Postchristian Introduction.* London: Colophon Books.

David, J. (ed.). 1972. *The American Indian: The First Victim.* New York: Morrow.

Davies, Robertson. 1975. *World of Wonders.* Harmondsworth: Penguin.

————. 1985. *What's Bred in the Bone.* Harmondsworth: Penguin.

————. 1987. "Keeping Faith." *Saturday Night* 102(1):187-192.

Davis, Kingsley. 1949. *Human Society.* New York: Macmillan.

DeMara, Bruce. 1992. "Scientologists infiltrated Metro police, trial told." *Toronto Star* (24 April).

Demerath, N.J. III, and Rhys H. Williams. 1992. "Secularization in a Community Context." *Journal for the Scientific Study of Religion* 31:189-206.

Denault, Bernard. 1986. "Un catholicisme discret." In Yvon Desrosiers (ed.), *Religion et culture au Québec: Figures contemporain du sacré.* Montreal: Fides.

"Development and Peace in Canada." 1988. *Global Village Voice* 13(Fall):8.

"Development and Peace Worries about Share Lent '91." 1991. *Catholic New Times.* (3 March):16.

Devine, E. 1923. *The Canadian Martyrs.* Montreal: Canadian Messenger.

Dobbelaere, Karel. 1987. "Some Trends in European Sociology of Religion: The Secularization Debate." *Sociological Analysis* 46:377-387.

————. 1981. "Secularization: A Multi-Dimensional Model," *Current Sociology* 29(2):1-216.

Dobryns, H. 1984. *Their Numbers Become Thinned: Native American Population Dynamics in Eastern North America.* Nashville: University of Tennessee Press.

Dobson, Andrew. 1990. *Green Political Thought.* London: Unwin Hyman.

Doely, S.B. (ed.). 1970. *Women's Liberation and the Church.* New York: Association Press.

Douglass, Jane Dempsey. 1974. "Women and the Continental Reformation." In Rosemary Radford Ruether (ed.), *Religion and Sexism.* New York: Simon and Schuster.

Dowell, Susan, and Linda Hurcombe. 1981. *Dispossessed Daughters of Eve: Faith and Feminism.* London: SCM Press.

Duffy, Dennis. 1985. "The Rejection of Modernity in Recent Canadian Fiction." *Canadian Issues, Themes Canadiens* 7:260-273.

Dunphy, Bill. 1992a. "Church Spy Web Alleged/Scientologists Trial." *Toronto Sun* (22 April):23.

————. 1992b. "Church Guilty in Spy Case." *Toronto Star* (26 June):1.

Durkheim, Emile. 1976. *The Elementary Forms of the Religious Life.* London: George Allen and Unwin.

Dyke, N. 1991. *What is the Indian "Problem"?* St. Johns: Memorial University, Institute of Social and Economic Research.

Ebaugh, Helen Rose Fuchs. 1988. *Becoming an Ex: The Process of Role Exit.* Chicago and London: University of Chicago Press.

ECSA (Episcopal Commission for Social Affairs). 1984. *Mandate.* Mimeo.

Ehrenfeld, David. 1978. *The Arrogance of Humanism.* New York: Oxford.

Eksteins, Modris. 1989. *Rites of Spring: The Great War and the Birth of the Modern Age.* Toronto: Lester and Orpen Dennys.

Eliot, T.S. 1945. *What is a Classic?* London: Faber and Faber.

Evans-Pritchard, E.E. 1965. *Theories of Primitive Religion.* Oxford: Clarendon Press.

Express (British Columbia). 1978. "Sect man guilty of defrauding public." (22 November).

Farley, Edward. 1990. "The Modernist Element in Protestantism." *Theology Today* 47(2):135.

Felt, L. 1975. "Nationalism and the Possibility of a Relevant Anglo-Canadian Sociology." *Canadian Journal of Sociology* 1(3).

Fenn, Richard. 1976. "Bellah and the New Orthodoxy." *Sociological Analysis* 37(1):160-166.

Ferm, Deane W. 1986. *Third World Liberation Theologies.* Maryknoll, NY: Orbis.

Festinger, Leon. 1964. *When Prophecy Fails: A Social and Psychological Study of a Modern Group that Predicted the End of the World.* New York: Harper Torchbooks.

Feuer, Lewis. 1975. *Ideology and the Ideologists.* New York: Harper and Row.

Feuerbach, Ludwig. 1957. *The Essence of Christianity.* Translated by George Eliot. New York: Harper and Row.

Fiorenza, Elisabeth Schussler. 1985. *In Memory of Her: A Feminist Theological Reconstruction of Christian Origins.* New York: Crossroads.

————. 1979. "Women in the Early Christian Movement." In Carol Christ and Judith Plaskow (eds.), *Womanspirit Rising.* San Francisco: Harper and Row.

Flanagan, T. 1979. *Louis "David" Riel: Prophet of the New World.* University of Toronto Press.

Fraser, Blair. 1967. *The Search for Identity.* Toronto: Doubleday.

Fraser, George. 1990. "Satanic Ritual Abuse: A Cause of Multiple Personality Disorder." *Journal of Child and Youth Care.* (Special Issue):55-66.

Frazer, James. 1922. *The Golden Bough.* New York: Macmillan.

Freed, Josh. 1980. *Moonwebs.* Toronto: Virgo Press.

Freire, Paulo. 1970. *Pedagogy of the Oppressed.* New York: Seabury.

Freud, Sigmund. 1957. *The Future of an Illusion.* Garden City: Doubleday.

Friedrichs, Robert W. 1970. *A Sociology of Sociology.* New York: The Free Press.

Friendenberg, Edgar Z. 1980. *Deference to Authority: The Case of Canada.* White Plains, NY: M.E. Sharpe Inc.

Fromm, Erich. 1957. "A Social Psychological Interpretation of Lutheranism and Calvinism." In J. Milton Yinger (ed.), *Religion, Society, and the Individual.* New York: Macmillan.

Frye, Northrop. 1971. *The Bush Garden: Essays on the Canadian Imagination.* Toronto: Anansi.

————. 1977. "Haunted by Lack of Ghosts: Some Patterns in the Imagery of Canadian Poetry." In David Staines (ed.), *The Canadian Imagination: Dimensions of a Literary Culture.* Cambridge, MA: Harvard University Press.

————. 1982. *Divisions on a Ground: Essays on Canadian Culture.* Toronto: Anansi.

Fukuyama, Francis. 1991. *The End of History and the Last Man.* New York: The Free Press.

Fuller, David Otis. 1961. *Valiant for the Truth.* London: Oliphants.

Fulton, John. 1987. "Religion and Politics in Gramsci: An Introduction." *Sociological Analysis* 48(3):197-216.

Gager, John G. 1975. *Kingdom and Community. The Social World of Early Christianity.* Englewood Cliffs, NJ: Prentice-Hall.

Gallup Canada, Ltd. 1992. *The Gallup Report.* Toronto. June 6.

Gallup, George Jr. 1992. *Emerging Trends.* Princeton: Princeton Research Center.

Gallup, George Jr., and Jim Castelli. 1989. *The People's Religion: American Faith in the 90's.* New York: Macmillan.

Gallup Poll Limited, Canadian. 1985. *Report to Sharelife, Archdiocese of Toronto.* Unpublished report.

Gannon, T. 1989. *World Catholicism in Transition.* New York: Macmillan.

Garfinkel, Harold. 1967. *Studies in Ethnomethodology.* Englewood Cliffs, NJ: Prentice-Hall.

Gault, John. 1988. "Sin and the Liberal Conscience." *Toronto Life* (September):39-80.

Gee, Ellen M., and Jean E. Veevers. 1989. "Religiously Unaffiliated Canadians: Sex, Age, and Regional Variations." *Social Indicators Research* 21:611-627.

―――. 1990. "Religious Involvement and Life Satisfaction in Canada: A Research Note." *Sociological Analysis* 51:387-394.

Geertz, Clifford. 1966. "Religion as a Cultural System." In Michael Banton (ed.), *Anthropological Approaches to the Study of Religion.* London: Tavistock.

Gehrig, Gail. 1979. *American Civil Religion: An Assessment.* Society for the Scientific Study of Religion, Monograph Series, No. 3.

Gellner, Ernest. 1985. *Relativism and the Social Sciences.* Cambridge: Cambridge University Press.

Gerth, Hans, and C. Wright Mills (eds.). 1958. *From Max Weber: Essays in Sociology.* London: Routledge and Kegan Paul.

Gifford, Paul. 1988. *The Religious Right in Southern Africa.* Harare: Baobab Books.

Glenn, Norval D. 1987. "The Trend to 'No Religion' Respondents in U.S. National Surveys, Late 1950s to Early 1980s." *Public Opinion Quarterly* 51:293-314.

Glock, Charles Y., and Phillip E. Hammond (eds.). 1973. *Beyond the Classics? Essays in the Scientific Study of Religion.* New York:

Harper and Row.

Glock, C.Y., and R. Stark. 1965. *Religion and Society in Tension.* Chicago: Rand McNally.

Gollnick, James. 1990. "The Merlin Archetype and the Transformation of the Self." *Studies in Religion/Sciences Religieuses* 19(3):319-329.

Gosselin, Jean-Pierre, et Denis Monière. 1978. *Le Trust de la Foi.* Montreal: Editions Quebec.

Gould, Stephen Jay. 1970. *The Mismeasure of Man.* New York: Norton.

Gouldner, Alvin W. 1955. "Metaphysical Pathos and the Theory of Bureaucracy." *American Political Science Review* 49(2):496-507.

———. 1958. "Introduction" to *Emile Durkheim, Socialism and Saint-Simon.* Translated by C. Sattler. Yellow Springs, OH: The Antioch Press.

Government of Canada, Senate Debates. 1987. "Private Bill. Regional Vicar for Canada of the Prelature of the Holy Cross and Opus Dei – Second Reading – Debate Adjourned." (April 7):852-853.

Government of Canada, The Senate of Canada. 1986-1987. "Bill S-7. An Act to incorporate the Regional Vicar for Canada of the Prelature of the Holy Cross and Opus Dei." 2nd Session, 33rd Parliament, 35-36 Elizabeth II. First Reading, April 2, 1987.

Graham, Ron. 1990. *God's Dominion: A Sceptic's Quest.* Toronto: McClelland and Stewart.

Graham, Billy. 1955. *Peace with God.* New York: Doubleday.

Grant, George. 1965. *Lament for a Nation: The Defeat of Canadian Nationalism.* Toronto: McClelland and Stewart.

———. 1969. *Technology and Empire.* Toronto: Anansi.

Grant, John Webster. 1967. *The Canadian Experience of Church Union.* London: Lutterworth Press.

———. 1955. "Asking Questions of the Canadian Past." *Canadian Journal of Theology* 1:98-104.

———. 1976. "Religious and Theological Writings." In *Literary History of Canada* (2nd ed.) vol. 2. Toronto: University of Toronto Press.

———. 1984. *The Moon in Wintertime.* University of Toronto Press.

———. 1988. "'They Don't Speak For Me': The United Church's Crisis of Confidence." *Touchstone* 6(3).

Greeley, Andrew M. 1972a. *The Denominational Society.* Glenview,

IL: Scott, Foresman.

――――. 1972b. *Unsecular Man: The Persistence of Religion*. New York: Schocken Books.

――――. 1976. *Ethnicity, Denomination, and Inequality*. Beverly Hills, CA: Sage.

――――. 1981. "Catholics and the Upper Middle Class." *Social Forces* 59 (March):824-830.

Greeley, Andrew M., and Gregory Baum (eds.). 1973. *The Persistence of Religion*. New York: Herder and Herder.

Greil, Arthur L., and David R. Rudy. 1990. "On the Margins of the Sacred." In Thomas Robbins and Dick Anthony (eds.), *In Gods We Trust*. New Brunswick and London: Transaction Publishers.

Griffith-Thomas, W.H. 1930. *The Principals of Theology*. Toronto: Longmans, Green & Co.

Gross, Rita M. 1979. "Female God Language in a Jewish Context." In Carol Christ and Judith Plaskow (eds.), *Woman-spirit Rising*. San Francisco: Harper and Row.

Gunn, Giles B. (ed.). 1971. *Literature and Religion*. London: SCM Press.

Gusfield, Joseph R. 1953. *Symbolic Crusade*. Urbana: University of Illinois Press.

Habermas, Jürgen. 1971. *Knowledge and Human Interests*. Translated by J.J. Shapiro. Boston: Beacon Press.

――――. 1974. *Theory and Practice*. Translated by John Viertel. London: Heinemann.

Hadaway, C.K. 1978. "Life Satisfaction and Religion: A Re-analysis." *Social Forces* 56:636-643.

――――. 1989. "Identifying American Apostates: A Cluster Analysis." *Journal for the Scientific Study of Religion* 28:201-215.

Haiven, Judith. 1984. *Faith, Hope, No Charity: An Inside Look At the Born Again Movement in Canada and the United States*. Vancouver: New Star Books.

Hamberg, Eva M. 1991. "On Stability and Change in Religious Beliefs, Practice, and Attitudes: A Swedish Panel Study." *Journal for the Scientific Study of Religion* 30:63-80.

Hamelin, Jean. 1984. *Le XXee siècle Tome 2: De 1940 à nos jours*. Nive Voisine, (ed.). *Histoire du catholicisme québécois*. Montreal: Boreal Express.

Hamilton Spectator. 1976. "Sect Fined for Soliciting." (18 December).

Hamilton Spectator. 1985. "Memory of cult [Hare Krishna] still haunts young mother." (11 January).

Hammond, Phillip E. (ed.). 1985. *The Sacred in a Secular Age: Toward Revision in the Scientific Study of Religion.* Berkeley: University of California Press.

Hammond, T.C. 1960. *In Understanding Be Men.* London: Inter-Varsity Press.

Hannigan, John A. 1991. "Social Movement Theory and the Sociology of Religion: Toward a New Synthesis." *Sociological Analysis* 52(4):311-331.

Harrington, Michael. 1983. *The Politics at God's Funeral.* New York: Viking Penguin.

Harris, Michael. 1990. *Unholy Orders: Tragedy at Mount Cashel.* Markham, ON: Penguin Books Ltd.

Harris, W. 1893. *History of the Early Missions in Western Canada.* Toronto: Hunter, Rose.

Harrison, Janet. 1983. *Attitudes to the Bible, Church and God.* London: Bible Society.

Harrison, P.M. 1959. *Authority and Power in the Free Church Tradition.* Princeton: Princeton University Press.

Haskell, Francis. 1959. "Art and Society." In *International Encyclopedia of the Social Sciences,* vol. 3.

Haworth, Larry. 1977. *Decadence and Objectivity.* Toronto, University of Toronto Press.

Hawthorne, H. (ed.). 1967. *A Survey of the Contemporary Indians of Canada.* Ottawa: Indian Affairs Branch, vol. II.

Heaton, Timothy. 1986. "Sociodemographic Characteristics of Religious Groups in Canada." *Sociological Analysis* 47(1):54-65.

Hegy, Pierre. 1987. "The Invisible Catholicism," *Sociological Analysis* 48:167-176.

Heirich, Max. 1977. "Change of Heart: A Test of Some Widely Held Theories about Religious Conversion." *American Journal of Sociology* 85(3):653-680.

Hervieu-Léger, Danièle. 1985. *Vers Un Nouveau Christianisme?* Paris: Cerf.

Hewitt, W.E. 1991. *Base Christian Communities and Social Change in Brazil.* Lincoln: University of Nebraska Press.

Hewitt, W.E., and D. Lewis. 1988. "Liberation Theology in First and Third World Countries: A Comparison." *Journal of Church and*

State 30(4):33-50.

Hexham, Irving, and Karla Poewe. 1986. *Understanding Cults and New Religions.* Grand Rapids, MI: Eerdmans.

Hexham, Irving, Raymond Currie, and J.B. Townsend. 1988. "New Religious Movements." In *The Canadian Encyclopedia*, 2nd ed. Edmonton, AB: Hurtig Publishers.

Hicks, Robert D. 1991. *In Pursuit of Satan: The Police and the Occult.* Buffalo, NY: Prometheus Books.

Hill, Daniel G. (Special Advisor). 1980. *Study of Mind Development Groups, Sects and Cults in Ontario.* Toronto: Government of Ontario.

Hill, Michael, and Richard Bowman. 1985. "Religious Aherence and Religious Practice in Contemporary New Zealand." *Archives de Sciences Sociales des Religions* 59:91-112.

Hiller, Harry. 1982. *Society and Change: S.D. Clark and the Development of Canadian Sociology.* Toronto: University of Toronto Press.

Hobsbawm, E.J. (ed.). 1983. *The Invention of Tradition.* Cambridge: Cambridge University Press.

Hobsbawm, Eric, and Terence Ranger (eds.). 1983. *The Invention of Tradition.* Cambridge: Cambridge University Press.

Hoffer, Eric. 1966. *The True Believer.* New York: Harper and Row.

Hoge, Dean. 1987. *Future of Catholic Leadership: Responses to the Priest Shortage.* Kansas City: Sheed and Ward.

―――. 1988. "Why Catholics Drop Out." In David G. Bromley (ed.), *Falling from the Faith: Causes and Consequences of Religious Apostasy.* Newbury Park, CA: Sage.

Holm, Nils G. 1989. "Religion in Finland and the Scandinavian Model." Presented at the annual meeting of the International Conference of the Sociology of Religion, Helsinki.

Holm, Olga. 1984. Personal communication.

Holton, Margaret Lindsay (ed.). 1983. *Spirit of Toronto.* Toronto: Image Publishing Inc.

Hornsby-Smith, Michael P. 1989. *The Changing Parish.* London and New York: Routledge.

Horton, Robin. 1968. "Neo-Tylorianism: Sound Sense or Sinister Prejudice?" *Man: The Journal of the Royal Anthropological Institute* 3:625-634.

Hospital, Clifford. 1989. "Christianity in a Multifaith World."

Mandate (Special Edition) 20(4):34-36.

Hostetler, John A. 1974. *Hutterite Society.* Baltimore: Johns Hopkins University Press.

Hughey, Michael W. 1983. *Civil Religion and Moral Order.* London: Greenwood Press.

Hultkranz, A. 1979. *The Religion of the American Indians.* Berkeley: University of California Press.

Hume, Stephen. 1987. "Lives Torn to Rout Demons." *Times Colonist* (13 June):A1, A6, (Victoria, BC) .

Hummelen, R., and K. Hummelen (eds.). 1985. *Stories of Survival.* New York: Friendship Press.

Humphries, Jefferson. 1983. *The Otherness Within.* Baton Rouge: Louisiana State University Press.

Hunsberger, Bruce E. 1980. "A Re-examination of the Antecedents of Apostasy." *Review of Religious Research* 21:158-170.

Hunsberger Bruce E., and L.B. Brown. 1984. "Religious Socialization, Apostasy, and the Impact of Family Background." *Journal for the Scientific Study of Religion* 23:239-251.

Hunter, James D. 1983. *American Evangelicalism: Conservative Religion and the Quandry of Modernity.* New Brunswick, NJ: Rutgers University Press.

Ice, Martha Long. 1987. *Clergywomen and Their World Views: Calling for a New Age.* New York: Praeger.

Innis, H.A. 1930. *The Fur Trade in Canada.* New Haven: Yale University Press.

————. 1933. *Problem of Staple Production in Canada.* Toronto: Ryerson Press.

Itwaru, Arnold Harrichand. 1990. *The Invention of Canada: Literary Text and the Immigrant Imaginary.* Toronto: TSAR Publications.

Jacquet, Constant H. Jr., and Alice M. Jones. 1992. *Yearbook of American & Canadian Churches 1991.* Nashville: Abingdon.

James, William. 1960. *The Varieties of Religious Experience.* London: Collins.

————. 1985. "Religious Symbolism in Recent English Canadian Fiction." *Canadian Issues/Themes Canadiens* 7:256-259.

Jay, Martin. 1973. *The Dialectical Imagination: A History of the Frankfurt School and the Institute of Social Research 1923-1950.* Boston: Little, Brown.

Jenness, Diamond. 1976. "Canadian Indian Religion." In Stewart

Crysdale and Les Wheatcroft (eds.), *Religion in Canadian Society.* Toronto: MacMillan.

Jewett, Paul K. 1980. *The Ordination of Women.* Grand Rapids: William B. Erdmans.

Johnson, Benton. 1963. "On Church and Sect." *American Sociological Review* 28:538-549.

Johnson, L. 1974. *Poverty and Wealth: The Capitalist Labour Market and Income Distribution in Canada.* Toronto: New Hogtown Press.

Johnson, Paul. 1988. *Intellectuals.* London: Weidenfeld and Nicolson.

Johnstone, Ronald. L. 1992. *Religion in Society.* Englewood Cliffs: Prentice-Hall.

Jones, D.G. 1970. *Butterfly on Rock: A Study of Themes and Images in Canadian Literature.* Toronto: University of Toronto Press.

Kalbach, W.E., and W.W. McVey, Jr. 1971. *The Demographic Bases of Canadian Society.* Toronto: McGraw-Hill Ryerson.

Kanter, Rosabeth. 1972. *Commitment and Community: Communes and Utopias in Sociological Perspective.* Cambridge, MA: Harvard University Press.

Kantrowitz, Barbara. 1992. "Sociology's Lonely Crowd." *Newsweek* (3 February):55.

Kehler, L. (ed.). 1969. *The Church and the Original Canadians.* Winnipeg: Mennonite Central Committee.

Kehoe, A. 1989. *The Ghost Dance: Ethnohistory and Revitalization.* Fort Worth, TX: Holt, Rinehart and Winston.

Kelly, Dean M. 1986. *Why Conservative Churches Are Growing.* Macon: Mercer University Press.

———. 1978. "Why Conservative Churches Are Still Growing." *Journal for the Scientific Study of Religion* 17:165-172.

Kendrick, Martyn. 1988. *Anatomy of a Nightmare: The Failure of Society in Dealing with Child Sexual Abuse.* Toronto: MacMillan.

Kenner, Hugh. 1954. "The Case of the Missing Face." In Malcolm Ross (ed.), *Our Sense of Identity.* Toronto: Ryerson Press.

Kenny, Gary. 1989. "The Mosaic and the Church." *Mandate* (Special Edition) 20(4):8-10.

Kent, Stephen A. 1982a. "Relative Deprivation and Resource Mobilization: A Study of Early Quakerism." *British Journal of Sociology* 33(4):529-544.

———. 1982b. "A Sectarian Interpretation of the Rise of Mahayana."

Religion 12:311-332.

———. 1990. "Deviance Strategies and Normative Designations Within the Canadian 'Cult/New Religions' Debate." *Canadian Journal of Sociology* 15(4):393-416.

———. 1991a. "International Social Control by the Church of Scientology." Paper presented at the Annual Meeting of the Society for the Scientific Study of Religion, November, Pittsburgh.

———. 1991b. "Religiously Ideological Organizations as International Social Movements." Paper Presented at New Religions in a Global Perspective Conference, May 16-17, Santa Barbara Centre for Humanistic Studies, CA.

———. 1992. "Deviant Scripturalism and Ritual Satanic Abuse." Paper Presented at the Canadian Sociology and Anthropology Association and the Canadian Society for the Study of Religion, June, Victoria.

Kenton, E. 1927. *The Indians of North America: Selected from "The Jesuit Relations."* New York: Harcourt, Brace.

Kermode, Frank. 1957. *Romantic Image.* London: Fontana Books.

Kohn, Rachael. 1983. "Dual-membership and Sectarian Status: The Case of a Hebrew Christian Group." *Studies in Religion* 12(2):1-57-166.

———. 1985. "Rejoinder to Roger O'Toole's 'Comment on Dual Membership and Sectarian Status...'" *Studies in Religion* 14(2):238-239.

Koop, Doug. 1991. "Are Canadians Really Going Back to Church?" *Christian Week* (September 10):1,4.

Korp, M. 1991. "Before Mother Earth: The Amerindian Earth Mound." *Studies in Religion* 19(1):17-25.

Krotz, L. 1982. "Native Spirituality." *The United Church Observer* 46(2):22-29.

Kuhn, Thomas S. 1962. *The Nature of Scientific Revolutions.* Chicago: University of Chicago Press.

———. 1970. *The Structure of Scientific Revolutions.* Chicago: University of Chicago Press.

Langley, Myrtle. 1983. *Equal Woman: A Christian Feminist Perspective.* Basingstoke: Marshall, Morgan and Scott.

Lasch, Christopher. 1978. *The Culture of Narcissism: American Life in an Age of Diminishing Expectations.* New York: Norton.

Leach, Edmund R. 1961. "Golden Bough or Gilded Twig?" *Daedalus*

90:371-387.

Leacy, F. (ed.). 1983. *Historical Statistics of Canada.* Ottawa: Department of Supply and Services.

Lee, John A. 1970. *Sectarian Healers and Hypnotherapy. A Study for the Committee on the Healing Arts.* Toronto: Queen's Printer.

Lehman, Edward C., Jr. 1980. "Placement of Men and Women in the Ministry." *Review of Religious Research* 22(1):18-40.

———. 1981a. "Organizational Resistance to Women in Ministry." *Sociological Analysis* 42(2):101-18.

———. 1981b. "Patterns of Lay Resistance to Women in Ministry." *Sociological Analysis* 41(4):317-38.

———. 1985. *Women Clergy: Breaking Through Gender Barriers.* New Brunswick: Transaction Publishers.

Lehman, Edward C., Jr. 1987. *Women Clergy in England: Sexism, Modern Consciousness, and Church Viability.* Lewiston: Edwin Mellen Press.

———. 1992. *Gender and Work: The Case of the Clergy.* Albany: State University of New York Press.

Lemert, Charles C. 1975. "Defining Non-Church Religion." *Review of Religious Research* 16:186-197.

Lemieux, Raymond. 1987. "Charisme, massmedia et religion populaire. Le voyage du Pape au Canada." *Social Compass* 34:11-31.

———. 1990. "Le catholicisme québécois: une question de culture." *Sociologie et sociétés* 22(2):145-164.

Lenski, Gerhard. 1966. *Power and Privilege: A Theory of Social Stratification.* New York: McGraw-Hill.

Levine, Daniel H. (ed.). 1980. *Churches and Politics in Latin America.* Beverly Hills: Sage.

Levine, Saul. 1984. *Radical Departures: Desperate Detours to Growing Up.* New York: Harcourt Brace Jovanovich.

Linteau, Paul-André, René Durocher, and Jean-Claude Robert. 1983. *Quebec: A History, 1867-1929.* Toronto: Lorimer.

Lippert, Randy. 1990. "The Construction of Satanism as a Social Problem in Canada." *Canadian Journal of Sociology* 15(4):417-439.

———. 1992. "Reply to Tucker." *Canadian Journal of Sociology* 17(2):191-192.

Lipset, S.M. 1950. *Agrarian Socialism.* Berkeley and Los Angeles:

University of California Press.

———. 1956. *Union Democracy*. Garden City, NJ: Doubleday.

———. 1963. *The First New Nation*. New York: Basic Books.

———. 1985. "Canada and the United States: the Cultural Dimension." In Charles F. Doran and John F. Sigler (eds.), *Canada and the United States: Enduring Friendship, Persistent Stress*. Englewood Cliffs, NJ, and Scarborough, ON: Prentice-Hall.

———. 1991. *Continental Divide: The Values and Institutions of the United States and Canada*. New York: Routledge.

Lofland, John. 1966. *Doomsday Cult*. Englewood Cliffs: Prentice-Hall.

Long, Charles H. 1967. "Prolegomenon to a Religious Hermeneutic." *History of Religions* 6(3):254-264.

Luckmann, Thomas. 1967. *The Invisible Religion: the Problem of Religion in Modern Society*. New York: Macmillan.

Luxton, Meg. 1980. *More Than A Labour of Love*. Toronto: Women's Press.

MacEoin, Gary. 1966. *What Happened at Rome?* New York: Holt, Rinehart, and Winston.

MacKendrick, Louis A. 1986. "God and His People in Modern English-Canadian Novels." In L. MacKendrick (ed.), *God and Man in Modern Literature*. Windsor, ON: Canterbury College.

Mackie, Marlene M. 1975. "Defection from Hutterite Colonies." In R.M. Pike and E. Zureik (eds.), *Socialization and Social Values in Canada*, vol. 2. Toronto: New Press.

Mackie, Marlene M., and Merlin B. Brinkerhoff. 1986. "Blessings and Burdens: the Reward-Cost Calculus of Religious Denominations." *Canadian Journal of Sociology* 11(2):157-181.

———. 1983. "Moonie Conferences: Dialog or Duplicity?" *Update* 7(3):22-37.

MacLeod, H.G. 1980. "The Transformation of the United Church of Canada 1946-1977: A Study in the Sociology of the Denomination." Unpublished Ph.D. dissertation, University of Toronto.

McAteer, Michael. 1981. "NFB film of Krishna devotees in Montreal upsets cult critics." *Toronto Star* (12 September).

———. 1988. "United Church Braces for Struggle over Gay Rights." *Toronto Star Saturday Magazine* (19 November 1988):M29.

McCallum, John. 1986. "The Dynamics of Secularization in Australia." Presented at the SAANZ '86 Conference, Armidale, New South Wales.

McCarthy, John D., and Mayer Zald. 1977. "Resource Mobilization and Social Movements: A Partial Theory." *American Journal of Sociology* 82(6):1212-1241.

McGowan, Mark G. 1990. "Coming Out of the Cloister: Some Reflections on Developments in the Study of Religion in Canada 1980-1990." *International Journal of Canadian Studies* 1(2):175-202.

McGowan, Mark G., and David B. Marshall (eds.). 1992. *Prophets, Priests, and Prodigals: Readings in Canadian Religious History, 1608 to Present.* Toronto: McGraw-Hill Ryerson.

McGuire, Meredith B. 1982. *Pentecostal Catholics: Power, Charisma, and Order in a Religious Movement.* Philadelphia: Temple University.

————. 1992. *Religion:The Social Context,* 3rd ed. Belmont, CA: Wadsworth Publishing Company.

McInnis, Troy, and Nancy Nason-Clark. 1989. "A Comparative Analysis of Non-Schismatic Movements in the Roman Catholic Church." Paper Presented at the Annual Meetings of the Society for the Scientific Study of Religion, October 26-29, Salt Lake City.

McLuhan, Marshall. 1977. "Canada: the Borderline Case." In David Staines (ed.), *The Canadian Imagination.* Cambridge, MA: Harvard University Press.

McMillan, A. 1988. *Native Peoples and Cultures of Canada.* Vancouver: Douglas and McIntyre.

McNicoll, Andre. 1982. *Catholic Cults.* Toronto: Griffin House.

McRoberts, Kenneth, and Dale Postgate. 1988. *Quebec: Social Change and Political Crisis.* 3rd ed. Toronto: McClelland and Stewart.

Maduro, Otto. 1977. "New Marxist Approaches to the Relative Autonomy of Religion." *Sociological Analysis* 38:359-367.

Magnuson, Roger. 1980. *A Brief History of Quebec Education: From New France to Parti Québécois.* Montreal: Harvest House.

Mandel, Arthur. 1979. *The Militant Messiah: Of The Flight from the Ghetto: The Story of Jacob Frank and the Frankist Movement.* Atlantic Highlands, NJ.

Manes, Christopher. 1990. *Green Rage: Radical Environmentalism and the Unmaking of Civilization.* Boston: Little, Brown.

Mann, W.E. 1955. *Sect, Cult and Church in Alberta.* Toronto: University of Toronto Press.

————. 1991. *The Quest for Total Bliss: a Psycho-Sociological Perspective.* Toronto: Canadian Scholars.

Mannheim, Karl. 1936. *Ideology and Utopia.* Translated by L. Wirth and E. Shils. London: Routledge and Kegan Paul.

————. 1952. "The Problem of Generations." In *Essays on the Sociology of Knowledge.* New York: Oxford University Press.

Manuel, Frank. 1965. *The Prophets of Paris: Turgot, Condorcet, Saint-Simon and Comte.* New York: Harper and Row.

Marron, Kevin. 1988. *Ritual Abuse.* Toronto: Seal Books.

————. 1989. *Witches, Pagans, & Magic in the New Age.* Toronto: Seal Books.

Marsden, George M. 1980. *Fundamentalism and American Culture: The Shaping of Twentieth-Century Evangelicalism, 1870-1925.* Oxford: Oxford University Press.

Marsh, James. 1985. "Niagara Falls." In *The Canadian Encyclopedia.* Edmonton: Hurtig.

Marshall, John. 1975. "Crown seeking appeal over scientologists lock-picking tools sentence." *Globe and Mail* (27 December):5.

Martin, David. 1962. "The Denomination." *British Journal of Sociology* 13(1):1-14.

————. 1965. "Towards Eliminating the Concept of Secularization." In J. Gould (ed.), *Penguin Survey of the Social Sciences.* Harmondsworth: Penguin Books.

————. 1966. "The Sociology of Religion: A Case of Status Deprivation." *British Journal of Sociology* 17:353-359.

————. 1967. *A Sociology of English Religion.* London: SCM Press.

————. 1978. *A General Theory of Secularization.* Oxford: Basil Blackwell.

Marx, Karl. 1959. *A World Without Jews.* Translated by Dagobert D. Runes. New York: Philosophical Library.

————. 1965. *The German Ideology.* Moscow: Foreign Languages Publishing House.

————. 1970. *Critique of Hegel's Philosophy of Right.* Translation 1970 by Annette Jollin and Joseph O'Malley. Cambridge: The University Press.

————. 1975. *Early Writings.* New York: Vintage.

Marx, Karl, and Frederick Engels. 1958. *On Religion.* Moscow: Foreign Languages Publishing House.

Masefield, Peter. 1985. "The Muni and the Moonies." *Religion*

15:143-160.

Matas, Robert. 1990. "Spicer Seeks Unity in Poetry." *Globe and Mail* (13 November):A1-2.

Mathews, Robin. 1988. *Canadian Identity*. Ottawa: Steel Rail Publishing.

Matthews, Robin, and James Steele (eds.). 1969. *The Struggle for Canadian Universities*. Toronto: New Press.

Mauss, Armand L. 1969. "Dimensions of religious defection." *Review of Religious Research* 10:128-135.

Medved, Michael. 1992. *Hollywood versus America*. New York: HarperCollins.

Melton, J. Gordon. 1986. *Encyclopedic Handbook of Cults in America*. New York: Garland Publishing.

————. 1987a. *Encyclopedia of American Religions,* 2nd ed., 2 vols. Detroit, MI: Gale Research Company.

————. 1987b. "How New Is New? The Flowering of the 'New' Religious Consciousness Since 1965." In David G. Bromley and Phillip E. Hammond (eds.), *The Future of New Religious Movements*. Macon, Georgia: Mercer University Press.

————. 1988. *Encyclopedia of American Religions, Religious Creeds*. Detroit, MI: Gale Research Company.

Michels, Robert. 1962. *Political Parties*. New York: Collier Books.

Millett, David. 1969. "A Typology of Religious Organizations Suggested by the Canadian Census." *Sociological Analysis* 30:108-119.

Mills, C. Wright. 1959. *The Sociological Imagination*. New York: Grove Press.

————. (ed.). 1960. *Images of Man*. New York: George Braziller.

Milner, Henry. 1986. *The Long Road to Reform: Restructuring Public Education in Quebec*. Kingston and Montreal: McGill-Queen's.

Moggridge, Donald M. 1992. *Maynard Keynes: An Economist's Biography*. London and New York: Routledge.

Moir, John S. 1959. *Church and State in Canada West: Three Studies in the Relation of Denominationalist Nationalism, 1841-1867*.

————. 1967. *Church and State in Canada*. Toronto: McClelland and Stewart.

————. 1983. "Coming of Age, but Slowly: Aspects of Canadian History Since Confederation." C.C.H.A. Study Sessions 50:89-98.

Mol, Hans. 1976a. *Identity and the Sacred: A Sketch for a New Social-Scientific Theory of Religion.* Agincourt: The Book Society.

———. 1976b. "Major Correlates of Churchgoing in Canada." In Stewart Crysdale and Les Wheatcroft (eds.), *Religion in Canadian Society.* Toronto: Macmillan.

———. 1985. *Faith and Fragility: Religion and Identity in Canada.* Burlington: Trinity Press.

———. 1988. "Canada, Australia, and New Zealand." In T. Gannon (ed.), *World Catholicism in Transition.* New York: Macmillan.

Montreal Calendar Magazine. 1981. "Moonstalking. Josh Freed's Expose Goes to the Movies." (October):32-33.

Montreal Gazette. 1985. "Krishna group fined for peddling phoney art." (13 March).

Mooney, J. 1896. *The Ghost Dance Religion and Wounded Knee.* New York: Dover.

Moore, Wilbert. 1965. *Industrialization and Labor: Social Aspects of Economic Development.* New York: Russell and Russell.

Moreux, Colette. 1973. "The End of a Religion?" In Gerald L. Gold and Marc-Adelard Tremblay (eds.), *Communities and Culture in French Canada.* Toronto: Holt, Rinehart and Winston.

Morton, W.L. 1972. *The Canadian Identity.* Toronto: University of Toronto Press.

Motz, Arnell (ed.). 1990. *Reclaiming a Nation: The Challenge of Re-Evangelizing Canada by the Year 2,000.* Richmond, BC: Church Leadership Library.

Muller, W. 1968. "North America." In Krickeberg et al. (eds.), *Pre-Columbian American Religions.* London: Weidenfeld and Nicolson.

Myrden, Judy. 1989. "Reports say Halifax-based group's leader spread virus." *Chronical-Herald* [Halifax, Nova Scotia] (22 February).

Naisbitt, John, and Patricia Aburdene. 1990. *Megatrends 2000.* New York: William Morrow and Company.

Nason-Clark, Nancy. 1984. *Clerical Attitudes Towards Appropriate Roles for Women in Church and Society: An Empirical Investigation of Anglican, Methodist and Baptist Clergy in Southern England.* Unpublished Ph.D. thesis, London School of Economics and Political Science, London, England.

———. 1986. "Sex Roles and the Clergy." Paper presented at the Annual Meetings of the Association for the Sociology of Religion,

August 20-24, Washington, D.C.

———. 1987a. "Ordaining Women as Priests: Religious vs. Sexist Explanations for Clerical Attitudes." *Sociological Analysis* 48(3):259-73.

———. 1987b. "Are Clergywomen Changing the Face of Ministry?: A Comparison of British and American Realities." *Review of Religious Research* 28(4):330-40.

———. 1991a. "Broken Trust: The Case of Roman Catholic Clergy in the Province of Newfoundland Charged with Child Sexual Assault." Paper Presented at the Annual Meetings of the Society for the Scientific Study of Religion, November 8-10, Pittsburgh, PA.

———. 1991b. "Progress or Stagnation on the Question of Women's Ordination to the Priesthood in the Church of England: Results from a Follow-up Study." Paper presented at the annual meetings of the Religious Research Association, 4-6 November, Pittsburg.

Neal, Marie Augusta. 1979. "Women in Religion: A Sociological Perspective." *Sociological Inquiry* 45(4):33-9.

Neill, S. 1964. *A History of Christian Missions.* Harmondsworth: Penguin.

Nesti, Arnaldo. 1990. "Implicit Religion: The Issues and Dynamics of a Phenomenon." *Social Compass* 37(4):423-438.

New Internationalist. August 1990.

Newman, Peter C. 1985. *Company of Adventurers.* 3 vols. Markham, ON: Viking.

Newsweek. 1976 (25 October).

Niebuhr, H. Richard. 1957. *The Social Sources of Denomination alism.* Cleveland: World Publishing.

Niehardt, J.G. 1932. *Black Elk Speaks.* New York: William Morrow.

Nock, David A. 1987. "Cult, Sect and Church: A Re-examination of Stark and Bainbridge." *Canadian Review of Sociology and Anthropology* 24(4):514-525.

———. 1989. "Differential Ecological Receptivity of Conversionist and Revolutionist Sects: A Reconsideration of Stark and Bainbridge." *Sociological Analysis* 50(3):229-246.

Nova Scotia Provincial Court. (Antigonish). 1983a. "Certificate of Conviction [for] Diane Phillips." Case 1417 (December 5).

———. 1983b. "Certificate of Conviction [for] Philip Phillips." Case 1416 (December 5).

"O Canada." 1990. *The Toronto Star* (30 June):M11.

Oliphant, John. 1991. *Brother Twelve. The Incredible Story of Canada's False Prophet.* Toronto: McClelland & Stewart.

Orr, James. *The Christian View of God and the World.* Grand Rapids: Eerdmans.

O'Toole, Roger. 1975. "Sectarianism in Politics: Case Studies of Maoists and De Leonists." In Roy Wallis (ed.), *Sectarianism: Analyses of Religious and Non-Religious Sects.* London: Peter Owen.

———. 1976. "'Underground' Traditions in the Study of Sectarianism." *Journal for the Scientific Study of Religion* 15:145-156.

———. 1977. *The Precipitous Path.* Toronto: PMA Associates.

———. 1984a. *Religion: Classic Sociological Approaches.* Toronto: McGraw-Hill Ryerson.

———. 1984b. "Some Good Purpose: Notes on Religion and Political Culture in Canada." In S.D. Berkowitz (ed.), *Models and Myths in Canadian Sociology.* Toronto: Butterworths.

———. 1985. "Society, the Sacred and the Secular: Sociological Observations on the Changing Role of Religion in Canadian Culture." *Canadian Issues* 7:99-117.

———. 1988. "Review of P.E. Hammond (ed.), *The Sacred in a Secular Age.*" *Sociological Analysis* 49(3):322-323.

O'Toole, Roger, D.F. Campbell, J.A. Hannigan, P. Beyer, and J.H. Simpson. 1991. "The United Church in Crisis: A Sociological Perspective on the Dilemmas of a Mainstream Denomination." *Studies in Religion* 10(2):151-163.

Ouston, Rick. 1989. "The departed children." *The Province* (Vancouver, BC) (30 July):28c-29.

Pagels, Elaine. 1979. *The Gnostic Gospels.* Harmondsworth, England: Penguin.

———. 1976. "What became of God the mother? Conflicting images of God in early Christianity." *Signs* 2(2):293-303.

Palard, Jacques. 1988. "La confessionalité scolaire au Québec: Enjeux politiques et religieux." *L'Année sociologique* 38:80-107.

Palmer, Susan J. 1976. "Shakti, The Spiritual Science of DNA." Master's Thesis, History and Philosophy, Concordia University, Montreal, Quebec.

———. 1980. "Performance Rituals in Meditation Rituals among the New Religions." *Studies in Religion* 9(4):403-413.

———. 1986. "Community and Commitment in the Rajneesh

Foundation." *Update* 10(4):3-15.

———. 1988. "Charisma and Abdication: A Study of the Leadership of Bhagwan Shree Rajneesh." *Sociological Analysis* 49(2):119-135.

Pape, Dorothy. 1976. *God and Women: A Fresh Look at What the New Testament Says About Women.* London: Mowbrays.

Parkman, Francis. 1867. *Jesuits in North America in the 17th Century.* Boston: Beacon, vol. 1.

Parsons, Talcott. 1949. *The Structure of Social Action.* Glencoe: The Free Press.

———. 1963a. "Introduction." In *Max Weber, The Sociology of Religion.* Boston: Beacon Press.

———. 1963b. "Christianity and Modern Industrial Society." In Edward Tiryakian (ed.), *Sociological Theory, Values, and Sociocultural Change.* Glencoe, IL: The Free Press.

———. 1964. "Durkheim's Contribution to the Theory of Integration of Social Systems." In K.H. Wolff (ed.), *Emile Durkheim: Essays on Sociology and Philosophy.* New York: Harper and Row.

———. 1966. *Societies: Evolutionary and Comparative Perspectives.* Englewood Cliffs, NJ: Prentice-Hall.

———. 1973. "Durkheim on Religion Revisited." In C.Y. Glock and P.E. Hammond (eds.), *Beyond the Classics?* New York: Harper and Row.

———. 1981. "Revisiting the Classics throughout a Long Career." In Buford Rhea (ed.), *The Future of the Sociological Classics.* London: George Allen and Unwin.

Parsons, Talcott, and E. Shils. 1965. *Toward a General Theory of Action.* New York: Harper Torchbooks.

Parvey, Constance. 1974. "The Theology and Leadership of Women in the New Testament." In Rosemary Radford Ruether (ed.), *Religion and Sexism.* New York: Simon and Schuster.

Pazder, Lawrence with Michelle Smith. 1980. *Michelle Remembers.* New York: Simon and Shuster.

Pelletier, Pierre. 1986. "est, une nouvelle religion?" *Studies in Religion* 15(1):3-15.

Penton, M. James. 1976. *Jehovah's Witnesses in Canada.* Toronto: Macmillan.

Perman, David. 1977. *Changes and the Churches.* Oxford: Bodley Head.

Peter, K., E.D. Boldt, I. Whitaker, and L.W. Roberts. 1982. "The

Dynamics of Religious Defection among Hutterites." *Journal for the Scientific Study of Religion* 21:327-337.

Pieper, Josef. 1987. *What is a Feast?* Waterloo, ON: North Waterloo Academic Press.

Pineo, Peter C., and John Porter. 1967. "Occupational Prestige in Canada." *Canadian Review of Sociology and Anthropology* 4:24-40. Jersey: The Humanities Press.

Pinnock, Clark H. 1985. *The Untapped Power of Sheer Christianity.* Burlington, ON: Welch.

Planas, Ricardo. 1986. *Liberation Theology.* Kansas City: Sheed and Ward.

Plantinga, Alvin. 1967. *God and Other Minds.* Ithaca: Cornell University Press.

Plaut, W. Gunther. 1988. *The Man Who Would be Messiah: A Biographical Novel.* Oakville, ON: Mosaic Press.

Plummer, Ken. 1983. *Documents of Life.* London: George Allen & Unwin.

Poewe, Karla. 1989. "Links and Parallels between Black and White Charismatic Churches in South Africa and the States." *Pneuma* 10(2):141-158.

———. 1988. "On the Metonymic Structure of Religious Experiences: The Example of Charismatic Christianity." *Cultural Dynamics* 2(4):361-380.

Polanyi, Karl. 1944. *The Great Transformation.* New York: Beacon Press.

Poloma, Margaret M. 1989. *The Assemblies of God at the Cross-roads: Charisma and Institutional Dilemmas.* Knoxville, TN: University of Tennessee.

Pomi, Massimo. 1990. "Le merveilleux comme paradigme du religieux implicite dans la culture du 20 eme siecle." *Social Compass* 37(4):439-454.

Porter, E. 1981. *The Anglican Church and Native Education.* Ph.D. Dissertation, University of Toronto.

Porter, John A. 1965. *The Vertical Mosaic: An Analysis of Social Class and Power in Canada.* Toronto: University of Toronto Press.

———. 1967. "Canadian Character in the Twentieth Century." *The Annals of the American Academy of Political and Social Science* 370 (March):48-56.

Ralston, Helen. 1988. "Strands of Research on Religious Movements in Canada." *Studies in Religion* 17(3):257-277.

Rawlyk, George A. (ed.). 1990a. *The Canadian Protestant Experience: 1760-1990.* Toronto: Walsh.

———. 1990b. *Champions of the Truth: Fundamentalism, Modernism and the Maritime Baptists.* Kingston: Queen's University Press.

Reny, Paul, and Jean-Paul Rouleau. 1978. "Charismatiques et Socio-politiques dans l'Eglise catholique au Québec." *Social Compass* 25:125-143.

Rhea, Buford (ed.). 1981. *The Future of the Sociological Classics.* London: George Allen and Unwin.

Richard, James T., Jan van der Lans, and Frans Derks. 1986. "Leaving and Labelling: Voluntary and Coerced Disaffiliation from Religious Social Movements." *Research in Social Movements, Conflicts and Change* 9: 97-126.

Richards, Caroline. 1990. "On Subduing the Earth: the Suzuki Critique." *Grail* 1 (December):95-100.

Richardson, Don. 1974. *Peace Child.* Glendale: Regal Books.

Richardson, James T., Joel Best, and David G. Bromley (eds.). 1991. *The Satanism Scare.* New York: Aldine De Gruyther.

Richler, Mordechai. 1992. *O Canada! O Quebec!: Requiem for a Divided Country.* Toronto: Penguin Books.

Rifkin, Jeremy. 1980. *The Emerging Order.* New York: Harper and Row.

Riordan, Michael. 1990. *The First Stone.* Toronto: McClelland and Stewart.

Riss, Richard M. 1987. *Latter Rain.* Mississauga, ON: Honeycomb Visual Productions.

Ritzer, George. 1975. *Sociology: A Multiple Paradigm Science.* Boston: Allyn and Bacon.

Robbins, Thomas. 1988. "Cults, Converts and Charisma: The Sociology of New Religious Movements." *Current Sociology* 36(1):1-25.

Robbins, Thomas, and Dick Anthony. 1979. "The study of contemporary religious movements." *Annual Review of Sociology* 5:75-89.

Robbins, Thomas, and Dick Anthony (eds.). 1981. *In Gods We Trust.* New Brunswick, NJ: Transaction.

Roberts, Keith A. 1984. *Religion in Sociological Perspective.* Homewood, IL: Dorsey Press.

Robertson, Roland. 1970. *The Sociological Interpretation of Religion.* New York: Schocken.

————. 1977. "Individualism, Societalism, Worldliness, Universalism: Thematizing Theoretical Sociology of Religion." *Sociological Analysis* 38:281-308.

Robertson, Roland, and Burkart Holzner (eds.). 1979. *Identity and Authority.* New York: St. Martin's Press.

Rochford, E. Burke, Jr. 1989. "Factionalism, Group Defection, and Schism in the Hare Krishna Movement." *Journal for the Scientific Study of Religion* 28:162-179.

Roof, Wade Clark, and Karen Loeb. 1990. "Baby Boomers and Religious Change." Presented at the Conference on Changing Patterns of Belief, Queens College, CUNY.

Roof, Wade C., and William McKinney. 1987. *American Mainline Protestantism: Its Changing Shape and Future.* New Brunswick, NJ: Rutgers University Press.

Roozen, D.A. 1980. "Church Dropouts: Changing Patterns of Disengagement and Re-entry." *Review of Religious Research* 21:427-450.

Roozen, D.A., William McKinney, and Wayne Thompson. 1990. "The 'Big Chill' Generation Warms to Worship." *Review of Religious Research* 31:314-322.

Rorty, Richard. 1984. "The Historiography of Philosophy." In R. Rorty, J.B. Schneewind, and Q. Skinner (eds.), *Philosophy in History.* Cambridge: Cambridge University Press.

Rose, Elliot. 1962. *A Razor for a Goat: A Discussion of Certain Problems in the History of Witchcraft and Diabolism.* Toronto: University of Toronto Press.

Ross, John Arthur. 1973. *Regionalism, Nationalism and Social Gospel Support in the Ecumenical Movement of Canadian Presbyterianism.* Unpublished Ph.D dissertation, McMaster University.

Ross, Malcolm Ross (ed.). 1954. *Our Sense of Identity.* Toronto: Ryerson Press.

Rostow, W.W. 1956. "The Take-Off into Self-Sustained Growth." *Economic Journal* (March):24-48.

Roy, Gilles. 1982. "Le clergé québécois: Une population vieillissante et en décroissance rapide." *Le Devoir* (8 April):32.

Roy, Marie-Andrée. 1990. "Le changement de la situation des

femmes dans le catholicisme québécois." *Sociologie et sociétés* 22(2):95-114.

Royle, Marjorie. 1987. "Using Bifocals to Overcome Blindspots: The Impact of Women on the Military and the Ministry." *Review of Religious Research* 28(4):341-350.

Ruether, Rosemary Rather (ed.). 1974. *Religion and Sexism: Images of Woman in the Jewish and Christian Traditions.* New York: Simon and Schuster.

———. 1979. *Mary: The Feminine Face of the Church.* London: SCM Press.

Rushdie, Salman. 1990. *Is Nothing Sacred?* New York: Granta.

Sacouman, R. James. 1977. "Underdevelopment and the Structural Origins of Antigonish Movement Co-operatives in Eastern Nova Scotia." *Acadiensis* 7:68-85.

St. Augustine. 1948. *The Lord's Sermon on the Mount.* Chapter 15: "Love and Hatred of Temporal Relationships," Ancient Christian Writers, No. 5. Translated by John Jepson. London: Longmans, Green and Company.

Saint John's Edmonton Report. 1978. "Develop your psyche the 'I am' way, and identify with the universe of energy." (9 June):30-31.

Sandomirsky, Sharon, and John Wilson. 1990. "Process of disaffiliation: Religious mobility among men and women." *Social Forces* 68:1211-1229.

Scheffel, David. 1991. *In the Shadow of the Antichrist: The Old Believers of Alberta.* Peterborough: Broadview Press.

Schmitt, Peter J. 1969. *Back to Nature.* New York: Oxford University Press.

Scotia Sun (Port Hawksbury, NS). 1983. "Former employees quit after training course." (9 November):3.

Scholem, Gershom. 1954. *Major Trends in Jewish Mysticism.* New York: Schocken Books.

———. 1973. *Sabbatai Sevi: The Mystical Messiah.* Princeton, NJ: Princeton University Press.

Schopflin, George. 1991. "Conservatism and Hungary's Transition." *Problems of Communism* 40:67-68.

Schumacher, E.F. 1973. *Small is Beautiful.* London: Blond and Briggs.

———. 1977. *A Guide for the Perplexed.* New York: Harper and Row.

Schutz, Alfred. 1967. *The Phenomenology of the Social World.*

Evanston, IL: Northwestern University Press.

Schweitzer, Albert. 1955. *Philosophy of Civilization.* Translated by C.T. Campion. New York: Macmillan.

Scott, Don (ed.). 1986. *Christian Resources Handbook: A Directory of Christian Organizations in Canada.* Mississauga, ON: World Vision.

Scott, Nathan. 1958. *Modern Literature and the Religious Frontier.* New York: Harper and Row.

Shankar, V. Gauri. 1980. *Taming the Giants: Transnational Corporations.* New Delhi: Intellectual Book Corner.

Shapiro, Ivor. 1990. "The Benefit of the Doubt." *Saturday Night* (April 1990):33-40.

Sharpe, Eric J. 1986. *Comparative Religion* (revised ed.). LaSalle, IL: Open Court.

Sheridan, E.F. 1987. *Do Justice! The Social Teaching of the Canadian Catholic Bishops.* Toronto: Editions Paulines and the Jesuit Centre for Social Faith and Justice.

Sherman, Lawrence W. 1974. "Uses of the Masters." *American Sociologist* 9:176-181.

Shiner, Larry. 1967. "The Concept of Secularization in Empirical Research." *Journal for the Scientific Study of Religion* 6:207-20.

Silcox, C.E. 1933. *Church Union in Canada.* New York: Institute of Social and Religious Research.

Simons, John. 1986. "The Religious Dimension of Literature: A Critical Appraisal." In L. MacKendrick (ed.), *God and Man in Modern Literature.* Windsor, ON: Canterbury College.

Simpson, John H. 1988. "Religion and the Churches." In James Curtis and Lorne Tepperman (eds.), *Understanding Canadian Society.* Toronto: McGraw-Hill Ryerson.

Sinclair-Faulkner, Tom. 1977. "A Puckish Reflection on Religion in Canada." In Peter Slater (ed.), *Religion and Culture in Canada.* Waterloo, ON: Canadian Corporation for Studies in Religion.

Skinner, B.F. 1971. *Beyond Freedom and Dignity.* New York: Alfred A. Knopf.

Skinner, Quentin. 1978. *The Foundations of Modern Political Thought* (2 vols.). Cambridge: Cambridge University Press.

Slater, Phil. 1977. *Origin and Significance of the Frankfurt School: A Marxist Perspective.* London: Routledge and Kegan Paul.

Smith, T. 1991. *Bridges and Barricades: In Defense of Mohawk*

Land. Montreal: Kanienkehaka Solidarity Group.

Smith, Thomas W. 1992. "Are Conservative Churches Growing?" *Review of Relgious Research* 33(4):305-329.

Somerville, J. 1991. "Residential Schools Project starts year's work." *Catholic New Times* (17 November):17.

Sorokin, Pitirim A. 1950. *Altruistic Love: A Study of American Good Neighbours and Christian Saints.* Boston: Beacon Press.

———. 1957. *Social and Cultural Dynamics.* Revised and abridged. Boston: Porter Sargent.

———. 1963. *A Long Journey.* New Haven, CN: College and University Press.

Spiritual Community. 1972. *Spiritual Community Guide.* San Rafael, CA: Spiritual Community Publications.

———. 1974. *Spiritual Community Guide.* San Rafael, CA: Spiritual Community Publications.

———. 1978. *Spiritual Community Guide #4.* San Rafael, CA. Spiritual Community Publications.

Spiro, Melford. 1966. "Religion: Problems of Definition and Explanation." In Michael Banton (ed.), *Anthropological Approaches to the Study of Religion.* London: Tavistock.

Stahl, William. 1979. "Symbols and Ethics: An Approach to the Civil Religion Debate." *Union Seminary Quarterly Review* 34(4):229-238.

———. 1981. "Civil Religion and Canadian Confederation." Berkeley, CA: unpublished doctoral dissertation, Graduate Theological Union.

———. 1984. "Coming to Terms: Defining Strucutres of Meaning in the Civil Religion and Nationality Debates." *Union Seminary Quarterly Review* 39(1-2):73-84.

Stanton, Elizabeth C. 1895. *The Woman's Bible.* New York: European Publishing.

Stapleton, Anne, and Nancy Nason-Clark. 1992. "The Power and the Pedestal: Roman Catholic Women in Newfoundland Reassess their Beliefs and Attitudes in the Aftermath of Scandal." Paper presented at the Annual Meetings of the Society for the Scientific Study of Religion, November 6-8, Washington, D.C.

Starhawk. 1982. *Dreaming the Dark.* Boston: Beacon.

Stark, Rodney. 1981. "Must All Religions Be Supernatural?" In Bryan Wilson (ed.), *The Social Impact of New Religious Movements.*

New York: Rose of Sharon Press.

Stark, Rodney, and Willam S. Bainbridge. 1985. *The Future of Religion.* Berkeley: University of California Press.

Stark, R. et al. 1980. "Rediscovering Moral Communities." In T. Hirschi et al. (eds.), *Understanding Crime.* Beverly Hills, CA: Sage.

———. 1983. "Beyond Durkheim: Religion and Suicide." *Journal for the Scientific Study of Religion* 22:120-131.

"Statement by the National Catholic Conference on Residential Schools." 1991. *Catholic New Times* (31 March):10.

Steeman, Theodore M. 1964. "Max Weber's Sociology of Religion." *Sociological Analysis* 25:50-58.

Steiner, George. 1989. *Real Presences.* Chicago: University of Chicago Press.

Stevens, Leslie. 1989. "Different Voice/Different Voices: Anglican Women in Ministry." *Review of Religious Research* 30(3):262-275.

Stiller, Brian. 1992. *Critical Options for Evangelicals.* Toronto: Faith Today.

Stott, John. 1958. *Basic Christianity.* London: Inter-Varsity Press.

———. 1984. *Issues Facing Christians Today.* Basingstoke: Marshal, Morgan and Scott.

Swanson, Guy E. 1960. *The Birth of the Gods.* Ann Arbor: University of Michigan Press.

"Szollosy Dismissal Raises Speculation about Justice Office." 1991. *Island Catholic News* (October):2.

Tanner, Tony. 1987. *Scenes of Nature, Signs of Men.* Cambridge: Cambridge University Press.

Tawney, R.H. 1938. *Religion and the Rise of Capitalism.* London: Pelican.

———. 1957. "The Social Setting of Calvinist Development." In Milton Yinger (ed.), *Religion, Society, and the Individual.* New York: Macmillan.

Tertullian. 1869. *Tertullian Writings.* Ante-Nicene Christian Library, edited by A. Roberts and J. Donaldson. Edinburgh: T and T Clark.

Thompson, Kenneth. 1975. "Religious Organization." In John B. McKinlay (ed.), *Processing People.* London: Holt, Rinehart and Winston.

Thumbadoo, Camilla. 1979. "A Directory of Religious/Spiritual Cults and Sects in Canada." Unpublished Mss. Presented to Department

Head, Social Sciences Department, Metropolitan Toronto Library.

Tilly, Charles. 1981. *As Sociology Meets History.* New York: Academic Press.

Todd, Douglas. 1984. "Religion...By Numbers." *The* [Vancouver] *Sun* (10 August):B1.

Toon, Peter. 1987. *Born Again: A Biblical and Theological Study of Regeneration.* Grand Rapids: Baker.

"Toward a Christian Understanding of Sexual Orientations, Lifestyles and Ministry." 1988. Toronto: United Church of Canada.

Trible, Phyllis. 1979. "Eve and Adam: Genesis 203 Reread." In Carol Christ and Judith Plaskow (eds.), *Womanspirit Rising.* San Francisco: Harper and Row.

Troeltsch, Ernst. 1931. *The Social Teaching of the Christian Churches.* Translated by Olive Wyon. London: George Allen and Unwin.

Trofimenkoff, Susan Mann. 1982. *The Dream of Nation: A Social and Intellectual History of Quebec.* Toronto: Macmillan.

Tucker, Robert. 1992. "Comment on Randy Lippert, 'The Construction of Satanism as a Social Problem in Canada.'" *Canadian Journal of Sociology* 17(2):184-190.

Tully, James (ed.). 1988. *Meaning and Context: Quentin Skinner and his Critics.* Princeton, NJ: Princeton University Press.

Turcotte, Paul-André. 1990. "Autour de l'intégralité intransigeante: la papauté, l'Eglise et la réception romaine au Canada français." *Social Compass* 37:225-238.

Turner, Bryan S. 1983. *Religion and Social Theory.* London: Heinemann.

Unamuno. 1954. *The Tragic Sense of Life.* New York: Dover.

Vaillancourt, Jean-Guy. 1984. "Les groupes socio-politiques progressistes dans le catholicisme québécois contemporain." In Jean-Paul Rouleau and Jacques Zylberberg (eds.), *Les mouvements religieux aujourd'hui: Théories et pratiques. Les cahiers de recherches en science de la religion*, vol. 5. Quebec: Laval University.

Vallee, F. 1976. "Religion of the Kabloona and Eskimo." In S. Crysdale and L. Wheatcroft (eds.), *Religion in Canadian Society.* Toronto: MacMillan.

Vandezande, Gerald. 1983. *Christians in the Crisis.* Toronto: Anglican Book Centre.

Varacalli, Joseph. 1983. *Toward the Establishment of Liberal Catholicism in America.* Lanham: University Press.

Veevers, Jean E. 1990. "Canadian Regional Differences in Religious Affiliation and the Catholic Protestant Factor." *Canadian Journal of Sociology* 15(1):77-83.

Veevers, Jean E., and F.D. Cousineau. 1980. "The Heathen Canadians: Demographic Correlates of Nonbelief." *Pacific Sociological Review* 23:199-216.

Veevers, Jean E., and Ellen M. Gee. 1988. "Religiously Unaffiliated Canadians: Demographic and Social Correlates of Secularization." *RSC Update* 5 (Winter):17-20.

Vernon, Glenn M. 1968. "The Religious 'Nones': A Neglected Category." *Journal for the Scientific Study of Religion* 7:219-229.

Vigod, Bernard L. 1986. *Quebec before Duplessis: The Political Career of Louis-Alexandre Taschereau.* Kingston and Montreal: McGill-Queen's University Press.

Wach, Joachim. 1944. *Sociology of Religion.* 1967 Reprint. Chicago: University of Chicago Press.

Wall Street Journal. 19 May 1978.

Wallace, A.F.C. 1956. "Revitalization Movements." *American Anthropologist* 58(2):264-281.

Wallace, Ruth. 1992. *They Call Her Pastor.* Albany: State University of New York Press.

Wallace, Ruth, and Alison Wolf. 1991. *Contemporary Sociological Theory: Continuing the Classical Tradition* (3rd ed.). Englewood Cliffs, NJ: Prentice-Hall.

Wallis, Roy. 1978. "The Rebirth of the Gods? Reflections on the New Religions in the West." Belfast: The Queen's University of Belfast (New Lecture Series No. 198).

Wallis, Roy, and Steve Bruce. 1984. "The Stark-Bainbridge Theory of Religion: A Critical Analysis and Counter Proposals." *Sociological Analysis* 45:11-28.

Ward, Barbara. 1979. *Progress for a Small Planet.* New York: Norton.

Warner, Marina. 1985. *Alone of All Her Sex: The Myth and the Cult of the Virgin Mary.* London: Picador.

Waterston, Elizabeth. 1986. "Rudy Wiebe and the Almighty Voice." In L. MacKendrick (ed.), *God and Man in Modern Literature.* Windsor, ON: Canterbury College.

Wearing, Joseph. 1988. *Strained Relations: Canadian Parties and Voters.* Toronto: McClelland and Stewart.

Weatherbe, Steve. 1987. "Of Opus Dei and self-flagellation." *Alberta Report* (29 June):38.

Weber, Max. 1904. "Die protestante Ethik und der 'Geist' des Kapitalismus." *Archiv fur Sozialwissenschaft und Sozialpolitik,* vol. XX and XXI:1-54; 1-110.

———. [1925] 1947. *The Theory of Social and Economic Organization.* London: William Hodge. (Chapter 12)

———. 1947. *The Theory of Social and Economic Organization.* New York: Free Press. (Chapter 13)

———. 1949. *The Methodology of the Social Sciences.* Translated by E.A. Shils and H.A. Finch. Glencoe: The Free Press.

———. 1951. *The Religion of China.* Translated by Hans Gerth. Glencoe: The Free Press.

———. 1952a. *The Religion of India.* Translated by Hans Gerth and Don Martindale. New York: The Free Press.

———. 1952b. *Ancient Judaism.* Translated by Hans Gerth and Don Martindale. Glencoe: The Free Press.

———. 1958a. *The Protestant Ethic and the Spirit of Capitalism.* Translated and edited by Talcott Parsons. New York: Charles Scribner's Sons.

———. 1958b. *The Religion of India.* New York: Free Press.

———. 1963. *The Sociology of Religion.* Translated by Ernest Fischoff. Boston: Beacon Press.

Weibe, Donald. 1989. "Is Science Really an Implicit Religion?" *Studies in Religion/Sciences Religieuses* 18(2):171-83.

Weidman, Judith. 1981. *Women Ministers.* San Francisco: Harper and Row.

Weiner, Jonathan. 1990. *The Next One Hundred Years: Shaping the Fate of Our Living Earth.* New York: Bantam.

Westfall, William. 1989. *Two Worlds: The Protestant Culture of Nineteenth-Century Ontario.* Kingston and Montreal: McGill-Queen's University Press.

Westhues, Kenneth. 1982. "Religion." In Kenneth Westhues, *First Sociology.* New York: McGraw-Hill.

Westley, Frances. 1978. "'The Cult of Man': Durkheim's Predictions and New Religious Movements." *Sociological Analysis* 39:135-145.

———. 1983. *The Complex Forms of the Religious Life: A*

Durkheimian View of New Religious Movements. Chico, CA: Scholars Press.

Wilkes, James. 1982. "Twin Valleys Centre: An Investigative Report." Report Prepared for the Ontario Ministry of Community and Social Services (October).

Williams, John R. (ed.) 1984. *Canadian Churches and Social Justice.* Toronto: Lorimer.

Williams, Robin. 1951. *American Society: A Sociological Interpretation.* New York: Knopf.

Wilson, Bryan R. 1969. *Religion in Secular Society.* Harmondsworth: Penguin Books.

———. 1973. *Magic and the Millennium.* New York: Harper and Row.

———. 1975. "The Debate Over 'Secularization.'" *Encounter* 45(10):77-83.

———. 1979. "The Return of the Sacred." *Journal for the Scientific Study of Religion* 18:268-280.

———. 1982. *Religion in Sociological Perspective.* London: Oxford University Press.

———. 1985. "Secularization: The Inherited Model." In Phillip E. Hammond (ed.), *The Sacred in the Secular Age.* Berkeley, CA: University of California Press.

———. 1987. "Secularization." In Mircea Eliade (ed.), *The Encyclopedia of Religion.* New York: Macmillan.

Winter, J. Alan. 1973. "The Metaphoric Parallelist Approach to the Sociology of Theistic Beliefs." *Sociological Analysis* 34:212-229.

Woodcock, George. 1977. "Possessing the Land: Notes on Canadian Fiction." In David Staines (ed.), *The Canadian Imagination.* Cambridge, MA: Harvard University Press.

Woodward, Kenneth, et al. 1990. "A Time to Seek: A Generation Returns to Religion." *Newsweek* (17 December):50-56.

Woolfolk, Alan. 1986. "The Artist as Cultural Guide: Camus' Post-Christian Asceticism." *Sociological Analysis* 47(2):93-110.

Wurmbrand, Richard. 1967. *Tortured for Christ.* New York: Bantam Books.

Wuthnow, Robert. 1976. "Recent Patterns of Secularization: A Problem of Generations?" *American Sociological Review* 41:850-8-67.

———. 1978. "Religious Movements and the Transition in World

Order." In Jacob Needleman and George Baker (eds.), *Understanding the New Religions.* New York: Seabury Press.

————. 1980. "World Order and Religious Movements." In Albert Bergesen (ed.), *Studies of the World System.* Toronto: Academic Press. Reprinted in Eileen Barker (ed.), *New Religious Movements: A Perspective for Understanding Society.* Lewiston, NY: Edwin Mellen Press.

Wuthnow, R., and C.Y. Glock. 1973. "Religious Loyalty, Defection, and Experimentation: A Longitudinal Analysis of University Men." *Review of Religious Research* 19:231-245.

Wuthnow, R., and C.Y. Glock. 1973. "Religious Loyalty, Defection and Experimentation among College Youth." *Journal for the Scientific Study of Religion* 12:157-180.

Yinger, J. Milton. 1957. "A Critique of Weber's Thesis." In J. Milton Yinger (ed.), *Religion, Society, and the Individual.* New York: Macmillan.

————. 1970. *The Scientific Study of Religion.* London: Macmillan.

Zald, Mayer N., and John D. McCarthy. 1980. "Social Movement Industries: Competition and Cooperation Among Movement Organizations." In Louis Kreisberg (ed.), *Research in Social Movements, Conflict and Change,* vol. 3. Greenwich, CT: JAI Press.

————. 1987. "Religious Groups as Crucibles of Social Movements." In Mayer N. Zald and John D. McCarthy (eds.), *Social Movements in an Organizational Society.* New Brunswick, New Jersey: Transaction Books.

Zylberberg, Jacques, and Jean-Paul Montminy. 1981. "L'Esprit, le pouvoir et les femmes, polygraphie d'un mouvement culturel québécois." *Recherches sociographiques* 22:49-104.

Zylberberg, Jacques, and Jean-Paul Rouleau (eds.). 1984. *Les mouvements religieux aujourd'hui.* Montreal: Bellarmin.

Index

A

Aboriginal religion, *see* Native peoples
Aburdene, Patricia, 69
Adams, Harold, 249
Adler, Margot, 57
Anglicans, 42, 43, 45, 46, 47, 72, 121, 226, 228, 243, 244, 248, 249, 290, 291-292, 293
Apostasy, *see* Religious nones
Atwood, Margaret, 164-165, 185

B

Bailey, Edward, 157
Bainbridge, William S., 45, 57, 58, 71-72, 74, 76, 78, 90-92, 101, 246
Baptists, 48, 54, 72, 226, 291, 292, 293, 295, 298
Barrett, Stanley, 101
Basic Christian communities, *see* Catholic Church, Canada
Baum, Gregory, 259, 263, 264, 269-270
Becker, Ernest, 200
Becker, Howard S., 29, 35
Beckford, James, 78
Bell, Daniel, 68-69
Bellah, Robert, 23, 174-182, 183, 185, 189, 190

Berger, Peter, 7, 66, 68, 74, 135
Bergeron, Richard, 93
Beyer, Peter, 307
Bibby, Reginald W., 15, 31, 32, 51, 54, 60, 90-91, 111-112, 115, 116, 117, 118, 121, 144, 155, 263, 270, 292, 297-298, 304
Bird, Frederick, 89-90, 94, 102, 103
Biteaux, Armand, 103
Blumstock, Robert, 306
Bookchin, Murray, 208
Bouchard, Alain, 102
Bozinoff, Lorne, 114
Braudel, Fernand, 36
Brinkerhoff, Merlin, 99, 112, 121, 123, 298
Bruce, Steve, 77
Brunet, Michel, 137
Buber, Martin, 200
Buddhism, 85, 96
Burke, K., 121

C

Calvin, John, 14, 256, 257
Calvinism, 24
Campbell, Douglas, 307
Canadian Conference of Catholic Bishops (CCCB),